EXPERTS, NETWORKS AND INTERNATIONAL LAW

Highlighting how the challenges raised by globalisation – from environmental management to financial sector meltdowns – have encouraged the emergence of experts and networks as powerful actors in international governance, the contributions in this collection assess the methods and effectiveness of these new actors. Unlike other books that have focused on networks or experts, this volume brings these players together, showing how they interact and share the challenges of establishing legitimacy and justifying their power and influence. The collection shows how experts and networks function in different ways to address diverse problems across multiple borders. The reader is provided with a broader and deeper practical understanding of how informal authority actually operates, and of the nature of the relationship between different actors involved in policy-making. Through a range of case studies, the contributions in this collection explain how globalisation is re-shaping traditional forms of power and authority.

HOLLY CULLEN is Adjunct Professor of Law at the University of Western Australia.

JOANNA HARRINGTON is Professor of Law at the University of Alberta.

CATHERINE RENSHAW is Associate Professor of Law at the Australian Catholic University.

EXPERTS, NETWORKS AND INTERNATIONAL LAW

Edited by

HOLLY CULLEN
University of Western Australia

JOANNA HARRINGTON
University of Alberta

CATHERINE RENSHAW
Australian Catholic University

CAMBRIDGE
UNIVERSITY PRESS

CAMBRIDGE
UNIVERSITY PRESS

University Printing House, Cambridge CB2 8BS, United Kingdom

One Liberty Plaza, 20th Floor, New York, NY 10006, USA

477 Williamstown Road, Port Melbourne, VIC 3207, Australia

4843/24, 2nd Floor, Ansari Road, Daryaganj, Delhi – 110002, India

79 Anson Road, #06–04/06, Singapore 079906

Cambridge University Press is part of the University of Cambridge.

It furthers the University's mission by disseminating knowledge in the pursuit of education, learning, and research at the highest international levels of excellence.

www.cambridge.org
Information on this title: www.cambridge.org/9781107184428
10.1017/9781316876923

First published 2017

A catalogue record for this publication is available from the British Library.

Library of Congress Cataloging-in-Publication Data
Names: Cullen, Holly, editor. | Harrington, Joanna, editor. | Renshaw, Catherine (Law teacher), editor.
Title: Experts, networks and international law / edited by Holly Cullen, University of Western Australia, Perth; Joanna Harrington, University of Alberta; Catherine Renshaw, University of Western Sydney.
Description: Cambridge, United Kingdom ; New York, NY, USA : Cambridge University Press, 2017. | Includes bibliographical references and index.
Identifiers: LCCN 2016051390 | ISBN 9781107184428 (hardback)
Subjects: LCSH: International law. | Evidence, Expert. | BISAC: LAW / International.
Classification: LCC KZ3410 .E974 2017 | DDC 341–dc23
LC record available at https://lccn.loc.gov/2016051390

ISBN 978-1-107-18442-8 Hardback

CONTENTS

CONTRIBUTORS

SUZANNE AKILA is Assistant Director in the International Legal Branch at the Australian Department of Foreign Affairs and Trade. She has been a Sir Roland Wilson Foundation scholar at the Centre for International Governance and Justice at the Australian National University. She has also served as a Senior Legal Officer at the Office of International Law in the Australian Attorney-General's Department and a criminal prosecutor with the Office of the Director of Public Prosecutions. She teaches Public International Law and convenes Critical Approaches to International Law in the LLM programme at the Australian National University. She completed her LLB at the University of Western Australia and her LLM at University College London, specialising in public international law, and holds a PhD from the Australian National University.

HOLLY CULLEN is Adjunct Professor of Law at the University of Western Australia, having been Professor of Law from 2010 to 2016. Prior to 2010, she was Reader in Law at Durham University. From 1998 to 2006, she was Deputy Director of the Durham European Law Institute and served as its Acting Director from 2003 to 2004. She is the author of *The Role of International Law in the Elimination of Child Labor* (2007), as well as numerous articles and chapters on international law issues. She was a member of the International Law Association's research committee on non-state actors in international law from 2007 to 2016, and has participated in international research projects on issues such as slavery and child soldiers. She holds a BCL and LLB from McGill University and an LLM in international human rights law from the University of Essex. She was an advocate of the Barreau du Québec from 1988 to 1992.

JOANNA HARRINGTON is Professor of Law at the University of Alberta and a former Fulbright Visiting Research Chair in Policy Studies at the University of Texas at Austin. In addition to journal articles and book chapters, she is a co-author of the second edition of *International Law: Doctrine, Practice, and Theory* (2014) and the author of the public international law title for the *Halsbury's Laws of Canada* series. Her teaching and research are infused by her experiences in practice, including a two-year secondment with the Legal Affairs Bureau of the Canadian Department of Foreign Affairs and International Trade. She has represented Canada at the United Nations, the Organization of American States and the Assembly of States Parties to the Rome Statute of the International Criminal Court, and served as a consultant with the British Council, the Canadian Human Rights Commission and the United Nations Development Programme. She has also assisted counsel in matters before national courts, the Human Rights Committee and the Inter-American Commission on Human Rights. From 2010 to 2015, she served as an associate dean with across-campus responsibilities for graduate students. She holds a BA from the University of British Columbia, a JD from the University of Victoria and a PhD in law from the University of Cambridge.

CAMERON S.G. JEFFERIES is Assistant Professor and Borden Ladner Gervais Energy Law Fellow at the Faculty of Law at the University of Alberta. His research and teaching interests include international environmental law, law of the sea and sustainability law. Currently, his research focuses on a critical assessment of Canada's regulatory climate change response and marine protected area strategy in light of international commitments. He is the author of *Marine Mammal Conservation and the Law of the Sea* (2016), as well as journal articles that examine international and domestic shark and marine mammal conservation, and climate change. Professor Jefferies holds a BSc and LLB from the University of Alberta, an LLM and an SJD from the University of Virginia and a diploma from the Rhodes Academy of Oceans Law and Policy.

PHILIPP KASTNER is Assistant Professor at the Faculty of Law of the University of Western Australia. His research and teaching interests include the resolution of armed conflicts, international criminal law, international human rights and humanitarian law, public international law, law of the sea, legal pluralism and legal theory. His current research focuses on the creation and role of legal norms in the context of peace negotiations aiming to end internal armed conflicts. His publications include *International Criminal Justice in Bello? The ICC between Law and*

Politics in Darfur and Northern Uganda (2012) and *Legal Normativity in the Resolution of Internal Armed Conflict* (Cambridge University Press, 2015). He holds an LLM and a DCL from McGill University and a Mag. iur. and Dr. iur. from the University of Innsbruck.

HITOMI KIMURA is Associate Professor at Otsuma Women's University, where she teaches international and domestic environmental law. From 2002 to 2004, she was a researcher at what is now Mitsubishi UFJ Research and Consulting, and from 2004 to 2010, she was a researcher, then Fellow from 2011 to 2013, at the Institute for Global Environment Strategies. She has also taught foreign students as a part-time lecturer with the Graduate Program on Human Security at the University of Tokyo's Graduate School of Arts and Sciences, and as a collaborator for the Global Environmental Leaders Special Education Program at Hiroshima University's Graduate School for International Development and Cooperation. Her research areas within international environmental law include matters of climate change law and policy, as well as the national implementation of international environmental law and policy. She holds a BA in law from Sophia University, an MA from the Graduate School of International Development at Nagoya University, an LLM from Temple University and a PhD in law from Waseda University.

MASAHIRO KUROSAKI is the Head of the Study of Law and Military Operations, an Associate Professor of International Law at the National Defence Academy of the Japanese Ministry of Defence and a Research Fellow at the Grotius Centre for International Legal Studies at Leiden University. In this capacity, he has also been active as a legal adviser to the Japanese Self-Defence Force and the Ministry of Foreign Affairs of Japan, at times representing the Japanese government in human rights and humanitarian law negotiations. He has published a range of articles and book chapters on the law of international security, the law of armed conflict, international criminal law and Japanese security laws. He holds an MA in international law from the University of Tokyo.

KEI NAKAJIMA is Associate Legal Officer at the International Court of Justice and a PhD candidate at the Graduate Institute of International and Development Studies in Geneva, specialising in international law, international economic law and the law of international dispute settlement, including both WTO dispute settlement and investment treaty arbitration. His current research interests include evidence and fact-finding before international courts and tribunals, as well as the international law of sovereign debt restructuring. From 2008 to 2013, he was a Research Fellow at the University of Tokyo and with the Japanese Society for the Promotion of Science. He also completed an internship with the Human Rights Committee established pursuant to the International Covenant on Civil and Political Rights, and served as an assistant to the editors of the *Japanese Yearbook of International Law*. He holds a BA in law from Waseda University and an LLM and LLD from the University of Tokyo.

TAHNEE PRIOR is a Trudeau Scholar, Vanier Canada Graduate Scholar and PhD candidate in global governance at the Balsillie School of International Affairs at the University of Waterloo. Her dissertation seeks to understand what a legalised international governance structure that could account for the complexity and rapid change of the Arctic could look like and how we could get there from here. Previously, she was the lead researcher of a project on climate change and human rights at the Northern Institute for Environmental and Minority Law at the Arctic Centre at the University of Lapland. She holds a BA in international relations from Franklin University Switzerland and an MA in global governance, specialising in multilateral institutions and diplomacy, from the Balsillie School of International Affairs.

PAMMELA QUINN is Associate Professor of Law at Drexel University. Her scholarly interests are focused on the regulation of institutions and actors across national borders. She has published a number of journal articles analysing the interactions of various types and forms of regulation on diverse international and transnational actors, including states, corporations and individuals. Her current research continues to explore the effectiveness of different strategies to regulate transnational and international actors. Before joining Drexel's Thomas R. Kline School of Law, Professor Quinn served as an attorney-adviser in the Office of the Legal Adviser of the US State Department, where she represented the United States in commercial arbitrations, real property transactions and diplomatic property disputes around the globe. She holds an AB from Dartmouth College and a JD from Duke University.

CATHERINE RENSHAW is Associate Professor of Law at the Australian Catholic University. Her research focuses on human rights and democracy in Southeast Asia. With Professor Ben Saul, she is the editor of *Human Rights in Asia and the Pacific* (2014). She is an editor of the *Journal of South Asian Law*, the author of numerous journal articles and book chapters, and from 2008 to 2010 was Director of an Australian Research Council project based at the Australian Human Rights Centre at the University of New South Wales. In 2011 and 2013 she carried out fieldwork in Myanmar as part of her doctoral research. She completed her law degree at the University of New South Wales, her LLM at the University of Sydney and her PhD at the University of Sydney. She is admitted to practice as a lawyer in the Supreme Court of New South Wales and the High Court of Australia.

CECILY ROSE is Assistant Professor at the Grotius Centre for International Legal Studies at Leiden University. She previously worked as an Associate Legal Officer at the International Court of Justice in The Hague, and at the Special Court for Sierra Leone in Freetown, Sierra Leone. She has also worked as an associate in the international regulation and compliance group of Steptoe & Johnson, LLP, in Washington, DC. Professor Rose holds a BA from Yale University, a JD from Columbia Law School and an LLM and PhD from the University of Cambridge.

JOSEPHINE TOOP is a PhD student at the University of Canterbury, where she is investigating the existence and operation of global administrative law principles (such as transparency, participation, review, reason-giving and impartiality) within multilateral environmental agreements (MEAs) and regional fisheries management organisations (RFMOs) and considering whether these principles bring effectiveness and legitimacy benefits. During the course of her research, she has undertaken a PhD exchange to the University of Oxford and has also worked for an MEA secretariat. She is the year-in-review contributor for New Zealand for the *Yearbook of International Environmental Law* and a year-in-review contributor on matters of international environmental law for the *New Zealand Yearbook of International Law*. She has also lectured and tutored at the university level and worked as a solicitor. She holds a BA and an LLB from the University of Otago and an LLM in international law from the University of Canterbury.

FOREWORD

This collection of essays is the outcome of the Four Societies workshop held at the Australian National University in July 2014. The goal of the Four Societies workshops, of which this event was the fifth, is to foster collaboration between early career scholars and practitioners of the four sponsoring societies – the American Society of International Law, the Australian and New Zealand Society of International Law, the Canadian Council on International Law and the Japanese Society of International Law. The theme of *Experts, Networks, and International Law*, the brainchild of my colleague Catherine Renshaw, was chosen to allow participants to explore shifting patterns and ways of understanding governance between and beyond states across a broad range of fields.

A decade earlier, Anne-Marie Slaughter had presented a novel answer to the question of how best to govern the world. In her influential book *A New World Order*, Slaughter had argued that global governance already existed, but not where most people expected. For Slaughter, rather than stop imagining ways of creating an imaginary international system that could bring unitary states closer together, it made more sense to start thinking about ways in which states had been 'disaggregated', with their now disaggregated parts (legislators, regulators, judiciaries) increasingly operating in functionally specialised 'government networks'. For Slaughter, the emergence of a 'world of government networks' is not just an 'underappreciated' fact of international life but also 'a more effective and potentially just world order' than either 'what we have today' or 'a world government in which a set of global institutions perched above nation-states enforced global rules'.[1] The Four Societies workshop invited participants to reflect upon how that vision of a new world order of government networks had held up over the intervening decade, in the face of major events such as the Global Financial Crisis and

[1] Anne-Marie Slaughter, *A New World Order* (Princeton: Princeton University Press, 2004), 1, 7.

the Arab Spring, and the challenges of achieving consensus on policy questions relating to pressing global issues such as climate change, agricultural liberalisation, the responsibility to protect or financial market reform.

The questions we posed to the participants were both empirical and normative. On the empirical side, participants were invited to explore whether international law does in fact increasingly operate through networks of experts rather than state-to-state encounters and negotiations. If so, what might empirical studies of networks reveal about their effectiveness as mechanisms of decision-making and governance, or the way that power operated to structure and constrain decision-making within those networks? Is strengthening governance by experts across fields such as policing, counter-terrorism, environmental protection, human rights promotion, food safety, public health, financial regulation, international criminal prosecution, investment liberalisation and security sector reform equally effective? On the normative side of the equation, participants were invited to explore the extent to which strengthening governance by experts was desirable across different settings. Do networks complement or compete with democratic institutions, and how does that vary across regimes? Should international lawyers support the development of global governance through government networks, or should they take a more critical approach to the rise of networked governance?

The chapters gathered in this book more than live up to our ambitions in convening the workshop. It is instructive and illuminating to see how the authors have gone to work to explore the idea of networked governance through disaggregated state agencies and other actors. The authors test the idea and ideal of networked governance both empirically and normatively, asking both what adopting the lens of networked governance allows us to see and how we should in turn assess the resulting picture of global governance which emerges. Is networked governance something to be supported, or something to be resisted, and if so why?

The great value of this collection is that it develops answers to those questions by painting a picture of the operation of networks within and across fragmented issue areas. We may respond quite differently to the successful establishment of efficient networks informed by expert knowledge operating outside domestic or democratic constraints if the focus of the resulting network is on environmental protection rather than financial market deregulation, or Arctic resource management rather than the securitisation of migration. Networked regulation or governance may make it possible for administrators or officials to provide more timely and efficient responses to global problems, by moving beyond clunky state-to-state mechanisms of bureaucratic negotiation, but in so doing create new problems – of unaccountable or partial expertise, forbiddingly technical knowledge or speed as the enemy of consultation. In addition, the collection offers new insights into how, through what procedures and techniques, networked governance is conducted, from coordination of policy positions, exchanging information, and consultation, through to more hands-on forms of training, capacity-building and standard setting. Throughout their analyses, the authors explore which frameworks, languages, concepts or theoretical apparatus are best suited to making sense of the resulting experiments in global governance that are taking place around us on an everyday basis.

In addition to making a significant, substantive contribution to debates about the place of networks and experts in international law, this volume also makes an important contribution to the relationship between the four societies of international law involved in this project. The goals of the Four Societies programme are to create international collaborations between scholars and practitioners, support new and exciting scholarship by early career researchers, and foster relationships between the four societies that share an ocean and a history of encounters to which both geographic proximity and shared values give rise. As president of the Australian and New Zealand Society of International Law at the time the Four Societies workshop was held and co-chair of the workshop organising committee, I witnessed the generosity and energy with which colleagues from each of the four societies worked collectively to convene the workshop, raise sponsorship, participate in discussions, support the early career researchers and build collaborations.

The resulting workshop, and the book to which it has given rise, are a testament to the collective effort of the mutually supportive and deeply engaged scholars and practitioners of international law who are members of the four societies. In particular, this book is the result of the hard work and dedication of the three editors, Holly Cullen, Joanna Harrington and Catherine Renshaw, who have successfully brought together this timely collection of imaginative and insightful essays by a new generation of international law scholars.

Anne Orford
The University of Melbourne

ABBREVIATIONS

ACCOBAMS	Agreement on the Conservation of Cetaceans in the Black and Mediterranean Sea
ACP	Asian Co-benefits Partnership
AECEN	Asian Environmental Compliance and Enforcement Network
AFP	Agence France-Presse
AMAP	Arctic Monitoring and Assessment Programme
ANCP	allegedly non-complying party
ANZSIL	Australian and New Zealand Society of International Law
AOSIS	Alliance of Small Island States
APAN	Asia Pacific Adaptation Network
APFED	Asia-Pacific Forum for Environment and Development
APN	Asia-Pacific Network for Global Change Research
ASCOBANS	Agreement on the Conservation of Small Cetaceans of the Baltic and North Seas
ASIL	American Society of International Law
AU	African Union
BASIC	Brazil, South Africa, India and China
BWU	Blue Whale Unit
CAC	collective action clause
CBD	Convention on Biological Diversity
CCAC	Climate and Clean Air Coalition
CCAMLR	Commission for the Conservation of Antarctic Marine Living Resources
CCIL	Canadian Council on International Law
CCOL	Coordinating Committee on the Ozone Layer
CDM	clean development mechanism
CILAE	Centro de Investigación Latinoamérica-Europa
CITES	Convention on International Trade in Endangered Species
COP	Conference of the Parties
DC	District of Columbia
EANET	Acid Deposition Monitoring Network in East Asia
ECJ	European Court of Justice
ECOWAS	Economic Community of West African States

EEA	European Environment Agency
EEZ	exclusive economic zone
EHRR	European Human Rights Reports
EIONET	European Environmental Information and Observation Network
EITI	Extractive Industries Transparency Initiative
ESM	European Stability Mechanism
FATF	Financial Action Task Force
FCPA	Foreign Corrupt Practices Act (United States)
FRELIMO	Front for the Liberation of Mozambique
FSC	Forest Stewardship Council
G7	Group of Seven
G8	Group of Eight
G20	Group of Twenty
GA	General Assembly
GAOR	General Assembly Official Records
GLOBE	Global Legislators Organisation for a Balanced Environment
IACHR	Inter-American Court of Human Rights
ICC	International Criminal Court
ICCAT	International Commission for the Conservation of Atlantic Tuna
ICJ	International Court of Justice
ICRC	International Committee of the Red Cross
ICRW	International Convention for the Regulation of Whaling
ICSID	International Centre for Settlement of Investment Disputes
IFOR	Implementation Force
IGO	intergovernmental organisation
ILA	International Law Association
ILC	International Law Commission
ILM	International Legal Materials
ILR	International Law Reports
IMF	International Monetary Fund
IMO	International Maritime Organization
INC	intergovernmental negotiating committee
INECE	International Network for Environmental Compliance and Enforcement
IOSCO	International Organization of Securities Commissions
IPBES	Intergovernmental Platform on Biodiversity and Ecosystem Services
IPCC	Intergovernmental Panel on Climate Change
ISO	International Organization for Standardization
ITLOS	International Tribunal for the Law of the Sea
IUCN	International Union for the Conservation of Nature
IUU	illegal, unreported and unregulated

IWC	International Whaling Commission
JARPA	Japanese Whale Research Program
JSIL	Japanese Society of International Law
LCS-RNet	International Research Network for Low Carbon Societies
LTTE	Liberation Tigers of Tamil Eelam
LoCARNet	Low Carbon Asia Research Network
MARPOL	marine pollution
MEA	multilateral environmental agreement
MEF	Major Economies Forum on Energy and Climate
MEM	Major Economies Meeting on Energy Security and Climate Change
METI	Ministry of Economy, Trade and Industry
MIT	Massachusetts Institute of Technology
MoE	Ministry of the Environment
MOFA	Ministry of Foreign Affairs
MOP	Meeting of the Parties
MoU	memorandum of understanding
MPA	marine protected area
MSY	maximum sustainable yield
NAFTA	North American Free Trade Agreement
NAMMCO	North Atlantic Marine Mammal Commission
NCADP	National Coalition to Abolish the Death Penalty
NCM	non-compliance mechanism
NEWREP-A	New Scientific Whale Research Program in the Antarctic Ocean
NGO	non-governmental organisation
OECD	Organisation for Economic Co-operation and Development
OSFI	Office of the Superintendent of Financial Institutions (Canada)
PLO	Palestine Liberation Organization
POP	persistent organic pollutant
RENAMO	Mozambican National Resistance
RFMO	regional fisheries management organisation
RMP	Revised Management Procedure
RMS	Revised Management Scheme
R.S.C.	Revised Statutes of Canada
S Ct	(United States) Supreme Court
S.C.	Statutes of Canada
SCAR	Scientific Committee on Antarctic Research
SCRS	Standing Committee on Research and Statistics
SDNY	Southern District of New York
SDRM	Sovereign Debt Restructuring Mechanism
SOLAS	International Convention for the Safety of Life at Sea
SPD	Social Democratic Party (Germany)
STRP	Scientific and Technical Review Panel

TEMM	Tripartite Environment Ministers Meeting
TVPA	Torture Victim Protection Act (United States)
UKTS	United Kingdom Treaty Series
UN	United Nations
UNCCD	United Nations Convention to Combat Desertification
UNCLOS	United Nations Convention on the Law of the Sea
UNCTAD	United Nations Conference on Trade and Development
UNEP	United Nations Environment Programme
UNESCO	United Nations Educational, Scientific and Cultural Organization
UNFCCC	United Nations Framework Convention on Climate Change
UNFSA	United Nations Fish Stocks Agreement
USC	United States Code
USCA	United States Court of Appeals
USTS	United States Treaty Series
UNTS	United Nations Treaty Series
VCCR	Vienna Convention on Consular Relations
VCLT	Vienna Convention on the Law of Treaties
WTO	World Trade Organization
WWF	World Wildlife Fund

1

Experts, Networks and International Law

HOLLY CULLEN, JOANNA HARRINGTON AND CATHERINE RENSHAW

In the early years of the current millennium, questions about the architecture of global governance occupied the attention of scholars of both international law and international relations. To many, it seemed as though the traditional approaches to international governance and the traditional institutions of international law would be ill-equipped to deal with the problems of a globalised world, including climate change, pandemics, migration, financial market instability and international crime. The problems are complex and transnational in nature. Identifying problems, interpreting data and charting paths of action require the expertise of specialists and technicians, while the implementation of solutions requires flexible and speedy responses from state and non-state actors working in concert across multiple borders.

I The Roles for Experts and Expertise

The difficulty in identifying issues and interpreting their significance points to an increasingly significant role for experts. At the domestic level, over the past century, the increasing bureaucratisation of the state has shifted the locus of governance from politics to expertise.[1] At the international level, in more recent times, a similar phenomenon has taken place. The conditions of uncertainty that characterise globalisation, where complex and interrelated variables heighten the unpredictability of policy choices, increase the authority and importance of experts as professionals with special knowledge and skills in given issue areas. Policy-makers and leaders increasingly rely upon experts to help them understand the nature of problems, identify relevant state interests,

[1] Peter M. Haas, 'Introduction: Epistemic Communities and International Policy Coordination' (1992) 46:1 *International Organization* 1–35, 8.

produce specialised information efficiently, frame issues for collective debate, chart the range of appropriate actions, propose specific policies and maintain the institutions necessary to implement policies. Experts become powerful, their power lying in their control over knowledge and information and their consequent capacity to determine policy. It is a power that David Kennedy has described as lying in 'the capillaries of social and economic life': the 'background' of world affairs.[2]

The net result is that patterns of global decision-making are not – or not solely – the result of interstate diplomacy reflecting the interests of sovereigns or legislators. They are also shaped by the work of specialists and technicians. These specialists and technicians are located inside international organisations and civil society groups, and within state bureaucracies where domestic experts engage with their foreign counterparts to implement policies of transnational reach. Experts are recognised as such by their membership in a group with shared professional beliefs, values and techniques. Networks of knowledge-based experts, also known as 'epistemic communities', have multiplied.[3] As Peter Haas has explained, these communities share: (1) a set of common practices associated with their professional competence; (2) a set of principled beliefs that provide a basis for the action of community members; (3) an understanding of the range of possible policy actions to achieve the desired outcomes; and (4) internally defined criteria for validating knowledge.[4] The language of international experts and epistemic communities is one of rationality: scientific objectivity, best practices, expert consensus and empirical necessity. The considerable influence of these actors in defining agendas, setting standards and affecting the way that states perceive their interests is facilitated by the structure of the international environment, where international institutions provide important forums through which information can be solicited and disseminated.

By the end of the 1990s, it was no longer questioned that experts and epistemic communities mattered as actors in international affairs.[5] Scholars had by then turned to the question of when, and under what conditions, they mattered, and to normative questions about whether their power undermined state autonomy or served the ends of global

[2] David W. Kennedy, 'Challenging Expert Rule: The Politics of Global Governance' (2005) 27 *Sydney Law Review* 5–28, 7. See further, David Kennedy, *A World of Struggle: How Power, Law, and Expertise Shaped Political Economy* (Princeton: Princeton University Press, 2016).

[3] Haas, above note 1, 2. [4] Ibid., 3. [5] Ibid.

justice.[6] The most obvious criticism was that experts and epistemic communities lacked democratic accountability. Experts were responsible for decisions that affected people in multiple ways, but they were not answerable to the people at the ballot box. They provided advice and implemented decisions according to a worldview that was not articulated (nor contested) within political discourse because experts did not use the language of interest and ideology.[7] By nature they were elitist; they excluded the opinions and perspectives of those outside the club. When experts operated within networks that reached across borders to address issues of transnational concern, questions arose about their motivations and their allegiances.

Scholarly interest in the role of experts in international law includes an examination of international lawyers themselves as experts.[8] Analyses of the role for international lawyers, particularly government legal advisers, have been published periodically in the past 50 years,[9] but recently a more critical, and self-critical, scholarship on how international lawyers use their expertise has emerged. Martti Koskenniemi has analysed the different ways in which international lawyers deploy their expertise in terms of a tension between commitment and cynicism.[10] He suggests that the mere choice of international law as a career path demonstrates commitment beyond that held, for example, by a commercial lawyer.[11] Indeed, practitioners of international law have asserted that the role is not only to advise their clients, but also to advance the cause of international law.[12] On the other hand, practitioners' comments about their role also support the charge of cynicism, where one accepts that advice is fed into an essentially political context, and legal advice is often not 'the end of the matter'.[13] For Koskenniemi, the commitment is continually under stress

[6] See, for example, Kennedy, above note 2. [7] Ibid., 27.

[8] Stephen Bouwhuis, 'The Role of an International Legal Adviser to Government' (2012) 61 *International and Comparative Law Quarterly* 939–960, 950 and 954.

[9] See, for example, Herbert C.L. Merillat, ed., *Legal Advisers and Foreign Affairs* (Dobbs Ferry: Oceana Publications, 1964).

[10] Martti Koskenniemi, 'Between Commitment and Cynicism: Outline of a Theory of International Law as Practice' in Martti Koskenniemi, ed., *The Politics of International Law* (Oxford: Hart Publishing, 2011), 271–293.

[11] Ibid., 274.

[12] James Crawford, 'International Law as Discipline and Profession' (2012) 106 *American Society of International Law Annual Meeting Proceedings* 471–486, 474; Bouwhuis, above note 8, 940–941.

[13] Daniel Bethlehem, 'The Secret Life of International Law' (2012) 1 *Cambridge Journal of International and Comparative Law* 23–26, 29.

as the hopes for international law are dashed.[14] Furthermore, the ways that the tensions between commitment and cynicism manifest themselves differ between the roles that international lawyers fill, and may place them in opposition to each other, such as the criticism of government lawyers by activists advocating particular causes.[15]

On the more pragmatic side, there appears to be an increase in the extent of legal expertise used by foreign affairs ministries. More government lawyers have advanced qualifications in international law, and government departments use outside experts to a greater extent than in the past.[16] Often the expertise of the government legal adviser operates behind the scenes, in what Daniel Bethlehem has described as 'the secret life of international law'.[17] International lawyers, and indeed international courts, also rely on non-legal expertise.[18] As James Crawford has said, 'a degree of interdisciplinarity to grasp complex non-legal ideas may be necessary . . . there is no expectation on the practical level that we go beyond that'.[19] Instead, the international lawyer relies on experts in a variety of fields governed by international law.

II The Roles for Networks and Networked Governance

As for the question of how to coordinate responses to complex issues involving multiple actors across many borders, the current reality points away from traditional institutions of international law (which were perceived as slow-moving, cumbersome and unwieldy) towards new forms of organisation.[20] Some have argued for the creation of a more legalised and powerful world order – such as a 'world government' for global problems[21] – but it remains difficult to see how this could be

[14] Koskenniemi, above note 10, 276–281. [15] Ibid., 289.

[16] Richard Rowe, 'International Law and Diplomacy: The Art of the Possible' (2014) 15 *Melbourne Journal of International Law* 318–329, 318 and 323; Bouwhuis, above note 8, 951–952.

[17] Bethlehem, above note 13, 23.

[18] Crawford, above note 12, 478–479. See also the discussion of the *Whaling in the Antarctic* case in the chapter by Cameron S.G. Jefferies.

[19] Crawford, above note 12, 479.

[20] Kal Raustiala, 'The Architecture of International Cooperation: Transgovernmental Networks and the Future of International Law' (2002) 43:1 *Virginia Journal of International Law* 1–92, 25.

[21] See, for example, Campbell Craig, 'The Resurgent Idea of World Government' (2008) 22:2 *Ethics & International Affairs* 133–142.

achieved in the absence of a global *demos*.[22] Moreover, many view a more powerful centralised global institution as a deeply undesirable prospect, denying the diversity of the world's peoples and threatening both democracy and individual liberty.[23] In a nutshell, this is the 'governance dilemma' so aptly described by political scientists: more international governance was necessary, but 'world government' was feared.[24]

A novel answer to this dilemma was presented by international law and relations scholar Anne-Marie Slaughter in her 2004 book *A New World Order*. In Slaughter's view, the future of global governance lay within existing and new 'transgovernmental networks', a term she used to refer to the 'patterns of regular and purposive relations among like government units working across the borders that divide countries from one another and that demarcate the "domestic" from the "international" sphere'.[25] Slaughter argued that these networks could carry out various aspects of global governance in new and informal ways, and indeed were already doing so.[26] Networked relations between regulatory and subject-matter experts occurred at the sub-state level and were not necessarily controlled or closely guided by the policies of cabinets or chief executives of governments.[27]

Slaughter's premise was that the state is not a unitary monolithic actor, but the sum of its aggregate parts (legislative, bureaucratic and judicial) and that these parts have the capacity (and the imperative) to interact with their foreign counterparts in order to address issues of transnational or common concern. Engagement results in horizontal networks of experts and policy-makers that are decentralised and dispersed, and incapable of exercising centralised coercive authority.[28] Slaughter[29] has

22 Anne-Marie Slaughter, *A New World Order* (Princeton: Princeton University Press, 2004), 8.
23 Ibid.
24 See Robert O. Keohane, 'Governance in a Partially Globalized World: Presidential Address' (2001) 95:1 *American Political Science Review* 1–13.
25 Slaughter, above note 22, 14.
26 See further, Anne-Marie Slaughter and David Zaring, 'Networking Goes International: An Update' (2006) 2 *Annual Review of Law and Social Science* 211–229. In recent years, government legal advisers have been more open about the degree of ongoing cooperation between the foreign ministries of allied states: see, for example, Rowe, above note 16, 326–327; Harold Hongju Koh, 'The State Department Legal Adviser's Office: Eight Decades in Peace and War' (2011–2012) 100 *Georgetown Law Journal* 1747–1781, 1756 and 1764.
27 Robert O. Keohane and Joseph Nye, 'Transgovernmental Relations and International Organisations' (1974) 1 *World Politics* 39–42.
28 Slaughter and Zaring, above note 26, 211.
29 See, for example, Emilie M. Hafner-Burton, Miles Kahler and Alexander H. Montgomery, 'Network Analysis for International Relations' (2009) 63 *International Organizations* 559–592.

argued, as have other network theorists, that domestic political decisions to implement global objectives (from resisting deforestation to conforming to global standards for securities trading) are the result of activities amongst regulators (coordinating information, policy and action) at the same hierarchical level within their own national structure. Direct engagement – including the dissemination and sharing of information and strategies, the discussion of joint approaches to common problems and the shared implementation processes for achieving solutions – was orchestrated below the state level by networks driven by the imperative to resolve a common issue. Slaughter argued that as a form of international governance, transgovernmental networks are more efficient and adaptable than the bureaucracies of international organisations.[30]

Slaughter identified three different types of network, whose functions sometimes overlap: (1) information networks, which provide a forum for the exchange of ideas, techniques, experiences, problems; (2) enforcement and capacity-building networks, which aim (through training and technical assistance) to enhance capacity so that states can enforce their own domestic regulation; and (3) harmonisation networks, which aim to bring different national systems into conformity with one another.[31] In each of these networks, the principal characteristic is the absence of vertical ties, which permits flexibility, informality and consensus-based decision-making processes.[32] In contrast, international organisations are characterised by a formal vertical structure, with centralised decision-making that is implemented at lower levels, and official mechanisms for dispute resolution.

Slaughter's theory of governance by networks drew on globalisation's central features to answer the governance dilemma, notably the accessibility of information and the speed of communication, which enables different actors to link across the world, as well as the complexity of national governance. For Slaughter, the emergence of a world of government networks was not just an underappreciated fact of international life, but it also offered 'a more effective and potentially more just world order; than either what we have today' or 'a world government in which a set a global institutions perched above nation-states enforced global rules'.[33] She also suggested that '[g]lobal governance through government networks is good public policy for the world' and that a 'world order

[30] Miles Kahler, ed., *Networked Politics: Agency, Power and Governance* (Ithaca, NY: Cornell University Press, 2009), 2.

[31] Slaughter, above note 22, 52–61.

[32] See also Raustiala, above note 20, 22.

[33] Slaughter, above note 22, 6–7.

self-consciously created out of horizontal and vertical government networks could ... create a genuine global rule of law without centralised global institutions'.[34] This approach to networks has been refined in some writings to include actors outside of government. In his reflections on the eightieth anniversary of the Legal Adviser's Office of the US State Department, Harold Koh recognised that after the end of the Cold War, '[t]he defining players ... may be networks of actors connected in countless tangible and intangible ways that challenge our traditional understandings of international relations and international law'.[35]

Some were, and continue to be, sceptical about Slaughter's claims. Transgovernmental networks aim to achieve domestic change that conforms to a global objective through the cooperation of government officials. Such networks thus bypass political processes normally triggered by government attempts to achieve change in traditional ways, such as through the negotiation of treaties complete with processes of national consultation and ratification. For these reasons, for some, transgovernmental networks represent an unacceptable surrender of the democratic accountability of states, which alone possess the legitimacy to act in the public interest.[36] Philip Alston, for example, has worried that power would congeal in '[t]he back rooms of the real new world order, where those with power consolidate it and make the decisions which will continue to determine the fate of the excluded.'[37] Others worry that enforcement networks will serve as a mask for preferences shaped by hegemonic interests,[38] while others are concerned about the ethics of a process which appears to enmesh illiberal states 'in a system of

[34] Ibid., 261.

[35] Koh, above note 26, 1772. Examples of complex networks of state and non-state actors are examined in the chapters by Suzanne Akila, Philipp Kastner and Josephine Toop.

[36] Kenneth Anderson, 'Squaring the Circle? Reconciling Sovereignty and Global Governance through Global Government Networks' (2005) 118:4 *Harvard Law Review* 1255–1312. For an alternative perspective, see the chapter by Cecily Rose in this collection.

[37] Philip Alston has written that if Slaughter's analysis is correct, 'it implies the marginalisation of governments as such and their replacement by special interest groups. It suggests a move away from arenas of relative transparency into the backrooms and the bypassing of the national political arenas to which the United States and other proponents of the importance of healthy democratic institutions attach so much importance.' Philip Alston, 'The Myopia of the Handmaidens: International Lawyers and Globalization' (1997) 8 *European Journal of International Law* 435–448, 441.

[38] Martii Koskenniemi, 'Carl Schmitt, Hans Morgenthau, and the Image of Law in International Relations' in Michael Byers, ed., *The Role of Law in International Politics. Essays in International Relations and International Law* (Oxford: Oxford University Press, 2000), 17–34.

transnational networks designed to ease them into the liberal-democratic legal order'.[39]

While some are concerned about the power *of* networks, others are concerned about the distribution and uses of power *within* networks. Some scholars suggest that networked governance is too often represented as inherently consensual and that the assumption that power within networks is always exercised in a benign way must be questioned. These critics point to the ability of some network nodes to exert disproportionate influence as a result of their position in the network; with 'power's second face, setting the network's agenda through (the) structural control of information'.[40] Slaughter had a threefold rejoinder to these concerns. First, she argued that government networks are primarily 'talking shops' and (traditional, political) accountability is not relevant to the 'soft power' of (only) giving and receiving ideas. Second, she argued that the (independent) nature of some domestic institutions (such as courts) is that they 'act legitimately without direct accountability'. Finally, she noted that accountability must be assessed comparatively; international organisations such as the UN, and civil society actors who sometimes wield considerable influence, are not very accountable themselves, yet both aim to effect domestic change and bypass domestic political processes.[41]

III About This Book

In this book, we reflect upon the role for both experts and networks in international law. We are interested in whether and how experts and epistemic communities have answered challenges about their democratic accountability, inclusiveness and transparency in the face of a new and demanding set of urgent contemporary problems, whether environmental or economic. We are also interested in how the vision of a new world order based upon networked, disaggregated state institutions has held up over the past ten years, and how experts and epistemic communities have addressed ongoing issues of governance such as human rights and individual criminal accountability. Does international law today in fact

[39] Gerry Simpson, 'The Ethics of the New Liberalism' in Christian Reus-Smit and Duncan Snidal, eds., *The Oxford Handbook of International Relations* (Oxford: Oxford University Press, 2009), 255–266.

[40] Kahler, above note 30, 3.

[41] Anne-Marie Slaughter, 'The Accountability of Government Networks' (2000) 8:2 *Indiana Journal of Global Legal Studies* 341–367, 347.

operate through diffused networks, and through the experts within those networks that one may consider influencers? How does power operate within and between transnational networks? Have the fears of sceptics of a 'new world order' proven justified? Do networks complement or compete with traditional institutions of global governance, and how do these dynamics vary in different institutional and substantive settings? What is the power of networks in setting global policy agendas, and how much control do global policy-makers really have over the implementation of those agendas?

Both experts and networks belong to the backstage world of international law. Our attention to what goes on behind the scenes is not new in international law and international relations scholarship.[42] But tracking the nature of the power exercised by actors that lies in the shadows remains an important task. In recent years, the reach and influence of both experts and networks have increased, as the complexity and interdependent nature of economic and environmental problems, as well as problems of individual and collective security, make coordinated international decision-making more important and more uncertain. Both experts and networks share the same fundamental vulnerability on the count of democratic legitimacy: neither is elected or answerable to a political constituency. Both experts and networks also share, potentially, the same remedy for this democratic deficit: greater inclusiveness and transparency. A little over a decade has elapsed since Anne-Marie Slaughter published *A New World Order*, and David Kennedy challenged experts to resist denying 'the political' in their work and thus abrogating both freedom and responsibility. It is a propitious time to assess whether and how experts and networks have changed their practices and patterns of influence.

This book brings to the fore the important role of experts both individually and as members of networks, as key facilitators of the exchange of material and immaterial resources (principally information), to network members. The contributors were given great latitude in terms of defining both experts and networks, and in determining their methodological approach, leading to differences in emphasis as well as varying conclusions, some more positive, others more critical. We view this intellectual diversity within the collection as a strength, and a benefit for future research. In relation to the power and influence of experts, this

[42] See further, Haas, above note 1; Kennedy, above note 2; Alan Boyle and Christine Chinkin, *The Making of International Law* (Oxford: Oxford University Press, 2007).

book is interested in the following questions. In whose interest are experts acting? To whom are they accountable? To what extent do experts 'govern' and is governance by experts across diverse fields such as environmental protection, human rights promotion, international criminal prosecution and financial sector reform desirable and effective? Recent conflicts within the International Labour Organization, for example, demonstrate the resistance that established actors, both state and non-state, may present to an increased role for experts in international governance.[43] With respect to networks, we are interested in the diversity of networks and the different contexts in which they operate. The informality of many networks allows for the participation of a wide range of actors, with international relations scholars having long identified the work of non-governmental organisations in the human rights field, for example, as a form of network.[44] The case studies on diplomatic protection, human rights litigation and peace negotiation included within this collection also demonstrate the contributions of networks of diverse participants in developing and implementing international legal norms.

IV Within the Book

This collection is organised into three parts. Part I examines the role for experts and networks in relation to advocacy, fact-finding, dispute resolution and mediation, particularly for matters of human rights. The three chapters within this part demonstrate the ways in which experts and networks enhance (rather than compete with) the effectiveness of international legal regimes, in particular by providing a structure in which both state and non-state actors can participate in international law-making, as well as its execution.

The chapter by Suzanne Akila demonstrates the complexity of interactions between networks of both state and non-state actors for the protection of citizens abroad. Using the *LaGrand* case before the International Court of Justice as an illustrative case study,[45] Akila examines how and why Germany sought to protect two of its nationals from the application of the death penalty in the United States and the role for both

[43] Claire La Hovary, 'Showdown at the ILO? A Historical Perspective on the Employers' Group's 2012 Challenge to the Right to Strike' (2013) 42:4 *Industrial Law Journal* 338–368.

[44] Margaret E. Keck and Kathryn Sikkink, *Activists Beyond Borders: Advocacy Networks in International Politics* (Ithaca, NY: Cornell University Press, 1998).

[45] *LaGrand (Germany* v. *United States of America)*, Judgment, [2001] ICJ Rep 466.

networks and expertise in influencing Germany's decision to intervene as well as how it chose to conduct that intervention. Drawing on interviews, as well as a review of court records, Akila's research also reminds us of the role for non-state actors in the international system, with the intersecting anti-death penalty networks able to have influence precisely because they offered technical expertise as well as constituent support. Akila's chapter also provides a critique of the state-focussed aspects of Slaughter's work on transgovernmentalism, with Akila concluding that a broader theory of networked governance is required to understand the interdependent roles of both government and non-governmental actors within the different processes used for the protection of citizens abroad.

Next, Pammela Quinn shows how experts with official monitoring and reporting responsibilities within the field of international human rights law might assist domestic courts in building factual records and gathering evidence for the purposes of human rights litigation. Building on Slaughter's identification of global regulatory networks as 'transmission belts for information', Quinn argues that transnational judicial conversations concerning legal information would be more effective with the inclusion and transmission of what she terms 'wider and deeper' factual records. Her chapter explores how the fact-finding activities of special rapporteurs, treaty monitoring bodies and truth and reconciliation commissions can enhance a domestic court's understanding of both the particular facts of a case (the record facts) and the broader context (the legislative facts). Ultimately, Quinn argues for greater recognition of the fact-finding role of experts tasked with reporting on violations of international human rights law as a means to enhance the contributions of transnational judicial networks for the protection of human rights, while concluding with some thoughts on the need for future research.

Part I concludes with a thought-provoking chapter by Philipp Kastner on a particular form of network within the field of international peace and security that he labels the epistemic community of peace mediators. As with Akila, Kastner relies on the international relations concept of epistemic communities to refer to networks of experts who may introduce new policy alternatives to governments, with the work of both scholars providing examples of networks, primarily horizontal in nature, that transcend the distinction between state and non-state actors. While each peace process can be seen as a distinct event, Kastner shows how networks of peace mediators are shaping the conduct and outcome of peace negotiations. These networks include international and regional intergovernmental and non-governmental organisations as well as experienced peace negotiators aligned with such bodies as the Centre for Humanitarian Dialogue. In particular, Kastner argues that these networks of peace mediators are shaping the normative environment for peace negotiations. In some cases, their influence is limited to upholding the neutrality and impartiality of peace negotiators themselves. But in other cases, the role for the mediators as transnational experts emphasises legitimacy-reinforcing norms such as individual accountability for crimes committed during conflict. Kastner, however, is not unaware that 'the boundaries of legitimate peace mediation styles . . . are malleable, and grey zones remain'.

International environmental law regimes are the focus of Part II. The discussion begins with Josephine Toop's examination of multilateral environmental agreements (MEAs) and regional fisheries management organisations (RFMOs) from the perspective of experts, networks and global administrative law principles. Toop considers how MEA and RFMO regimes may be considered networks in and of themselves, while also recognising the networks and sub-networks of various actors that operate within and around them. She also suggests that synergies between MEAs and RFMOs can operate as a wider network of influence and strength. Toop's chapter explores the institutional architecture of both MEA and RFMO regimes, as well as the role for secretariats, scientific bodies and compliance committees. She shows how networks within the MEA and RFMO frameworks exchange information and facilitate capacity-building and the transfer of technology, while also encouraging ongoing dialogue to facilitate the implementation of treaty obligations and encourage improvements in compliance. She argues that networking, and the drawing upon expertise, can bring a number of benefits that are integral to the functioning of MEA and RFMO regimes. But she also identifies some potential drawbacks, arguing that these may be mitigated, to some extent, by the application of global administrative law principles to enhance a regime's legitimacy and effectiveness.

Next, Cameron S.G. Jefferies considers the role for science, and scientific expertise, within international environmental decision-making, using the international legal regimes for the management and conservation of whales as a timely case study. Like others, Jefferies questions the effectiveness of the current regulatory system, which is hampered by political and ideological disagreements. As with Kastner's work on peace mediators, he also looks at scientists as epistemic communities capable of influence, but his research demonstrates how science, and scientific uncertainty, have been used to support both commercial use and preservation within the International Whaling Commission. However, for Jefferies, there is a need to improve the institutionalisation of these competing perspectives, rather than deny that scientific experts may hold differing views, and he argues for the pragmatic option of crafting parallel arrangements to reframe the role for experts within a more robust Scientific Committee, which could also incorporate the regional networks discussed by Toop for improved implementation. Recognising the practical obstacles to amending the International Convention for the Regulation of Whaling (ICRW),[46] Jefferies relies on articles 65 and 120 of the United Nations Convention on the Law of the Sea (UNCLOS)[47] to support the creation of a new cetacean management regime with an improved role for scientific expertise. He also considers the need to address matters of accountability, recognising that scientific experts, as with other experts, can be co-opted.

Following on from Jefferies' work is Tahnee Prior's analysis of the insufficiency of both hard and soft law regimes to address environmental change in the Arctic. Prior's work explains how a 'transformative shift' has led to networks of collaboration, the recombining of resources and the institutionalisation of novel governance structures for the Arctic region. But the Arctic is not static, and Prior fears that the region is reaching a new threshold of biophysical and socio-economic change that imposes constraints on the existing, and largely informal, governance arrangements that renders them inadequate. Prior argues for a more comprehensive and resilient governance framework that cuts across policy domains, state and international organisations, political interests and administrative jurisdictions, to address the full range of social and environmental problems. She looks to resilience theory for a framework to address the dilemmas of Arctic governance and argues for a 'reflexive legal system' to account for the region's changing complexity. Her chapter suggests that the flexibility and informality of networks create opportunities for both state and non-state actors to engage in interactions that may lead, in turn, to creative and diverse solutions to problems, which are sensitive to the particular contexts in which they will be applied. However, she also recognises that governance structures, such as the Arctic Council, can also raise questions of longevity, influence and accountability.

Part II of the collection concludes with Hitomi Kimura's typology of environmental government networks with Asian examples, demonstrating

[46] 2 December 1946, 161 UNTS 74, in force 10 November 1948.

[47] 10 December 1982, 1833 UNTS 3, in force 16 November 1994.

that various networks play an increasingly important role in the sharing of information and in building capacity for the domestic development of environmental standards and the promotion of international cooperation for the mitigation of diplomatic tensions. Kimura's chapter explains how structural differences between different network types allow them to function in diverse ways: as transgovernmental regulatory organisations, intergovernmental organisational networks, government-supported research-oriented networks and regional networks. Kimura also discusses why networks are particularly effective in Asia, where language obstacles and differences between national legal systems often lead to a preference for using non-legally binding approaches – with the subsequent chapter by Cecily Rose exploring this preference more generally within the field of international finance law. Kimura's chapter also discusses how some government networks develop in parallel with international conventional obligations, and rise to prominence after the adoption of these conventions in order to oversee their compliance. She also mentions the downside of transnational networking through government sub-divisions to address international problems requiring a holistic solution. With respect to the issue of democratic accountability, Kimura notes that there is an increasing role for parliamentarians working as experts within environmental networks in countries such as Japan, where, she advises, government officials draft the majority of legislative bills. Kimura also aims to show how participation in networks improves state performance in relation to international environmental agreements, minimising the 'implementation gap' that can arise when states ratify treaties, but lack the capacity or the will to implement all their obligations.[48]

Finally, in Part III of this collection, the contributors examine the role for experts and networks within the context of institutional evolution and change, examining developments in such fields as the international regulation of finance and investment, transnational crime, insolvency and sovereign debt restructuring, and international accountability for atrocity crimes.

The chapter by Cecily Rose examines the creation of new and effective international standards by government officials and other experts through the adoption of non-binding instruments, such as recommendations and guidelines, drawing on examples from the work of the Organisation for Economic Co-operation and Development (OECD),

[48] See, for example, the work of Beth Simmons, *Mobilizing for Human Rights: International Law in Domestic Politics* (Cambridge: Cambridge University Press, 2009).

the Basel Committee on Banking Supervision and the Extractive Industries Transparency Initiative (EITI). In particular, Rose is focussed on the sub-set of non-binding instruments that, in her words, 'bring about' domestic implementation, such as through existing legislation, regulations or executive action, and the questions then raised about the resulting impact on democratic governance at the domestic level. While non-binding instruments, in comparison with treaties, represent a speedier and more efficient method for influencing both domestic legal systems and state compliance, Rose also recognises the need to address whether or not the trade-off for speed and efficiency is an undermining of the role of the legislature and democratic representation. Rose argues that any loss of accountability that results from the use of non-binding instruments is not as great as it might first appear, with her chapter aptly demonstrating how such loss is mitigated by other mechanisms, such as legislative oversight, the approval of implementing legislation and public consultation processes that serve as a means for ensuring external accountability. She thus concludes that the use of non-binding instruments, often developed by horizontal networks of government officials serving as experts, does not necessarily raise serious accountability concerns.

Next, Kei Nakajima examines the vexing but timely issue of sovereign debt restructuring through a review of past proposals made by experts to address the consequences of state insolvency through an international governance framework. As Nakajima explains, there are no international legal mechanisms to address the techniques used by states in financial distress to change a debt's original terms, notwithstanding the impact of associated austerity measures and conditional loans. Through his review of both traditional and modern designs for an international mechanism to regulate sovereign debt restructuring, Nakajima identifies a tendency for experts to favour a centralised approach, often involving the creation of an international bankruptcy court. But for Nakajima, a decentralised approach is more apt for a defragmented legal order, albeit one that retains the best advice from the experts who developed the traditional models. He also makes clear that the traditional debtor/creditor dichotomy does not reflect the full complexity of sovereign debt restructurings, with more modern designs bringing us back to the focus underlying Part I by taking into account human rights considerations as well as overlapping regional and bilateral arrangements.

In this collection's final chapter, we turn to international criminal law and the strengthening of cooperation with the International Criminal

Court, with a chapter by Masahiro Kurosaki reflecting upon the role for an expert body, such as the International Law Commission, in developing international law to further the fight against impunity. Kurosaki's chapter examines the regime of aggravated state responsibility, as finalised in article 41 of the Commission's articles on state responsibility,[49] as a means for securing wider state cooperation in the suppression of core international crimes. Characterising the regime as a product of the interactive law-making process between the Commission and the International Court of Justice,[50] Kurosaki's analysis focusses on the obligations of cooperation, non-recognition and non-assistance that have been developed by the Commission as providing a potential foundation for a general obligation to cooperate with the International Criminal Court.

Conclusions

The contributions to this book demonstrate how experts and transnational networks are capable of promoting change at the domestic level and orchestrating regimes of cooperation at the international level. Experts and networks (often facilitated by experts) are able to set standards of independence and effectiveness for members, disseminate information and ideas amongst members, and catalyse action in relation to the domestic implementation of international rules and standards. Networks seem most effective in relation to problems that require flexible approaches and an ability to harmonise and coordinate government responses quickly between counterpart national officials, and where the creation of a centralised coercive authority is impractical or politically impossible. Within a network, it is also possible for network members to vary their levels of commitment to different issues; to play a prominent role in relation to implementing some decisions and to withdraw from others. As the chapters on environmental governance show, networks can also operate to complement international treaties, by assisting in the creation of institutions through alliances of interested parties who work towards their establishment, and by facilitating implementation through standard setting and monitoring. Networks may also allow for the participation of a wide range of actors in global governance processes, and may include significant roles for non-state actors.

[49] Adopted in 2001 and reproduced in *Report of the International Law Commission*, UN GAOR, 56th Sess, Supp No 10, ch. IV, 43–59, UN Doc A/56/10 (2001).

[50] This approach is echoed by Crawford, above note 12, 472.

It is less clear from contributions to this book, however, whether networks are a more just way of global governance. In *A New World Order*, Slaughter concluded: 'Global governance through government networks is good public policy for the world . . . [a] world order self-consciously created out of horizontal and vertical government networks could . . . create a genuine global rule of law without centralised global institutions'.[51] On this point, our contributors are ambivalent. While the effectiveness of networks, and of experts working within these networks, as mechanisms of decision-making and governance is generally viewed positively, further reflection is needed on the way power operates within and between transnational networks and in whose name this power is exercised.

We conclude this introduction with thanks to the 'Four Societies' initiative that brought together the contributing authors in this collection. The 'Four Societies' initiative aims to foster a scholarly network among primarily early career scholars of international law, with the encouragement of the American Society of International Law (ASIL), the Australian and New Zealand Society of International Law (ANZSIL), the Canadian Council on International Law (CCIL) and the Japanese Society of International Law (JSIL). Without the support of these four societies, and the members from each who formed the steering committee to select the contributing authors, this collection would not have come to fruition. A special note of thanks is owed to ANZSIL for hosting a two-day workshop for the discussion of initial drafts. ANZSIL members from academia and government also provided invaluable feedback. We also extend our thanks to Elizabeth Spicer at Cambridge University Press and to the anonymous reviewers for their helpful comments.

[51] Slaughter, above note 22, 261.

PART I

Experts, Networks, Advocacy and Mediation

2

Networks of Protection

SUZANNE AKILA

The protection of citizens abroad is commonly understood as an exclusively state enterprise. However, participation in international law activities is, in reality, no longer limited to states. This chapter considers the protection of citizens abroad as a far more complex network of interactions. I explore the actors who drive and deliver the protection of nationals, the behaviours that constitute the practice of protection and the motivating factors for protective behaviour. The focus for this exploration rests on the case known as *LaGrand* that was brought by Germany against the United States before the International Court of Justice (ICJ).[1] The chapter explores how and why Germany sought to protect two of its citizens from the application of the death penalty and the role of networks and expertise in generating Germany's decision to intervene and the conduct of its intervention.

The chapter is organised into three sections. Section I outlines the international legal framework for the protection of citizens abroad and some of the analytical problems it poses. It considers Anne-Marie Slaughter's theory of transgovernmentalism as a framework for addressing these issues and explains the limitations of her approach. Section II traces the actions that state and non-state actors took in their attempt to protect the LaGrand brothers. It also explores Germany's motivations in bringing the case, drawn from interviews conducted in 2013 with state and non-state actors connected with the legal proceedings.[2] Section III

Thanks are due to Hilary Charlesworth, Holly Cullen, Fiona Haines, Merhdad Payandeh and the participants at the fifth 'Four Societies' workshop held in July 2014 for their helpful feedback.

1 *LaGrand (Germany v. United States of America)*, Judgment [2001] ICJ Rep 466.

2 Interviews were conducted in Germany, Belgium, Australia and the United Kingdom from 2013 to 2014 with counsel involved in the *LaGrand* case, German government officials and civil society organisations. Transcripts of these interviews are on file with the author.

examines how those networks of protection applied different techniques to motivate state intervention on behalf of the LaGrand brothers, including the manner in which some actors harnessed their expertise to shape the course of action. It also examines the different components of protecting citizens abroad and how the traditional state functions are distributed across a network of actors.

I conclude that protecting citizens abroad can be understood as the actions of a network: a disaggregated state, where various parts of the state interact with a variety of non-state actors and respond to a variety of pressures, not all of them legal in nature. This more complex model of networks allows the process of coordination between actors within the network to be more visible, as well as the ability of networks to generate substantive values and norms.

I The Protection of Nationals Abroad in International Law

A Diplomatic Protection

International legal scholars typically regard the protection of citizens abroad as falling within the exclusive domain of states.[3] In Western legal thought, Emer de Vattel presented the protection of citizens abroad as an issue related to the law of nations, in 1758.[4] Vattel characterised the protection of citizens abroad as a right of states. He opined that there were some kinds of harm against a citizen that were of such a nature that they could be considered to be harm against the state itself.[5] In this sense, states can choose to stand in the place of their nationals to seek a remedy

[3] See generally Edwin M. Borchard, *The Diplomatic Protection of Citizens Abroad: Or The Law of International Claims* (New York: Banks Law Publishing, 1915); Richard B. Lillich, ed., *International Law of State Responsibility for Injuries to Aliens* (Charlottesville: University Press of Virginia, 1983); Francisco V. García-Amador, *The Changing Law of International Claims*, vols. 1 and 2 (New York: Oceana Publications, 1984); Carmen Tiburcio, *The Human Rights of Aliens Under International and Comparative Law* (The Hague: Martinus Nijhoff, 2001); Chittharanjan F. Amerasinghe, *Diplomatic Protection* (Oxford: Oxford University Press, 2008). See also 'Text of the Draft Articles [on Diplomatic Protection] with Commentaries thereto' in *Report of the International Law Commission*, UN Doc A/61/10 (2006), ch. IV, 22–100.

[4] Emer de Vattel, *The Law of Nations or Principles of the Law of Nature, Applied to the Conduct and Affairs of Nations and Sovereigns* (1758, Béla Kapossy and Richard Whatmore, eds., Indianapolis: Liberty Fund, 2008).

[5] For further discussion of Vattel and diplomatic protection, see Kate Parlett, *The Individual in the International Legal System* (Cambridge: Cambridge University Press, 2011), 49–50; M. Sornarajah, *International Law on Foreign Investment*, 3rd ed. (Cambridge: Cambridge University Press, 2010), 121.

for the harm inflicted by the offending foreign state. This concept of transforming an individual injury to a state injury coupled with the ability of states to pursue action on a national's behalf is referred to as the doctrine of diplomatic protection. The proximity of state and citizen interests and Vattel's characterisation of protection as a matter related to the law of nations have shaped the way in which protection is regulated in international law.

Since Vattel's characterisation of protection, international law has been the main vehicle for addressing the protection of citizens abroad.[6] Protection of citizens has been addressed in the law of state responsibility, the law on the treatment of aliens, the law of diplomatic protection, the law on nationality, international human rights law and international investment law.[7] The International Law Commission (ILC), a body established within the United Nations for the purpose of codifying and developing international law,[8] undertook programmes of study to codify the rules of diplomatic protection.[9] This ILC process ultimately concluded with the adoption of draft articles on Diplomatic Protection in 2006, which reflect, for the most part, the customary international rules of diplomatic protection.[10]

[6] See, for example, Borchard, above note 3; Frederick Sherwood Dunn, *The Protection of Nationals: A Study in the Application of International Law* (1932) (New York: Klaus Reprint, 1970); Alwyn V. Freeman, *The International Responsibility of States for Denial of Justice* (1938) (New York: Klaus Reprint, 1970); Chittharanjan F. Amerasinghe, *State Responsibility for Injuries to Aliens* (Oxford: Clarendon Press, 1967); Lillich, above note 3; García-Amador, above note 3; Tiburcio, above note 3; John Dugard, 'Diplomatic Protection' (2009) in Rüdiger Wolfrum, ed., *Max Planck Encyclopedia of Public International Law* (Oxford: Oxford University Press, 2012), vol. 3, 114–134; Annemarieke Vermeer-Künzli, *The Protection of Individuals by Means of Diplomatic Protection: Diplomatic Protection as a Human Rights Instrument* (PhD thesis, Leiden University, 2007), online at: https://openaccess.leidenuniv.nl/; Amerasinghe, *Diplomatic Protection*, above note 3.

[7] See, for example, García-Amador, above note 3; Amerasinghe, *Diplomatic Protection*, above note 3.

[8] *Establishment of an International Law Commission*, GA Res 174(II), UN Doc A/RES/174(11) (1947), Annex, *Statute of the International Law Commission 1947*, art. 1(1).

[9] For a broader discussion of the ILC's work on state responsibility, see James Crawford, *The International Law Commission's Articles on State Responsibility* (Cambridge: Cambridge University Press, 2002). For a discussion of diplomatic protection, see John Dugard, 'Diplomatic Protection' in James Crawford, Alain Pellet and Simon Olleson, eds., *The Law of International Responsibility* (Oxford: Oxford University Press, 2010), 1051–1072.

[10] See 'Text of the Draft Articles on Diplomatic Protection' in *Report of the International Law Commission*, UN Doc A/61/10 (2006), ch. IV, 16–22. See also John Dugard, 'Articles on Diplomatic Protection 2006' in United Nations, *Audiovisual Library of International*

The 'ILC Draft Articles on Diplomatic Protection' define diplomatic protection as

> the invocation by a State, through diplomatic action or other means of peaceful settlement, of the responsibility of another State for an injury caused by an internationally wrongful act of that State to a natural or legal person that is a national of the former State with a view to the implementation of such responsibility.[11]

This definition reveals two features of the legal regime regulating the protection of citizens abroad. The first is that responsibility for breaches of international law against individuals is invoked by and between states.[12] Second, the 'ILC Draft Articles on Diplomatic Protection' recognise the right of states to invoke protection in favour of their citizens, meaning that there is no obligation on states in international law to intervene if their citizens experience a human rights violation abroad.[13] States can exercise their right to intervene in a number of ways, such as through consular assistance, diplomatic representations, negotiations, mediation, arbitration, judicial settlement and the severance of diplomatic ties.[14]

B Problems with the International Law Framework

The framework of protection in international law has encouraged scholarly analysis and practice to over-emphasise the exclusive role of states in the protection of citizens abroad. The structure of international law recognises only two actors: the individual and the state (with only states

Law, online at: www.un.org/law/avl/. The draft articles themselves are not binding; however, they refer to and codify customary international law principles, which are binding. As the Special Rapporteur for the topic of diplomatic protection for the ILC, Professor Dugard also attempted to develop progressively some aspects of the law of diplomatic protection beyond the existing rules of customary international law.

11 ILC Draft Articles on Diplomatic Protection, above note 10, art. 1.

12 The ILC's work on diplomatic protection takes the position that there is some scope for the individual to seek a remedy in his or her own right given that the position of the individual in the international legal system has changed: 'Text of the Draft Articles [on Diplomatic Protection] with Commentaries thereto', above note 3, 25–26.

13 There are three requirements before a state may intervene: the commission of an internationally wrongful act or omission, the existence of a bond of nationality between the injured individual and the intervening state and the exhaustion of all domestic remedies within the foreign state. See further, the discussion of C. John R. Dugard in 'First Report of the Special Rapporteur on Diplomatic Protection', UN Doc A/CN.4/506 and Add.1 (2000). See also *Report of the International Law Commission*, UN Doc A/55/10 (2000), ch. V, 72–74 and 76–77.

14 Amerasinghe, *Diplomatic Protection*, above note 3, 27.

bearing full rights and duties under international law). This approach reinforces the role of the state as the sole decider and provider of protection for citizens abroad. As a result, some scholars advocate for states to use diplomatic protection more frequently to protect human rights and even for the creation of an obligation on states to intervene on behalf of their citizens in circumstances of human rights violations.[15] This state-centric view assumes that only states can or do perform the functions of protection.

Another problem that emerges from the classic approach to diplomatic protection is the narrow focus on judicial decisions. Studies on the protection of citizens abroad have relied, almost exclusively, on judgments from international courts and tribunals to describe the phenomenon of protection.[16] Scholars have shown interest primarily in the doctrinal aspects of ICJ and arbitral cases, rather than the broader question of how and why litigation has been used as a tool to protect. The nature of doctrinal analysis also has the effect of rendering invisible the participation or contribution of non-state actors by focusing only on the narrative of the states. While case law is important for doctrine, past studies overlook state systems and their diplomatic practice, even though they underpin and precede any legal action in international forums.

Finally, diplomatic protection entrenches the classic international law formulation of states as monolithic entities. The protection of citizens abroad will necessarily include a series of political decisions and actions, diplomatic efforts and negotiations between states as well as within states. Government, in many states, is an organisation of many actors, including courts, government departments and politicians. Where a state is understood as a single entity, these complexities of international governance and regulation remain invisible in scholarly analysis.

C *Network Theory: A Solution?*

An exclusive focus on legal doctrine and the behaviour of states precludes actors that influence, participate in and generate processes or actions

[15] See, for example, 'First Report of the Special Rapporteur on Diplomatic Protection', above note 13. See also Vermeer-Künzli, above note 6; Darren O'Donovan et al., 'An Analysis of Home-State Obligations to International Migrants', 1 June 2013, online at: http://papers.ssrn.com/sol3/papers.cfm?abstract_id=2276741.

[16] See, for example, Borchard, above note 3; Amerasinghe, *Diplomatic Protection*, above note 3.

from analysis. How can we resolve the shortcomings of state-centricity when addressing the protection of citizens abroad? One solution for the intellectual barriers imposed by the monolithic state paradigm is to conceive of the state as multiple actors and units. In her book entitled *A New World Order*, Anne-Marie Slaughter draws on the work of regulatory theorists, sociologists and political scientists to 'disaggregate' the state and to identify networks of decision-making.[17] The intention of this disaggregation is to identify connections between actors that previously would go unseen in the international law model. Slaughter suggests new connections between actors and attempts to reveal new networks for decision-making and concentrations of power.

Slaughter's model of global order focuses on the networks established between government counterparts across national borders. The emphasis is placed on relationships between government agencies – she describes these connections as 'government networks' or the theory more broadly as 'transgovernmentalism'.[18] Transgovernmentalism can be understood as the connections between sub-units of governments and the networks formed through their interaction. This section will consider how to apply models of networks, including Slaughter's model of transgovernmentalism, to the protection of citizens abroad in international law.

Slaughter asserts that relying on the state as an exclusive unit of analysis limits our understanding of global governance. She argues that disaggregating the state is a useful analytical tool for identifying nodes of power and generators of action. Slaughter instructs her reader on how to better view the world as follows:

> Stop imagining the international system as a system of States – unitary entities like billiard balls or black boxes – subject to rules created by international institutions that are apart from, 'above' these States. Start thinking about a world of governments, with all the different institutions that perform the basic functions of governments – legislation, adjudication, implementation – interactions both with each other domestically and also with their foreign and supranational counterparts. States still exist in this world; indeed, they are crucial actors.[19]

States have growing regulatory responsibility in social, political, economic and legal relations, and this increased responsibility is coupled with an increase of actors executing state functions. In light of this, it is

[17] Anne-Marie Slaughter, *A New World Order* (Princeton: Princeton University Press, 2004).

[18] Ibid., 145. [19] Ibid., 5.

possible to disaggregate and re-aggregate the state in a number of ways. This intellectual process could result in groupings along function, subject matter, level (local, national, regional, international), geography, membership composition or structure. How the state is disaggregated and who is included and excluded in this exercise has consequences for how we characterise global governance and explain actions by states and non-states alike.

Slaughter's vision disaggregates and re-aggregates the state through networks between similar agencies of different states. She suggests that there are two kinds of networks: horizontal and vertical. The horizontal order she describes refers to the connections directly between government agencies and their counterparts in other states. The vertical order refers to the connections that occur between states and supranational organisations or institutions. Within the horizontal networks, there are 'direct interactions across sub-units of different governments that are not controlled or closely guided by the policies of the cabinets or chief executives of those governments'.[20] For example, foreign ministries in different countries may exchange information and set standards for consular practice without ministerial or executive approval. These networks include executive, judicial and legislative networks running at the sub-state level. The objectives of these networks vary, according to Slaughter. Based on their function, they can be characterised as information networks, harmonisation networks, coordination networks and enforcement networks.[21]

Transgovernmentalism, and the networks Slaughter describes, can be understood as a map for tracing forms of international cooperation. Kal Raustiala has identified a similar vision of cooperation, contributing case studies in the fields of securities regulation, competition policy and environmental regulation.[22] He observes that there is a coordinating value to these transgovernmental networks, noting that

> [t]he state is instead disaggregating for purposes of cooperation: domestic officials are reaching out to their foreign counterparts regularly and directly through networks, rather than through state-to-state negotiation of the kind that dominated 20th century cooperation. This notion of 'disaggregated sovereignty' is at the center of transgovernmental theory.[23]

[20] Ibid., 10. [21] Ibid., 144.

[22] Kal Raustiala, 'The Architecture of International Cooperation: Transgovernmental Networks and the Future of International Law' (2002) 43:1 *Virginia Journal of International Law* 1–92.

[23] Ibid., 10–11.

Raustiala and Slaughter emphasise the role of networks as vehicles for information exchange and the coordination of activity. The benefit of transgovernmentalism is that it provides a framework for unveiling the connections shared by sub-units of state actors between different states. It also identifies a broader range of government actors and their connections than the traditionally monolithic state-centred model. Transgovernmental networks can also, at least in part, explain global cooperation in relation to transnational problems.

However, transgovernmentalism has some limitations, particularly as it relates to the protection of citizens abroad. First, it remains a fundamentally state-centric model for understanding participation in the international legal order. In this regard, Slaughter's analysis does not fully address the role of non-state actors in the international system. Transgovernmentalism as envisaged by Slaughter recognises the existence of non-state actors, but it does not go beyond placing them as a phenomenon outside of the networks formed between state agencies where, in her view, power is generated and exerted. In Slaughter's vision, non-state actors have their own separate networks that interact with transgovernmental networks. However, this analysis replicates an emphasis on the state, with non-state actors on the periphery. Yet a reality of global governance and cooperation is the presence and power of multi-actor networks. What the transgovernmental model cannot achieve is an explanation of how different actors (state and non-state) employ modes of influence and how they interact with one another, sometimes within the same network, to achieve their goals.

1 Networked Governance

There are several theories of governance, regulation and networks that provide a framework for disaggregating the state into its composite actors, yet they also recognise the participation of actors outside of formal state structures. Common to all the modes of governance is an underlying assumption of a pluricentric rather than unicentric model of networks.[24] Rachel Parker observes that many actors participate in regulation: 'individual actors, firms, social groups, civic organisations and

[24] Kees Van Kersbergen and Frans Van Waarden, '"Governance" as a Bridge between Disciplines: Cross-disciplinary Inspiration Regarding Shifts in Governance and Problems of Governability, Accountability and Legitimacy' (2004) 43:2 *European Journal of Political Research* 143–171, 151; Clifford Shearing and Jennifer Wood, 'Nodal Governance, Democracy, and the New "Denizens"' (2003) 30:3 *Journal of Law and Society* 400–419, 403.

policy makers interact with each other . . . to implement and enforce public policies and to improve private-sector coordination'.[25] These theories focus on the connections between actors, rather than their formal status. David Kennedy's work on governance exemplifies this emphasis on the relationships between actors by asking: 'who functions in this hidden world where rules are made, how do they become powerful, what kinds of rules and principles travel from one domain to another and which are left behind?'[26] A greater emphasis on actors and values means that the state does not occupy a more privileged position than other actors, but is instead 'merely one – albeit an important – actor among many others'.[27] In his study on network power, Manuel Castells suggests that 'even the most powerful states, have some power (mainly destructive), but not all the power'.[28] These scholars suggest that the traditional monopoly of power exercised by the state through coercion, command and control has been superseded by a more nuanced expression of power through cooperation and alliance formation within networks.[29]

Some writers have suggested that this matrix of actors, agendas and complex relationships of power and influence requires empirical tracing. Reinforcing this point, Kennedy stated, 'Simply mapping the modes of global power and identifying the channels and levers of influence remains an enormous sociological challenge'.[30] In their work on peace building in Timor Leste, John Braithwaite, Hilary Charlesworth and Adérito Soares endorse empirical approaches to governance. In their words:

> The networked governance tradition in political theory is primarily a descriptive one. It is about the empirical observation in a world of global business networks, trans-governmental networks and global NGO networks that governance can be more important than government (by a state), that networked power can be more important than hierarchical bureaucratic power.[31]

[25] Rachel Parker, 'Networked Governance or Just Networks? Local Governance of the Knowledge Economy in Limerick (Ireland) and Karlskrona (Sweden)' (2007) 55:1 *Political Studies* 113–132, 118.

[26] David Kennedy, 'The Mystery of Global Governance' (2008) 34:3 *Ohio Northern University Law Review* 827–860, 842.

[27] Van Kersbergen and Van Waarden, above note 24, 152.

[28] Manuel Castells, 'A Network Theory of Power' (2011) 5 *International Journal of Communication* 773–787, 776.

[29] Van Kersbergen and Van Waarden, above note 24, 152.

[30] Kennedy, above note 26, 828.

[31] John Braithwaite, Hilary Charlesworth and Adérito Soares, *Networked Governance of Freedom and Tyranny: Peace in Timor-Leste* (Canberra: Australian National University Press, 2012), 8.

The governance and network frameworks that these scholars describe explore how issues of public interest are resolved through a decision-making lens. Yet, the state-centricity of the transgovernmentalism theory does not allow for decision-making processes to be seen as 'interactive, fragmented, multidimensional policy-making involving a range of state and non-state actors' in the way that many writers analysing networks would envisage.[32] Inclusion of a broader range of actors is necessary for a pluralistic view of influence where actors are both subjects and objects of regulation.[33]

II Background to the *LaGrand* Case

In 1999, Germany commenced proceedings in the ICJ against the United States for breaches of the Vienna Convention on Consular Relations (VCCR).[34] Germany invoked its right of diplomatic protection on behalf of two German nationals, brothers Karl and Walter LaGrand. The LaGrands were convicted of violent crimes and consequently sentenced to death by an Arizona court. Following numerous appeals and interventions by Germany, their death sentence was not set aside. Germany made a request for the indication of provisional measures to halt the executions until the ICJ issued a judgment on the alleged international law violations.[35] However, before the merits of the ICJ case had even been heard, the LaGrand brothers were executed. Section II of this chapter aims to investigate the participation and actions of state and non-state actors prior to Germany's ICJ intervention.

A Karl and Walter LaGrand: A Life before Death Row

The progeny of a German woman, Karl and Walter LaGrand moved from Germany to the United States as young children. Unbeknownst to them, they never acquired US citizenship during their residence. An American serviceman – and their mother's partner at the time of their emigration from Germany – adopted the brothers and gave them the surname LaGrand. Many years later, in January 1982, Walter and Karl LaGrand

32 Parker, above note 25, 116.

33 See generally, John Braithwaite and Peter Drahos, *Global Business Regulation* (Cambridge: Cambridge University Press, 2000).

34 24 April 1963, 596 UNTS 261, in force 19 March 1967, art. 36(1)(b).

35 *LaGrand (Germany v. United States of America)*, Provisional Measures, Order of 3 March 1999, [1999] ICJ Rep 9.

committed a bank robbery in Arizona. They killed one person and inflicted serious injuries on another. At the time of their arrest they informed police that they were Americans, on the assumption that they had been naturalised. Karl and Walter LaGrand were convicted of armed robbery and murder by an Arizona court and were sentenced to death. The LaGrands appealed their sentences from 1987 until 1998.[36]

It is not clear at what point in the domestic criminal proceedings the revelation about their German nationality occurred. At some point during their custody they met another German incarcerated in the same facility and he informed the brothers that an official from the German consulate had visited him and provided some support during his criminal proceedings.[37] Once the LaGrand brothers were in contact with their consulate, Germany began making representations on their behalf. Germany intervened through a series of political and diplomatic measures, including representations at their appeals and at every level in the US political and legal system.[38] It became apparent that Germany's diplomatic and political efforts had failed when Karl LaGrand was executed on 24 February 1999.

B The International Court of Justice Proceedings

Once domestic remedies in the United States had been exhausted, Germany commenced legal proceedings in the ICJ. Germany filed for provisional measures in the ICJ to prevent the execution of the second brother, Walter LaGrand, on 3 March 1999. The Court granted provisional measures on 2 March 1999, but Walter LaGrand was executed the next day.[39] Despite the execution of both Karl and Walter LaGrand prior to the merits stage of the case, Germany proceeded with its action against the United States.

Germany's case was brought on the basis of a breach of the VCCR and its right of diplomatic protection. There are two obligations that flow from article 36 of the VCCR. The first requires states to notify one

[36] *Arizona v. Walter LaGrand*, 153 Ariz 21 (1987); *Arizona v. Karl Hinze LaGrand*, 152 Ariz 483 (1987).

[37] Interview with counsel 1 for Germany in *LaGrand*, June 2013.

[38] These interventions included an application in the Supreme Court of the United States for an injunction against the execution of Walter LaGrand in compliance with the international court's order of provisional measures. See *Federal Republic of Germany v. United States*, 526 US 111 (1999).

[39] Roger Cohen, 'U.S. Execution of German Stirs Anger', *New York Times* (4 March 1999), online at: www.nytimes.com/1999/03/05/us/us-execution-of-german-stirs-anger.html.

another when foreign nationals come into their custody and the second is to inform foreign nationals of their right to have consular access. These obligations allow states to provide consular assistance to their nationals and make representations about the conditions of their custody to the detaining state if needed. Article 36 (1)(b) of the VCCR states:

> [I]f he so requests, the competent authorities of the receiving State shall, without delay, inform the consular post of the sending State if, within its consular district, a national of that State is arrested or committed to prison or to custody pending trial or is detained in any other manner. Any communication addressed to the consular post by the person arrested, in prison, custody or detention shall be forwarded by the said authorities without delay. The said authorities shall inform the person concerned without delay of his rights under this subparagraph.[40]

In its claim before the ICJ, Germany argued that the LaGrand brothers had not been informed of their right to contact the German consulate without delay and that the German consulate was not notified of their custody. The US government acknowledged that they had failed to notify Germany that the LaGrands were in US custody and issued a formal apology in relation to the breach. However, Germany argued that if it had received consular notification of the LaGrands' detention without delay, it could have provided the brothers with assistance in their proceedings, leading to the possibility of an outcome less than the death penalty. Under Arizona's criminal law, the doctrine of 'procedural default' prevented any new legal grounds being raised in appeals that had not previously been raised. The practical impact of this procedural rule meant that the issue of consular notification could not be relied upon as a ground for appeal because the LaGrand brothers had not raised it in their trials or in previous appeals.[41]

On the substantive legal issues, the ICJ decided in favour of Germany. It held that the failure of the United States to inform Germany that the LaGrand brothers were in its custody was a breach of the VCCR. The Court ordered review and reconsideration as the remedy.[42] Germany also alleged violations of its right in customary international law to diplomatic protection. In its memorial, Germany claimed that the United States had 'injured Germany *indirectly* through its failure to

[40] VCCR, above note 34, art. 36(1)(b).

[41] *LaGrand (Germany v. United States of America)*, Counter-Memorial of the United States of America (27 March 2000), para 76, online at: www.icj-cij.org/docket/files/104/8554.pdf.

[42] *LaGrand* (Judgment), above note 1, 512–513, para 124.

accord to German nationals in the United States the treatment to which they were entitled under international law'.[43] By pleading diplomatic protection, and not just the treaty violation under the VCCR, Germany adopted the injury against the LaGrands as its own. However, the ICJ saw no need to decide on the question of diplomatic protection in its judgment.[44]

C Germany's Interventions on Behalf of Karl and Walter LaGrand

Interventions by Germany can be divided into actions taken before and after 1998, as this year corresponds with elections in Germany and a change of government. Routine consular actions were taken by Germany on behalf of the brothers prior to 1998. However, after 1998, the actions taken by Germany included a range of consular, diplomatic and political measures.[45] In addition to routine consular measures, Germany made 'energetic moral and political appeals'.[46] These appeals included

> every diplomatic means at its disposal in order to prevent the carrying out of the death sentences . . . [b]oth the President and the Chancellor of the Federal Republic of Germany appealed to the President of the United States, the latter also to the Governor of Arizona. Foreign Minister Fischer and Minister of Justice Däubler-Gmelin raised the issue with their respective counterparts in the United States Administration and with the Governor of the State of Arizona. Démarches were undertaken by the German Ambassador to the United States. A further démarche followed on behalf of the European Union. Both the German Ambassador and the German Consul-General in Los Angeles explained the German position to the Board of Executive Clemency of the State of Arizona on the days prior to the execution of the brothers. In his second letter to United States Secretary of State Albright, dated 22 February 1999, the German Foreign Minister, Joschka Fischer, raised the issue of a violation of the Vienna Convention [on Consular Relations] – to no avail.[47]

43 *LaGrand (Germany v. United States of America)*, Memorial of the Federal Republic of Germany (16 September 1999), para 4.86, online at: www.icj-cij.org/docket/files/104/8552.pdf.

44 *LaGrand* (Judgment), above note 1, 494, paras 77–78.

45 This was a point of criticism raised by the United States in the ICJ case, where it noted that Germany's efforts escalated after 1998. See Counter-Memorial of the United States of America, above note 41, paras 30–36.

46 Memorial of the Federal Republic of Germany, above note 43, para 1.03.

47 Ibid., para 2.11 [references omitted].

German officials and politicians attended and made representations in the clemency hearings.[48] Claudia Roth, president of the Green Party and chair of the *Bundestag*'s Human Rights Committee, travelled to Arizona to attend the LaGrand brothers' hearings in person.

Germany's efforts to save the LaGrands were frustrated by the allocation of powers between the state of Arizona and the federal government of the United States. Arizona had jurisdiction for state-based criminal matters, including decisions on clemency. The US government faced a domestic deadlock with Arizona whose judiciary and politicians disregarded the VCCR and the LaGrands' claim that it had been breached. The US government did not have the power to prevent the application of the death penalty to Karl and Walter LaGrand or force Arizona to review the matter.

D *State and Non-state Actor Participation*

1 State Actors

In the German bureaucracy the two major ministries concerned, the Federal Ministry of Justice and the Federal Ministry of Foreign Affairs, did not agree on whether Germany should proceed with judicial action against the United States.[49] Concerned with maintaining their relationship with the United States, the Ministry of Foreign Affairs opposed the idea of taking Germany's ally to the ICJ.[50] Use of the ICJ mechanism contributed to elevating the matter from the privacy of diplomacy to the publicity of global legal action; moreover, the public nature of the case risked endangering US–German relations in the foreign ministry's view. The Justice Ministry, however, was more concerned with the legal case and the technical grounds available to Germany under the VCCR.[51] Within the German ministries, the United States was both a military ally and legal foe. On one front Germany had a military alliance with the United States and on another it was challenging US death penalty values in a public and international forum. The differing positions of the ministries were ultimately resolved by the Federal Chancellor's office, which instructed them to proceed with an action in the ICJ.[52]

This decision by the political classes of government may be explained by reference to political forces present in Germany in 1998–1999. The

[48] Ibid., para 2.10. [49] Interview with counsel 2 for Germany in *LaGrand*, July 2013.
[50] Ibid. [51] Interview with German official 1, August 2013.
[52] Interview with counsel 1 for Germany in *LaGrand*, June 2013.

political environment in Germany contributed to elevating the LaGrand brothers' situation from a matter of consular concern to a matter of international judicial concern. In 1999 the Social Democratic and Green parties ousted the conservatives from power in the German federal election, making it the first time that these parties formed government in Germany. Prior to the handover by the right-of-centre Christian Democrat-led government to the incoming Social Democratic and Greens government, a vote passed in the German Parliament (*Bundestag*) committing Germany to participation in Kosovo as part of the broader NATO intervention. The consequence of this decision was that it would be the first occasion that Germany would participate in an armed conflict since World War II. The incoming Social Democratic and Greens government upheld the decision to join the NATO forces – a decision that was hugely unpopular with the German public. In their examination of Germany's policy in Kosovo, Aubrey Hamilton and Engjellushe Morina situate this decision within its domestic context as follows:

> This decision was made at a time when the center-left 'Social Democratic Party' (SPD) still distinguished between measures to preserve peace, which were considered good, and measures to create peace, which many rejected. Ready to normalize Germany's military role in geopolitics and 'create peace' in Kosovo, the coalition government of the SPD and Greens pushed through a positive vote for German intervention in Kosovo.[53]

As a result of the government's decision to participate in the armed conflict in Kosovo, the newly formed government lost support from their core constituency early in their incumbency.[54] Historically a pacifist party, the Greens' support for military participation was unpopular with their voters.[55] This controversy echoed in the media and public; it manifested in protests and physical attacks on Greens ministers,

[53] Aubrey Hamilton and Engjellushe Morina, *Germany's Foreign Policy Towards Kosovo: A Policy Perspective* (Prishtina, Kosovo: Group for Legal and Political Studies and Prishtina Council on Foreign Relations, 2014), 7, online at: http://legalpoliticalstudies.org/download/Policy%20Report%2002%202014.pdf.

[54] Interview with counsel 2 for Germany in *LaGrand*, July 2013.

[55] 'Schröder on Kosovo: "The Goal Was Exclusively Humanitarian"' *Speigel Online* (26 October 2006), online at www.spiegel.de/international/schroeder-on-kosovo-the-goal-was-exclusively-humanitarian-a-444727.html; 'German Greens Avoid Political Crisis' BBC News (14 May 1999), online at: http://news.bbc.co.uk/1/hi/world/europe/343503.stm.

including Foreign Minister Joschka Fischer.[56] The decision to intervene on behalf of the LaGrands may have been an attempt to win back the coalition's base in a strong move towards human rights protection and anti-death penalty values (values more akin to their political ideology and that of their voters).[57]

2 Non-state Actors

The ICJ memorials and judgment reveal little about the participation of non-state actors in Germany's interventions on behalf of the LaGrand brothers. Non-state actors played a critical role in attracting public attention to the situation of the LaGrands and mobilising an existing network of anti-death penalty actors. The involvement of non-state actors in Germany pivots on the attention generated by the media around the execution of the brothers. The LaGrand plight came into German public consciousness sometime in 1999. Steffen Ufer, a German lawyer from Munich, had been involved in the *LaGrand* criminal cases in Arizona. Some suspected that Ufer leaked the case to the German media in order to raise the profile of the issue and to apply some pressure on the German government to act.[58] Ufer's action changed the case from an obscure Arizona criminal trial to a contest of values relating to the death penalty. The case generated a great deal of public attention in Germany, particularly as it related to Germany's values as a rule-of-law state. It led to several developments for the LaGrands: the mobilisation of an existing global anti-death penalty campaign, the formation of a network of state and non-state actors, and public support for action.

The anti-death penalty campaign gained momentum, within Europe, with the entry into force of *Protocol No. 6 to the Convention for the Protection of Human Rights and Fundamental Freedoms*,[59] and beyond Europe, with the entry into force in 1991 of the *Second Optional Protocol to the International Covenant on Civil and Political Rights* aiming at the abolition of the death penalty (Second Optional Protocol).[60] Germany is a party to both treaties, having ratified Protocol No. 6 on 1 August 1989

[56] The foreign minister at the time, Joschka Fischer, was attacked with cans of red paint by protesters, resulting in a perforated eardrum: 'German Greens Avoid Political Crisis' (ibid.).

[57] Interview with counsel 2 for Germany in *LaGrand*, July 2013.

[58] Interview with counsel 1 for Germany in *LaGrand*, June 2013.

[59] 28 April 1983, 1496 UNTS 281, ETS No 114, in force 1 March 1985, in force for Germany 1 August 1989.

[60] 15 December 1989, 1642 UNTS 414, in force 11 July 1991.

and the Second Optional Protocol on 18 August 1992. Following ratification, Germany formed part of the broader European campaign against the death penalty, which served as a springboard for a larger global campaign for its abolition. Girling describes the transition of the anti-death penalty campaign from a European to a global phenomenon as the point when 'a very vocal and evangelical European voice gained prominence on the international stage'.[61] Civil society organisations Amnesty International and Human Rights Watch launched specialised international campaigns addressing the death penalty as part of the momentum.[62] Germany also took part in the campaign for the abolition of the death penalty, drawing attention to its actions and campaign activities in its memorial submitted to the Court.[63]

Once the imminence of the brothers' executions became apparent, the German section of Amnesty International received daily enquiries about activities and possible action that the organisation would take to address their situation.[64] In response, it launched the 'National Coalition to Abolish the Death Penalty' (NCADP), a national campaign addressing the use of the death penalty globally. As the domestic public campaign gained momentum, so did Germany's advocacy on behalf of the LaGrands in the United States. Karen Bagge, a representative of Amnesty International, was sent to Arizona to conduct appeals on behalf of the LaGrands. She appeared alongside Steffen Ufer, the German ambassador Jürgen Chrobog, Green Party president and parliamentarian Claudia Roth, lawyer Carla Ryan (counsel for Karl LaGrand) and Bruce Burke (counsel for Walter LaGrand) in the LaGrands' clemency hearings in 1999. Prior to the clemency appeals, Bagge recounted that she met with the lawyers for the brothers, the German ambassador, Steffen Ufer, Claudia Roth and Matthias Lemphul (representative of the NCADP). Both state and non-state actors strategised together about their collective approach and the angle that each actor would take in the clemency

[61] Eva Girling, 'European Identity and the Mission against the Death Penalty in the United States' in Austin Sarat and Christian Boulanger, eds., *Cultural Lives of Capital Punishment: Comparative Perspectives* (Stanford: Stanford University Press, 2005), 112–128, 114.

[62] Information on Amnesty International's campaign against the death penalty can be found online at: www.amnesty.org/en/what-we-do/death-penalty/. Information on Human Rights Watch's efforts can be found online at: www.hrw.org/tag/death-penalty.

[63] Memorial of the Federal Republic of Germany, above note 43, footnote 3.

[64] Karen Bagge, 'Die Selbstherrlichkeit der Grossmacht' [The Arrogance of the Super Power] *Amnesty International Journal (German Section)* (April 1999), online at: www.amnesty.de/umleitung/1999/deu05/223.

hearings.[65] These actors also presented 50,000 signatures from the German public petitioning the Governor of Arizona for clemency for the LaGrand brothers.

In the anti-death penalty campaign it is possible to identify three networks of actors: the transnational or global network, the European network and the German network. The domestic non-state actors in Germany harnessed existing network advocacy to further their own campaigns for the LaGrands. Moreover, Amnesty International's Germany office, through Karen Bagge, was able to harness existing expertise and experience from the broader anti-death penalty campaigns and put forward a policy position on the LaGrands. The actors in the intersecting anti-death penalty networks can be described as epistemic communities (or networks of experts) that the government relied upon. Peter Haas argues that '[e]pistemic communities may introduce new policy alternatives to their governments, and depending on the extent to which these communities are successful in obtaining and retaining bureaucratic power domestically, they can often lead their governments to pursue them'.[66] Haas argued that regimes can contribute to the empowerment of new groups of actors. In the case of Germany, the existing international and European human rights regime, coupled with the success of the international campaign against the death penalty, served as a platform for the empowerment of NGOs and individual actors to lobby for the LaGrands' case to be juridified as an alternative policy measure.

E *Germany's Legal Framework for the Protection of Citizens*

Another source of pressure on the German government to intervene on behalf of the LaGrand brothers may be found in Germany's domestic legal framework for protection of citizens. The provision of consular assistance and the protection of citizens abroad are governed by Germany's constitution, the Basic Law of 1949 (*Grundgesetz*), and the Consular Law of 1974.[67] The Consular Law sets out a number of arrangements relevant to the protection of German citizens, including

[65] Ibid.

[66] Peter M. Haas, 'Do Regimes Matter? Epistemic Communities and Mediterranean Pollution Control' (1989) 43:3 *International Organization* 377–403, 402.

[67] *Grundgesetz für die Bundesrepublik Deutschland* [Basic Law of the Federal Republic of Germany], 23 May 1949, as amended, and *Consular Law* (Germany), 11 September 1974, Federal Law Gazette I, 2317.

that assistance may include legal protection.[68] Framed in general terms, the Consular Law creates a conditional obligation on consular officers to 'help Germans in their consular district requiring assistance if the state of distress cannot be resolved in any other way'.[69] The generality of the language in the legislation ensures a wide margin for consular officers to exercise discretion in the provision of assistance to German citizens.

The Basic Law contains a number of protections for citizens, which are directly binding law.[70] The Basic Law creates a foundation for Germany as a rule of law and democratic state, which is reflected in its constitutional provisions.[71] With a rigorous and active court system, this constitutional document is an important component of government decision-making and civic participation. The Basic Law in Germany guides a range of government action. Werner Ebke and Matthew Finkin describe the Basic Law as setting minimum goals and that these standards 'have to play a role in decision-making on all levels of state action'.[72] Edward Eberle argues that human dignity is at the centre of the German constitutional framework; 'it infuses throughout the whole constitutional order, obligating the state both to protect and realize it'.[73] He goes on to argue that 'the systematization of German legal science, centers around the human person as a "spiritual-moral" individual, and her dignity, including especially her ability to realize human capacity and satisfaction. Human values are thus the focal point of the legal order.'[74]

Article 2(2) of the Basic Law, entitled 'Rights of Liberty', states, 'Everyone has the right to life and to inviolability of his person. The freedom of the individual is inviolable. These rights may only be encroached upon pursuant to a law.'[75] Within this right is the obligation on the German government to protect the lives of nationals, including the provision of consular assistance. There is an important role for German courts in interpreting the Basic Law in accordance with the protection of

[68] Basic Law of the Federal Republic of Germany, above note 67, art. 5(3).

[69] Ibid., art. 5(1).

[70] Werner F. Ebke and Matthew Finkin, eds., *An Introduction to German Law* (Leiden: Kluwer Law International, 1996), 67.

[71] Ibid., 47. [72] Ibid., 55.

[73] Edward J. Eberle, 'Observations on the Development of Human Dignity and Personality in German Constitutional Law: An Overview' (2012) 33 *Liverpool Law Review* 201–233, 206.

[74] Ibid., 229. [75] Basic Law of the Federal Republic of Germany, above note 67, art. 2(2).

human dignity and the right to life.[76] In a case concerning Rudolph Hess, the Federal Constitutional Court held that the German government is 'constitutionally obliged to a duty to protect German nationals and their interests against foreign States'.[77] While the judgment does not specify to which articles this obligation would apply, it would seem that it confers a general obligation on the government to protect the rights of its citizens, particularly those fundamental rights such as the right to life. Some scholars have interpreted this judgment to be a constitutional enshrinement of the right to diplomatic protection by Germany.[78]

In the case of the LaGrand brothers, the threat of a domestic constitutional challenge against the government may have contributed to a more motivated response to their plight.[79] This may also explain the Ministry of Justice's approach to the case as a legal necessity whereby it attributed more weight to the constitutional legal obligations to protect the right to life than to the political considerations raised by the Foreign Ministry about the American–German relationship.

III Networked Governance, Values and Law

As discussed above, the commencement of the *LaGrand* case in the ICJ cannot be explained through the actions of state actors alone, but must implicate a broader network of actors. A network of protection intervened on the LaGrands' behalf that included components of a disaggregated state as well as actors falling outside of state structures. Actors including NGOs, judicial institutions, public constituencies, media and individuals influenced the decisions of the government through moral pressure, political mechanisms and law. The competing values of Germany's government departments, as well as non-state actors, like civil society and individual lawyers, provide a more nuanced explanation for why Germany intervened on the brothers' behalf. Section III will consider three things: how those networks formed, law as a technique of protection and the significance of disaggregation for protection in the LaGrand action.

[76] Eberle, above note 73, 206.

[77] *Rudolph Hess*, Federal Constitutional Court, 16 December 1980, reprinted in 90 ILR 387, 396.

[78] See, for example, Annemarieke Vermeer-Künzli, 'Restricting Discretion: Judicial Review of Diplomatic Protection' (2006) 75:2 *Nordic Journal of International Law* 279–307, 282.

[79] Interview with counsel 1 for Germany in *LaGrand*, June 2013.

A Formation, Function and Techniques of the LaGrand Protection Network

1 Network Formation: The Role of Epistemic Communities and Expertise

How did the network between state actors and non-state actors in the LaGrand action form? One explanation is that changes in government policy can occur when states become 'porous' to civil society influence.[80] Christopher Pallas and Anders Uhlin argue that civil society organisations are not able to achieve change without access to the state and alignment to its interests.[81] Pallas and Uhlin also observe that in order for there to be success in civil society efforts to influence a state, they must offer 'technical expertise or constituent support'.[82] The civil society and private actors involved in the LaGrand proceedings in the United States were able to offer the German government expertise on US domestic law, international human rights law and the anti-death penalty campaign, and to deliver the support of the mass public in Germany.

Another important aligning interest that contributed to forming the network were the attempts by different actors to gain legitimacy with their respective audiences. Mark Suchman notes that legitimacy affects the way that people respond, relate and understand an organisation or entity.[83] He identifies two dimensions related to seeking legitimacy: one of continuity versus credibility, and another of active versus passive support.[84] Organisations that have legitimacy are considered by their target audience to be more trustworthy and more meaningful (credibility and continuity), and this legitimacy may be gained through active approval of the decisions or directions or acquiescence (active and passive support).[85] After the newly elected government's decision to commit Germany to the Kosovo war contributed to a deficit in its moral legitimacy, the government needed to display its capacity to 'do the right thing'.[86] In the face of falling popularity, the German government sought to assert its human rights credentials, particularly with its disenchanted voters, through the LaGrand action. Even after the

[80] Christopher L. Pallas and Anders Uhlin, 'Civil Society Influence on International Organizations: Theorizing the State Channel' (2014) 10:2 *Journal of Civil Society* 184–203, 188.

[81] Ibid., 186–187. [82] Ibid., 199.

[83] Mark C. Suchman, 'Managing Legitimacy: Strategic and Institutional Approaches' (1995) 20:3 *Academy of Management Review* 571–610, 575.

[84] Ibid., 574. [85] Ibid., 575. [86] Ibid., 579.

execution of both brothers, the ICJ case served as a 'hollow symbolic gesture' to the German public about Germany's values.[87] Conversely, civil society in Germany was seeking legitimacy within their broader anti-death penalty regime as the leader in the transnational and global campaign. The ICJ effort translated into a concrete 'win' for the campaign and reinforced the moral legitimacy of the anti-death penalty message.

2 Function

The network of protection in the LaGrand action disrupts pre-existing notions of what 'protection' is and its characterisation as an exclusive state function. The LaGrand example helps to diffuse the protection of citizens abroad into several components or tasks. Two components of protection emerge. The first component is generating the motivation to intervene on a citizen's behalf. This motivation may be generated by moral or political values including political expediency, national values, human rights, security or the rule of law.

The aim or value of intervention on behalf of the LaGrand brothers is complex. Actors were driven by different values, but shared a common objective of intervention. Germany did not internally generate the value or motivation to protect the LaGrand brothers until domestic criticism of the government's values emerged. Civil society actors were motivated by the global publicity an ICJ case would attract, as well as the prospect of obtaining a binding judgment to bolster their campaign. It is evident that it was not civil society pressure alone that motivated action, but an alignment of the interests of the government with civil society to take action, united by the shared goal of gaining legitimacy with their respective audiences.

The second task involves the modalities of protection: the practical aspects of representations, making consular visits and negotiating. Within the multi-actor protection network that emerged on behalf of the LaGrand brothers, actors undertook these tasks, irrespective of their status as a state or non-state actor. Throughout Germany's active period of intervention, civil society organisations were making representations directly to the Governor of Arizona and the US government. It is not atypical for civil society actors to adopt protective state functions, including oral and written representations to other states. State and non-state actors distribute and claim traditional state functions of protecting citizens abroad for a range of reasons. Multi-actor action within a network

[87] Ibid.

can assist with burden sharing between actors. In the case of the LaGrands, the actors were able to harness existing expertise and political capital effectively to win popular support in Germany and achieve leadership in the anti-death penalty movement.[88]

John Braithwaite and Peter Drahos have explored this phenomenon in global business where states and business corporations (and other actors) act as agents for one another. This reflexive agency reconstitutes both agents and principals continually.[89] The idea of co-agency may also be applied to the protection of citizens abroad. The traditional state functions of protecting citizens abroad (both generating motivation and the modalities) are reassigned to civil society, media and individual actors within a multi-actor network depending on the shared objectives of the network. Actors may perform tasks interchangeably to achieve the goals of the network.

B Law as a Technique of Protection: Law to Mobilise, Law to Neutralise

Studies on the protection of citizens abroad often fail to interrogate the different ways in which law manifests itself in protective actions. However this case study reveals how law operates as a tool for actors to achieve their aims in different ways. Law is deployed as a tool in two ways: law as an instrument of mobilisation and law as an instrument of neutralisation. Civil society actors advocating for the LaGrand brothers relied on international human rights standards to campaign for increased intervention. Civil society mobilised the public, media and parts of the German government around the LaGrand plight on the grounds that it was based on, supported and required by law. In this respect, human rights law emerges as a mobilising force, where actors engage the authority of law, through the technique of litigation, to pursue claims and enforce rights. These actors drew on the perceived authority of law to compel action and negotiate standards for state behaviour.

Conversely, the various German government actors relied on law as a neutralising force. Counsel for *LaGrand* emphasised the technicality of the case under article 36 of the VCCR, noting in Germany's memorial that the case was not one about values.[90] Germany's reliance on the formality and objectivity of law occurred for a number of reasons. One

[88] Slaughter, above note 18, 16. [89] Braithwaite and Drahos, above note 33, 479.

[90] Memorial of the Federal Republic of Germany, above note 43, para 1.08.

of those reasons related to US pressure on Germany to ensure that the case did not turn into a global anti-US platform.[91] By framing the dispute in a technical manner the German government could preserve its bilateral relationship with the United States, and the NATO alliance. Germany deployed the law as a neutral and mediating force focused on the application of the VCCR and not a comparison between national values on human rights. Germany and the United States attempted to strip the case of culture, moral norms and national values by situating the ICJ proceedings as a matter of technical legal interpretation. Moreover, by presenting the case within this aura of technicality, Germany discouraged other states from joining the claim, thereby avoiding the risk of politicising the action with more parties opposing the United States publicly.

The technicality of the legal action also served to neutralise its characterisation as a political or national claim. While diplomatic protection is understood as a claim based on nationality, the case avoided pause on nationality and, even more so, nationalism. Instead, the action was framed as a legal requirement, based on the values entrenched in the German constitution. This sensitivity around nationalism in Germany can be explained by what some German scholars refer to as 'constitutional patriotism'.[92] This substitution of values, from the nationalist to the constitutional, is evident in the manner in which Germany avoided making a nationalistic claim about the treatment of its citizens, but instead based its claim on the way in which the VCCR is applied, and compliance with the constitutional requirement of protection.

Simultaneously, *LaGrand* served as a vehicle for Germany to express its political and moral values about the death penalty, even though the ICJ case related to consular notification. Anti-American sentiment was embedded in German society at the time of *LaGrand* and grew at the announcement of participation in Kosovo.[93] The title of Karen Bagge's article for the *Amnesty International Journal* on *LaGrand* – 'The Arrogance of the Super Power' – is an example of the anti-Americanism present in Germany in the lead-up to the case.[94] The case allowed the contestation of values to occur under the guise of law as a neutral arbiter. While at the

[91] Interview with counsel 1 for Germany in *LaGrand*, June 2013.

[92] See generally Jan-Werner Müller, *Constitutional Patriotism* (Princeton: Princeton University Press, 2007).

[93] Interview with counsel 1 for Germany in *LaGrand*, June 2013.

[94] Bagge, above note 64.

international level, and within its memorials, Germany claimed the pursuit of a legal technicality under the VCCR, the message for Germany's domestic audience conveyed a contest of values about the death penalty. Germany's values of human rights and the protection of life were juxtaposed against the US application of the death penalty, with success in the ICJ being both a win for Germany's values and an opportunity to distinguish itself from the United States in the view of the German public.

C Aggregation, Disaggregation, Re-aggregation

Internal discord between agencies of government on particular issues is commonplace. While Slaughter's theory of disaggregation gives visibility to the different branches of government, her theory does not properly address how the parts of a state interact with one another on common issues. Within government, a great deal of time is committed to reconciling different positions between bureaucratic departments, ministries, agencies and stakeholders (including ministerial offices, national human rights institutions and parliamentarians). Government departments often hold different values, as evinced by Germany's Foreign Ministry and the Ministry of Justice. Slaughter's model as developed in 2004 overlooks this tension and the considerable bureaucratic energy and resources that are committed to reconciling and developing a consensus position on an issue. More importantly, it highlights that there is no single manner in which disaggregation can occur.

The LaGrand example provides two disaggregating lenses that warrant close attention. In Germany, the interaction and tension between bureaucracies, the executive, individual politicians and diplomats representing Germany in the United States are not atypical of how democratic and developed states resolve policy issues domestically. What seems even more interesting is that these sub-state actors formed alliances with actors outside of the state structure. The German Foreign Ministry aligned itself with NATO and the German Ministry of Justice aligned itself with civil society and the public – each respectively forming their own network of resistance and protection.

Federalism appears as a second fracture of disaggregation. The source of the dispute between Germany and the United States can be traced to the disunity between the US government and the state of Arizona. Implementation of the VCCR and the ICJ's decision continues as a point of contention between some states and the US government.

These two examples, US federalism and Germany's multi-actor network, demonstrate how disaggregation can be harnessed in different ways to achieve aims or support positions. In the case of Germany, this disaggregation was used to bring a range of actors into a network of shared values and interests for the purpose of acting on behalf of the LaGrands. In the United States, the disaggregation created an opportunity for the US government to set limits on its ability to act, arguing that power resided with Arizona. These examples show us how disaggregation is not merely an exercise of drawing lines between actors, as Slaughter had suggested, but rather a much more complex endeavour to harness and repudiate political claims and achieve governance outcomes.

Conclusion

States still operate as the most important unit of analysis in many areas of human life and society; however, multi-actor participation is a reality of the international legal system. The state is an important feature of regulation in the lives of citizens and most often is the unit that is criticised or praised for changes in society or failures to make meaningful change. However, state-centricity can inhibit our understanding of a phenomenon like the protection of citizens abroad. While a theory of disaggregation of the state is useful as a first step, it is necessary to consider how sub-units of the state interact with one another, as well as units and actors outside the state. The *LaGrand* case demonstrates that there are a number of actors involved in generating and motivating action to protect citizens abroad. In the earlier stages, state action was generated by non-state actors through the media. Civil society actors capitalised on the momentum of the global anti-death penalty campaign. Once an alignment of interests was achieved between the non-state actors and state actors, juridification of the death penalty value emerged as a credible policy avenue. Networks of state and non-state actors shared information, expertise and strategy. An assessment of the existence and operation of networks cannot be limited to a consideration of their coordinating aspect alone, but rather must include a substantive analysis of norm and value generation.

3

Advancing the Conversation

Non-judicial Voices and the Transnational Judicial Dialogue

PAMMELA QUINN

Over a decade ago, Anne-Marie Slaughter sketched out the emerging reality of a networked international order and explored its future potential. As she described them, global networks operate mainly as 'transmission belts for information'.[1] While the prototypical examples of these 'information networks' are transnational groups of regulators[2] who transmit expert, factual information that falls within the core of regulatory expertise, judicial networks are also a type of information network. As Slaughter has written: 'The networks of national constitutional courts are explicitly focused on the provision and exchange of information and ideas'.[3] Through these networks, domestic courts serve as important transnational actors, with the 'power to persuade, with the formal powers of legal office serving as leverage points and bargaining chips in a discursive, norm-creating process'.[4] In short, judicial actors can impact judges across national borders by engaging

I am indebted to Anil Kalhan, Fernanda Nicola and Melissa Waters for encouraging me to undertake this project. I am very grateful to the American Society of International Law for giving me the opportunity to present an early draft of this chapter at the fifth 'Four Societies' workshop held in Canberra, Australia. Thanks to all the Four Societies participants for their very helpful comments.

1 Anne-Marie Slaughter, *A New World Order* (Princeton: Princeton University Press, 2004), 48–49 ('Most important is regulation by information ... Government networks create regional and even global transmission belts for information ...') and 85 ('The glue of any transgovernmental network is the exchange of information and ideas').

2 See, for example, ibid., 86. Commentators have long described and lauded the rise of global governance tied together by networks of experts coordinating policy across transnational borders (with Slaughter citing the works of Peter M. Haas).

3 Ibid., 148.

4 Harold Hongju Koh, 'Why Do Nations Obey International Law?' (1997) 106 *Yale Law Journal* 2599–2659, 2638.

in 'judicial conversations' and through these conversations engage in global law-making.[5]

The potential power of judicial networks has particularly excited human rights scholars and advocates.[6] The notion that these norms can be transmitted and then made effective through a strong system of legal enforcement is appealing in the context of rights that often lack strong commitments and enforcement mechanisms.

Although the transmission of human rights norms through judicial networks is a type of 'information' transmission, the type of information being transmitted is often assumed to belong to a fundamentally different genre than the information transmitted through regulatory networks. Unlike regulators, judges are viewed frequently as disseminators of *legal* information and expertise. Citations to foreign or international legal opinions[7] (or, sometimes, to international legal sources themselves[8]) are the currency of judicial networks. These citations demonstrate the impact of those judges in one jurisdiction of legal norms and the persuasive reasoning underpinning them that were articulated by judges from another.[9]

While focusing on legal norms and analysis makes sense given the judicial context, doing so may overlook important context. Using the example of international human rights – the type of international norm that is the predominant focus of judicial network scholarship – this chapter explores the fact-finding aspects of transnational judicial decision-making to illuminate the importance of factual information to

[5] For instance, the interactions between domestic European courts and the European Court of Justice (ECJ) constrained domestic politicians throughout Europe who disliked ECJ decisions that curtailed their policy preferences. As Alter explains: 'Because of national judicial support for ECJ jurisprudence, national governments were forced to frame their response [opposing ECJ decisions with which they disagreed] in terms which could persuade a legal audience, and thus they became constrained by the legal rules of the game': Karen J. Alter, 'Who Are the "Masters of the Treaty"?: European Governments and the European Court of Justice' (1998) 52:1 *International Organization* 121–147, 124.

[6] See, for example, Melissa A. Waters, 'Mediating Norms and Identity: The Role of Transnational Judicial Dialogue in Creating and Enforcing International Law' (2005) 93:2 *Georgetown Law Journal* 487–574, 490. See also Margaret E. McGuinness, '*Medellín*, Norm Portals, and the Horizontal Integration of International Human Rights' (2006) 82:2 *Notre Dame Law Review* 755–842, 759–761 (describing 'norm portals' that facilitate the transmission of human rights standards into US law through domestic judicial decisions).

[7] Waters (ibid.).

[8] See, for example, Melissa A. Waters, 'Creeping Monism: The Judicial Trend Toward Interpretive Incorporation of Human Rights Treaties' (2007) 107:3 *Columbia Law Review* 628–705.

[9] Waters, 'Mediating Norms', above note 6.

transnational judicial networks. By no means is this meant to suggest that transmitting legal norms or legal analyses is unimportant. The point is, simply, that facts are also an important, and in some cases essential, component of the legal decision-making process. Moreover, although fact-finding is important to judicial networks, because judges are not always ideally positioned to uncover relevant factual information, citations among domestic courts *alone* are not the optimal way for judicial networks to operate. Instead, at least in the human rights context, judicial networks would be more effective if they encouraged the inclusion and transmission of more factual information than the closed universe of judicial opinions typically allows.

This chapter illuminates the importance of fact-finding and incorporating non-traditional fact-finding into judicial networks by, first, unpacking the important role of fact-finding in judicial decision-making (Section I), and second, describing the significant and growing universe of official entities dedicated to human rights reporting and the advantages such entities have compared to courts when it comes to developing factual records related to human rights compliance (Section II). The chapter concludes with some thoughts on how this under-theorised aspect of global judicial networks can be further explored in future projects.

I Unpacking Judicial Decision-Making and the Role of Fact-finding

The typical broad-lens conception of judicial networks and the information that sustains them is understandable. Law and reasoning, not fact-finding, are the sine qua non of judging. Learning to read judicial decisions to find legal rules – and to understand the analyses of those rules – is the essence of learning to be a lawyer.

Yet, this broad understanding of what constitutes the 'information' critical to judicial networks fails to grapple with the reality that facts and fact-finding are frequently crucial to the human rights cases on which scholars and advocates of judicial networks are focused.[10] A party able to

[10] To be sure, while the assumption that judicial networks mainly convey legal norms and reasoning pervades most discussions of such networks, there are occasional statements recognising how critical factual information can be. For example, Slaughter notes that engaging with factual, rather than legal-judicial, sources of information can alter judicial approaches and outcomes: the 'significance of allowing judges to cite sources other than pure case law, such as scientific reports, policy analyses, and other non-legal materials' is

persuade a judge to accept that she has a legal right remains doomed to lose if she is unable to establish the underlying facts necessary to sustain the legal claim. Likewise, convincing a judge to rule that a broad principle of human rights law applies to a particular case often requires establishing important contextual facts.

As critical as facts and fact-finding are to judicial decision-making, courts are often poorly equipped to unearth them.[11] The very nature of legal decision-making – and the rules governing it – forces judges to make determinations based only on the admissible facts the parties (and, sometimes, *amici* or other third parties who become involved) are able to find and bring to the court's attention. But the facts brought to a court's attention are often limited by the parties' lack of access to relevant information that is not directly related to their dispute, or which is so old and stale that it has become difficult or impossible to unearth.[12] Even when facts are readily discoverable, they may be rendered suspect by the adversarial nature of adjudication.[13]

But though judicial systems are not adept at generating deep or accurate factual records, other entities are. In particular, in the context of international human rights, many formal institutional actors who are tasked with enforcing human rights norms do so not through adjudication but through intensive fact-finding and publication. Truth and reconciliation commissions, special rapporteurs and other *ad hoc* appointees are called upon to intervene in particular contexts where human rights violations are suspected.[14] Many committees created under the auspices of human rights treaties undertake routine investigations of all the

that exposure to such information will expand 'a judge's universe of information' which in turn 'makes it possible to make a wider range of arguments for or against a particular decision': Slaughter, *A New World Order*, above note 1, 314.

[11] See Edward K. Cheng, 'Independent Judicial Research in the *Daubert* Age' (2007) 56 *Duke Law Journal* 1263–1318, 1283. See also Kenneth Culp Davis, 'Judicial, Legislative, and Administrative Lawmaking: A Proposed Research Service for the Supreme Court' (1986) 71:1 *Minnesota Law Review* 1–18, 4; Allison Orr Larsen, 'Confronting Supreme Court Fact Finding' (2012) 98:6 *Virginia Law Review* 1255–1312, 1290, footnote 175 ('most agree at the outset of that debate that the judiciary faces significant institutional weaknesses in its ability to gather facts').

[12] Cheng (ibid.).

[13] Pammela Quinn, 'The Integrated Enforcement of Human Rights' (2012) 45:1 *New York University Journal of International Law and Politics* 97–174, 121.

[14] Ibid., 162–164 (describing the numerous special rapporteurs and committees on which the Inter-American Court of Human Rights relied in The Cotton Field Case, discussed *infra*.

contracting states on an ongoing, periodic basis.[15] Like judges, these types of legal actors also make findings regarding whether legal violations have occurred. But unlike judges, they are able to make these decisions against a deep factual record that considers state conduct across a large number of cases, rather than in connection with the facts of a single case a litigant has brought to its attention.

These decision-makers – and the factual records they generate and rely upon – have the potential to serve as important 'voices' in the transnational judicial conversation about human rights. In some cases, they have already been brought into the judicial conversation: domestic courts do sometimes cite official, non-judicial entities such as those described above and render decisions they would not have been able to reach in the absence of the factual records they developed. But in other cases, domestic courts may lack the capacity to integrate these non-judicial sources of factual information or be unaware that these sources are available to aid them in uncovering important information relevant to decisions regarding human rights.

Most scholarly accounts of judicial networks focus on citations between and among courts and the transmission thereby of legal norms and legal analysis – the quintessential products of judicial decision-making.[16] While not all scholarly engagement with networks focuses primarily or exclusively on courts rather than other types of international actors, most do.[17] And even with scholars whose works promote the engagement in judicial dialogue of entities other than courts (such as treaty monitoring bodies), there tends to be a focus on the legal conclusions reached, rather than the factual conclusions drawn.[18] At best, discussions conflate the two

[15] Ibid., 101–102 (describing the adoption of the Universal Periodic Review process at the UN).

[16] See, for example, Anne-Marie Slaughter, 'A Typology of Transjudicial Communication' (1994) 29:1 *University of Richmond Law Review* 99–138; Anne-Marie Slaughter, 'Judicial Globalization' (2000) 40:4 *Virginia Journal of International Law* 1103–1124; Anne-Marie Slaughter, 'A Global Community of Courts' (2003) 44:1 *Harvard International Law Journal* 191–220; Waters, 'Mediating Norms', above note 6; Waters, 'Creeping Monism', above note 8.

[17] See, for example, Joanna Harrington, 'The Democratic Challenge of Incorporation: International Human Rights Treaties and National Constitutions' (2007) 38:2 *Victoria University of Wellington Law Review* 217–235 (pointing out at 220 'the irony of [a Canadian judge's] admonishment of the United States Supreme Court [for not citing to other countries' case law and engaging thereby in the international dialogue on human rights issues] given that the Supreme Court of Canada rarely mentions in its judgments the jurisprudence of the United Nations human rights treaty monitoring bodies [to which Canada has given its consent] . . .').

[18] Ibid. See also Joanna Harrington, 'The Absent Dialogue: Extradition and the International Covenant on Civil and Political Rights' (2006–2007) 32:1 *Queen's Law Journal* 82–134; Machiko Kanetake and André Nollkaemper, 'The Application of

functions of legal decision-making without considering fact-finding as an independently important aspect of these decisions. That is, even when other types of tribunals are included in network analyses, the products of these entities are considered because they are viewed as roughly akin to the product produced by courts: a statement and explanation (ideally a persuasive one) of a legal principle.

Of course judicial decisions do contain statements of legal norms supported by legal analyses. But these products of judicial decision-making include ingredients other than the legal text itself. Probably no legal decision relies solely on the interpretation of a text or rule in a vacuum. Legal decision-making is inextricably intertwined with factual determinations.

The significance of record facts to a legal decision may seem obvious. Clearly, a court cannot ultimately determine that a legal violation has occurred in a given case without an established factual predicate to which the finding relates. Yet, in the human rights context – the very context in which transnational judicial networks are frequently discussed and considered particularly important for norm transmission – the ability of plaintiffs to establish relevant facts may be compromised. As discussed in detail below, the ability of plaintiffs to convince courts to rule in their favour in some cases can be hampered (or altogether precluded) by the reality that, though they have a persuasive argument for the legal rule they are advancing, the relevant rules of evidence prevent them from establishing the necessary factual predicate. This practical impediment to individual plaintiffs compromises the network. If a plaintiff cannot establish a legal entitlement, the chances that his case will lead to a judicial opinion creating a norm that may be transmitted are diminished.

The impact of legislative fact-finding on transnational judicial networks is perhaps less obvious, but no less important. Even when record facts can be established, a party may be unable to convince a judge to conclude that a legal right has been violated without the establishment of contextual facts favouring the adoption of the legal argument being advanced. In the domestic context, for instance, cases about contested rights often turn on fact-based policy questions, such as: 'Is a partial-birth abortion ever medically necessary? Can one effectively discharge a locked gun in self-defence? Are African American children stigmatized by segregated schools?'[19]

Informal International Instruments Before Domestic Courts' (2014) 46:4 *George Washington International Law Review* 765–807.

[19] Larsen, 'Confronting Supreme Court Fact Finding', above note 11, 1255–1256 (citing *Gonzales* v. *Carhart*, 550 US 124, 165–166 (2007); *District of Columbia* v. *Heller*,

In addition to the factual understanding a judge must develop to answer related policy questions, judges considering what legal rule to adopt or apply to a specific fact pattern may need to understand the factual context from which the rule emerged and the impact the rule will have in a broader sense than the specific factual context which serves as the vehicle for the legal determination. The ways that legislative fact-finding in its various forms can also drive legal decision-making in the international human rights context, and thereby impact the network of which the judge and judicial system are a part, are explored in detail below with reference to illustrative examples.

Putting the essential ingredients of judicial decisions under an even more powerful microscope, we see that the factual determinations comprising legal decisions fall into (at least) two distinct categories. The first category of facts includes those that most of us are probably apt to think of when we hear the word 'fact-finding' in connection with litigation: the 'record facts' to be decided by a judge or jury (who did what to whom and when).[20] But a second category of fact-finding is also important to legal decision-making. The determination of the relevant contextual or 'legislative'[21] facts, referring to a fact that '"transcend[s] the particular dispute" and provides descriptive information about the world which judges use as foundational "building blocks" to form and apply legal rules',[22] is often vital to legal decisions implicating policy questions, as decisions deciding whether or not to recognise claimed rights nearly always do.

A The Importance of Record Facts to Judging International Human Rights Cases

The importance of record facts to the pronouncement of human rights norms is not often considered explicitly. Yet a lack of factual support may

128 S Ct 2783, 2818 (2008); *Parents Involved in Community School* v. *Seattle School District No 1*, 551 US 701, 733 (2007); and *Brown* v. *Board of Education*, 347 US 483, 493–494 (1954)).

20 Ibid., 1255.

21 Ibid., 1256, footnote 5 (discussing origins of terms 'legislative fact' and similar types of background facts, sometimes called 'constitutional facts', 'social facts' and 'foundational facts').

22 Ibid., 1256–1257 (quoting David L. Faigman, '"Normative Constitutional Fact-Finding": Exploring the Empirical Component of Constitutional Interpretation' (1991) 139 *University of Pennsylvania Law Review* 541, 552). 'Legislative' facts are so called not because they are facts that are necessarily found by a legislature but because they are facts that are related to the legislative or policy-making function: ibid., 1256.

be a more significant hurdle than a failed effort to convince a judge to interpret a legal norm in a particular way. Instead, in at least some cases, judicial enforcement of human rights norms may be difficult or impossible because of a much deeper and more structural problem than failure to persuade the judge. As Yonatan Lupu has explained: 'Much of the [factual] information one may have about [certain human rights] violations may be inadmissible in courts'.[23] Achieving an adequate evidential record in human rights cases may be hampered by a number of potential obstacles, including the admissibility of available evidence and the costs and difficulties associated with obtaining it.

To be sure, factual information about these types of violations is often unearthed and disclosed by non-governmental organisations (NGOs) and the media, who 'perform crucial roles in monitoring governments, collecting information from victims and educating the domestic and international public about abuses'.[24] But the information that is disseminated generally does not meet the standards for admissibility in court proceedings. Thus, while many scholars have focused on the importance of information and information disclosure as an end in itself,[25] the corresponding and underlying assumption that such information can be filtered through a court to check illegal conduct needs to be unpacked.

In fact, when working in isolation (or even in conversation with other judicial entities), it appears that domestic judicial systems 'are less compatible [with certain types of human rights claims] than much of the literature implicitly assumes'.[26] In particular, according to Lupu: 'Courts are unlikely to be effective enforcers in areas where evidence of violations is especially costly to obtain – even if actors outside the judicial process have significant amounts of information about such violations'.[27] For this reason, certain human rights violations are particularly difficult to prosecute. Namely, because 'evidence-production costs and standards of proof are high with respect to [human rights] violations . . . such as torture, extrajudicial killings, political imprisonment and disappearances', courts may lack the capacity 'to constrain

[23] Yonatan Lupu, 'Best Evidence: The Role of Information in Domestic Judicial Enforcement of International Human Rights Agreements' (2013) 67:3 *International Organization* 469–503, 471.

[24] Ibid.

[25] See generally Beth A. Simmons, *Mobilizing for Human Rights: International Law and Domestic Politics* (Cambridge: Cambridge University Press, 2009).

[26] Lupu, above note 23, 471. [27] Ibid.

governments into reducing these violations', regardless of whether those governments have made 'an international commitment to do so'. By contrast, evidence-production costs and standards of proof in the context of rights such as the freedoms of association and assembly are lower.[28]

The particular evidentiary and other procedural rules typically utilised by judicial systems may create obstacles for victims of human rights abuses involving physical harm who come forward and file claims in domestic courts.[29] Evidence may be difficult for victims to obtain when the human rights violation has taken place in a context 'in which the government has control of the victim and the surrounding evidence'.[30]

In addition, the type of factual information that does come to light through investigations and reporting of NGOs and the media is frequently of a type that either is unlikely to be utilised in court proceedings or would be inadmissible if it were to be proffered. For instance, Lupu explains that 'Individuals too fearful to be named in a newspaper article, for example, are unlikely to be willing to provide the same information in a legal proceeding'.[31] Relying on earlier work by David Weissbrodt and James McCarthy,[32] Lupu makes the point that NGOs that create reports documenting violations 'often need to rely upon hearsay statements, documents which are not fully authenticated, and justifiable inference from indirect evidence'.[33]

[28] Ibid., 483.

[29] Even if physically able to bring a claim, a victim that has been subjected to torture, or has otherwise had his or her physical integrity violated in the past, is much more likely to be intimidated and fearful of further abuse by the government and therefore to choose not to come forward: ibid., 478–479.

[30] Ibid., 479. Because the government is in a good position to hide evidence easily, the rules of evidence can impact the ability of the judicial branch to serve a checking function: ibid., 479.

[31] Ibid., 481.

[32] David Weissbrodt and James McCarthy, 'Fact-Finding by Nongovernmental Organizations' in Bertrand G. Ramcharan, ed., *International Law and Fact-Finding in the Field of Human Rights* (The Hague: Martinus Nijhoff, 1982), 186–230.

[33] Lupu, above note 23, 481. Lupu also notes at 481 that, even when NGOs 'have developed policies in order to avoid relying excessively on hearsay, they do rely substantially on interviews of witnesses who are neither under an obligation to speak with the NGO nor under an obligation to tell the truth', citing Diane F. Orentlicher, 'Bearing Witness: The Art and Science of Human Rights Fact-Finding' (1990) 3 *Harvard Human Rights Journal* 83–135.

B The Importance of Legislative Facts to Judging International Human Rights Cases

Legal decision-making also relies upon other types of facts in addition to the record facts about the parties themselves. In order to make legal determinations, judges often need to find answers to preliminary factual questions, the answers to which will drive legal decision-making. These facts are not about what happened between the parties to the case. Instead, they include more generic facts about the world that inform judges' legal decisions.

Such background facts may be dispositive to the outcome of a case. For instance, in *Baze* v. *Reese*, the decision of the US Supreme Court as to whether lethal injection constitutes cruel and unusual punishment turned on the question of whether it creates a 'substantial risk of pain'[34] – a question that Chief Justice Roberts, for one, answered by citing a book chapter concerning euthanasia protocols in the Netherlands.[35]

Even when they are not dispositive, legislative facts may help judges to write more persuasive opinions. Deciding or referencing legislative facts that are related to the legal argument and claiming empirical support for them 'protects and entrenches the [related legal conclusion] by elevating its validity with a stamp of scientific imprimatur'.[36] For example, in order to bolster its associated legal arguments and holdings, the Supreme Court decided 'the factual claim in *Citizens United* v. *Federal Election Commission* that corporate independent expenditures do not corrupt politics' and 'the factual claim in *Grutter* v. *Bollinger* that racially diverse viewpoints improve a law school education'.[37]

In human rights litigation, legislative facts are sometimes critical to interpreting the frequently broad legal principles invoked by individual

[34] As discussed in Larsen, 'Confronting Supreme Court Fact Finding', above note 11, 1284, footnote 139. Other examples include (at 1284–1285): 'whether homegrown medical marijuana will affect the larger marijuana market – a dispositive question of fact in *Gonzales* v. *Raich*'; whether 'striking the ball and not walking from hole to hole was the "essence" of golf' in deciding *PGA Tour* v. *Martin*, 'a case involving whether, under the *Americans with Disabilities Act*, a professional golfer's physical handicap should excuse him from the requirement that he walk and carry his golf clubs'.

[35] *Baze* v. *Reese*, 553 US 35, 58 (2008) (citing G.K. Kimsma, 'Euthanasia and Euthanizing Drugs in the Netherlands' in M. Pabst Battin and Arthur G. Lipman, eds., *Drug Use in Assisted Suicide and Euthanasia* (New York: Pharmaceutical Products Press, 1996) 193–210, 193, 200 and 204).

[36] See Larsen, 'Confronting Supreme Court Fact Finding', above note 11, 1270.

[37] Allison Orr Larsen, 'Factual Precedents' (2013) 162:1 *University of Pennsylvania Law Review* 59–116, 94.

litigants. For example, in order to determine whether medical student Layla Şahin's human rights were violated when she was forbidden to wear a headscarf in her university classes, the judges of the human rights court adjudicating her claims needed to know facts other than those involving what the parties did. Certainly it was *necessary* for Şahin to establish that she had a religiously based desire to wear an Islamic headscarf to class, that the university regulations prohibited her from doing so and that she was in fact disciplined for failing to follow those regulations.[38] But the European Court of Human Rights also needed to understand background facts about Turkey and the context in which the dispute between Ms Şahin and the university arose. Thus, the history of Turkey's secular policies, as well as the impact of those policies on how the university carried out its ban on religious dress, was directly relevant to the court's legal determination. While the disagreement among the judges reflects the controversial nature of the outcome,[39] the background facts regarding Turkey's history and relationship with secularism and the political nature of religious dress being worn in public were critical to the majority's conclusion that Turkey's policy did not violate Ms. Şahin's rights – even though an identical incident that occurred against a different factual and historical backdrop might well be found to constitute a human rights violation.[40]

II Fact-finding and Judicial Networks

The above discussion regarding the importance of facts to legal decision-making suggests that citations between and among courts alone are not

[38] See, for example, *Leyla Şahin* v. *Turkey*, App No 44774/98, (2005) 44 EHRR 99 (Grand Chamber), para 22 ('the dean of the faculty declared that her attitude and failure to comply with the rules on dress were not befitting of a student' and issued her a warning); para 23 ('an unauthorised assembly gathered outside the deanery of the Cerrahpaşa Faculty of Medicine to protest against the rules on dress'); and para 24 ('the dean of the faculty began disciplinary proceedings against various students, including the applicant, for joining the assembly . . . [A]fter hearing her representations, he suspended her from the university for a semester').

[39] See further Karima Bennoune, 'Secularism and Human Rights: A Contextual Analysis of Headscarves, Religious Expression, and Women's Equality Under International Law' (2007) 45:2 *Columbia Journal of Transnational Law* 367–426, 371, noting that: 'Some human rights groups sharply criticized the ruling [in the *Şahin* case] as failing to defend women's rights to manifest their religion'.

[40] *Leyla Şahin* v. *Turkey*, above note 38, paras 154 and 157–158, discussing and applying a margin of appreciation and balancing interests of state against restriction of applicant's rights.

the optimal way for judicial networks to be structured. Judicial networks could be more effective if they also integrated the work done by those official entities better situated to generate and transmit relevant factual information than a closed universe of court-to-court citations typically allows. The work done by investigating and reporting mechanisms created in lieu of judicial mechanisms by many human rights treaties (for example, the Human Rights Committee, the Committee on the Elimination of All Forms of Discrimination Against Women and several others) has the unique potential to enhance the ability of judicial networks to create and enforce international human rights norms. In particular, non-judicial mechanisms are able to elicit a wider and deeper factual background, over a longer time horizon, than judicial fact-finding can, thereby enabling such mechanisms to better flesh out the contours of specific rights.

It is true, of course, that domestic judicial opinions contain certain facts that may be useful, especially as they specifically relate to the legal norm and analysis in the case being cited. But for at least two distinct reasons, judicial opinions are not the optimal vehicle for generating and transmitting facts.

First, the common law judicial process is designed to limit fact-finding and may not allow judges to access all relevant facts – much less allow them to put all the relevant facts in the record to pass along to the judge in the next case. In general, individual claimants who bring claims before adjudicative tribunals will focus on their own, individual factual circumstances and will frequently lack the resources and capacity to investigate and bring forth relevant facts outside of their control, especially ones that are old or stale. In any event, as Schauer has argued, the focus on the facts involved in a particular, concrete case is 'more often distorting than illuminating'; judges focus on the 'this-ness' of particular facts while ignoring or misunderstanding the nature of future similar controversies.[41]

Nor are courts, which 'have relatively weak monitoring powers', doing much under their current rules.[42] To the extent claimants attempt to

[41] Frederick Schauer, 'Do Cases Make Bad Law?' (2006) 73:3 *University of Chicago Law Review* 883–918, 884.

[42] Lupu, above note 23, 471 and 475. Reforms have been proposed to provide courts with access to a broader range of information than they are typically exposed to. For example, Gorod suggests that *amici* should be more involved earlier in cases. She argues that it is better 'to bring those organizations and individuals with relevant facts into the process at the trial court stage when the information they have to offer can be subjected to some

demonstrate the broader impact of a challenged policy, the information they present may not be admissible; even when it is, it may be viewed critically or sceptically, because it will be presented against an adversarial backdrop that incentivises advocacy and the selective presentation of facts and evidence that most strongly supports the claimant's position.[43] Moreover, as noted previously, rules of evidence and procedure often constrain courts in human rights cases.

Even civil law criminal courts, where judges have much more control over the investigation of the facts, are also limited (albeit less so) in what information they can uncover and rely upon.[44] Furthermore, precisely because judges control the investigation, fewer facts are likely to be uncovered. Judges are likely to focus fact-finding efforts more economically than in common law systems that 'investigate everything that could possibly come up at trial'.[45] Instead, fact-finding will reasonably focus on areas strictly necessary to adjudicate the dispute before it.[46]

When courts in any system engage in fact-finding, they may be not the most reliable or expert sources of factual information. Larsen reports that, although lower courts frequently cite US Supreme Court opinions for factual propositions, we should be concerned about this practice,

form of scrutiny and testing': Brianne J. Gorod, 'The Adversarial Myth: Appellate Court Extra-Record Factfinding' (2011) 61:1 *Duke Law Journal* 1–80, 69–73.

43 As I have written previously: 'In part to try to compensate for this structural downside, adjudicative tribunals have become increasingly receptive to permitting evidence from *amici* [or intervenors]. Still . . . the adversarial format may make it easier to dismiss an *amicus* because of a perception that it is acting more as an advocate and less as an issue-area expert. This may be less true in the monitoring context, when third-party interest groups that serve an *amicus*-like role are likely to be engaged in a back-and-forth conversation with a monitoring committee in a less-formal, investigative setting': Quinn, above note 13, 121 (notes omitted).

44 For instance, 'German law exhibits expansive notions of testimonial privilege, especially for potential witnesses drawn from the family': John H. Langbein, 'The German Advantage in Civil Procedure' (1985) 52:4 *University of Chicago Law Review* 823–866, 829.

45 Ibid., 831.

46 It is also not clear whether inquisitorial fact-finding is more or less accurate than adversarial. As explained by Samuel R. Gross in 'The American Advantage: The Value of Inefficient Litigation' (1987) 85:4 *Michigan Law Review* 734–757, 740: 'Langbein believes that the German [civil law] system is more likely than [the American common law system] to reach factually correct results. While this is a plausible consequence of his description of the superior rationality of German procedure, I am unconvinced . . . [I]ts accuracy is almost always unknown since we rarely have any external evidence by which to judge it'. See also Hyun Song Shin, 'Adversarial and Inquisitorial Procedures in Arbitration' (1998) 29:2 *RAND Journal of Economics* 378–405 (arguing that an adversarial fact-finding model produces more accurate outcomes than an inquisitorial model).

because the facts relied on in judicial opinions are frequently 'employed instrumentally ... for persuasive rhetoric ..., may not be carefully deliberated, may not have garnered the support of [the majority who decided the case], and may be selected for reasons other than that they are the most reliable sources'.[47]

Although Larsen, for one, has proposed that courts could engage in better fact-finding by acting more like administrative agencies – i.e. by enacting rules allowing them to solicit opinions and evidence from all interested parties and encouraging public participation, similar to the notice and comment rule-making process that agencies use[48] – the reality remains that the rules by which courts (and entities that we conceive of as court-like) operate do not permit this. Instead, courts are constrained to engage in fact-finding as described above. Instead of undertaking their own investigations, domestic courts rely on the parties and, in some cases, on the fact-finding done by administrative agencies.[49]

While courts (both domestic and international) cannot engage in administrative-style fact-finding in the transnational and international context either, some entities *do* act more like administrative agencies and engage in fact-finding at a much deeper and broader level – with more public input. The vast majority of human rights treaties rely on entities that conduct and report on factual investigations that serve as these treaties' primary compliance mechanism.[50] Human rights treaty bodies utilise state self-reporting in conjunction with additional reporting from NGOs, UN special procedures and other states to compile a comprehensive factual record of state practices relating to human rights treaty obligations. Formal external monitoring committees analyse these records and then base comprehensive reports regarding the state party's human rights practices on the factual data they compile.[51] A similar,

[47] Larsen, 'Factual Precedents', above note 37, 63.

[48] Allison Orr Larsen, 'The Trouble with Amicus Facts' (2014) 100:8 *Virginia Law Review* 1757–1818, 1809.

[49] Indeed, even when courts are acting simply as reviewing courts respecting administrative fact-finding, they subject such facts to much less scrutiny than facts found through the judicial process precisely because the administrative fact-gathering process produces more reliable facts than the judicial process. See Slaughter, *A New World Order*, above note 1, 68–69 (describing regulators as those with 'specialized expertise ... that often guarantees a measure of deference from judges, legislators, and fellow regulators').

[50] Quinn, above note 13, 110.

[51] See, for example, ibid., 133–138 (discussing the structure of Framework Convention for the Protection of National Minorities, 1 February 1995, 2151 UNTS 243, in force 1 February 1998).

formal investigation and review by a neutral monitor also occurs in cases where a special rapporteur is appointed by the Human Rights Council and when official treaty monitoring bodies appoint outside monitors to conduct an investigation of a state party in circumstances suggesting that such an investigation is warranted.[52]

For example, a decision by the Inter-American Court of Human Rights (IACHR) reflects a number of reports generated in connection with such investigations, all of which impacted the decision by the IACHR. After national and international attention became focused on a culture of violence against women in Ciudad Juárez that 'has prevailed since 1993, and the deficient state response to these crimes',[53] a number of human rights bodies undertook investigations. These included the UN special rapporteur on extrajudicial, summary or arbitrary executions, who visited and reported on Mexico in 1999 after having requested an invitation from the Mexican government to conduct a fact-finding country visit for several years;[54] the UN special rapporteur on the independence of judges and lawyers who in 2001 investigated allegations relating to the situation in Ciudad Juárez;[55] the special rapporteur on the rights of women, established by the Inter-American Commission on Human Rights, who visited Mexico in 2002 to gather information relating to the rights of women in Ciudad Juárez;[56] the Committee on the Elimination of Discrimination against Women, which travelled to Mexico to meet with various politicians, diplomats, NGOs and individuals nearly a year later in 2003;[57] and the UN special rapporteur on violence against women, who

[52] Ibid., 162–164, discussing some examples of this type of reporting in connection with *Gonzalez et al* v. *Mexico* (The Cotton Field Case), Case Nos 12.496, 12.497 and 12.498, Judgment, Inter-Am. Ct. H.R., Series C, No 206 (16 November 2009).

[53] The Cotton Field Case (ibid.), para 114 (quoting the Commission).

[54] *Report of the Special Rapporteur on Extrajudicial, Summary or Arbitrary Execution . . .: Visit to Mexico*, UN Doc E/CN.4/2000/3/Add.3 (25 November 1998), 3. This special rapporteur is specifically tasked with responding to alleged cases of improper executions, including those for which the state is directly responsible, as well as those that occur because the state has not fulfilled its obligation to actively prevent and respond to extrajudicial killings carried out by private parties who are not instrumentalities of the state. See further, Office of the High Commissioner for Human Rights, 'Special Rapporteur on Extrajudicial, Summary or Arbitrary Executions' (undated), online at: www.ohchr.org/EN/Issues/Executions/Pages/SRExecutionsIndex.aspx.

[55] *Report of the Special Rapporteur on the Independence of Judges and Lawyers . . .: Report on the Mission to Mexico*, UN Doc E/CN.4/2002/72/Add.1 (24 January 2002).

[56] *The Situation of the Rights of Women in Ciudad Juárez, Mexico: The Right To Be Free From Violence and Discrimination* OAS Doc OEA/Ser.L/V/II.117, doc 44 (7 March 2003), online at: www.cidh.org/annualrep/2002eng/chap.vi.juarez.htm.

[57] Ibid.

travelled to Mexico in 2005 to investigate widespread allegations of violence against women.[58] The significant factual records compiled by these various entities were critical to the ability of the plaintiffs to prevail in court.[59]

Because such entities – to which I will refer, for simplicity's sake, as 'reporting and monitoring' entities – collect information from a wide range of sources, including the states themselves, rights advocates, issue experts and others, they are able to situate their legal judgments against a much richer and more comprehensive factual backdrop than are courts adjudicating claims based only on the admissible evidence produced by disputing parties.[60] The ongoing nature of the responsibilities of some reporting and monitoring entities enables the creation of comprehensive historical records. For instance, the universal periodic review process occurs every five years for every UN member state, while a similar review undertaken by the committee tasked with monitoring compliance with the Framework Convention for the Protection of National Minorities[61] takes place every four years.[62] The periodic nature of these investigations allows the monitoring committees to build upon facts developed in the prior iterations and assess whether changes have occurred over time. A similar historical record would be difficult to develop in the context of an individual claim in which relevant historical facts would typically no longer be available or would be hard to reconstruct.

In particular, as documented below, reporting and monitoring entities may be able to generate both of the types of facts discussed in Section I in cases where courts alone cannot. First, putative record facts that are hard for claimants to discover on their own, and/or admit into evidence, have become part of reports documenting in-depth investigations undertaken by special rapporteurs or others appointed by treaty bodies to

58 *Report of the Special Rapporteur on Violence against Women, its Causes and Consequences . . .: Mission to Mexico*, UN Doc E/CN.4/2006/61/Add.4 (13 January 2006). See further, Office of the High Commissioner for Human Rights, 'Special Rapporteur on Violence Against Women, Its Causes and Consequences' (undated), online at: www.ohchr.org/EN/Issues/Women/SRWomen/Pages/SRWomenIndex.aspx.

59 Quinn, above note 13, 166–168.

60 In some cases, courts may also have evidence from expert witnesses or *amici*, or both. This may well provide more factual inputs than the parties alone can provide, but the nature of an adversarial proceeding, and the evidentiary limits imposed by the relevant rules limit the extent to which courts can develop a factual record.

61 Above note 51.

62 Quinn, above note 13, 122 (discussing the ongoing mandate of many monitoring committees).

undertake human rights investigations, such as UN-sponsored truth commissions.[63] For legislative facts, periodic reports often provide contextual factual evidence that is useful to courts looking for generalised facts that are relevant to making or justifying a decision. Both types of facts, when found in such official reports, are in fact sometimes used by domestic courts adjudicating cases where such facts are relevant.

A *Reports and Record Fact-finding in Human Rights Cases*

While attention paid to transnational judicial networks has focused predominantly on citations between and among courts,[64] there are in fact examples of citations by domestic courts to official reports produced by reporting and monitoring entities.[65] As the examples below reflect, domestic courts have cited such reports. Moreover, they have done so in cases where plaintiffs might not otherwise have been able to establish sufficient facts to support their legal claims for the reasons just discussed.

For example, in the context of cases brought pursuant to a US federal law, the Torture Victim Protection Act (TVPA), plaintiffs (including both American citizens and aliens) may bring claims in US courts against any individual 'who, under actual or apparent authority, or color of law, of any foreign nation subjects an individual to torture ... [or] extrajudicial killing'.[66] Thus, plaintiffs bringing TVPA claims have to prove several elements to establish liability, including that the defendant was (1) acting

[63] See, for example, *Chavez* v. *Carranza*, 559 F.3d 486 (USCA 6th Cir 2009) (considering and rejecting the claim that the district court abused its discretion in admitting into evidence the final report of the Commission for the Truth for El Salvador, an entity established under the 1992 United Nations sponsored peace agreements).

[64] See the works by Slaughter and Waters, cited at note 16, for scholarly accounts of transnational judicial dialogue looking at decisions between courts, although a few exceptions exist, for example, Harrington, 'The Absent Dialogue', above note 18; Harrington, 'The Democratic Challenge', above note 17.

[65] Previously, I have documented the use of official reports issued by reporting and monitoring entities by international human rights courts and demonstrated how this type of 'integrated enforcement' leads to better human rights enforcement than either type of entity can achieve alone. See Quinn, above note 13.

[66] Public Law 102–256 (12 March 1992), codified at 28 U.S.C. §1350. TVPA claims may be brought only by victims who are unable to utilise the judicial system in the place where the torture occurred: 'A court shall decline to hear a claim under [the TVPA] if the claimant has not exhausted adequate and available remedies in the place in which the conduct giving rise to the claim occurred'. See also *Mohamad* v. *Palestinian Authority*, 132 S Ct 454 (2011), holding that only an individual, not an organisation or other collective entity, is a proper defendant to a suit under the TVPA.

under 'color of law' of a foreign nation; and (2) subjected the plaintiff (or the person on whose behalf the plaintiff is bringing the claims) to torture or extrajudicial killing.

For the reasons noted above, admissible evidence sufficient to meet a plaintiff's burden of proof may be difficult to obtain. This situation may be particularly true in cases where the events occurred long ago; some TVPA cases have been brought more than two decades after the events in question occurred.[67]

In some cases, plaintiffs have used official reports to help meet their evidentiary burden. One such example is *Chavez* v. *Carranza*[68] concerning a jury decision holding a defendant liable and awarding USD $1.5 million in damages to each of several plaintiffs. The defendant, Carranza, had served as El Salvador's Vice Minister of Defence and Public Security, in which capacity he 'exercised operational control over the Salvadoran Security Forces' in the early 1980s, before moving to Memphis, Tennessee, where he eventually gained American citizenship.[69] The plaintiffs brought claims more than a decade later, each asserting that Carranza was responsible for acts of torture and extrajudicial killing committed when they, and some of their family members, were in official custody during his tenure.[70] The evidence supporting all of these plaintiffs' claims was based in part on a report:

> prepared by the Commission on the Truth for El Salvador, an entity established under the 1992 United Nations-sponsored peace agreements between the Government of El Salvador and the *Frente Farabundo Marti para la Liberación Nacional*. The Truth Commission Report sets forth the

[67] Although the statute has a ten-year limit on claims, courts typically extend the statute of limitations through a practice known as tolling in cases where the claim could not be brought because a repressive regime was still in power. See, for example, *Jean* v. *Dorelien*, 431 F.3d 776, 780 (USCA 11th Cir 2005) ('Litigation will often not be possible until there has been a regime change in the plaintiff's country of origin, after which the plaintiff can compile evidence without fear of reprisal against him, his family and witnesses'). See also *Arce* v. *Garcia*, 434 F.3d 1254, 1262–1264 (USCA 11th Cir 2006) (concerning a claim of torture in El Salvador); *Cabello* v. *Fernandez-Larios*, 402 F.3d 1148 (USCA 11th Cir 2005) (tolling a claim, for 26 years, until a post-junta government assumed power in Chile).

[68] 559 F.3d 486 (USCA 6th Cir 2009). [69] Ibid., 491.

[70] In particular, plaintiff Cecilia Santos 'was tortured and assaulted while in custody at the National Police headquarters in San Salvador'; plaintiff Jose Calderon was forced to the ground by 'members of the National Police [who] entered [his] home . . . and murdered [his] father'; plaintiff Erlinda Franco brought a claim on behalf of her 'husband, Manuel, [who] was abducted, tortured, and killed . . . [by] members of the Security Forces'; and plaintiff Daniel Alvarado 'was abducted by members of the Treasury Police [and] tortured [for] . . . four days [and unjustly] imprisonment for over two years': ibid.

> factual findings that the Truth Commission discovered through its investigation of El Salvador – an investigation mandated by the peace agreements sponsored by the UN.[71]

Defendant Carranza objected to the trial court's decision to admit the Truth Commission Report into evidence and appealed, contending specifically 'that the report is not timely and, therefore, is not trustworthy'.[72] While the report had been admitted by the lower court under the 'Public Records and Reports' exception to the hearsay rule, which allows reports of 'public offices or agencies' setting forth 'factual findings resulting from an investigation made pursuant to authority granted by law', the rule specifically provides that such reports are admissible 'unless the sources of information or other circumstances indicate lack of trustworthiness'.[73] Ultimately, the court of appeals rejected the argument that the report was not timely, or otherwise untrustworthy, noting that, although the 'investigation on which it was based did not begin until at least eight years after Carranza's association with the El Salvador military was over, and ended seven years after he moved to the United States . . . the timeliness factor focuses on how much time passed between the events being investigated and the beginning of the investigation'.[74] Thus, because 'the Peace Accord was signed on January 1, 1992, and the Truth Commission began its investigation on July 13, 1992, seven months later . . ., the timeliness of the investigation suggests the Report is trustworthy'.[75] Furthermore, the court also rejected the argument that the report was untrustworthy because the commission had not held any hearings in preparing it. As the court explained: 'Even though the Truth Commission did not conduct a formal hearing, it interviewed numerous witnesses, victims, and relatives associated with the events described in the Report. In addition, the Truth Commission reviewed thousands of complaints of acts of violence, examined documents, interviewed members of the military, and visited locations of acts of violence.'[76]

To be sure, the report was not the only evidence used by the *Chavez* plaintiffs. However, as the defendant's targeting of the report in his appeal demonstrated, the report constituted a significant piece of evidence that would have been independently sufficient to support many of the jury's factual findings in the case.[77] In addition, the official report

[71] Ibid., 496. [72] Ibid. [73] United States, Federal Rules of Evidence, § 803(8)(C).
[74] *Chavez* v. *Carranza*, above note 68, 496. [75] Ibid. [76] Ibid.
[77] Interestingly, as will be noted below, the same report used to establish record facts in *Chavez* v. *Carranza* was also used as part of another plaintiff's case-in-chief under the TVPA: *Arce* v. *Garcia*, above note 67, 1264.

undoubtedly bolstered the facts that were introduced through the plaintiffs' other witnesses, thereby strengthening the plaintiffs' claims and helping them to prevail.

B *Reports and Legislative Fact-finding in Human Rights Cases*

While the factual information necessary to establish legislative facts might be available from various sources, official treaty body reports interpreting the right in question are a source that can be used to establish legislative facts that bolster legal conclusions (just as they may be able to bolster record fact-finding, as in the cases discussed above). For instance, in The Cotton Field case, the families of women whose mutilated bodies were found in a cotton field in Juárez, Mexico, brought human rights claims against the Mexican government based on allegations that the deaths were attributable to dilatory investigative policies and practices motivated by gender animus.[78] Establishing the predicate for these claims required far more than looking at what the authorities had said and done in the cases of the individual murdered women. Legislative facts about the historical practices of the police department, their actions in numerous other cases and statistical evidence regarding murder rates in the region were crucial to the judges' ability to put the specific claims brought by a few families into a context that enabled them to conclude that the deaths were in fact femicides for which the state of Mexico was legally responsible.[79]

Examples of this type of use of reports can also be found in domestic judicial opinions from around the world. For example:

In Australia, the Family Court considered an application by the Australian beneficiaries of an illegal surrogacy contract to obtain a judicial order recognising their 'parental responsibility' for children born to a surrogate mother in Thailand.[80] At the outset of its opinion, the court noted that 'much of the evidence required to determine the children's identity and their best interests was obtained' from the Independent Children's Lawyer appointed by the court and not by the applicant parents. The court expressed concern that this factual evidence was critical to ensure that the children were not 'victims of child trafficking for whom unidentified parents searched in vain' – a

[78] The Cotton Field Case, above note 52.

[79] See also Quinn, above note 13, 168–170 (discussing the facts relied upon by the court to justify its legal conclusions).

[80] *Ellison and another* v. *Karnchanit*, [2012] FamCA 602 (Australia).

concern that the court noted was not 'fanciful' but was consistent with a number of 'credible' reports including those of the former UN Commission on Human Rights and the reports of two separate special rapporteurs.[81]

In Canada, a provincial trial court found that the government had violated a prisoner's rights under the Canadian Charter of Rights and Freedoms for having placed him in solitary confinement pending trial on murder charges.[82] In support of its decision, the court quoted at length from an interim report of the special rapporteur on torture and other cruel, inhuman or degrading treatment or punishment.[83] In particular, the court not only noted the legal conclusions of the special rapporteur under international law, but also discussed at length the interim report's factual findings with respect to the 'psychological and sometimes physiological ill effects of solitary confinement'[84] in bolstering its own conclusion that keeping the plaintiff in solitary confinement violated Canadian law.

In Hong Kong, the Court of First Instance concluded that an adjudicator's decision dismissing the applicant's torture claim had failed to consider relevant materials and therefore erred as a matter of law.[85] The court based its decision on a number of UN reports finding relevant facts contrary to those cited by the adjudicator in dismissing the claim.[86]

In the United States, a federal court of appeals affirmed a district court's factual findings in support of its decision to toll a statute of limitations in a case brought under the TVPA (the US statute discussed above).[87] The court concluded that the facts which the court had relied upon as the basis for its legal conclusion were supported by the evidence in the record and bolstered this conclusion by noting that the evidence on which it was relying was consistent with a report that had been submitted to the UN Security Council.[88]

81 Referring to reports by the special rapporteur on the sale of children, child prostitution, and child pornography and the special rapporteur on violence against women its causes and consequences, dated 8 March 2005 and 18 March 2005 respectively.

82 *Bacon* v. *Surrey Pretrial Services Center (Warden)*, 2010 BCSC 805 (Canada).

83 Ibid., para 279. 84 Ibid.

85 *MDB* v. *Betty Kwan*, [2014] HKEC 497 (Court of First Instance).

86 Ibid., para 61, citing several sources, including UN, US Department of State and NGO reports.

87 See *Arce* v. *Garcia*, above note 67, 1264.

88 Ibid., citing *From Madness to Hope: The 12-year War in El Salvador: Report of the Commission on the Truth for El Salvador* (15 March 1993), 22, annexed to *Letter Dated*

These examples are just a brief survey of the case law in various jurisdictions around the world. Each case demonstrates the existence of networks between judicial and non-judicial actors, as well as the influence of non-judicial actors on judicial fact-finding. The fact that such incorporation can and does happen suggests the potential for non-judicial fact-finding to make human rights litigation more effective.

Conclusion: What Next?

The tendency of judicial networks scholars and advocates to overlook the factual records developed by reporting and monitoring entities as an important component of judicial networks may or may not be descriptively correct. As the above examples reflect, courts do sometimes integrate facts in their decisions and these facts appear to bolster the legal decision-making underlying the norm transmission that is at the heart of transnational judicial networks.

On the other hand, how widespread the practice is – or how easily courts can access factual information or rely upon it in a manner consistent with domestic rules of evidence and procedure – is far from clear. Future research investigating the integration of factual information into human rights networks should focus on the uses made of official reports by domestic courts deciding human rights claims. Which domestic courts use these reports? When they are used, are they used primarily for the legal analyses they contain (as has been typically assumed), for the factual information they contain (as in the cases discussed above), for a combination of the two or in some other way?

Furthermore, the importance of factual information to human rights decision-making suggests a need for a comprehensive analysis of the evidentiary and other procedural rules that may limit the ability of victims to use official reports. A comprehensive account parsing when and how domestic courts can use these reports would be illuminating. For example, can courts cite reports only to bolster legal analysis or can they also rely on them as a source of factual evidence? If they can rely on them as a source of factual evidence, can they do so only if the evidence independently meets admissibility requirements or do they grant an exception for official reports, as in US federal courts? These

29 March 1993 from the Secretary-General Addressed to the President of the Security Council, UN Doc S/25500 (1 April 1993).

and many related questions are ripe for examination. Understanding current practices, as well as constraints that may exist, can help more fully elucidate the potential of judicial networks, particularly to the extent they serve as a global enforcement mechanism for international human rights protections.

4

International Peace Mediators

The Normative Involvement of an Epistemic Community

PHILIPP KASTNER

International mediators are regularly involved and assist in the negotiated resolution of internal armed conflicts. However, so far, there has been little discussion on their normative involvement. This chapter argues that relying on a pluralistic understanding of law and on the concept of epistemic communities developed in international relations theory is useful to explore these phenomena. In the absence of formal rules governing their involvement, peace mediators, in interaction with the negotiating parties and other stakeholders, must find ways to ascertain their own legitimacy. Moreover, mediators have a significant normative impact on peace negotiations. This impact may be manifest when mediators consciously and explicitly vindicate their normative ambition; it may also be more latent and unrelated to a deliberate strategy pursued by the mediator, as in the case of facilitative mediators concerned with encouraging party self-determination and upholding their own neutrality and impartiality throughout the process. Though rarely recognised, this normative impact is, nonetheless, omnipresent. In the fairly new transnational field of peace mediation, mediators thus contribute to building a shared set of knowledge about peace mediation and to generating, both individually and collectively, the legal-normative framework of peace negotiations.

The chapter claims that without recognising the existence of, and without analysing, process-related norms and associated obligations, the conduct of mediators is neither legitimate nor illegitimate and can therefore not be assessed from a normative perspective; conformity with legal obligations, moreover, confers legitimacy. A consideration of the normative

Parts of this chapter build on Philipp Kastner, *Legal Normativity in the Resolution of Internal Armed Conflict* (Cambridge: Cambridge University Press, 2015).

role of mediators also has wider implications for the theory and practice of peace negotiations. Recognising and adequately conceiving the normative basis of the conduct of mediators and their normative impact on the negotiations are essential to grasp the normative framework of peace negotiations. The role of mediators is, indeed, highly illustrative of these normative dynamics. Mediators take part in the negotiations; as normative actors, they influence and are influenced by the normative framework constructed in this specific context. At the same time, they are, at least to some extent, outsiders who introduce into the negotiations preconceived norms and normative beliefs. In other words, mediators cannot be concerned exclusively with the specific context of negotiations in which they are involved and rely solely on the respective norms generated in interaction with the negotiating parties. They also operate within a larger normative framework where international legal norms are highly influential, with respect to both their own behaviour and, more generally, the manner in which the negotiations are conducted. One of the results is that peace mediators increasingly bear a normative ambition vis-à-vis the negotiating parties and are committed to norm-promotion.

In this sense, the peace mediator symbolises the archetypical normative actor: actively and constantly involved in the process of norm-creation and norm-application, in interaction with the negotiating parties and other stakeholders in a specific context of negotiations; yet inevitably inspired and directed by largely external normative influences, such as international legal norms and related obligations, that are consciously or unconsciously internalised and assumed. The concept of 'epistemic communities' elucidates the role of and especially the interaction among peace mediators. The term, coined in international relations theory, refers to knowledge-based transnational networks, often in relation to technical or scientific matters, through which shared interpretations, understandings and normative beliefs and commitment are constructed and transmitted in the absence of a hegemonic world order.[1] Despite the typically confidential or even secret nature of mediation

[1] For the concept of epistemic communities in international relations, see, in particular, the 1992 special issue of the journal *International Organization* published by MIT Press. Within this issue, Peter Haas refers to epistemic communities as 'a network of professionals with recognised expertise and competence in a particular domain and an authoritative claim to policy-relevant knowledge within that domain or issue-area': Peter M. Haas, 'Introduction: Epistemic Communities and International Policy Coordination' (1992) 46:2 *International Organization* 1–35, 2. He discusses shared normative commitments of epistemic communities at 19.

efforts, peace mediators have started to form a loose network by cooperating with and learning from each other. While some of these exchanges might only have an indirect impact, it is remarkable that several actors, including the UN, regional organisations and some non-governmental organisations, actively and intentionally provide mediation support to other actors involved in mediating peace negotiations, notably by sharing experiences and knowledge.

The Centre for Humanitarian Dialogue, for instance, aspires to 'further the debate on the challenges facing the mediation community' and 'develops practical information resources, including training material, which it makes available to the wider mediation community'.[2] Through the language used, the Centre for Humanitarian Dialogue clearly underlines its conviction that such a 'mediation community' exists. The formal status of mediation organisations within this community appears secondary: non-governmental organisations work with, support and are supported by states and international and regional organisations.[3] The community experienced a certain institutionalisation with the establishment, in 2008, of the Mediation Support Network,[4] a global network of primarily non-governmental organisations intended to support mediation in peace negotiations and share information among peace organisations. Hence peace mediators not only draw on experiences shared by other mediating organisations but also contribute to building a shared set of knowledge about peace mediation.

As the examples in this chapter illustrate, the epistemic community of peace mediators transcends the traditional state versus non-state actor divide and is best analysed from a pluralistic perspective. This community, although operating in a 'disaggregated world order', to borrow from Anne-Marie Slaughter, does not constitute a 'parallel network'; nor are peace mediators 'monitors and interlocutors for specific government networks'.[5]

[2] Centre for Humanitarian Dialogue, 'Mediation Support' (undated), online at: www.hdcentre.org/en/our-work/mediation-support/.

[3] By way of example, the Crisis Management Initiative supports the European Union in peace mediation: Crisis Management Initiative, 'CMI Closely Supports the EU in Peace Mediation' (undated), online at: www.cmi.fi/media-2/news/europe/657-cmi-closely-supports-the-eu-in-peace-mediation. Similarly, the Centre for Humanitarian Dialogue collaborates with regional organisations, such as the African Union and ECOWAS: Centre for Humanitarian Dialogue, 'Support to Regional Organizations' (undated), online at: www.hdcentre.org/en/our-work/mediation-support/current-activities/support-to-regional-organisations/.

[4] Online at: http://mediationsupportnetwork.net/.

[5] This language draws on Anne-Marie Slaughter, *A New World Order* (Princeton: Princeton University Press, 2009), 258–259.

Rather, mediators form a novel and primarily horizontal network of experts, which is – despite its hybridity – the principal structure in the field of today's peace negotiations. Through this network, mediators, whose activity becomes increasingly professionalised, contribute to generating, both individually and collectively, the legal-normative framework governing the peaceful resolution of internal armed conflicts.

This chapter analyses the place and role of mediators in the normative framework of peace negotiations along two aspects. The first relates to the subtle yet increasingly noticeable normative basis of the conduct of peace mediators. Without formal rules authorising and governing their involvement, these actors, in interaction with the negotiating parties and other stakeholders, must find ways to ascertain their own legitimacy. While the normative framework of peace negotiations eschews straightforward claims with respect to the legitimacy of mediators, some aspects that are explicitly identified in definitions of mediation can provide guidance as to what appear to be legitimate ways for peace mediators to get involved. Furthermore, more implicit, underlying principles about the motives, the morality and the ethics of peace mediators may have given or may give rise to certain norms regarding the involvement of mediators and their legitimacy.

The second aspect concerns the significant normative impact mediators have on negotiations, regardless of their various possible functions and roles. This impact is related to the fact that mediation in the context of the resolution of internal armed conflicts distinguishes itself from more common forms of mediation, such as in the fields of family, employment and community disputes, in several ways. A mediator will often have to address difficult questions, such as the representation of the belligerents and the participation of civil society actors at the negotiations. Furthermore, internal armed conflicts are usually highly asymmetrical in several aspects, which creates specific challenges for a mediator and his or her impartiality.

I Possible Functions and Scope of Action of Mediators: Seizing the Normative Impact

Peace mediators may assume various functions and pursue very different styles. In this regard, the large literature on mediation in the domestic context[6] and its theorisation of different mediation styles is helpful to

[6] It should be noted that what is called 'domestic mediation' here is not necessarily limited to a national context. International business and commercial mediation can be considered an

some extent. While mediation has spread to various fields since the 1980s, including to business and commerce, the mediation styles described – notably facilitative, evaluative and transformative mediation[7] – are shaped by concepts that have been developed in well-defined and rather limited fields, such as family, employment and community disputes. Moreover, mediation in the domestic context is one form of so-called alternative dispute resolution, which can replace or precede litigation. Mediation is, therefore, usually considered an alternative to court proceedings, which is why the literature often focuses on comparing its benefits and shortcomings to judicial mechanisms.[8] However, in the absence of a state-like legal system embracing and enforcing judicial decisions, adjudication is not an alternative in the context of the resolution of internal armed conflicts. As a result, peace negotiations are never conducted against the backdrop of a possible decision made by a judge, which would be binding on the parties. It is also impossible to conceive the dispute in question as primarily private due to the very public nature of armed conflicts, which affect large portions of or the whole population of a state or region and regularly threaten regional or even global peace and security.

In spite of these differences, the two main styles that characterise mediation more generally, namely facilitative and interventionist mediation, are also present in the context of peace negotiations, and the subsequent analysis will be pursued along these two styles. The conceptualisation of these styles is borrowed from the mediation literature and can easily be applied to the more specific situation of peace mediation. Facilitative mediation, which is sometimes also called pure mediation, focuses on party self-determination and mediator impartiality. It can be

expansion of domestic mediation to the transnational level. However, the very concept of mediation, the different styles of mediators, proposed standards of ethics and other attributes characterising the domestic mediation process hardly change. Moreover, contrary to the context of peace mediation, litigation and arbitration usually remain genuine alternatives.

[7] See, for example, Leonard L. Riskin, 'Mediator Orientation, Strategies and Techniques' (1994) 12:9 *Alternatives to the High Cost of Litigation* 111–114. For a thorough overview, see also Susan Nauss Exon, 'The Effect That Mediator Styles Impose on Neutrality and Impartiality Requirements of Mediation' (2008) 42:3 *University of San Francisco Law Review* 577–620, 589–594.

[8] It is worth noting that contrary to the determinedly voluntary nature of mediation, the fairly recent popularity of so-called *alternative* dispute resolution mechanisms in domestic systems has led, somewhat paradoxically, to mandatory mediation. In some jurisdictions, certain cases must now undergo a mediation procedure as a prerequisite for litigation. See further John W. Cooley, *The Mediator's Handbook: Advanced Practice Guide for Civil Litigation*, 2nd ed. (Louisville, CO: National Institute for Trial Advocacy, 2006), 21.

formulative to a certain extent and include elements of norm-promotion. Non-governmental actors and small, neutral states typically pursue this mediation style. The second style, sometimes called principal mediation, is more interventionist, generally also more formulative and at times even coercive. The normative impact of powerful states, which characteristically pursue this second style and can make use of their leverage on the negotiating parties as mediators, may be more visible than in the case of primarily facilitative mediation; in reality, as it will be argued, this impact is not necessarily more significant. While vindicating a more neutral and disinterested image, facilitative mediators may also bear an important normative ambition and influence peace negotiations in a significant way.

Distinguishing these two styles in their ideal forms should only be seen as serving to facilitate the analysis of the possible functions and the normative impact of mediators. In fact, these mediators always act along a continuum. Everything is a question of degree: clear boundaries neither should nor can be drawn, and one specific negotiation context can rarely be associated exclusively with one mediation style. A mediator may as well pursue several styles subsequently or even simultaneously – with respect to different issues – in the same situation. Facilitative and interventionist mediation styles are therefore not fixed categories but reflect tendencies in mediation theory and practice.

A Facilitative Mediation: Beyond Neutrality and Impartiality?

The most basic purpose of facilitative mediation is to bring the parties to the negotiating table and to enable communication between them. The mediator focuses on procedural issues to ensure that the parties meet and talk to each other but plays otherwise a rather passive role. This means that the negotiating parties themselves have the main responsibility to initiate substantive discussions about agenda items and possible compromises on substantive matters. Respect for party autonomy and the parties' own personal evaluations, and even the application of the parties' own benchmarks and standards of fairness, shape the mediator's role.[9]

Model examples of this kind of mediation in the context of peace negotiations include the mediation by the Community of Sant'Egidio of

[9] David A. Hoffman, 'Paradoxes of Mediation' in Daniel Bowling and David A. Hoffman, eds., *Bringing Peace into the Room: How the Personal Qualities of the Mediator Impact the Process of Conflict Resolution* (San Francisco: Jossey-Bass, 2003), 167–181, 178; Exon, above note 7, 591.

the negotiations leading to the 1992 Mozambican peace agreement and, by the Norwegian government and a non-governmental organisation, of those leading to the 1993 Oslo Peace Accords between Israel and the Palestine Liberation Organization. The mediators' reputation for neutrality has been highlighted as one of the key factors of successful mediation in these cases: the Norwegian mediators, for instance, had clear procedural rules on how to maintain their neutrality, throughout the negotiations, as 'active facilitators' and not as 'interested mediators'.[10] Perfectly equal treatment of the parties on all procedural matters, even with respect to providing equivalent rooms and meals, was a major concern.[11] Moreover, the main goal of the intervention was not to alter the negotiation structure or the extant power dynamics but to help the parties improve their communication.[12]

This type of mediation resembles most forms of mediation in the domestic context, where the mediator usually remains in the sphere of facilitation and is committed, as generally expected by the parties, to strictly maintaining his or her neutrality. Here, the mediator does not assume an interventionist role by actively proposing solutions to the parties. Small states and non-governmental organisations usually pursue such a facilitative mediation style. Surprisingly, the academic literature on international negotiations[13] reflects an apparently still common assumption that non-governmental organisations play an important role as advocates but not as actors that are directly involved and participate in the negotiations, either as negotiators[14] or mediators. However, in recent years, several non-governmental organisations have become specialised in the peaceful resolution of armed conflicts, such as the Centre for Humanitarian Dialogue,[15] Conciliation Resources,[16] the Centre for

[10] William J. Bien, 'The Oslo Channel' in Melanie C. Greenberg, John H. Barton and Margaret E. McGuinness, eds., *Words over War: Mediation and Arbitration to Prevent Deadly Conflict* (Lanham: Rowman & Littlefield, 2000), 109–136, 129–130. See also Karin Aggestam, 'Mediating Asymmetrical Conflict' (2002) 7:1 *Mediterranean Politics* 69–91, 77.

[11] Bien (ibid.), 130. [12] Aggestam, above note 10, 77.

[13] See, for example, Brigid Starkey, Mark A. Boyer and Jonathan Wilkenfeld, *Negotiating a Complex World: An Introduction to International Negotiation*, 2nd ed. (Oxford: Rowman & Littlefield, 2005).

[14] It has been pointed out that the direct influence of local non-governmental organisations on peace negotiations is understudied: Susan Burgerman, 'Voices from the Parallel Table: The Role of Civil Sectors in the Guatemalan Peace Process' in Oliver P. Richmond and Henry F. Carey, eds., *Subcontracting Peace: The Challenges of NGO Peacebuilding* (Aldershot: Ashgate, 2005), 85–91, 85.

[15] Online at: www.hdcentre.org. [16] Online at: www.c-r.org.

Conflict Resolution,[17] the Crisis Management Initiative,[18] International Alert[19] and the Carter Center.[20]

It has rightly been pointed out that much attention has been given to religion as a source of conflict but not to religion as a source of peace-making.[21] Yet some faith-based non-governmental organisations also get involved as mediators in peace negotiations. This does not necessarily result in religion itself turning into the main framework for the negotiations, but, as it will be argued, such mediators certainly introduce principles and concepts rooted in their religion. The Catholic Church, for instance, has played a key role in the peace negotiations in Mozambique and Colombia. Widely respected in the country, the Catholic Church has been a moral guide for the peace process in Colombia.[22] In Mozambique, the Catholic Church assisted in the negotiations of the Front for the Liberation of Mozambique (FRELIMO) with the colonial power Portugal, which resulted in Mozambique's independence in 1975.[23] Having started to provide humanitarian aid to Mozambique in the 1980s,[24] the Roman Catholic Community of Sant'Egidio became actively involved in 1990 as a mediator in the peace negotiations between the FRELIMO government and its rival, the Mozambican National Resistance, in the civil war. These negotiations culminated in the conclusion of the Rome Accords in 1992.[25]

17 Online at: ccrweb.ccr.uct.ac.za. 18 Online at: www.cmi.fi.

19 Online at: www.international-alert.org.

20 Online at: www.cartercenter.org/peace/conflict_resolution/index.html.

21 David Smock, 'Divine Intervention, Regional Reconciliation through Faith' (2004) 25:4 *Harvard International Review* 46–50, 46. The Pope has traditionally played an important role as an intermediary. For examples of the involvement of the Holy See as peace mediator, see Janne Haaland Matlary, 'The Just Peace: The Public and Classical Diplomacy of the Holy See' (2001) 14:2 *Cambridge Review of International Affairs* 80–94, 89–91.

22 For more information on the peace process, see José E. Arvelo, 'International Law and Conflict Resolution in Colombia: Balancing Peace and Justice in the Paramilitary Demobilization Process' (2005–2006) 37 *Georgetown Journal of International Law* 411–476.

23 For more information, see Pierre Anouilh, 'Sant'Egidio au Mozambique: de la charité à la fabrique de la paix' (2005) 3:59 *Revue internationale et stratégique* 9–20, 13.

24 Ibid., 15.

25 *General Peace Agreement for Mozambique*, 4 October 1992, on file with the United States Institute of Peace, online at: www.usip.org/files/file/resources/collections/peace_agreements/mozambique_1991-92.pdf. For a more general analysis of the Mozambique negotiations, see Ibrahim Msabaha, 'Negotiating an End to Mozambique's Murderous Rebellion' in I. William Zartman, ed., *Elusive Peace: Negotiating an End to Civil Wars* (Washington, DC: Brookings Institution, 1995), 204–230.

While the Community of Sant'Egidio benefits from its location in Rome and its ties to the Vatican and Italian diplomacy, it remains, as a non-governmental actor, independent in its policy decisions.[26] The mediation strategy of the Community of Sant'Egidio tries to combine the official, or 'institutional', with the flexibility of a more informal approach to mediation.[27] However, as a member of the Community has noted, 'The real factor behind the success of this formula is the fact that St Egidio is interested solely in putting an end to the conflict; it has no other interests to defend and considers any contribution that can work to this end useful and welcome'.[28] Compared to the typical motives of third parties getting involved in a peace process, a 'low' agenda, besides altruism and humanitarian interests, stands out in this case. The triggering cause for the Community was the realisation that its humanitarian aid to Mozambique would not be effective without reaching a lasting peace agreement, which meant for the Community 'leaving the field of simple solidarity and development work and entering the conflictual world of politics and war'.[29]

Small, peaceful states that are driven by humanitarian interests but do not have other major interests in the respective conflict region may assume a similar role. Comparative advantages of Switzerland as a mediator, for instance, have been described as lying in her credibility, proficiency and reliability.[30] Regarding internal armed conflicts in Africa, Switzerland has the additional intrinsic assets of not having a colonial past or particular economic interests. Similarly, Norway's approach to mediation has been portrayed as benefiting from 'impartiality, consistency, and confidentiality with the resources of an industrialised state'.[31] Oslo's close collaboration with non-governmental organisations to

[26] Mario Giro, 'The Community of Saint Egidio and Its Peace-Making Activities' (1998) 33:3 *International Spectator* 85–100, 87.

[27] Ibid., 89.

[28] Ibid. Giro also notes at 86 that: 'The Community's approach to peace-making is based on [a] fundamental social commitment to the poor and the dispossessed'.

[29] Ibid., 89.

[30] Damiano Sguaitamatti and Simon J.A. Mason, 'Vermittler im Vergleich: Bedeutung für die Schweiz als Mediatorin' (2011) 83 *Zürcher Beiträge zur Sicherheitspolitik* 69–109, 100. The fact that Switzerland is not part of a strong regional organisation, the missing cultural proximity to most conflict regions and an underdeveloped tradition of leadership because of Switzerland's consensus-based politics are cited as comparative disadvantages at 101.

[31] Daniel Lieberfeld, 'Small Is Credible: Norway's Niche in International Dispute Settlement' (1995) 11:3 *Negotiation Journal* 201–207, 201. Norway has been involved, inter alia, in the peace processes in Israel–Palestine, Guatemala and Sri Lanka.

conduct peace talks, as for instance in Sri Lanka and Sudan,[32] also confirms the assumption that a clear and generalised distinction between the role and mediation approach between state actors and non-state actors cannot be made. Although the coercive potential of non-governmental actors and small states may be limited, their normative ambition, combined with their legitimacy and credibility, may have an equally or even more significant and long-lasting normative impact on the negotiations than power-based and more interventionist mediation.

Even a somewhat minimalist view on the role and impact that a facilitative mediator has or might have bears two important *caveats*. First, the mere presence of mediators inevitably influences the negotiating parties.[33] The behaviour of the negotiating parties changes with the presence of an intermediary, even if he or she does not have a clear normative ambition regarding, for instance, fair and equal representation at the negotiating table or the inclusion of human rights and transitional justice elements on the agenda. A certain procedure, which may be suggested explicitly or implicitly by the mediator, may nevertheless have to be followed by the parties, and the style of communication and negotiation strategies of the parties may change simply because of the presence of a mediator.

Second, neutrality itself cannot be taken for granted, even if the mediator is perceived as neutral or impartial by the parties and actively tries to preserve this perception. As already mentioned, the neutrality and impartiality of a mediator have often been cited as crucial elements of successful peace negotiations. With respect to the mediator's role in the negotiations leading to the 1992 Mozambican peace agreement, for instance, a member of the Community of Sant'Egidio emphasised the importance of 'the [mediator's] ability to convince the parties to the conflict of one's impartiality, an essential premise for mediation'.[34] Maintaining an image of impartiality represents a particular challenge for mediators in the case of internal armed conflicts, which are

32 See Ann Kelleher and James Larry Taulbee, 'Building Peace Norwegian Style: Studies in Track 1½ Diplomacy' in Oliver P. Richmond and Henry F. Carey, eds., *Subcontracting Peace: The Challenges of NGO Peacebuilding* (Aldershot: Ashgate, 2005), 69–84, 78.

33 Daniel Bowling and David A. Hoffman, 'Bringing Peace into the Room: The Personal Qualities of the Mediator and Their Impact on the Mediation' in Bowling and Hoffman, eds., *Bringing Peace into the Room*, above note 9, ch. 1, 21. Bowling and Hoffman draw (at 20) an interesting parallel between the mediation context and the discovery of the physicist Werner Heisenberg that the observation of particles influences their behaviour.

34 Giro, above note 26, 100 [emphasis omitted].

characterised by a multidimensional asymmetry.[35] These asymmetries include the legal status of the parties, with non-state actors seeking international recognition through the negotiation process, uneven military and material capabilities as well as negotiation capacities.[36] Mediators can accept an imbalance between the parties and pursue a strategy of 'even-handedness', or they can try to empower the weaker party through an 'equalising strategy' based on the assumption that strictly facilitative mediation in situations of important power imbalances only allows the stronger party to dominate the weaker party and is, therefore, ineffective.[37] While mediation researchers disagree on whether equal power is a necessary prerequisite for effective and fair mediation,[38] the mediator must take a stance in an uneven situation and make a decision between maintaining or attempting to equalise the imbalance. A legal asymmetry can be levelled by conferring some legitimacy to non-state actors,[39] who may be regarded as mere 'insurgents' or 'criminals' by the state actor. This may turn out to be a challenging endeavour for the mediator. Indeed, in situations of asymmetrical conflicts, '[m]aintaining a perception of neutrality becomes, over time, close to impossible'.[40] Describing the involvement of the Norwegian government as a mediator in the Sri Lankan peace process and the contribution of the Nordic countries[41] to the Sri Lanka Monitoring Mission in the early 2000s, Höglund and Svensson provide a good account of the challenges that an a priori neutral third party might experience. Despite the clear objective of remaining neutral and being continuously perceived as neutral,

[35] Kristine Höglund and Isak Svensson, '"Damned if You Do, and Damned if You Don't": Nordic Involvement and Images of Third-Party Neutrality in Sri Lanka' (2008) 13:3 *International Negotiation* 341–364, 343. On the resolution of asymmetrical conflicts, see generally Christopher R. Mitchell, 'Asymmetry and Strategies of Regional Conflict Resolution' in I. William Zartman and Victor A. Kremenyuk, eds., *Cooperative Security: Reducing Third World Wars* (Syracuse: Syracuse University Press, 1995), 25–60. On the asymmetrical nature of internal armed conflicts and its implications for the reciprocal nature of international humanitarian law, revealing 'the emptiness of a purely positivistic grounding of these norms', see René Provost, 'Asymmetrical Reciprocity and Compliance with the Laws of War' in Benjamin Perrin, ed., *Modern Warfare: Armed Groups, Private Militaries, Humanitarian Organizations, and the Law* (Vancouver: UBC Press, 2012), 17–42, 37.

[36] Höglund and Svensson, above note 35, 344.

[37] Ibid., 345. Exon points out that such a more directive mediation style 'may infringe on the parties' rights of self-determination, which in turn may affect the mediator's neutrality and impartiality': Exon, above note 7, 595.

[38] See Höglund and Svensson, above note 35, 345, footnote 6.

[39] Ibid., 346.

[40] Ibid., 359.

[41] Norway, Sweden, Denmark, Finland and Iceland contributed to this mission.

the Nordic mission faced harsh criticism of bias, for instance after making a proposal to the Sri Lankan government to recognise the Sea Tigers, the naval unit of the Liberation Tigers of Tamil Eelam, as a de facto naval unit.[42]

In addition to the difficulties of maintaining an image of neutrality and impartiality that a mediator might experience in practice, it should be highlighted that the involvement of a human being, whether in a more personal capacity or as a representative of an institution, is based on assumptions, values and norms that might differ from those of the negotiating parties. Whether implicitly or explicitly, consciously or unconsciously, a mediator will always have to manage some tensions between the parties' objectives and his or her own normative beliefs and principles.[43] These beliefs and principles may be evident; more often, however, they are latent, albeit not necessarily less powerful. In the context of a discussion on the morality of mediators, it has been argued that 'The act of mediation is not a neutral act . . . The mediator may claim to be neutral with respect to the values and demands of the combatants, but the activity of mediating is still a declaration of values held by the mediator'.[44] A commitment to neutrality, impartiality and objectivity, in line with prevalent Western dispute resolution practice and evoking a Rawlsian 'veil of ignorance',[45] can certainly not hide cultural assumptions.[46] Good examples are faith-based organisations, such as the Community of Sant'Egidio, which may claim to be strictly neutral in mediating peace negotiations. Yet they certainly stand for and introduce certain values into the negotiations and shape, at least to a certain extent, both the procedure and the substance of the negotiations accordingly. In the words of Catherine Morris, the '"objective" mediator is a mythical

42 Höglund and Svensson, above note 35, 351–353.

43 Bowling and Hoffman, above note 33, 23.

44 Keith Webb, 'The Morality of Mediation' in Christopher R. Mitchell and Keith Webb, eds., *New Approaches to International Mediation* (New York: Greenwood Press, 1988), 16–28, 16. This phenomenon is also recognised by practitioners involved in peace negotiations. See, for instance, the brief prepared by the Public International Law and Policy Group for USAID's Office of Conflict Management and Mitigation: 'Technical Brief: Key Considerations when Supporting Peace Processes' (March 2013), 2, online at: www.usaid.gov/sites/default/files/documents/1866/Peace%20Processes%20Technical%20Brief%20FINAL.pdf.

45 John Rawls, *A Theory of Justice* (Cambridge, MA: Harvard University Press, 1971), 136–142.

46 For this argument, see Catherine Morris, 'The Trusted Mediator: Ethics and Interaction in Mediation' in Julie Macfarlane, ed., *Rethinking Disputes: The Mediation Alternative* (Toronto: Edmond Montgomery, 1997), 301–348, 313, 329–330.

creature removed from the realities of interaction among human beings who live in communities'.[47]

Furthermore, and related to the degree of intervention, mediation practice has shown that mere facilitation is not always the best path to follow.[48] In the context of peace mediation, more powerful states are often more ready to go beyond facilitation. They may have a considerable coercive potential and may even use their leverage to pursue a proactive 'carrots and sticks' mediation style, which may lead to more tangible results than merely facilitative mediation.

B *Interventionist Mediation and Its Limits*

Compared to non-governmental organisations and small, neutral states that do not have particular interests in the respective conflict region, the mediation style and strategy as well as the normative ambition of more powerful third states are more frequently linked to their political, military and economic influence on the negotiating parties. Moreover, since non-compliance with projected norms may be sanctioned by an interventionist powerful mediator, the normative impact on the negotiations is regularly more visible than in the case of non-governmental organisations, whose normative ambition must be voiced and implemented through more subtle means.

Internal armed conflicts, due to their typically asymmetrical nature, may arguably not be prone to strictly facilitative mediation but may warrant a more interventionist approach. Besides the traditional concepts of party self-determination, consensuality, mediator neutrality and impartiality, newer ethical standards reflect a trend towards fair results and related concepts of fairness, such as balancing the parties' power.[49] In

47 Ibid.

48 An explicit acknowledgement that a strictly non-interventionist approach may lead to an impasse can be found in the 2005 version of the Model Standards of Conduct for Mediators, an initiative of the American Arbitration Association, the American Bar Association, and the Society of Professionals in Dispute Resolution: 'Although party self-determination for process design is a fundamental principle of mediation practice, a mediator may need to balance such party self-determination with a mediator's duty to conduct a quality process'. See Standard I.A.1. of the Model Standards of Conduct for Mediators (September 2005), online at: www.americanbar.org/content/dam/aba/migrated/2011_build/dispute_resolution/model_standards_conduct_april2007.authcheckdam.pdf.

49 Exon, above note 7, 613. Exon shows that embracing fairness concepts leads to tensions with the impartiality requirement.

situations of asymmetrical conflict, the weaker party may be more willing to accept a mediation style that goes beyond facilitation. While some critics have called such a more evaluative mediation style, because it jeopardises mediator neutrality, an oxymoron,[50] other mediation scholars argue that certain elements of evaluation – and not only facilitation – can, or even must, be part of a mediation.[51]

This consideration, for instance, can explain why the Palestinian negotiators have accepted the United States, despite its general backing of Israel and support of Israel's interests, as a mediator. Washington's potential leverage over Israel, combined with a more directive and evaluative mediation style that goes far beyond mere facilitation, certainly reduces the parties' self-determination and discards mediator neutrality as a central attribute.[52] It may also contribute to balancing asymmetry between the parties, which can be considered vital for the Palestinian side. The mediation efforts made by the United States in the situation of Bosnia, resulting in the 1995 Dayton Peace Agreement, illustrate these aspects related to such an evaluative and formulative, and at times also coercive-manipulative, mediation style.[53]

Contrary to the earlier attempt of the European Community led by David Owen and Cyrus Vance, which has been characterised as 'an exercise in classical mediation', with the mediators having 'no leverage or power other than the parties' goodwill',[54] Dayton went far beyond facilitative mediation. As the chief mediator, Richard Holbrooke, has noted, '"Dayton" has entered the language as shorthand for a certain type of diplomacy – the Big Bang approach to negotiations: lock everyone up

[50] Kimberlee K. Kovach and Lela P. Love, '"Evaluative" Mediation is an Oxymoron' (1996) 14:3 *Alternatives to the High Cost of Litigation* 31–32. According to Maureen E. Laflin, 'mediators who approach the process as "advocates of a good solution" are necessarily adopting an attitude of power and control over the outcome, an attitude which cannot but compromise the principles of self-determination and impartiality': Maureen E. Laflin, 'Preserving the Integrity of Mediation through the Adoption of Ethical Rules for Lawyer-Mediators' (2000) 14 *Notre Dame Journal of Law, Ethics & Public Policy* 479–526, 498.

[51] For more details, see Exon, above note 7, 604.

[52] For more information on this debate, see ibid., 603.

[53] For a more thorough discussion of formulative and manipulative mediation styles, see Starkey, Boyer and Wilkenfeld, above note 13, 38.

[54] Melanie C. Greenberg, John H. Barton and Margaret E. McGuinness, 'From Lisbon to Dayton: International Mediation and the Bosnia Crisis' in Greenberg, Barton and McGuinness, eds., *Words over War*, above note 10, 35–75, 47. According to these authors, the subsequent Owen-Stoltenberg plan similarly 'expose[d] the true failure of classical mediation': ibid.,54.

until they reach agreement'.[55] Formulative mediation may be particularly important if the negotiating parties lack or have asymmetrical diplomatic and legal drafting skills. In Dayton, the mediation team not only shuttled between the parties and tried to facilitate communication between them but assumed, as 'experts', the responsibility to draft the texts to be negotiated. In one of the key moments at Dayton, it was the mediation team that handed each delegation the draft annexes pertaining to the constitution, the electoral system and the NATO-led Implementation Force.[56] Regarding the coercive-manipulative component, Holbrooke recalled this power approach to mediation repeatedly in his account of the negotiations. For instance, he describes threatening the Bosnian Foreign Minister that Washington would hold him publicly responsible if the conclusion of a pre-agreement to Dayton failed.[57] At a later meeting, US Secretary of State Warren Christopher similarly warned that 'the situation would have to be cleared up right away if Sarajevo wanted to avoid serious consequences to its relations with the United States'.[58] The Bosnian context also shows that the negotiating parties might willingly acknowledge the leverage that a powerful mediator has on the other parties, or even contribute to building a common perception of this leverage. Dismissing concerns that the Bosnians might not agree to a US proposal, President Milosevic expressed his perception of the leverage of the United States to Holbrooke in the following way: '[y]ou are the United States. You can't let the Bosnians push you around this way. *Just tell them what to do.*'[59]

Such a highly interventionist involvement of a mediator can push the limits of an acceptable mediation environment and challenge the very notion of mediation. Moreover, the policy of the US mediation team to support the continuation of some fighting, such as a Croatian offensive 'valuable for the negotiating process',[60] and to press for a military intervention by NATO and, subsequently, for an extension of the bombing campaign,[61] which supposedly created 'ripeness' for a negotiated solution

[55] Richard Holbrooke, *To End a War* (New York: Random House, 1998), 232. For a more general analysis of US approaches to negotiation, see Richard H. Solomon and Nigel Quinney, *American Negotiating Behavior: Wheeler-Dealers, Legal Eagles, Bullies, and Preachers* (Washington, DC: United States Institute of Peace, 2010). Solomon and Quinney (at 19–45) identify, for instance, four mindsets – businesslike, legalistic, moralistic and superpower negotiation – that shape US negotiating behavior.

[56] Holbrooke (ibid.), 240. [57] Ibid., 139. [58] As cited by Holbrooke (ibid.), 183.

[59] As cited in ibid., 306 [emphasis added]. [60] Ibid., 68.

[61] In Holbrooke's words: 'Give us bombs for peace': ibid., 132.

of the conflict,[62] appears hardly compatible with the notion of a peace mediator who is committed to avoiding more violence.

In line with the mediation literature focused on domestic contexts, an 'overly zealous' peace mediator who exercises excessive influence or coercion should be viewed critically[63] and remain an exception. Not only are agreements concluded under external pressure often breached as soon as this pressure lessens;[64] there simply does not seem to exist a widely shared consensus – especially not within the mediation community itself – as to the compatibility of such conduct with the very notion of peace mediation. Exploring the principles of justice and fairness in international negotiation and emphasising the 'voluntary acceptance by parties of whatever arrangements are proposed' as a core criterion,[65] Cecile Albin has maintained that negotiations should never take place in a coercive or manipulative context.[66] According to her, '[a]greements held in place by force are clearly seen as illegitimate'.[67] While Albin argues convincingly that upholding justice and fairness improves the chances of reaching a widely respected agreement, some flexibility might be required in balancing these principles. Coercion is certainly antithetical to mediation. Although the conduct of the US mediation team in the Bosnian situation must therefore be considered incompatible with the traditional notion of requiring a mediator to remain impartial and to honour party self-determination, Dayton has nevertheless shown that some coercion may be constructive to make the parties engage in serious negotiations and accept certain compromises. Dayton thus pushed the limits of the notional concept of mediation in a rather exceptional manner that was, however, consented to both by the negotiating parties and the international community. In this sense, this process contributed to transforming the normative framework of peace negotiations by diluting, in a fairly unequivocal way, a widely shared

[62] Greenberg, Barton and McGuinness, 'From Lisbon to Dayton', above note 54, 63.

[63] See Exon, above note 7, 608. [64] Sguaitamatti and Mason, above note 30, 74.

[65] Cecile Albin, *Justice and Fairness in International Negotiation* (Cambridge: Cambridge University Press, 2001), 12. For an example of the debate on how mediators should deal with justice and fairness, see Jonathan M. Hyman, 'Swimming in the Deep End: Dealing with Justice in Mediation?' (2004) 6:19 *Cardozo Journal of Conflict Resolution* 19–56.

[66] Albin (ibid.), 12. See also Avishai Margalit, *On Compromise and Rotten Compromises* (Princeton: Princeton University Press, 2010), 92–93 (who argues more generally that 'an agreement based on coercion is not a compromise').

[67] Albin (ibid.), 12.

commitment to neutral, impartial, non-coercive and non-manipulative peace mediation.

In sum, the boundaries of legitimate peace mediation styles certainly are malleable, and grey zones remain. What can be concluded is that a forceful imposition of the text of a peace agreement on the parties would certainly go beyond the acceptable scope of action of a mediator and would be considered manifestly illegitimate conduct. In addition, the foregoing analysis along facilitative and interventionist mediation styles has not only shown that different actors mediate in different manners but that, depending on the status and the style pursued, the legitimacy of a mediator and compliance of the negotiating parties with projected norms may be more or less difficult to ascertain. Yet peace mediation is always a normative and increasingly expert-driven enterprise. From powerful states or strong regional organisations to small non-governmental organisations, mediators never act in a legal vacuum and may also assume an active norm-promoting role.

II The Normative Ambition and Increasing Professionalisation of Peace Mediators

In the absence of a hierarchical legal order readily available, the legal-normative framework of peace negotiations is generated primarily by the negotiating parties, with a mediator guiding them through the process and influencing the negotiations more or less directly and intentionally. It is evident, however, that an armed conflict, which affects the population at large and possibly threatens regional and international peace and security, is not a private dispute between relative equals. Moreover, protective norms and fundamental values of concern to the global community as a whole may be at stake, which is why mediators increasingly – and appropriately – acknowledge that existing international legal norms are relevant in peace negotiations. Mediators have therefore started to exercise more consciously a highly normative influence on the negotiating parties not only regarding the perception of the legality and legitimacy of peace negotiations, but also on the respect of legal norms by the parties throughout the process. Two groups of actors that are a central part in the network of peace mediators, namely international organisations and non-governmental organisations, illustrate well this normative consciousness and ambition of mediating organisations.

Because of the high number of peace processes in which it has been involved, the UN plays a pivotal role with respect to mediation in the context of internal armed conflicts.[68] Furthermore, the conduct of its representatives must correspond to standards the organisation itself stands for. By way of example, the signature of a UN representative, such as a special representative of the Secretary-General, on a peace agreement signals 'some type of UN endorsement, meaning that the UN should have audited the agreement in terms of the normative requirements which it promulgates and claims to uphold'.[69]

In the 2000s, the mediation strategy of the UN has experienced an increasing normalisation, with the field of transitional justice and the trend towards individual accountability for core crimes being the most visible element. While the UN had participated in several peace negotiations with amnesties on the agenda, thus giving such amnesties 'a kind of international legitimacy',[70] the organisation now regularly assumes transitional justice obligations with respect to its role as a mediator in peace negotiations, as confirmed in several documents. Most notably, in 1999, following the signing of the Lomé Agreement and the disclaimer of the Special Representative of the Secretary-General with respect to amnesties for grave crimes committed in the conflict in Sierra Leone, the Secretary-General issued guidelines to his envoys and representatives regarding the respect of human rights in peace negotiations.[71] Although these guidelines were not published, they represented a first step in addressing the assumed dilemma of a mediator between aspiring to honour the necessity of punishing perpetrators of core crimes and

[68] A list of recent situations in which the UN led or supported mediation is included in *Strengthening the Role of Mediation in the Peaceful Settlement of Disputes, Conflict Prevention and Resolution: Report of the Secretary-General*, UN Doc A/66/811 (25 June 2012), para 22. To render its mediation activities more effective, the UN established in 2006 the Mediation Support Unit within the Department of Political Affairs: UN, Department of Political Affairs, 'Diplomacy and Mediation' (undated), online at: www.un.org/undpa/diplomacy-mediation.

[69] Christine Bell, 'Peace Agreements and Human Rights: Implications for the UN' in Nigel D. White and Dirk Klaasen, eds., *The UN, Human Rights and Post-Conflict Situations* (Manchester: Manchester University Press, 2005), 241–266, 250.

[70] Kai Ambos, 'The Legal Framework of Transitional Justice: A Systematic Study with a Special Focus on the Role of the ICC' in Kai Ambos, Judith Large and Marieke Wierda, eds., *Building a Future on Peace and Justice: Studies on Transitional Justice, Peace and Development: The Nuremberg Declaration on Peace and Justice* (Berlin: Springer, 2009), 19–104, 57, footnote 240.

[71] 'Press Release: Secretary-General Comments on Guidelines Issued to Envoys', UN Doc SG/SM/7257 (10 December 1999).

doing everything feasible to end the hostilities. They also reflect the UN's appreciation of the obligations of an international mediator to bear a normative ambition vis-à-vis the negotiating parties. In line with one of the main arguments of this chapter, the importance of these guidelines does not lie in determining a specific outcome but in providing a normative tool that shapes the process and contributes to the development of a legal-normative framework for peace negotiations, in this case with UN participation.

The role of the UN as a peace mediator can, indeed, be conceived as norm-promoting. The mandate of the UN does not only consist in raising awareness about fundamental human rights norms but also in supporting their respect throughout the process as well as in seeking to construe them, at least partly, as the normative basis of a peace agreement. Because of this involvement, the negotiating parties are continuously encouraged to consider, internalise and eventually comply with the respective norms projected. The Secretary-General's 2012 report on the UN's mediation activities evokes a successful example of the implementation of this norm-promotional approach. The Secretary-General's Special Advisor for Yemen is said to have 'explained United Nations principles and standards relating to women and peace and security to government officials and stressed that a transition process must include the participation of women. As a result of those efforts, the 2011 Yemen Transition Agreement called for women to be represented in key institutions'.[72] In the same report, the Secretary-General underlines as well that the participation of women must be further promoted and that the 'United Nations will continue to do its part to push for the adequate representation of women and availability of gender expertise in peace process'.[73] The 'Guidance for Effective Mediation', annexed to this report, is remarkable for its ambition to guide not only UN mediators but also other mediators involved in peace negotiations. In this sense, the UN clearly aims to be the central pillar within the network of peace mediators and to regulate, to some extent, this network. In a norm-entrepreneurial manner, the UN has thus underlined the need for a more professional approach to mediation – 'mediation is a specialized activity'[74] – and advised peace mediators that they, among others,

[72] *Strengthening the Role of Mediation*, above note 68, para 25. [73] Ibid., para 77(b).

[74] Ibid., Annex I: Guidance for Effective Mediation, para 12. Regarding the professional approach to mediation, the Guidelines also state that '[a] good mediator promotes exchange through listening and dialogue, engenders a spirit of collaboration through problem solving, ensures that negotiating parties have sufficient knowledge, information

'[e]nsure and seek to demonstrate that the process and the treatment of the parties is fair and balanced'[75] and '[e]nsure that the parties understand the demands and limits of applicable conventions and international laws'.[76] Mediators, in other words, ought to be experts.

The mediation approach of the UN is probably the most visible example of the normatisation of a peace mediator's strategy that aspires to have a normative impact on the negotiating parties. However, other mediators, as exemplified by the norm-promoting role of the Catholic Church in the Colombian peace process,[77] also bear a similar normative ambition. Indeed, several non-governmental mediation organisations have outspokenly acknowledged that a willingness to educate the negotiating parties about their legal obligations and to advocate for their respect – for instance, in the field of justice and accountability – may determine the negotiations significantly. As noted in a report by the Centre for Humanitarian Dialogue, 'Of course the positions of the parties are key, but even where negotiators are ambivalent or initially resistant, much can be achieved through a proactive mediator ... The mediator should be clear in advising on the demands and limits of international law, and use expert input where necessary.'[78] Similarly, International Alert, a peace-building non-governmental organisation, expresses at greater length in its code of conduct its commitment to advocate for the inclusion of human rights standards in peace agreements and the establishment of accountability mechanisms:

> *We are committed to* pressing for international human rights standards to be recognised and incorporated in settlement agreements ... *We are also committed to* supporting measures which address the problems of impunity

and skills to negotiate with confidence and broadens the process to include relevant stakeholders from different segments of a society. Mediators are most successful in assisting negotiating parties to forge agreements when they are well informed, patient, balanced in their approach and discreet.'

75 Ibid., para 28. 76 Ibid., para 42.

77 The 1990 agreement characterises the Catholic Church as 'moral and spiritual guide': *Acuerdo político entre el gobierno nacional, los partidos políticos, el M-19, y la iglesia católica en calidad de tutora moral y espiritual del proceso* [Accord between the National Government, the Political Parties, the M-19 and the Catholic Church in the capacity of a moral and spiritual guide for the process], 9 March 1990 (Colombia), online at: http://peacemaker.un.org/sites/peacemaker.un.org/files/CO_900309_Acuerdo%20Pol%C3%ADtico%20Entre%20El%20Gobierno%20Nacional%20los%20Partidos%20Pol%C3%ADticos%20y%20El%20M-19.pdf.

78 Priscilla Hayner, *Negotiating Justice: Guidelines for Mediators* (Geneva: Henry Dunant Centre for Humanitarian Dialogue, 2009), 20–21, online at: www.hdcentre.org/uploads/tx_news/43Negotiatingjusticereport.pdf.

> and injustice, historical truth and compensation for victims.[79] ... Where appropriate, *promoting awareness* of the International Criminal Court and related institutions and mechanisms should also be encouraged.[80]

These examples illustrate that a strong normative element may be introduced into the negotiations through the mediator's assertion of certain values and principles, for instance regarding the respect of norms projected by international human rights law and international criminal law. Often, the normative bearing that the relatively new network of mediation experts has on the negotiations is not necessarily directed at a specific outcome but primarily at the process. It is a process-related norm that provides the parties and the mediator with a legitimate zone of possible agreement.

Conclusion

This chapter has shown that both facilitative and more interventionist mediators shape the process of the negotiations and may influence the substance of a peace agreement significantly. It is at this stage that a mediator's normative ambition, that may be latent or openly proclaimed, reveals itself most forcefully.

As it has been argued, the involvement of mediators in peace negotiations and ways to legitimise this involvement are norm-creative endeavours. Generalised, universally applicable norms are rare; even principles like mediator neutrality and impartiality cannot be taken for granted. They have to be dealt with by the mediators, who are normative actors, in interaction with other normative actors involved in every context of peace negotiations. At the same time, the actors do not have to reinvent the normative wheel every time. By forming an influential epistemic community, it is above all the mediators themselves who ensure interaction and exchange of normative knowledge between different contexts. If the right balance between facilitative and interventionist mediation cannot be reached in the abstract, some normative trends are developing through and within this network of experts: it is necessary to go beyond strictly facilitative mediation in certain situations, especially in the context of asymmetrical conflicts. Moreover, there is no clearly delineated yet

[79] International Alert, 'Code of Conduct' (1998), 5 [emphasis added], online at: http://international-alert.org/sites/default/files/publications/Code%20of%20Conduct.pdf.

[80] Ibid., 10 [emphasis added]. Similarly, the Centre for Humanitarian Dialogue proclaimed that: 'The HD Centre's operational work suggests that justice and the rule of law play a central role in sustainable conflict resolution': online at: http://archive-org-2012.com/org/h/2012-10-26_527283_5/Israeli-Palestinian-Conflict-HD-Centre.

nevertheless an existing boundary as to the acceptable behaviour of an interventionist peace mediator.

The examples analysed in this chapter, taken from various contexts and including states, the UN and non-governmental organisations as peace mediators, show that these mediators do not only assist the negotiating parties in generating their proper normative framework but also form a network of norm-promoters and norm-creators who may introduce predominantly external norms into the negotiations. Fundamental requirements for the open pursuit of such normative mediation are the acknowledgement by the mediator of his or her potential to have a normative impact on the negotiations, his or her aspiration to go beyond mere facilitation, and a commitment to put into practice this normative ambition. Moreover, latent forms of normative commitments and effects are omnipresent and not necessarily less influential in the context of peace negotiations.

While it is difficult to measure the direct effects of a mediator's normative commitment to include, for instance, issues of justice and accountability into the negotiations and raise awareness about the International Criminal Court, such a commitment shapes the normative framework of peace negotiations and can be highly influential for the conduct of the negotiating parties. Clearly, the respect of legal norms introduced into the negotiations cannot be enforced by a norm-promoting mediator in the absence of a coercive sanction-based system. These norms, nonetheless, may shape the negotiations significantly and may provide considerable guidance with a view to rendering them more legitimate. Furthermore, mediators do not operate in isolation but always interact, in some way or another, with other mediation actors. The direct and indirect sharing of experiences, knowledge and normative beliefs within the epistemic community of peace mediators thus contributes to the development of shared norms and facilitates their promotion.

Shifting our lens to the process and to an aspirational view, and beyond static requirements like 'neutrality' and 'impartiality', may again be helpful. Such requirements should not be considered according to a binary 'either-or' logic but as something that a mediator should, self-reflectively[81] and in interaction with the parties, strive for throughout the process;[82] being satisfied with the fulfilment of pre-established standards is simply

[81] For a discussion of self-awareness and self-reflectivity in mediation, see Hilary Astor, 'Mediator Neutrality: Making Sense of Theory and Practice' (2007) 16:2 *Social and Legal Studies* 221–239, 230.

[82] For this perspective and associated difficulties, see ibid., 227–228.

insufficient. Similarly, party self-determination and their control over the process are relative variables that do not predetermine the process. Because a mediator should generally not impose his or her views against the will of the parties, one of the objectives of a mediator should be the maximisation of party self-determination.[83] Yet a mediator should also make conscious decisions as to his or her intervention that may be required, such as to balance the typically unequal capacities of the negotiating parties in the context of an asymmetrical internal armed conflict.

Especially when emphasising process over outcome, it is apparent that mediators increasingly assume an internalised commitment to play a norm-promotional role, most notably regarding the respect of international human rights and humanitarian law. This shapes the behaviour of the negotiating parties and can have a significant effect on their compliance with the respective norm projected. It also contributes to identifying the contours of a legal framework that can be used as a parameter to assess the conduct of both mediators and the negotiating parties, as well as the legitimacy of peace negotiations more generally, thus increasing their effectiveness.

[83] Ibid., 234–235.

PART II

Experts, Networks and International Environmental Law

5

Multilateral Environmental Agreements and Regional Fisheries Management Organisations

Experts, Networks and Global Administrative Law Principles

JOSEPHINE TOOP

In *A New World Order*, Anne-Marie Slaughter argues that we need to stop imagining the international system as purely one in which states are unitary actors and the main activity is being carried out by heads of state and foreign ministers negotiating formally at diplomatic conferences.[1] Other actors and processes are at work, including networks. Networks may be understood 'as informal institutions linking actors across national boundaries and carrying on various aspects of global governance in new and informal ways'.[2] As networks have grown in size and taken on ever more important tasks, many have become more formal in their structure and operations.[3] Networks can exist both within and alongside formal organisations in a wide variety of modes.[4] Slaughter focuses on exploring networks in their transgovernmental form, by which she means domestic regulatory agencies and departments with expertise in relevant subject matters linking directly with their foreign counterparts, revealing in her view the disaggregated state.[5] She suggests that networks occupy 'a middle place between traditional international organisations and *ad hoc* communication'.[6]

Thanks are due to Karen N. Scott, the editors and the participants at the fifth 'Four Societies' workshop for their feedback and ideas, and to New Zealand's University of Canterbury and the Australian and New Zealand Society of International Law for their funding of my research-related activities.

1 Anne-Marie Slaughter, *A New World Order* (Princeton: Princeton University Press, 2005), especially 5–6, 32.

2 Anne-Marie Slaughter and David Zaring, 'Networking Goes International: An Update' (2006) 2 *Annual Review of Law and Social Science* 211–229, 215.

3 Ibid. 4 Slaughter, *A New World Order*, above note 1, 152. 5 Ibid., 5–6 and 32.

6 Anne-Marie Slaughter and Thomas N. Hale, 'Transgovernmental Networks and Multi-level Governance' in Henrik Enderlein, Sonja Wälti and Michael Zürn, eds., *Handbook on Multi-level Governance* (Cheltenham: Edward Elgar, 2011), 358–369, 358.

Slaughter further notes that since networks have arrived on the scene, 'many have adopted some of the administrative trappings – notice and comment, transparency through the electronic publication of minutes and reports – that are marked traditionally as features of democratically governed domestic systems of administrative law'.[7] Others, in their work on the concept of 'global administrative law', similarly suggest that principles somewhat comparable to those found within domestic administrative law are appearing within global governance mechanisms to varying extents.[8] The potential of global administrative law has not, as yet, attracted the attention of many scholars with respect to multilateral environmental agreements (MEAs) and regional fisheries management organisations (RFMOs). This is a surprising omission given that certain MEA and RFMO regime features, like non-compliance mechanisms (NCMs), seem particularly amenable to the global administrative law concept.[9]

In this chapter, I examine MEA and RFMO regimes in light of the above considerations. MEA and RFMO regimes may be considered networks in and of themselves, since they are neither traditional international organisations nor ad hoc communication, but something in between. They are more informal and more flexible than traditional organisations, but hold a higher degree of structure than intergovernmental negotiating conferences and subsequent review conferences. In addition, networks and sub-networks operate in and around MEA and RFMO regimes.

This chapter is organised in three sections. In Section I, I discuss the evolution, core features and the informal, dynamic and flexible nature of MEA and RFMO regimes. In Section II, I consider various networks and sub-networks, from the informal to the more formal, involving both state and non-state actors, including experts, within the MEA and

[7] Slaughter and Zaring, above note 2, 215, citing David Zaring, 'Informal Procedure, Hard and Soft, in International Administration' (2005) 5:2 *Chicago Journal of International Law* 547–603.

[8] See further Benedict Kingsbury, Nico Krisch and Richard B. Stewart, 'The Emergence of Global Administrative Law' (2004) 68:15 *Law and Contemporary Problems* 15–61.

[9] See Karen N. Scott, 'Non-compliance Procedures and Dispute Resolution Mechanisms under International Environmental Agreements' in Duncan French, Matthew Saul and Nigel D. White, eds., *International Law and Dispute Settlement: New Problems and Techniques* (Oxford: Hart, 2010), 225–270, 230. Taking up this challenge, I am considering the administrative law-style principles of participation, transparency, reason-giving, impartiality and review in a broad selection of MEA and RFMO regimes in a wider research project.

RFMO context. I uncover numerous instances of networking and the use of experts (and indeed, networks of experts) and draw out some trends. I consider, in particular, the conference of the parties and commission meetings as frameworks for annual, biannual or tri-annual networking, and I consider how MEAs and RFMOs tend to institutionalise expertise through subsidiary bodies, including secretariats, scientific bodies, and non-compliance mechanisms. I also explore the synergies between MEAs and RFMOs and how these can operate as wider networks.

In Section III, I argue that networking and drawing on expertise can bring a number of benefits; indeed, networks, sub-networks and experts are integral to the operation of many MEA and RFMO regimes. I suggest that the application of global administrative law principles may help to mitigate some of the potential associated drawbacks to the use of networks and experts. Global administrative law principles may help improve effectiveness and legitimacy. To this end, I investigate the ways in which the principles of participation, transparency, review, reason-giving and impartiality currently operate within MEA and RFMO regimes. Many of these networks have adopted something akin to Slaughter's 'administrative trappings' and I offer some thoughts on employing these principles more extensively. I also suggest that further work needs to be done to ascertain where these principles may be most beneficial and which principles, in what modified forms, are most appropriate for the various MEA and RFMO regimes, and indeed, the various bodies and processes within them, as well as for the networks and sub-networks operating within and around MEAs and RFMOs.

I MEA and RFMO Networks

A Evolution

Early MEAs tended not to establish institutional machinery and then found their effectiveness curtailed since amending agreements through traditional procedures, such as ad hoc diplomatic conferences followed by ratification, takes time. There was no easy way to update obligations in light of changed circumstances, such as adding new species for protection. As a result, MEAs began to create institutional frameworks to provide 'for the adoption of administrative decisions of various kinds for the filling of gaps in the treaty law or for its formal or informal adjustment to changed circumstances'.[10] The 1971 Convention on Wetlands of International Importance Especially as Regards Waterfowl Habitat (Ramsar Convention)[11] was the first to incorporate an embryonic conference of the parties, which evolved over time.[12] MEAs and RFMOs now tend not to be a static set of rules, but rather mark the beginning of a flexible and dynamic norm-creating process. If basic obligations can be agreed initially, more detailed measures can be developed later through collaboration and ongoing dialogue within various regime bodies.

Despite this, a number of regimes still struggle to respond adequately to the problems that necessitated their creation. For example, notwithstanding the long-standing existence of the Convention on International Trade in Endangered Species of Wild Fauna and Flora (CITES),[13] the illegal trade in wildlife has registered as the fourth-largest criminal global trade, behind narcotics, counterfeiting and human trafficking.[14] Improving the effectiveness of environmental regimes is accordingly a very important goal.

B Core Features

Although the specific institutional framework differs among regimes, there are some core features which can be identified.[15] MEA regimes create a conference of the parties (COP), and agreements establishing RFMOs create a commission meeting. COP/Commission meetings are the supreme decision-making fora, and provide the institutional core of each MEA and RFMO network through annual, biannual or tri-annual meetings. Whilst COP/Commission meetings are the governing bodies of each system, they are less formal than the plenary organs of an intergovernmental organisation (IGO). COPs usually depend upon parties offering to host meetings. These meetings are attended by the parties,

[10] Thomas Gehring, 'Treaty-Making and Treaty Evolution' in Daniel Bodansky, Jutta Brunnée and Ellen Hey, eds., *The Oxford Handbook of International Environmental Law* (Oxford: Oxford University Press, 2007), 467–497, 479.

[11] 2 February 1971, 996 UNTS 246, in force 21 December 1975.

[12] Robin Churchill and Geir Ulfstein, 'Autonomous Institutional Arrangements in Multilateral Environmental Agreements: A Little-Noticed Phenomenon in International Law' (2000) 94:4 *American Journal of International Law* 623–659, 629.

[13] 3 March 1973, 993 UNTS 243, in force 1 July 1975.

[14] World Wildlife Fund, *Fighting Illicit Wildlife Trafficking: A Consultation with Governments* (Washington, DC: World Wildlife Fund, 2012), 9.

[15] Churchill and Ulfstein, above note 12, is a leading article on these arrangements.

whether represented by heads of government, foreign and other ministers (especially environmental ministers), their delegates, various domestic agencies or all of the above. A bureau or committee may also be created in MEAs (less common in RFMOs) to plan and organise the meeting agenda and to give guidance between meetings. MEA and RFMO regimes also invariably contain a secretariat, which is a permanent office usually housed within an existing international organisation. MEA and RFMO regimes also contain a number of other subsidiary bodies, which can include scientific, financial, technical and compliance bodies, which work to provide advice and recommendations to the governing body. Subsidiary bodies exhibit a high degree of institutional innovation, differing in composition, form and function depending upon the needs of the regime. Subsidiary bodies may be involved in developing recommendations, providing advice and reviewing compliance and treaty implementation.

Regulatory complexity, scientific detail and other technicalities have stimulated the network of institutions in MEA and RFMO regimes. As has been explained by Benedict Kingsbury:

> the continuous increase in regulatory complexity means that only experts can draft workable technical rules and amend them in response to practical experience and new knowledge. The real work of detailed rule-making must be done administratively (not by national legislatures and not by international treaties).[16]

In the MEA and RFMO context, subsidiary bodies have been created to do the technical work required. Since subsidiary bodies are usually able to consider matters more extensively than the COP/Commission meeting, and can often draw upon special expertise, the advice of subsidiary bodies may amount to a powerful proposal for decision-making at the COP/Commission level.[17]

C *Informal, Dynamic and Flexible*

MEA regimes hold 'a higher degree of organisational structure and differentiation than is the case with intergovernmental negotiating

[16] Benedict Kingsbury, 'Global Environmental Governance as Administration: Implications for International Law' in *Oxford Handbook of International Environmental Law*, above note 10, 63–84, 68.

[17] Volker Röben, 'Institutional Developments under Modern International Environmental Agreements' (2000) 4 *Max Planck Yearbook of United Nations Law* 363–443, 394.

conferences complemented by subsequent review conferences'.[18] They are also not international organisations in the traditional sense since they take 'a distinct and different approach to institutionalised collaboration between states, being both more informal and more flexible, and often innovative in relation to norm creation and compliance'.[19] Typically, RFMOs are also much less formal and bureaucratic than their global counterparts and RFMO organisational structures may share similarities with those of MEA regimes.[20] Given their characteristics, MEA and RFMO institutions can be considered as being somewhat 'freestanding and distinct' from the parties and for this reason they have been dubbed 'autonomous institutional arrangements' by commentators.[21] The word 'autonomous' should not, however, be taken to mean that states do not guide the arrangements. States give general consent because they are themselves the creators of these regimes, and through their continuing participation within these ongoing governance systems, as well as giving more specific consent by opting in to, or having the ability to opt out of, COP/Commission decisions.[22]

In sum, MEA and RFMO institutional arrangements add up to more than diplomatic conferences and ad hoc communication, and yet are more informal and flexible than many IGOs. For this reason, MEA and RFMO regimes may be considered networks in and of themselves. As I discuss below, networks and sub-networks are also operating in and around MEAs and RFMOs.

II Networks and Experts

A COP/Commission Meetings and Intersessional Interaction

The functions of COP/Commission meetings include establishing, guiding and supervising subsidiary bodies and mechanisms. Other functions include adopting rules of procedure and taking decisions on internal matters; progressively implementing the agreement and developing new substantive obligations by amending the treaty or its annexes; developing new protocols; determining consequences of non-compliance; and acting

[18] Ibid., 365. [19] Churchill and Ulfstein, above note 12, 625. [20] Ibid., 631.

[21] Ibid., 623 and 625.

[22] On general consent as a concept distinct from specific consent, see Daniel Bodansky, 'The Legitimacy of International Governance: A Coming Challenge for International Environmental Law?' (1999) 93:3 *American Journal of International Law* 596–627, 604.

externally to make arrangements with organisations, states and other actors.

Majority decision-making often features in these arrangements, usually after efforts to achieve consensus have been exhausted. To amend the agreement, consensus is first attempted and if that fails, voting ensues, with majorities of two-thirds or three-quarters being common. Amendments do not usually enter into force until ratified by a specified number of parties, and are then only in force for those parties that have ratified them ('opting in'). As for annexes and appendices, these usually contain technical measures and lists of protected species, sites, banned chemicals or other substances, and require updating as a result of new information or political agreement on tightening or altering obligations. The amendment of annexes usually follows the same majority decision-making procedure as for amendments to the agreement; however, rather than 'opting in', 'opt out' provisions (with time limits ranging from 3 to 12 months) are used for states that do not wish to be bound.[23] In general, voting makes it easier to develop the regime and may also help promote reason-based decisions, both of which may prove fruitful to the overall aims of the treaty. For instance, within the CITES regime, even powerful states have accepted listing decisions after being outvoted. When listing decisions are based on expert recommendations and good reasons they become persuasive. A desire to preserve reciprocity in future listing interactions may also be a factor.[24]

COP/Commission meetings provide an opportunity for networking among states on an annual, biannual or tri-annual basis. They also provide a forum for NGOs and other actors to network with state actors, and among themselves. Indeed, regimes often encourage NGO networking. The Convention on Access to Information, Public Participation in Decision-Making and Access to Justice in Environmental Matters (Aarhus Convention)[25] and the United Nations Framework Convention on Climate Change (UNFCCC)[26] regimes, for instance, encourage NGOs with common goals and interests to form a single delegation to present

[23] The exception is the Montreal Protocol on Substances that Deplete the Ozone Layer (Montreal Protocol), 16 September 1987, 1522 UNTS 3, in force 1 January 1989, which requires voting on a two-thirds majority basis without an 'opt out' provision. States, however, remain free to withdraw from the Protocol if they wish.

[24] Thomas Gehring and Eva Ruffing, 'When Arguments Prevail over Power: The CITES Procedure for the Listing of Endangered Species' (2008) 8:2 *Global Environmental Politics* 123–148, 138

[25] 25 June 1998, 2161 UNTS 447, in force 30 October 2001.

[26] 9 May 1992, 1771 UNTS 107, in force 21 March 1994.

their views through one representative, in order to facilitate proceedings.[27] This kind of networking allows NGOs to pool expertise, minimise costs of sending multiple NGO delegations, prioritise certain agenda items to push and help with venue capacity issues especially where a large number of NGOs wish to be present. Independent experts usually appear as observers at COP/Commission meetings. However, often, COP/Commission meetings are also attended by state representatives who have some degree of expertise, such as representatives from domestic agencies that are engaged with the subject matter of the treaty, who accompany foreign ministries.

Networking can occur on both a large and small scale, with the potential to establish sub-networks among domestic agencies and their foreign counterparts for future COP/Commission meetings and for intersessional interaction. The same applies to the subsidiary bodies in which the parties meet. These sub-networks tend to be composed of fewer states than the number of states who are party to the wider MEA or RFMO, and these sub-networks can work to progress the regime. For example, Australia and New Zealand worked intersessionally in 2013 to develop conservation and management measures in respect of bottom fishing to replace interim measures in the area governed by the Convention on the Conservation and Management of High Seas Fishery Resources in the South Pacific Ocean.[28]

There are also numerous networks related to various MEA and RFMO subject areas that are more loosely associated with the regime. In the climate area, for instance, the Climate and Clean Air Coalition to Reduce Short Lived Climate Pollutants[29] was formed by the governments of Bangladesh, Canada, Ghana, Mexico, Sweden and the United States, along with the United Nations Environment Programme, to focus on action relating to methane, black carbon and hydrofluorocarbons to

[27] Aarhus Convention, *Decision I/1: Rules of Procedure*, adopted at the first Meeting of the Parties held in Lucca, Italy, on 21–23 October 2002, UN Doc ECE/MP.OO/2/Add.2 (2 April 2004), rule 27(4); UNFCCC, 'Non-governmental Organization Constituencies' (undated), online at: http://unfccc.int/files/parties_and_observers/ngo/application/pdf/constituency_2011_english.pdf.

[28] 14 November 2009, UNTS No. 50553, in force 24 August 2012. On the intersessional work, see the *Report of the First Meeting of the Commission of the South Pacific Regional Fisheries Management Organisation*, held in Auckland, New Zealand, 28 January-1 February 2013, para 20, online at: www.sprfmo.int/assets/Meetings/Meetings-2013-plus/Commission-Meetings/1st-Commission-Meeting-2013-Auckland-New-Zealand/SPRFMO-Commission-FINAL-REPORT.pdf.

[29] See further Climate and Clean Air Coalition (CCAC), online at: www.ccacoalition.org/en.

'complement and supplement' efforts under the UNFCCC. In the fisheries area, the Pacific Maritime Surveillance Partnership network between Australia, France, New Zealand and the United States works to improve cooperation and coordination on aerial and surface maritime surveillance to combat illegal, unreported and unregulated (IUU) fishing, which is complementary to the goals of a number of RFMO regimes.[30] There are also examples of government networks, as envisaged by Slaughter, working to mobilise a wide range of non-governmental actors.[31] For instance, New Zealand and the European Union worked together in 2013 to co-host the 'Pacific Energy Summit' to mobilise public and private investment in renewable energy and energy efficiency in the region.[32]

Countries working together with other countries in sub-networks within MEA or RFMO regimes can also try to influence and shape the wider network. A good example is the relationship between Australia, France, New Zealand, the United States and the European Union within the Commission on the Conservation of Antarctic Marine Living Resources (CCAMLR),[33] which led to the issuance of a joint statement calling for the annual 2013 CCAMLR meeting to establish marine protected areas (MPAs) in the Ross Sea region and in East Antarctica.[34] No MPA has yet been agreed, but this network is continuing to engage with other CCAMLR members to try to secure agreement to the proposal. Another example is the group of countries that chose not to accept new targets under the Kyoto Protocol in the second commitment period. New Zealand was one such country, with its media releases of the time indicating a desire to align its climate change efforts with Brazil, Canada, China, India, Japan, Russia and the United States,[35] the group collectively responsible for 85 per cent of world emissions. New Zealand

[30] Government of New Zealand, Minister of Foreign Affairs, Murray McCully, 'Pacific Maritime Surveillance Partnership Statement', Media Release, 1 September 2012, online at: http://beehive.govt.nz/release/pacific-maritime-surveillance-partnership-statement.

[31] Slaughter, *A New World Order*, above note 1, 32–33.

[32] Government of New Zealand, Minister of Energy and Resources, Simon Bridges, 'Address to the Pacific Energy Summit', Media Release, 26 March 2013, online at: www.beehive.govt.nz/speech/address-pacific-energy-summit.

[33] 20 May 1980, 1329 UNTS 48, in force 7 April 1982.

[34] Government of New Zealand, Minister of Foreign Affairs, Murray McCully, 'Joint Statement on Establishment of Marine Protected Areas in the Southern Ocean, Antarctica', Media Release, 16 October 2013, online at: www.beehive.govt.nz/release/joint-statement-establishment-marine-protected-areas-southern-ocean-antarctica.

[35] Government of New Zealand, Minister for Climate Change Issues, Tim Groser, 'New Zealand Commits to UN Framework Convention', Media Release, 9 November 2012,

subsequently hosted informal dialogues between climate change negotiators,[36] although details of who attended and what was discussed are scarce. This scarcity of information highlights one difficulty with this sort of loosely associated networking; with transparency to be discussed in Section III.

B Secretariats

MEA and RFMO secretariats are given their mandate by states through the agreement text and/or through subsequent COP/Commission decisions. Secretariat roles range from preparing draft decisions and other documentation for COP/Commission meetings and meetings of subsidiary bodies, to coordinating between the parties, conducting research, helping with policy development, receiving and disseminating reports on the implementation of commitments, facilitating data and information collection, cooperating with other relevant MEAs and RFMOs as well as other international bodies, promoting the convention and its objectives, and generally performing all other work that the COP/Commission may require. It has been said that MEA and RFMO secretariats are essentially 'international bureaucracies that are being operated by international civil servants'.[37]

Slaughter does not discuss MEA nor RFMO regimes in depth in *A New World Order*, but she does mention one MEA secretariat in passing. She suggests that the CITES Secretariat (and secretariats in a number of other areas) are best described as 'information agencies' with the principal purpose of making networks run more smoothly and efficiently, and responding to the needs of their members.[38] She notes the lack of independent governing authority and suggests that such agencies 'are not counterparts to national government officials, but rather handmaidens [to national government officials]'.[39] The word 'handmaiden'

online at: www.beehive.govt.nz/release/new-zealand-commits-un-framework-convention.

[36] See, for example, Government of New Zealand, Minister for Climate Change Issues, Tim Groser, 'Minister Welcomes International Climate Change Negotiators', Media Release, 10 September 2013, online at: www.beehive.govt.nz/release/minister-welcomes-international-climate-change-negotiators.

[37] Steffen Bauer, Per-Olof Busch and Bernd Siebenhüner, 'Treaty Secretariats in Global Environmental Governance' in Frank Beirmann, Bernd Siebenhüner and Anna Schreyögg, eds., *International Organizations in Global Environmental Governance* (Abingdon: Routledge, 2009), 174–192, 174.

[38] Slaughter, *A New World Order*, above note 1, 156–157.

[39] Ibid.

implies to 'serve' and 'assist', and certainly has some merit. Secretariats are ultimately constrained by their mandate. The idea of 'information agencies' is also valid since many MEA and RFMO secretariats do perform 'information hub' functions. However, secretariats often do more than just provide information. This description may understate, to some extent, the importance of secretariats to the functioning of MEA and RFMO regimes. Indeed, the parties have given the CITES Secretariat the mandate, inter alia, to work to secure compliance with treaty commitments[40] and make important recommendations to the COP on various appendix listing proposals. In respect of the latter, the secretariat draws upon scientific evidence to assess whether a species is actually endangered or not and makes a recommendation about listing or delisting to the COP, along with its reasons. This work is clearly of great value to the COP. For example, when the outcomes of a recent CITES COP meeting (COP 16 in 2013) and the secretariat's recommendations are compared, there is approximately 70 per cent convergence.[41]

Secretariats are also engaged in a great deal of networking, both vertically and horizontally. They can reach into states vertically to provide technical assistance to relevant government departments to help them with both implementation and compliance, since not all countries possess the requisite level of technical, legal or scientific expertise. The expertise that secretariats can offer is reflected in the fact that they have increasingly divided into sub-units, with branches offering technical support, scientific support, compliance support; or the secretariat has a dedicated compliance officer. Secretariats are also engaged in what might be loosely styled horizontal networking, involving other MEA and RFMO secretariats as well as other institutions.

C Scientific Bodies

MEA and RFMO regimes usually contain one or more scientific bodies with the chief function of providing advice to the COP/Commission

[40] An area in which it has been active. See further Rosalind Reeve, 'The Convention on International Trade in Endangered Species of Wild Flora and Fauna CITES)' in Geir Ulfstein, ed., *Making Treaties Work: Human Rights, Environment and Arms Control* (Cambridge: Cambridge University Press, 2007), 134–160.

[41] Decisions of the CITES COP can be found online at: www.cites.org/eng/dec/index.php. A 'List of Proposals to amend Appendices I and II and CITES Secretariat Recommendations', CoP16/Doc 77/Annex 1 can be found online at: www.cites.org/eng/cop/16/doc/Proposals_with_Secretariat_comments.pdf.

meeting. Reflecting the advisory function, the mode of decision-making in scientific bodies primarily rests on consensus, although some regimes have gone further and incorporated voting provisions for when consensus fails. Where consensus cannot be achieved, a common requirement is that differing views should be set out in the report to the governing body. Often, there is a larger overarching scientific body as well as smaller scientific bodies which meet in respect of specific issues.

The main scientific bodies mostly comprise government representatives competent in the relevant field of expertise, or are composed of scientists nominated by the parties. Many also allow representatives to be accompanied by experts and advisers with suitable scientific, environmental or technical competence. Some primary scientific and technical bodies have a reduced number of representatives and pay attention to geographical representation. Networking and expertise are key, as demonstrated in the Ramsar Convention's Scientific and Technical Review Panel. Candidates must have 'demonstrated capacity for networking with wetland conservation and wise use experts at local, national and international scales, and demonstrated engagement in such expert networks', and, once on the panel, are required to 'leverage their own networks of wetland experts nationally and internationally to contribute to the work of the Panel'.[42]

MEA and RFMO regimes also exhibit a tendency to create a series of smaller, often ad hoc, scientific bodies or working groups to examine particular issues. Here every party is less likely to have a representative, with these more flexible arrangements often making greater use of independent experts. These bodies can get very small indeed, with the Scientific Assessment Panel of the Montreal Protocol[43] being composed of only four individuals from universities or science divisions of domestic administrative agencies, who work in conjunction with lead authors to create scientific assessment of ozone depletion reports every 3 or 4 years. However, they are aided by a large body of researchers worldwide, which shows how science bodies can draw together the members of the body and the wider scientific community.

As observed by Volker Röben, '[t]he structure and mandate of each of these bodies reflects the degree to which parties have decided to allow the discipline of scientific or other expertise to direct political action'.[44]

[42] *The Modus Operandi of the Scientific and Technical Review Panel (STRP) 2013–2015*, paras 5 and 8, online at: www.ramsar.org/sites/default/files/documents/pdf/strp/STRPmod-op-2013–2015.pdf.

[43] Above note 23. [44] Röben, above note 17, 394.

Scientific bodies that do not comprise all parties, or which are made up mostly of independent experts, may make scientific debate easier and enable greater focus on science than politics. After all, the raison d'être for MEA and RFMO scientific bodies is to provide the governing body with progressive and quality scientific advice. This 'focus on the science' idea is supported by the fact that there appears to be an emerging requirement in the rules governing scientific bodies for 'peer review', a fact which would tend to suggest some movement towards 'the scientific' and away from 'the political'.

D Compliance and Non-compliance Mechanisms

In regard to compliance, Slaughter argues that 'government networks can improve compliance with international treaties' through 'technical assistance flowing through horizontal networks [which] can build ... capacity in states where there may be a willingness to enforce international legal obligations but the infrastructure is weak'.[45] This idea is certainly borne out in MEA and RFMO regimes, many of which envisage states cooperating with one another in networks to facilitate technical assistance, information exchange and capacity building in order to implement obligations. However, it may not only be 'government' networks performing these tasks. MEA and RFMO regimes also often envisage a role for other actors, ranging from non-party states and secretariats to international organisations, NGOs, academic institutions, the scientific community, and individuals in the private and public sectors, either on their own or in collaborative networks with others. Wider networks of this kind are perhaps particularly useful in the environmental sphere, given frequent funding and human resource limitations.

MEAs often contain dispute settlement procedures that favour the use of negotiations, and thereafter the use (with consent) of arbitration or the services of the International Court of Justice. These provisions, are, however, used infrequently. Instead, parties increasingly resort to innovative means to facilitate compliance, such as the adoption of NCMs. NCMs differ in several respects from traditional dispute settlement. NCMs are future-oriented and proactive, and they are facilitative and non-confrontational. Usually, the main NCM objective is to identify the causes of the non-compliance, enable dialogue between the relevant

[45] Slaughter, *A New World Order*, above note 1, 24.

parties and offer appropriate solutions. This approach fits with managerial theories which posit that the main reason for non-compliance with commitments is often a lack of capacity rather than bad will.[46] Accordingly, outputs tend to be facilitative or advisory. However, a few NCMs are empowered to take stronger measures, usually after facilitative measures are exhausted, such as recommendations, cautions, statements of concern, declarations of non-compliance and suspending rights and privileges.[47]

NCMs are 'still undergoing an evolutionary phase'.[48] Most MEAs assign a supervisory role for compliance to the COP/Commission meeting, and there is an increasing trend towards the establishment of compliance committees to make recommendations to the COP/Commission meeting on non-compliance issues. Compliance committees tend to have between 8 and 15 members, who are nominated to serve by the parties, with attention given to the geographic and regional distribution of the committee membership. Compliance committees can usually consider both general issues of implementation and compliance with treaty obligations as well as the compliance of an individual state through a specific submissions process.

NCMs are composed of persons with recognised competence in the fields related to the regime, including scientific, technical, socio-economic or legal expertise, or a combination of these qualities. Although some NCMs have a political bent, most require their committee members to serve in their personal, individual or independent capacities, or to serve objectively and in the best interests of the particular regime. This requirement may even go so far as to require an oath to be sworn about performing functions objectively, independently and impartially. A number of regimes also have conflict of interest requirements, requiring members to avoid direct or indirect conflicts of interest.

[46] Abram Chayes and Antonia Handler Chayes, 'On Compliance' (1993) 47:2 *International Organization* 175–205, especially 176 and 188.

[47] The enforcement branch under the Kyoto Protocol, for instance, can make declarations of non-compliance and decide on consequences such as a suspension of eligibilities: *Decision 27/CMP.1: Procedures and mechanisms relating to compliance under the Kyoto Protocol*, UN Doc FCCC/KP/CMP/2005/8/Add.3 (9–10 December 2005), 92–103, Annex, 'XV. Consequences applied by the Enforcement Branch', paras 1(a) and 5(c).

[48] Attila Tanzi and Cesare Pitea, 'Non-compliance Mechanisms: Lessons Learned and the Way Forward' in Tullio Treves, et al., eds., *Non-compliance Procedures and Mechanisms and the Effectiveness of International Environmental Agreements* (Cambridge: Cambridge University Press, 2009), 569–580, 570.

E Synergies: The Wider Network/s

Some authors have suggested that multiple MEAs are collectively engaged in a wider network. This 'interlocking system with a complex network structure' creates an overarching web of MEAs.[49] It is certainly true that MEA and RFMO regimes are engaging in horizontal synergies with other regimes. The idea behind such networking is to maximise efficiency, enhance information exchange, avoid duplication of effort and ensure that the various MEA and RFMO instruments and processes are coherent and mutually supportive.[50] A fairly standard directive is for the secretariat to coordinate its activities with the secretariats of other relevant conventions and international bodies. COP/Commission participant lists reveal that MEA and RFMO secretariat officials sometimes attend the COP/Commission meetings of other MEAs/RFMOs as observers. Relationships for ongoing engagement may also be more formalised, as in, for instance, the Regional Fishery Body Secretariats Network, which brings together a number of fishery bodies, including RFMO secretariats, to facilitate information exchange.[51]

There is an increasing trend towards horizontal networking involving a programme of joint meetings between regimes which have similar subject matter. For instance, there is a formal synergies programme leading to special coordinated COP meetings for the three chemicals conventions.[52] As another example, the Biodiversity Liaison Group provides a coordination mechanism for the executive heads of a number of biodiversity-related regimes.[53] Subsidiary bodies are also interacting

[49] Rakhyun E. Kim, 'The Emergent Network Structure of the Multilateral Environmental Agreement System' (2013) 23:5 *Global Environmental Change* 980–991, 980.

[50] Karen N. Scott, 'International Environmental Governance: Managing Fragmentation through Institutional Connection' (2011) 12 *Melbourne Journal of International Law* 177–216, 181.

[51] See further Food and Agriculture Organization of the United Nations, Fisheries and Aquaculture Department, 'Regional Fishery Body Secretariats Network (RSN)' (undated), online at: www.fao.org/fishery/rsn/en.

[52] Basel Convention on the Control of Transboundary Movements of Hazardous Wastes and their Disposal, 22 March 1989, 1673 UNTS 126, in force 5 May 1992 (Basel Convention); Convention on Prior Informed Consent Procedure for Certain Hazardous Chemicals and Pesticides in International Trade, 10 September 1998, 2244 UNTS 337, in force 24 February 2004 (Rotterdam Convention); Convention on Persistent Organic Pollutants, 23 May 2001, 2256 UNTS 119, in force 17 May 2004 (Stockholm Convention).

[53] Convention on Biological Diversity, 5 June 1992, 1760 UNTS 79, in force 29 December 1993; CITES, above note 13; Convention on the Conservation of Migratory Species of Wild Animals, 23 June 1979, 1651 UNTS 333, in force 1 November 1983; Ramsar

where they have a similar remit. For instance, the Persistent Organic Pollutants Review Committee for the Stockholm Convention regime[54] and the Chemical Review Committee for the Rotterdam Convention regime[55] both review chemicals (sometimes the same chemicals) for listing in annexes and so work together to share information and expertise.[56]

Synergies between NCM procedures can also be found. For instance, the compliance committees of the Aarhus Convention and the Convention on the Protection and Use of Transboundary Watercourses and International Lakes[57] are directed to communicate, as appropriate, with other MEA compliance bodies to enhance synergies.[58] Under the Convention on the Conservation and Management of Highly Migratory Fish Stocks in the Western and Central Pacific Ocean,[59] the compliance committee may, in the exercise of its functions, where appropriate, consult any other fisheries management organisation.[60] On occasion, MEAs have networked in respect of a specific submission of non-compliance, as happened in relation to Ukraine's decision to construct the Danube–Black Sea canal. In that case, a number of closely related obligations were alleged to have been breached, and so the matter was brought to the NCM of five different MEAs, and a joint fact-finding mission was subsequently conducted.[61]

Convention, above note 11; International Treaty on Plant Genetic Resources for Food and Agriculture, 3 November 2001, 2400 UNTS 303, in force 29 June 2004; Convention Concerning Protection of the World Cultural and Natural Heritage, 16 November 1972, 1037 UNTS 15511, in force 17 December 1975 (World Heritage Convention).

54 Above note 52. 55 Ibid.

56 See Secretariat of the Basel, Rotterdam and Stockholm Conventions, 'Synergies among the Basel, Rotterdam and Stockholm Conventions' (undated), online at: http://synergies.pops.int/Decisionmaking/SubsidiaryBodiesCoordination/Overview/tabid/3585/language/en-US/Default.aspx.

57 17 March 1992, 1936 UNTS 269, in force 17 January 2000.

58 See, for example, Aarhus Convention, Report of the First Meeting of the Parties, *Decision I/7: Review of Compliance*, adopted 21–23 October 2002, UN Doc ECE/MP.PP/2/Add.8 (2 April 2004), Annex, 'XIV. Enhancement of Synergies', para 39 and Protocol on Water and Health, Report of the First Meeting of the Parties, *Decision I/2: Review of Compliance*, UN Doc ECE/MP.WH/2/Add.3 and EUR/06/5069385/1/1Add.3 (3 July 2007), para 37.

59 5 September 2000, 2275 UNTS 43, in force 19 June 2004. 60 Ibid., art. 11(5).

61 The MEAs concerned were the Aarhus Convention; the Convention on Environmental Impact Assessment in a Transboundary Context, 25 February 1991, 1989 UNTS 310, in force 10 September 1997; the Ramsar Convention; the Convention on the Conservation of European Wildlife and Natural Habitats, 19 September 1979, 1284 UNTS 209, in force 1 June 1982; and the Convention on the Conservation of Migratory Species of Wild Animals, 23 June 1979, 1651 UNTS 333, in force 1 November 1983. On the Danube-Black Sea canal case, see Karen N. Scott, above note 9, 252–253.

III Global Administrative Law Principles

A Networks and Experts: Importance and Drawbacks

As demonstrated above, there are multiple actors and complex processes at work within MEA and RFMO regimes, which could not function effectively without their subsidiary bodies or without drawing on expertise. As Jessica Lawrence has explained within the context of the World Trade Organization (WTO), 'Experts are not something that can be "added to" or "subtracted from" the WTO . . . their [inputs] are the fabric from which the organisation is cut'.[62] The same point can be made regarding both scientific experts and science bodies, and legal experts and NCMs; experts are part of the very fabric of MEAs and RFMOs.

As noted by Daniel Esty (drawing on the logic of Max Weber's writing on bureaucratic decision-making), expertise and the ability to generate 'right answers' is one established basis for the acceptance of governing authority.[63] Legitimacy may derive from the expertise of the policymaker and the ability to generate right answers and good outcomes or social welfare gains.[64] Weber focused on 'the virtues of bureaucratic governance processes that delegate some policy choices to experts whose knowledge, focus, neutrality, and insulation from politics promise systematically superior decision-making outcomes'.[65] Quality brings legitimacy. Involving experts is often perceived as necessary in technical and scientific areas. Decisions tend to be better accepted if they are considered rational not arbitrary. Esty suggests that 'Weberian legitimacy is especially important in the international realm' where '[a] demonstrated capacity to deliver good outcomes has been the main attraction to nation-states of delegating elements of policymaking to supranational bodies'.[66]

Networks and sub-networks between states, NGOs, experts and subsidiary bodies offer numerous benefits within the MEA and RFMO context. Among other things, networks can be flexible to specific needs, help progress matters between meetings and reach into states to provide technical assistance, information exchange and capacity building to relevant government departments to assist both implementation and

[62] Jessica Lawrence, 'The Structural Logic of Expert Participation in WTO Decision-making Processes' in Monika Ambrus, et al., eds., *The Role of 'Experts' in International and European Decision-Making Processes: Advisors, Decision Makers or Irrelevant Actors?* (Cambridge: Cambridge University Press, 2013), 173–193, 174.

[63] Daniel Esty, 'Good Governance at the Supranational Scale: Globalizing Administrative Law' (2006) 115 *Yale Law Journal* 1490–1562, 1495.

[64] Ibid., 1517. [65] Ibid. [66] Ibid.

compliance. These activities are crucially important to a regime's effectiveness. Experts can provide more objective assessments than might otherwise be the case and increase the acceptance of ideas based upon what is considered to be rational criteria. Networking between NGOs to present ideas collectively can mean pooling expertise and minimising cost, as well as helping with venue capacity. Encouraging synergies between MEAs and RFMOs through information exchange and joint meetings can maximise efficiency, avoid duplication of effort and ensure that MEA and RFMO instruments and processes are mutually supportive.

However, there may also be potential dangers and drawbacks to delegating roles to subsidiary bodies, networks, sub-networks and experts. Not all networking and the use of experts can be assumed to be positive. Fears which stalk domestic administration may also be applicable, such as principal–agent problems, lack of public scrutiny, lack of accountability or manipulation by special interests. Companies might use opaque networks to try to subvert the goals of the regime to their own ends; groups of states might band together in networks to justify and solidify each other's positions and bully others into halting regime progression and the tightening of obligations; and experts might represent just one perspective, but be relied upon nonetheless by virtue of their qualifications. These are certainly dangers to be kept in mind. However, we should also remember the 'softness' of the outputs that subsidiary bodies, networks and experts tend to produce in the MEA and RFMO context. The COP/Commission is the forum in which decisions are made (many of which are formally non-binding), and the input from subsidiary bodies and experts is, for the most part, advisory. The COP/Commission and the states within it largely remain free to draw on subsidiary body and expert recommendations and advice as they see fit. In addition, while it may not provide a complete panacea, I argue that global administrative law principles might work to mitigate some of these dangers and drawbacks.

B The Potential of Global Administrative Law

Global administrative law scholars note that structures beyond the state have arisen to assume a variety of regulatory functions that were traditionally the preserve of state administrations, and thus subject to administrative law procedures at that level. Global regulation is not always so constrained. Yet principles which appear to have some similarities to those of domestic administrative law seem to be emerging in some areas.

Domestically, administrative law principles such as participation, transparency, reason-giving and review aim to make administration more responsive, enhance perceptions of legitimacy and improve the quality of norms developed. Delegation is necessary in modern governance, and so principles have been adopted with both negative power-checking functions (constraining the authority of officials who overreach) and affirmative power-directing functions (improving outcomes). Controls on the exercise of public power focus on citizens' rights, protection of private autonomy, and acting as a brake on state action, including through court-based controls.[67] This has been called the red light theory of administrative law.[68] Administrative law may also function affirmatively to ensure responsiveness. Since the 'public interest is a texture of multiple strands' and 'not a monolith',[69] participation is necessary to ensure that many interests, views and ideas are put forward. Accordingly, green light theories focus on how administrative procedures help public bodies meet certain policy objectives in an efficient manner; indeed, '[i]f properly developed and implemented, administrative procedures [can] promote careful rulemaking, efficient delivery of public goods, and fair treatment'.[70] Participation, for instance, taps into the creativity and knowledge of a broad constituency, and helps bring forward relevant considerations that can improve the quality of information available to decision-makers, which may ultimately result in better decisions. Participation can also help identify potential problems that may have been overlooked. The process of public participation accordingly improves the substantive outcomes of decision-making processes. Most domestic administrative systems reflect aspects of both red and green light theories.

Global administrative law scholars have noted that almost every public institution of global governance faces demands to increase the openness of its decision-making processes. Most of the justifications relate to improving the quality of the law or decision made (through better information, reduced risk of regulatory capture or improving the overall quality and

[67] Carol Harlow and Richard Rawlings, *Law and Administration*, 3rd ed. (Cambridge: Cambridge University Press, 2009), 6 and 31 onwards.

[68] Ibid.

[69] Richard B. Stewart, 'The Reformation of American Administrative Law' (1975) 88:8 *Harvard Law Review* 1667–1813, 1683, citing Justice Frankfurter in dissent in *Federal Power Commission* v. *Hope Natural Gas*, 320 US 591, 627 (1944).

[70] Esty, above note 63, 1496. On green light, see also Harlow and Rawlings, above note 67, 31 onwards.

impact of the laws or decision), or strengthening the legitimacy of the institution and the support for it.[71] While MEA and RFMO regimes have not yet received much attention from this perspective, global administrative law appears to offer some exciting potential in this area.

Delegation to subsidiary bodies within the MEA and RFMO context echoes the domestic tendency to create ever more technical agencies. MEA and RFMO regimes are performing a number of public functions; activity that could be considered administrative in nature. My research reveals that corresponding administrative law-style principles (or what Slaughter called 'administrative trappings') are emerging in this context. Some MEA and RFMO regimes, such as the Aarhus Convention, widely embrace these principles, while others, such as the ASEAN Agreement on Transboundary Haze Pollution,[72] utilise them less often. It is, however, a very diverse picture with regard to where and in what forms they appear. Some of the principles have already been touched upon; the next section offers a few further thoughts.

C *Principles of Global Administrative Law*

1 Transparency

Slaughter suggests that increasing the visibility, accessibility and monitoring of networks may be able to accord a similar degree of accountability as it does for administrative agencies domestically.[73] In the global sphere it is often more difficult to obtain the basic details of policy and decision-making. Indeed, '[u]nlike domestic administrative law, where the responsible agency is generally clearly identifiable, [for] international regulation ... the information about relevant policy and decision making processes is often unknown to all but the cognoscenti, including NGOs and business interests, who closely follow specific global regulatory issues'.[74] This situation may create an even greater need for transparency than domestically.

[71] Benedict Kingsbury, 'The Concept of "Law" in Global Administrative Law' (2009) 20:1 *European Journal of International Law* 23–57, 48.

[72] 10 June 2002, in force 25 November 2003, online at: http://haze.asean.org/?wpfb_dl=32.

[73] Anne-Marie Slaughter, 'Agencies on the Loose? Holding Government Networks Accountable' in George A. Bermann, Matthias Herdegen and Peter L. Lindseth, eds., *Transatlantic Regulatory Co-operation: Legal Problems and Political Prospects* (Oxford: Oxford University Press, 2000), 521–546, 528 and 531.

[74] Eleanor D. Kinney, 'The Emerging Field of International Administrative Law: Its Content and Potential' (2002) 54:1 *Administrative Law Review* 415–433, 429.

Most MEA and RFMO regimes have rules about notifying states, observers and other actors about upcoming meetings, and there is a strong practice of listing upcoming meetings on websites. Many have also adopted default rules requiring governing body meetings (and sometimes subsidiary body meetings) to be held in public unless a decision is taken to the contrary. NCM meetings, however, tend to be more private, although a few NCMs decide about openness on a case-by-case basis. In practice, many NCMs utilise closed meetings.

Secretariats run websites and therefore have a large role in the facilitation of regime transparency. MEA and RFMO websites tend to be good at providing brief explanations of environmental problems and the areas of work of the various bodies. After meetings, reports are commonly produced and made available, particularly on MEA websites (although this is less so for NCM meetings). While many meeting documents are available online, there is often a lack of plain language summaries of what occurred. Newsfeeds containing short summaries of developments are also not always up to date. A few regimes use real-time transparency through live webcasts. In general, most MEAs, although not all, seem to be trending towards greater transparency, but this is not true for NCMs to the same extent. In 2000, Slaughter described the internet as 'the ultimate network'.[75] It does certainly have this potential. Websites are the easiest way of allowing access to documents, with frequent updates, and they can provide a potential avenue for public involvement. However, as billions of people are still without internet access,[76] supplementary activity may also be necessary to truly make MEA and RFMO regimes transparent.

The more informal networks associated with MEA and RFMO regimes tend to have lower visibility. Indeed, there is likely to be networking going on that receives no publicity whatsoever. Even where such a network's existence and outcomes are publicised, this tends to be done in a fragmented way on various government or NGO websites. While opacity may occasionally be appropriate to some degree, if we are not aware of a network's existence then it will be difficult to assess what functions are being performed, how effective it is and whether or not it should be constrained by certain principles. A suggested first step is therefore increased publicity. Where confidentiality is an issue, it might

[75] Slaughter, 'Agencies on the Loose?', above note 73, 529.

[76] 'Billions of people in developing world still without Internet access, new UN report finds', *UN News Centre* (21 September 2015), online at: www.un.org/apps/news/story.asp?NewsID=51924#.Vo96sbH2-Uk.

be possible to produce only a basic description of a network, but even this would help. It is possible actors will choose to publicise those examples of networking which can be given a positive spin as being complementary to MEA and RFMO regimes, and remain quiet on networking that does not. Accordingly, it seems inadequate to leave sole responsibility for publicity to network participants. It appears desirable to have these kinds of networks publicised centrally, perhaps on the MEA or RFMO website where they are sufficiently connected to the regime, or possibly on a separate environmental network database.

2 Participation

Participation in MEA and RFMO networks is variable. Almost all MEAs and RFMOs make provision for observer attendance at regime meetings, and usually some degree of qualification or expertise in the subject matter is required. By far the most common phrase is that any agency or body, whether national or international, governmental or non-governmental, qualified in matters covered by the agreement, or in named specified areas (like hazardous wastes, which is potentially more restrictive), which has informed the secretariat of its wish to attend, may be admitted unless at least one-third of the parties present object. MEAs do not usually require that NGOs be non-profit, or have a democratically adopted constitution delineating an authority to speak for its members. Private organisations are not excluded explicitly by the wording of the observer rules. Indeed sometimes they are explicitly contemplated. For instance, the South Pacific Regional Fisheries Management Organisation and the Western and Central Pacific Fisheries Commission include fishing industry organisations and similar entities with an interest in the work of the respective commissions.[77] The UN Convention to Combat Desertification[78] admits business and industry representatives that have expressed interest in participating, have relevant expertise and participate in the United Nations Global Compact.[79] The UN, non-party states and, to a lesser extent, other IGOs usually have a stronger right to be

[77] SPRFMO Convention, above note 28, art. 18(4); Western and Central Pacific Fisheries Commission, *Rules of Procedure*, 10 December 2004, rule 36, online at: www.wcpfc.int/system/files/Rules_of_Procedure.pdf.

[78] 14 October 1994, 1954 UNTS 3, 26 December 1996.

[79] *Revised Procedures for the Accreditation of Civil Society Organizations and Representatives from the Private Sector to the Conference of the Parties and their Participation in Meetings and Processes of the United Nations Convention to Combat Desertification: Note by the Secretariat*, UN Doc ICCD/COP(11)/4 (3 July 2013).

present than NGOs, with NGOs being more often subject to invitation or objection requirements. Compliance meetings may be open to qualified observers, although less so in regard to specific submissions, but in practice NCM meetings are more likely to be private than COP/ Commission meetings.

Observers typically participate without the right to vote. Often they may speak, submit documents, and sometimes engage in other activities. Many MEAs allow information, analysis and views to be presented, ranging from allowing provision of written statements, particularly opening statements, which can form part of the official documentation, to allowing information documents and reports to be distributed to meeting participants or left on general information tables. Some similarities are evident between these avenues of participation and domestic 'notice and comment' procedures. The level and quality of such participation can differ not just between MEA regimes, but also within them. For instance, observers may be allowed to attend and speak at plenary meetings, but not at other meetings. In practice, some regimes call upon NGOs to speak frequently, while others do not. Participation without the right to vote tends to be conditional upon no party, or not more than one-third of parties, objecting, or upon the discretion or invitation of the chair, especially for NGOs.

Some regimes give greater roles to special status organisations (whether IGOs, NGOs or a hybrid mixture), or other experts, delegating them roles as advisers, or drawing on them in other ways that are helpful to the regime. For example, the Polar Bear Specialist Group of the International Union for the Conservation of Nature (which brings together NGOs, governments and scientists in a worldwide partnership) provides scientific advice within the context of the Agreement on the Conservation of Polar Bears,[80] and the NGO 'TRAFFIC' (a wildlife trade monitoring network) is contracted to monitor wildlife trade and provide data to the CITES Secretariat.

3 Reason-giving, Review and Impartiality

Reason-giving is a key feature of the work of scientific bodies. CCAMLR, for example, has a scientific committee whose 'report shall include and provide the rationale for all findings and recommendations and shall include any minority reports'.[81] Impartiality, as was shown above, is also

[80] 15 November 1973, UNTS No. 50540, (1974) 3 ILM 13, in force 26 May 1976.

[81] Commission for the Conservation of Antarctic Marine Living Resources, *Rules of Procedure of the Scientific Committee* (undated), rule 17, online at: www.ccamlr.org/en/system/files/e-pt4.pdf.

a feature. It can be found in the membership rules for many NCMs. Members of scientific bodies are often asked to serve objectively and impartially. An increasing number of scientific bodies now have conflict of interest rules that make it clear that financial and 'other' usually unspecified conflicts of interest must be declared. Emerging requirements of peer review suggest a move towards the scientific, at least for advisory purposes. Peer review has the advantage of reducing the risk of co-option of scientists by special interests, strengthening information or arguments, or taking issue with them, and producing better-quality advice. However, it would be a mistake to assume that all scientific bodies, especially the larger ones, are free of political influence.[82]

Review does not presently feature in many MEA or RFMO regimes. The Kyoto NCM allows for appeal to the COP, subject to some limitations, 'if that party believes it has been denied due process'.[83] Such review does not extend to the substance of the decision. So far this seems to be the only NCM to have incorporated such a right of review. Another emerging review procedure can be found in the Kyoto clean development mechanism (CDM), where executive body decisions directly impact the property interests and commercial expectations of private legal entities participating in the CDM (and also the wider communities in which projects are situated), but the procedure lacks review mechanisms.[84] The CDM has responded to this criticism, no doubt fearing project participants and investors might cease participating, and is developing appeal rights. The future of the CDM is, however, uncertain with the expected entry into force of the Paris Agreement in 2016.[85]

4 Non-compliance Mechanisms and Administrative Law-style Features

A number of quasi-judicial, administrative law-style features appear to be emerging in NCMs, especially in respect of the specific submissions process, although NCMs are dealing with states rather than individuals

[82] See further, the chapter in this collection by Cameron S.G. Jefferies.

[83] *Decision 27/CMP.1: Procedures and mechanisms relating to compliance under the Kyoto Protocol*, UN Doc FCCC/KP/CMP/2005/8/Add.3 (9–10 December 2005), 92–103, Annex, XI. Appeals, para 1.

[84] Charlotte Streck and Jolene Lin, 'Making Markets Work: A Review of CDM Performance and the Need for Reform' (2008) 19:2 *European Journal of International Law* 409–442, 441. See also Jacob Werksman, 'Defending the "Legitimate Expectations" of Private Investors under the Climate Change Regime: In Search of a Legal Theory for Redress' (2007–2008) 39 *Georgetown Journal of International Law* 679–692, 689.

[85] UN Doc FCCC/CP/2015/L.9/Rev.1 (12 December 2015).

or companies. The process itself is interesting when considered with a view towards domestic analogy (and divergence). For specific submissions, the process begins with an initial phase during which cases may be 'triggered' by states themselves ('self-trigger') or by other parties (termed 'party-to-party trigger'). The extent to which parties must be affected by the non-compliance varies, with some regimes requiring an interest affected, or likely to be affected, by the alleged non-compliance. A number of regimes also allow the secretariat to trigger the NCM. Far less commonly, NGOs are allowed to trigger the specific submission process, or the committee is given the power to initiate a case (i.e. to act *proprio motu*). Once the NCM has been triggered, some regimes screen for admissibility. The allegedly non-complying party (ANCP) is given notice of the NCM being triggered. Following trigger, the next step, or middle phase, is one in which the relevant information is collected and cases are considered, discussed and examined, sometimes across multiple meetings. Some regimes allow the participation of other actors in terms of information provision or observer status, or both. The ANCP has the opportunity to state its case. A few regimes explicitly refer to 'hearings' and use other trial-related terminology. For instance, the Kyoto procedure allows the ANCP to present expert testimony or opinion, and the enforcement branch may put questions to the party[86] and the Barcelona regime makes clear that the compliance committee 'shall be guided by the principle of "due process" in order to ensure fairness and transparency'.[87] One distinction from domestic contexts is that due process rights do not always extend to the other state when the party-to-party trigger has been used. Where NGO or public trigger is permitted, such as in the Aarhus Convention and the Protocol on Water and Health regimes,[88] participation of those actors is envisaged, and indeed, the NGO or public may participate on somewhat equal terms to the ANCP. Finally there is a deliberating phase, usually in closed session. The ANCP is almost always excluded from participating in the elaboration of the recommendations or findings, as would be a party to a domestic proceeding.

Despite these quasi-judicial and administrative law-style features it should be emphasised that NCMs are generally not adversarial, and try to

[86] *Decision 27/CMP.1*, above note 47, 'IX. Procedures for the Enforcement Branch', para 3.

[87] *Procedures and Mechanisms on Compliance under the Barcelona Convention and its Protocols* (Consolidated Text of Decision IG 17/2: modified by Decision IG. 21/1), para 28, online at: www.unepmap.org/index.php?module=content2&catid=001001005.

[88] Above note 58.

be facilitative and advisory. NCMs aim to work towards greater compliance rather than punishment. Nonetheless, due process elements such as notification, fair hearing, the opportunity to be heard and impartiality appear to be emerging. Some NCM rules use terminology familiar from domestic contexts.

The review available under the Kyoto NCM for lack of due process has already been mentioned. In the context of its one and only use by Croatia in 2010, the secretariat produced a technical paper which suggested that even though we are dealing with states, not individuals, there might be a certain core of due process applicable, such as 'a fair hearing by an impartial organ, the right to be heard and the duty to give reasoned decisions' as well as 'consistency in decision-making'.[89] The case was, however, dropped before it could be considered further.

The Aarhus Convention NCM is perhaps the most extreme and refers to 'the right to comment, right to be heard and the right to have comments taken into account by the Committee',[90] extending these rights to both parties concerned, and the participating public. NGOs may propose candidates to the Aarhus Convention NCM, and a public or NGO trigger is also allowed for specific submissions. However, it should be noted that the Aarhus Convention is not generally representative of what happens in other regimes. The very subject matter of that convention – namely access to information, public participation and access to justice in environmental matters – makes it unsurprising that it is particularly strong on these values within its own operation.

5 Concluding Remarks on Global Administrative Law Principles

The principles discussed in this chapter are far from uniformly adopted; indeed, some, like review, appear less frequently than others. Nonetheless, they appear, to some degree, to be trying to achieve

[89] *Procedural Requirements and the Scope and Content of Applicable Law for the Consideration of Appeals under Decision 27/CMP.1 and Other Relevant Decisions of the Conference of the Parties Serving as the Meeting of the Parties to the Kyoto Protocol, as well as the Approach Taken by Other Relevant International Bodies relating to Denial of Due Process*, UN Doc FCCC/TP/2011/6 (15 September 2011), para 52.

[90] United Nations Economic Commission for Europe, *Guidance Document on the Aarhus Convention Compliance Mechanism* (undated), 12–13, online at: www.unece.org/fileadmin/DAM/env/pp/compliance/CC_GuidanceDocument.pdf; Aarhus Convention, Meeting of the Parties, *Report on the First Meeting*, UN Doc MP.PP/C.1/2003/2 (16 June 2003), para 16.

somewhat similar functions to their domestic counterparts. While domestic analogies must be viewed with some caution, the administrative law-style principles (or what Slaughter called 'administrative trappings') in MEA and RFMO regimes appear to be trying to achieve power-checking and power-directing functions. At least in some measure they aim to enhance perceptions of MEA and RFMO regimes and build higher-quality norms.

Article 3.7 of the Aarhus Convention provides that parties shall promote the application of convention principles in international environmental decision-making processes and within the framework of international organisations in matters relating to the environment. The subsequently adopted Almaty Guidelines on Promoting the Application of the Principles of the Aarhus Convention in International Forums of 2005[91] advocate public participation on the basis that it 'generally contributes to the quality of decision-making on environmental matters in international forums by bringing different opinions and expertise to the process and increasing transparency and accountability',[92] and on the basis that access improves the implementation of decisions.[93] This quote shows that effectiveness, quality and thus legitimacy provide rationales for adoption of administrative law-style principles. The Aarhus Convention is important in that 46 states plus the European Union can be seen to have taken a stand on the value of participation and other administrative law-style principles in international environmental matters by becoming Convention parties.[94]

It is not appropriate, however, to advocate wholesale adoption of global administrative law principles without attention to the needs of the various regimes, their disparate bodies and functions, and the specifics of the networks and sub-networks operating within and around them. Further work is necessary here. It is beyond the scope of this chapter to consider in detail whether the principles mentioned should be more widely adopted, although some preliminary thoughts can be offered. Some activities appear to lend themselves more to openness and to the application of other principles, but in some cases, the adoption of principles may have undesirable effects. It may not, for instance, be

[91] The guidelines are found annexed to *Report of the Second Meeting of the Parties: Addendum*, UN Doc ECE/MP.PP/2005/2/Add.5 (20 June 2005).

[92] Ibid., para 28. [93] Ibid., para 12.

[94] Eric Dannenmaier, 'A European Commitment to Environmental Citizenship: Article 3.7 of the Aarhus Convention and Public Participation in International Forums' (2008) 18:1 *Yearbook of International Environmental Law* 32–64, 49.

appropriate to introduce transparency when the NCM committee prepares a decision (in a specific submissions case) since debate as to the appropriate outcome and/or wording may occur more freely in private. However, greater transparency in the lead-up to a compliance decision being made as well as more transparency of NCM outcomes, and the reasoning behind outcomes, may be beneficial, providing this does not get in the way of the facilitative function of the NCM. Complete participation may not be appropriate if the costs of hosting an indefinite number of interested participants would force regime collapse. Participation of private non-state actors may be useful; indeed, there are companies whose interests may be affected, whose ends are served by encouraging the regime towards its goals or who may be able to assist the regime in helpful ways. But the potential for private interests to try to subvert the goals of a regime for their own ends should not be forgotten. Closer attention may need to be paid to the effects of participation by private non-state actors. NGO trigger appears a useful tool for making NCMs more effective. If more widely adopted, it might increase the use of NCMs particularly where states have been reluctant to trigger. NGOs are sometimes in a good position to monitor compliance, mobilise political pressure to address issues or act unencumbered by the diplomatic ramifications that can constrain states.[95] Use of admissibility screening could provide a safeguard to weed out frivolous, vexatious or groundless claims. Opening processes up to further public participation (perhaps by increased use of webcasts) might aid in transparency, and potentially allow other experts outside the process to dispute or feed into facts or arguments, thus improving the eventual advice. Finally, it is somewhat surprising that appeal for denial of due process is only available in the UNFCCC NCM. Wider availability of due process review, for both states and other actors, appears desirable, as it is likely to increase perceptions of fair treatment and consistency, leading to increased confidence in NCMs.

Conclusion

This chapter explored the phenomena of networks and the use of experts within and around MEA and RFMO regimes. I have suggested that both drawing upon expertise and networking can bring a number of benefits, but there may also be potential drawbacks. It is useful to consider

[95] Tanzi and Pitea, above note 48, 577.

whether and to what extent principles akin to those which constrain and inform administrative law at the national level are appearing where the exercise of public functions is occurring beyond the state. Within MEA and RFMO regimes, steps have been taken to secure participation through notice and comment processes, and improve transparency, primarily through holding open meetings and allowing observer participation, and the publication of outcomes and other material on websites. Experts have found roles, and are indeed essential to the operation of some regimes, especially in regard to the provision of technical, scientific or legal advice. A greater reliance on peer review is emerging, along with a practice of providing for reasons, and, to some extent, impartiality in regard to scientific mechanisms, as well as due process considerations within some NCMs.

The principles identified in this chapter are unevenly employed in MEA and RFMO networks. I have offered some preliminary thoughts as to whether these principles should be more widely adopted than is currently the case, finding that the principles do appear to have potential to perform power-checking and power-directing functions, and enhance legitimacy and its effectiveness. However, further research needs to be done to ascertain exactly where these principles may be most beneficially employed, and which principles, in what forms, are most appropriate for the various MEA and RFMO regimes, taking into account the diversity of bodies and processes, as well as the networks and sub-networks operating within and around them.

6

Institutional Expertise

Reconsidering the Role of Scientific Experts in the International Conservation and Management of Cetaceans

CAMERON S.G. JEFFERIES

The scientific order 'cetacea' is comprised of 88 extant whale, dolphin and porpoise species – collectively, the cetaceans.[1] Despite varying in size, feeding habits and distribution, cetaceans are all generally long-living with late onset of sexual maturity and low reproductive rates.[2] These life-history characteristics impact conservation and management decisions because they explain both the rate of population depletion and the extended time period required for replenishment.

International cetacean management is fragmented and hindered by political and ideological disagreement. It is also a highly interdisciplinary field, being both informed and complicated by scientific, anthropological, sociological and philosophical considerations.[3] The management of large whales ranks amongst the most controversial of international environmental issues. The dominant international organisation responsible

Thanks are due to the peer reviewers for their valuable insights. Earlier versions of parts of this chapter appear in Cameron S.G. Jefferies, *Marine Mammal Conservation and the Law of the Sea* (New York: Oxford University Press, 2016).

[1] Society for Marine Mammology, Committee on Taxonomy, List of Marine Mammal Species and Subspecies, online at: www.marinemammalscience.org/species-information /list-of-marine-mammal-species-subspecies/. See also Dale W. Rice, 'Classification (Overall)' in William F. Perrin, Bernd Wursig and J.G.M. Thewissen, eds., *Encyclopedia of Marine Mammals*, 2nd ed. (Burlington: Elsevier, 2009), 234–237.

[2] William Burke, *The New International Law of Fisheries: UNCLOS 1982 and Beyond* (New York: Cambridge University Press, 1994), 257; Ana D. Davidson et al., 'Drivers and Hotspots of Extinction Risk in Marine Mammals' (2012) 109:9 *Proceedings of the National Academy of Sciences* 3395–3400, 3395.

[3] See Cinnamon Pinon Carlarne, 'Saving the Whales in the New Millennium: International Institutions, Recent Development and the Future of International Whaling Policies' (2005–2006) 24:1 *Virginia Environmental Law Journal* 1–48, 2.

for large whales is the International Whaling Commission (IWC), established by the International Convention for the Regulation of Whaling (ICRW).[4] The IWC has arguably become ineffective as its contracting governments fail to compromise on key management issues, including the appropriateness of any regulated commercial whale take. This disagreement has impeded progress in addressing the impacts of modern threats, which include climate change,[5] environmental pollution,[6] habitat destruction,[7] by-catch,[8] ship-strikes,[9] anthropogenic noise[10] and even cetacean-based tourism.[11]

As stated in its preamble, the objective of the ICRW is to 'establish a system of international regulation for the whale fisheries to ensure proper and effective conservation and development of whale stocks'. To that end, the ICRW established the IWC, but the IWC's functionality has morphed significantly since its inception, transitioning from a 'whalers' club' into a preservationist organisation.[12] Science, and scientific uncertainty, have featured predominately in these developments and have been used to justify both over-exploitation and preservation.[13] In 2014, the International Court of Justice (ICJ) released its judgment concerning Australia's application instituting proceedings against Japan, with New Zealand intervening, alleging that Japan was in

[4] 2 December 1946, 161 UNTS 74, in force 10 November 1948.

[5] William C.G. Burns, 'From the Harpoon to the Heat: Climate Change and the International Whaling Commission in the 21st Century' (2001) 13:2 *Georgetown International Environmental Review* 335–359.

[6] Davidson et al., above note 2, 3395.

[7] John Harwood, 'Marine Mammals and their Environment in the Twenty-First Century' (2001) 82:3 *Journal of Mammalogy* 630–640.

[8] Andrew Read, Phebe Drinker and Simon Northridge, 'Bycatch of Marine Mammals in the U.S. and Global Fisheries' (2006) 20:1 *Conservation Biology* 163–169, 164; Randall Reeves, Kate McClellan and Timothy Werner, 'Marine Mammal Bycatch in Gillnet and Other Entangling Net Fisheries, 1990–2011' (2013) 20 *Endangered Species Research* 71–97.

[9] Angelia S.M. Vanderlaan et al., 'Probability and Mitigation of Vessel Encounters with North Atlantic Right Whales' (2009) 6 *Endangered Species Research* 273–285, 274.

[10] Karen N. Scott, 'International Regulation of Undersea Noise' (2004) 53:2 *International and Comparative Law Quarterly* 287–323; Karen N. Scott, 'Sound and Cetaceans: A Regional Response to Regulating Acoustic Marine Pollution' (2007) 10:2 *Journal of International Wildlife Law and Policy* 175–199.

[11] Erich Hoyt, 'Whale Watching' in *Encyclopedia of Marine Mammals*, above note 1, 1226.

[12] Gerry Nagtzaam, *The Making of International Environmental Treaties: Neoliberal and Constructivist Analyses of Normative Evolution* (Northampton: Edward Elgar, 2009), 172.

[13] William Aron, 'Science and the IWC' in Robert L. Friedheim, ed., *Toward a Sustainable Whaling Regime* (Seattle: University of Washington Press, 2001), 105–122, 118.

breach of its obligations under the ICRW.[14] The judgment addressed Australia's assertion that the program of whaling carried out under the second iteration of the Japanese Whale Research Program under special permit in the Antarctic (known as JARPA II) was inconsistent with the provisions on special permit whaling provided for by the ICRW. It also cast a spotlight on the validity of lethal scientific research.

As Sheila Jasanoff has written, 'it is well to remember that the institutions we have built are meant to serve us, and not forget that neither scientific nor legal expertise sits beyond questioning or beyond reform'.[15] In my view the international community should continually strive to promote law reform and the rule of law in the oceans, and to achieve long-term conservation, sustainability and ecosystem-based management, the latter referring to holistic, integrated management that recognises the uncertainty and natural variability of ecosystems and seeks to maintain ecosystem structure and function.[16] In light of these goals, this chapter considers the role of scientific experts and scientific expertise within the ICRW legal regime, and questions the sufficiency of the status quo. Effectively empowering experts may increase the possibility of reconciling competing perspectives; moreover, the efficacy of the international conservation and management of whales, and perhaps all cetaceans, could be further bolstered by reconsidering how the contributions of scientific experts are presently institutionalised. This may be achieved within an amended ICRW/IWC regime or, more suitably, through a successor treaty regime that advances a new mandate, reframes the role of experts and seeks to limit the shortcomings of regulatory science. This ICRW/IWC case study also stresses the importance of regional cooperation and implementation of conservation measures and the possibility of establishing a global network of scientific experts.

The chapter is organised in three sections. In Section I, I discuss the role of scientific expertise in international decision-making. In Section II, the current international cetacean governance framework is surveyed and the role of scientific experts and scientific evidence within the

[14] *Whaling in the Antarctic (Australia* v. *Japan: New Zealand Intervening)*, Judgment, [2014] ICJ Rep 226.

[15] Sheila Jasanoff, 'A World of Experts: Science and Global Environmental Constitutionalism' (2013) 40:2 *Boston College Environmental Affairs Law Review* 439–452, 452.

[16] See further, Duncan Currie, *Ecosystem-Based Management in Multilateral Environmental Agreements: Progress towards Adopting the Ecosystem Approach in the International Management of Living Marine Resources* (Rome: WWF-International, 2007), 1–4, online at: assets.panda.org/downloads/wwf_ecosystem_paper_final_wlogo.pdf.

ICRW/IWC is considered. Then, in Section III, I offer a principled justification for altering the manner in which scientific experts are currently institutionalised within the regime, and introduce the key aspects of the role that scientific experts could play. I conclude that scientific experts, and scientific expertise, remain crucial elements for any future governance regime for cetacean conservation and management.

I The Role of Scientific Expertise and Evidence in International Decision-Making

A Why Science?

Scientific experts offer knowledge that is widely employed in different legal systems. As noted by Jasanoff, the legal community has come to increasingly believe that scientific evidence is one of the more reliable forms of evidence, that scientific experts provide important insights into legal matters and that science assists in the pursuit of truth.[17] Science is attractive as an alternative to value-based regulation[18] because it is, at least in theory, objective, neutral, rational and forward-looking. Through the application of the scientific method,[19] it is said that 'Science seeks truth and approaches it through a long process of experimentation; it is often most comfortable giving answers as ranges of probability rather than bottom line, linear causal relationships'.[20] Society has its own interpretation of science, expecting that 'modern science support[s] the search for *an* exclusive truth'.[21]

Science and scientific experts serve many functions within international environmental law. Fundamentally, the product of scientific endeavour is capable of demonstrating the extent and potential consequences of environmental problems and is also a source of potential solutions.[22] Problems

[17] Sheila Jasanoff, 'Just Evidence: The Limits of Science in the Legal Process' (2006) 34:2 *Journal of Law, Medicine and Ethics* 328–341, 330.

[18] See generally A. Dan Tarlock, 'Environmental Law: Ethics or Science?' (1996) 7:1 *Duke Environmental Law and Policy Forum* 193–224 [Tarlock, 'Environmental Law'].

[19] See further, Kristin Carden, 'Bridging the Divide: The Role of Science in Species Conservation Law' (2006) 30:1 *Harvard Environmental Law Review* 165–259, 170–172.

[20] A. Dan Tarlock, 'Who Owns Science?' (2001–2002) 10:2 *Penn State Environmental Law Review* 135–154, 139 [Tarlock, 'Who Owns Science?'].

[21] Ibid., 136 [emphasis in original].

[22] Steiner Andresen, 'The Role of Scientific Expertise in Multilateral Environmental Agreements: Influence and Effectiveness' in Monika Ambrus, Karin Arts, Ellen Hey and Helena Raulus, eds., *The Role of 'Experts' in International and European Decision-Making Processes* (Cambridge: Cambridge University Press, 2014), 105–125, 106.

such as ozone depletion, climate change and biodiversity loss are all contextualised by our ability to understand the consequences of human activity and our capability to craft a meaningful response – tasks that rely heavily on scientific knowledge. Additionally, science-based decision-making remains the most appropriate paradigm for wildlife management[23] because without the application of science, regulatory decision-making is too speculative.[24] Achieving science-based decision-making necessitates recourse to scientific experts.

With respect to cetaceans, scientific understanding continues to improve. Scientific investigation has progressed to include surveys of global distribution, identification of habitats in need of protection, estimates of the impact of other threats to cetacean populations, such as fisheries by-catch, and even assessment of cetacean intelligence and culture.[25] Marine mammal scientists constitute a robust epistemic community of 'knowledge producers'[26] that must continue to focus its work on addressing areas of uncertainty.[27] One may ask, however, whether the mere existence of this epistemic community satisfies the need to incorporate scientific expertise into international decision-making concerning cetacean conservation and management, with the answer requiring consideration of the limits of science as well as the ways for expert knowledge to have influence.

B *The Limits of Regulatory Science*

Even if science is accepted as the appropriate basis for international cetacean management and conservation, it must be conceded that

[23] Carden, above note 19, 125. [24] Andresen, above note 22, 112.

[25] See, for example, Sandra Pompa, Paul R. Ehrlich and Gerardo Ceballos, 'Global Distribution and Conservation of Marine Mammals' (2011) 108 *Proceedings of the National Academy of Sciences* 13600–13605, 13602 (wherein 'global [marine mammal] species richness, irreplaceable sites, endemism, and threatened species' is investigated and 20 key conservation sites are identified. The impact of climate change, pollution, shipping, fisheries and by-catch is assessed for each site). See also Davidson et al., above note 2, 3397–3398 (identifying marine mammal extinction hotspots and contributing factors, and critically observing that 'hotspots of risk overlap little with current Marine Protected Areas'). See also Peter T. Fretwell, Iain J. Staniland and Jaume Forcada, 'Whales from Space: Counting Southern Right Whales by Satellite' (2014) 9:2 *PLOS ONE* e88655 (demonstrating a new technique in determining whale population size – a problem that has historically been quite difficult). Cetacean intelligence is also debated. For an introduction, see Lori Marino et al., 'Cetaceans Have Complex Brains for Complex Cognition' (2007) 5:5 *PLOS Biology* e139.

[26] Andresen, above note 22, 107.

[27] Pompa, Ehrlich and Ceballos, above note 25, 13604. See further, Cameron S.G. Jefferies, *Marine Mammal Conservation and the Law of the Sea* (New York: Oxford University Press, 2016), ch. 6.

recourse to scientific experts and the use of science has limits as a regulatory tool.[28] For example, while it seems reasonable to 'demand that regulators should use "good science" as a basis for their standardizing decisions ... what counts as science (let alone good science) for policy purposes is frequently contested'.[29] It is common for international instruments to refer to the application of the 'best scientific evidence available', but this phrase does not sufficiently guide inclusion and exclusion. For example, articles 61 and 119 of the United Nations Convention on the Law of the Sea (UNCLOS)[30] on the conservation of living resources in the exclusive economic zone (EEZ) and the high seas, respectively, stipulate that catch measures will take into account (article 61) or be designed using (article 119) the 'best scientific evidence available'. Unfortunately, UNCLOS does not offer guidance on what constitutes best scientific evidence. The commentaries tracking the negotiating history of these articles demonstrate the intention that utilising scientific evidence is mandatory, but do not detail what evidence qualifies. It is also clear that scientific evidence is not the only factor to be considered.[31]

It is also not clear to what extent experts should participate in the regulatory decision-making process and which experts should participate. Regulatory science is also limited when the scientific basis conflicts with other regulatory justifications, including ethical or political preferences.[32] Reconciling such conflicts is a daunting task.[33] Indeed, 'the use of science as the basis for policy making ... is by no means a simple or straightforward means of establishing a consensus-based and, therefore, workable environmental management regime'.[34] Even if scientists control the production of science, its application as a regulatory tool raises 'ownership

[28] See further, Jefferies, above note 27, 221–223.

[29] Shelia Jasanoff, 'Science and Judgment in Environmental Standard Setting' (1998) 11:1 *Applied Measurement in Education* 107–120, 112.

[30] 10 December 1982, 1833 UNTS 3, in force 16 November 1994.

[31] See Myron H. Nordquist, Satya Nandan and Shabtai Rosenne, eds., *United Nations Convention on the Law of the Sea 1982: A Commentary* (Norwell, MA: Kluwer, 1985), vol. II, 594–611; Myron H. Nordquist et al., eds., *United Nations Convention on the Law of the Sea 1982: A Commentary* (Norwell, MA: Kluwer, 1995), vol. III, 304–313.

[32] See further, Jefferies, above note 27, 221–223.

[33] For a discussion of the competing justifications for environmental regulation, see Tarlock, 'Environmental Law', above note 18.

[34] Michael Heazle, 'Scientific Uncertainty and the International Whaling Commission: An Alternative Perspective on the Use of Science in Policy Making' (2004) 28 *Marine Policy* 361–374, 367.

issues'[35] because its use may be influenced, or even co-opted, by lobby groups, political actors, and by the reality that ultimate discretion remains with the states that are represented within a particular regime's law-making body.[36]

The final limitation introduced here is scientific uncertainty. Scientific experts are rarely able to conclusively answer the 'bottom line' questions that society poses[37] or to deliver clear solutions – a product of the fact that science develops incrementally. Uncertainty in the context of renewable marine resource management is attributable to error associated with 'sampling and monitoring resources', 'lack of knowledge of population dynamics', 'seemingly unpredictable natural variability in population parameters' and 'problems in [the] enforcement of measures taken' to conserve the resource.[38] The international community has responded to uncertainty through the development of the precautionary principle, which requires that 'Where there are threats of serious or irreversible damage, lack of full scientific certainty shall not be used as a reason for postponing cost-effective measures to prevent environmental degradation'.[39] The precautionary principle has gained operational strength in international environmental law, but Viñuales has succinctly identified the challenges in its effective implementation. He writes:

[35] See Tarlock, 'Who Owns Science?', above note 20, 142 (considering the ownership of science within domestic American environmental law).

[36] A leading example of politics trumping science is the work of the International Commission for the Conservation of Atlantic Tuna (ICCAT). Established pursuant to the International Convention for the Conservation of Atlantic Tuna, 14 May 1966, 673 UNTS 63, in force 21 March 1969, and tasked with quota setting, the ICCAT is a 'controversial caretaker ... often spectacularly failing to meet its responsibilities': Joseph Paul Heffernan, 'Dealing with Mediterranean Bluefin Tuna: A Study in International Management' (2014) 50 *Marine Policy* 81–88, 82. Bluefin tuna are highly commercially prized and for a number of years the ICCAT set quotas well above the limits recommended by the scientists in its Standing Committee on Research and Statistics (SCRS). The ICCAT has recently reduced quotas in alignment with the SCRS's recommendations, signalling that it might be willing to prioritise sustainability moving forward. See further, John G. Phyne, Michael J.W. Stokesbury, Montana F. McLean and Phillip M. Saunders, 'Sustainability and the Atlantic Bluefin Tuna: Science, Socioeconomic Forces, and Governance' (2013) 16:2–3 *Journal of International Wildlife Law and Policy* 198–226.

[37] Tarlock, 'Who Owns Science?', above note 20, 139.

[38] Andre E. Punt and Greg P. Donovan, 'Developing Management Procedures that are Robust to Uncertainty: Lessons from the International Whaling Commission' (2007) 64:4 *ICES Journal of Marine Science* 603–612, 603.

[39] Rio Declaration on Environment and Development, UN Doc A/CONF.151/5/Rev.1 (14 June 1992), Principle 15.

> precaution is a multi-layered concept involving both a broad consensual meaning and more specific controversial ones. It is hard to disagree with the adage that it is better to prevent the occurrence of disaster than to deal with it once it has occurred. But when one tries to move beyond this broad meaning to more operational characterisations of precaution, controversy becomes the rule.[40]

In addition to precautionary reasoning, Viñuales reminds us that law can respond to uncertainty in various ways, including the use of a framework-then-protocol approach to treaty making, the use of advisory scientific bodies by treaty bodies and the use of specialised evidence during dispute resolution.[41]

C Where Science?

The identification of effective methods for bringing scientific expertise to bear on international environmental problems is a topic debated within international relations, among other fields. Some stress the importance of seeking consensual knowledge,[42] premised on the idea that '[c]onsensual knowledge has the power to mould the interests of the [regime's] actors'.[43] Accordingly, experts inside or outside of the regime can influence decision-making by helping develop consensus and by moving decision-makers towards 'successful environmental cooperation'.[44] Conversely, 'institutionalists'[45] focus on the contributions of states as 'rational actors ... trying to satisfy their own interests' and the role that experts play in informing state positions.[46] This debate is contextualised further by the status of any given regime. Here, experts act as an 'input to the process of bargaining with limited opportunity to modify

[40] Jorge Viñuales, 'Legal Techniques for Dealing with Scientific Uncertainty in Environmental Law' (2010) 43:2 *Vanderbilt Journal of Transnational Law* 437–503, 448–449.

[41] Ibid., 446–448.

[42] See Peter M. Hass, 'Do Regimes Matter? Epistemic Communities and Mediterranean Pollution Control' (1989) 43:3 *International Organization* 337–403; Peter M. Hass, 'Introduction: Epistemic Communities and International Policy Coordination' (1992) 46:1 *International Organization* 1–35.

[43] See Rolf Lidskog and Göran Sundquist, 'The Role of Science in Environmental Regimes: The Case of LRTAP' (2002) 8:1 *European Journal of International Relations* 77–101, 81.

[44] Ibid.

[45] For example, Oran R. Young et al., 'Subsistence, Sustainability, and Sea Mammals: Reconstructing the International Whaling Regime' (1994) 23:1 *Ocean and Coastal Management* 117–127.

[46] Lidskog and Sundquist, above note 43, 81.

the usually stable interests of the actors'.[47] The applicability of each theory will vary based on whether it is a 'regime formation' situation, where a new regime is being negotiated and constructed, or a 'regime transformation' situation, where an existing regime struggles to avoid scientific obsolescence.[48]

From a positivist international law perspective, and recognising the importance of both consensual knowledge and informed state positions, it falls to international governance structures established through negotiation to institutionalise and thereby embed scientific expertise within their decision-making processes. The goal, then, is to afford specialised knowledge sufficient weight without usurping the decision-making authority of the regime's law-making body. This aim is particularly important in the field of cetacean conservation and management where political pressure and competing interpretations of scientific evidence have been used by states and by non-governmental organisations to advance particular agendas.[49]

II The Prevailing International Regulatory Framework for Cetaceans

Currently, there is no single international agreement that comprehensively governs human interaction with all cetaceans, and regulation is fragmented by issue or by species, or both. The international trade in species is addressed by the Convention on International Trade in Endangered Species of Wild Fauna and Flora (CITES),[50] while certain migratory cetacean species are protected by the Convention on the Conservation of Migratory Species of Wild Animals,[51] and its two

[47] Ibid. [48] See Viñuales, above note 40, 445.

[49] See generally Gerry Nagtzaam, 'The International Whaling Commission and the Elusive White Whale of Preservationism' (2009) 33:2 *William and Mary Environmental Law and Policy Review* 375–447. See also Stefan Ásmudsson, 'Whaling' in Myron H. Nordquist, Ronán Long, Tomas H. Heidar and John Norton Moore, eds., *Law, Science and Ocean Management* (Leiden: Martinus Nijhoff, 2007) 459–468, 463 asserting that:

> One could say that throughout its history the IWC generally has had a bad track record of fulfilling its role of ensuring sustainable whaling on a scientific basis. For the first few decades of its existence, this was because of its failure to stop over-harvesting and since then because of its blatant disregard for science by refusing to accept anything but a zero-quota for whale stocks that everyone agrees have been demonstrated as being abundant.

[50] 3 March 1973, 993 UNTS 243, in force 1 July 1975.

[51] 23 June 1979, 1651 UNTS 333, in force 1 November 1983.

affiliated sub-agreements, the Agreement on the Conservation of Small Cetaceans of the Baltic and North Seas (ASCOBANS)[52] and the Agreement on the Conservation of Cetaceans of the Black Sea, Mediterranean Sea and Contiguous Atlantic Area (ACCOBAMS).[53] The Agreement on Cooperation in Research, Conservation and Management of Marine Mammals in the North Atlantic (NAMMCO Agreement)[54] establishes a forum for dialogue and cooperation in pursuit of rational conservation and management within the region,[55] while certain regional fisheries management organisations (RFMOs) regulate by-catch.[56] But notwithstanding these arrangements, UNCLOS and the ICRW remain the two key global regimes worthy of further discussion in this context.[57]

A UNCLOS

As the primary convention on the law of the sea, UNCLOS famously represents a 'constitution for the oceans' that was designed to 'stand the test of time'.[58] The two articles addressing marine mammals in UNCLOS

52 17 March 1992, 1772 UNTS 217, in force 29 March 1994.

53 24 November 1996, 2183 UNTS 303, in force 1 June 2001.

54 9 April 1992, in force 8 July 1992, online at: www.nammco.no/webcronize/images/Nammco/659.pdf.

55 Ibid., preamble. See also Brettny Hardy, 'A Regional Approach to Whaling: How the North Atlantic Marine Mammal Commission Is Shifting the Tides for Whale Management' (2006) 17:1 *Duke Journal of Comparative and International Law* 169–198, 180.

56 See, for example, the Costa Rica-United States Convention for the Establishment of an Inter-American Tropical Tuna Commission, 31 May 1949, 80 UNTS 3, in force 3 March 1950, as amended by the Antigua Convention, 27 June 2003, in force 27 August 2010, online at: www.iattc.org/PDFFiles2/Antigua_Convention_Jun_2003.pdf.

57 The decision to focus on UNCLOS and the ICRW is based on my opinion that the goal ought to remain a functional unitary international organisation, and that these two regimes present the most suitable mechanism to pursue this outcome. I am not suggesting that important regional arrangements have not helped advance the global cetacean management agenda since the opposite is true, especially in the case of small cetacean habitat protection and management under ASCOBANS and ACCOBAMS. See, for example, Scott, 'Sound and Cetaceans', above note 10, 199, making the point that in the absence of an effective global treaty to address a novel problem such as marine noise pollution, 'regulatory action at the regional level can, in the short term, go some way towards addressing this lacuna. Moreover, rules, guidelines, procedures and strategies adopted regionally can in order to address acoustic marine pollution will serve to inform, advance and evolve the global agenda.'

58 'Statement of Ambassador Tommy T.B. Koh, President of the Conference, at its final session in Montego Bay, Jamaica, 10 December 1982' reprinted in *The Law of the Sea: Official Text of the United Nations Convention on the Law of the Sea* (New York: United Nations, 2003), xxxiii–xviii.

are framework provisions.[59] Article 65 engages marine mammal conservation and management within the 200 nautical mile EEZ where coastal states have 'sovereign rights' over natural resources.[60] Operatively, it exempts marine mammals from the 'optimum utilisation' management regime that generally prevails in the EEZ,[61] recognises the potential for an international organisation to exert prescriptive jurisdiction over marine mammals 'as appropriate' and requires cooperation with respect to marine mammal conservation – with a heightened obligation to 'work through the appropriate international organisations for their conservation, management and study' for cetaceans. Article 120 extends the operation of article 65 to the high seas.[62]

Together, articles 65 and 120 embody an ambiguous compromise capable of varied interpretation.[63] How does an international organisation gain competence to regulate marine mammals within EEZs? What is the content of the duty to 'cooperate' with respect to marine mammal conservation generally or to 'work through the appropriate international organisations' regarding cetaceans? What makes an international organisation 'appropriate' for this purpose and what is the significance of the plurality of 'organisations'?[64] These questions have been discussed within the literature, but UNCLOS has not contributed significantly to international marine mammal conservation and management. The possibility of enhancing its contribution is considered later in this chapter in connection with a proposal to negotiate a new implementing agreement that would give a more certain meaning to these provisions.[65]

[59] Kimberly S. Davis, 'International Management of Cetaceans under the New Law of the Sea Convention' (1985) 3:2 *Boston University International Law Journal* 477–518, 508–509.

[60] UNCLOS, above note 30, art. 56(1)(a). [61] Ibid., art. 61(3).

[62] See further, Jefferies, above note 27, 38 and 176–199.

[63] Johanna Matanich, 'A Treaty Comes of Age for the Ancient Ones: Implications of the Law of the Sea for the Regulation of Whaling' (1996) 8:1 *International Legal Perspectives* 37–72, 71 (noting that UNCLOS provides a 'measure of hope that whalers and protectionist states will find a way to compromise').

[64] For example, the United States took the position during the negotiation of articles 65 and 120 that the plurality of 'organisations' was meant to capture the IWC (or its potential successor) and those regional organisations that helped regulate by-catch concerns. See Letter from John Norton Moore, Walter L. Brown Professor of Law and Director of the Center for Oceans Law and Policy, University of Virginia, to the Honorable Elliot L. Richardson, 15 August 1979, cited in Patricia Forkan, Executive Vice President, Humane Society of the United States, 'The Legislative History and Interpretation of Article 65 of the Law of the Sea Convention', testimony submitted 14 October 2003, online at: www.hsi.org/assets/pdfs/HSUS_testimony_LOS.pdf.

[65] Ted L. McDorman, 'Canada and Whaling: An Analysis of Article 65 of the Law of the Sea Convention' (1998) 29:2 *Ocean Development and International Law* 179–194;

B *The ICRW/IWC Regime*

The ICRW/IWC regime has served as the primary international legal framework for the management of large whales for nearly 70 years. As set out in the preamble, the ICRW seeks to 'establish a system of international regulation for the whale fisheries to ensure proper and effective conservation and development of whale stocks'. To this end, the ICRW includes a schedule as an integral part of the treaty, which enables the treaty regime to evolve through the promulgation of action-oriented regulatory provisions.[66] Article V establishes that the schedule shall house the major regulatory measures, including, inter alia, which species can be taken, when they can be taken, where they can be taken and how they can be taken. Article V(1) makes clear that the IWC is the decision-making body tasked with implementing and revising the schedule, with the latter action requiring a three-quarters majority vote, while article V(2) requires that any amendment to the schedule is to be undertaken so as to 'provide for the conservation, development, and optimum utilisation of the whale resources'. Amendments must also consider the interests of the whaling industry and whale consumers, and shall be based on 'scientific findings'.[67] Contracting governments may also lodge reservations and opt out of any schedule amendment.[68]

The ICRW/IWC regime has undergone significant transformation. From 1946 to 1981, the regime was characterised by a failure to prevent continued over-exploitation[69] and, especially in its earliest years, witnessed the 'depletion of nearly all the world's [whale] populations ... [a]nd the whaling industry ... experienced a disorderly, though long-drawn out, collapse'.[70] Since 1982, its attention has been focused on a moratorium on commercial whaling and use of the special permit

Steven Freeland and Julie Drysdale, 'Co-Operation or Chaos? – Article 65 of United Nations Convention on the Law of the Sea and the Future of the International Whaling Commission' (2005) 2:1 *Macquarie Journal of International and Comparative Environmental Law* 1–36; Patricia Birnie, 'Marine Mammals: Exploiting the Ambiguities of Article 65 of the Convention on the Law of the Sea and Related Provisions: Practice under the International Convention for the Regulation of Whaling' in David Freestone, Richard Barnes and David Ong, eds., *The Law of the Sea: Progress and Prospects* (New York: Oxford University Press, 2006), 261–280, 261.

66 ICRW, above note 4, arts. I and V. 67 Ibid., art. V(2). 68 Ibid., art. V(3).

69 See Adrienne M Ruffle, 'Resurrecting the International Whaling Commission: Suggestions to Strengthen the Conservation Effort' (2001–2002) 27:2 *Brooklyn Journal of International Law* 639–672, 647–649 (proposing this theoretical division for the functioning of the IWC).

70 See Carlarne, above note 3, 4.

exception.[71] A commercial whaling moratorium was first proposed at the United Nations Conference on the Human Environment in 1972 and came in the form of a ten-year ban.[72] The moratorium became a topic of discussion for the IWC throughout the 1970s, which coincided with the emergence of vocal environmental non-governmental organisations, and, by the end of that decade, several contracting governments openly supported a commercial whaling ban.[73] Then, in 1982, the IWC voted in favour of instituting a commercial moratorium,[74] to be implemented in 1986.[75] Despite purporting to be temporary, the moratorium has essentially become permanent.[76] Both Iceland and Norway have utilised the ICRW's opt-out mechanism to continue a commercial take, while Japan has pursued special permit whaling pursuant to article VIII to take whales in the Antarctic and North Atlantic waters.[77]

The ICRW/IWC regime currently features a political and ideological divide between a pro-whaling bloc of nations who oppose the commercial moratorium and an anti-whaling bloc of nations who oppose any future lethal utilisation of whales. The pro-utilisation bloc includes Iceland, Japan and Norway, while the anti-whaling bloc includes Australia and many European Union and South American countries. Analysis from the Pew Charitable Trusts suggests that:

> There is a significant group of countries, currently holding a majority of the votes at the IWC, who supports the continuation of the moratorium on commercial whaling as a necessary and legitimate decision under international law, entirely compatible with the principle of science-based policy and rule-making … Opposed to this view, the group of countries opposing the continuation of the moratorium on commercial whaling (currently in the minority within the IWC) argues that the moratorium by definition was meant to be a temporary measure and

[71] See Ruffle, above note 69, 647.

[72] *Report of the United Nations Conference on the Human Environment*, 5–16 June 1972, UN Doc A/Conf.48/14/Rev.1, 12, Recommendation 33. See also A.W. Harris, 'The Best Scientific Evidence Available: The Whaling Moratorium and Divergent Interpretations of Science' (2004–2005) 29:2 *William and Mary Environmental Law and Policy Review* 375–450, 377.

[73] Harris (ibid.), 377–378. See also Davis, above note 59, 485 (noting that by 1977, less than half of IWC nations commercially whaled).

[74] International Whaling Commission, *Chairman's Report of the Thirty-Fourth Annual Meeting*, Brighton, United Kingdom, 19–24 July 1982, 3.

[75] ICRW, above note 4, schedule, para 10(e).

[76] See Robert L. Friedheim, 'Introduction: The IWC as a Contested Regime' in Friedheim, *Toward a Sustainable Whaling Regime*, above note 13, 3–48, 5.

[77] See further, Jefferies, above note 27, 45.

> that whaling should be allowed to resume because certain whale populations are showing signs of recovery, and others according to them are not endangered.[78]

As a result, the IWC's decision-making process has devolved into value-based conflict.[79] This division has also limited the IWC's effectiveness, evidenced most recently by the failed 'Future of the IWC' process. Conducted by a small working group, working in tandem with a support group of 12 representative states, and officially spanning the period between the 2007 and 2010 annual meetings, the 'Future of the IWC' initiative sought to address the IWC's relevance as the international organisation charged with large whale conservation.[80] Making use of inter-sessional meetings, unofficial conferences[81] and sideline discussions,[82] it was hoped that the process would bridge the divide between pro-whaling and anti-whaling nations. When the process concluded in 2010, the IWC introduced a 'Proposed Consensus Decision to Improve the Conservation of Whales' that emphasised compromise, but the document was not adopted, and the process concluded without making significant headway.[83]

1 The IWC's Scientific Committee

The use of an advisory scientific body is common in international environmental law and in the context of cetacean conservation and management such bodies exist in the regimes established by the Convention on Migratory Species and the ASCOBANS, ACCOBAMS

[78] *Turning the Page: Bringing Whale Conservation into the 21st Century* (Philadelphia: Pew Charitable Trusts, 2009), 4–5.

[79] Andresen, above note 22, 117.

[80] Mike Iliff, 'The Hogarth Initiative on the Future of the International Whaling Commission' (2010) 34:3 *Marine Policy* 360–366, 360 [Iliff, 'The Hogarth Initiative']. See also International Whaling Commission, 'Future of the IWC' (undated), online at: http://iwc.int/future.

[81] Examples include the 'Normalization of the International Whaling Commission' conference held in Tokyo in February 2007, referred to in *Turning the Page*, above note 78, 2, and the 'Pew Commission on Whale Conservation in the 21st Century' conference, held in Lisbon, 9–10 February 2009: International Institute for Sustainable Development, *News: Pew Commission on Whale Conservation Holds Third Meeting*, online at: http://water-l.iisd.org/news/pew-commission-on-whale-conservation-holds-third-meeting/.

[82] The so-called 'Safety Net Initiative', for example, envisioned a new international organisation to manage the use of plentiful species and ensure the recovery of depleted species. See further, Mike Iliff, 'Contemporary Initiatives on the Future of the International Whaling Commission' (2010) 34:3 *Marine Policy* 461–467, 462–463 [Iliff, 'Contemporary Initiatives'].

[83] On previous reform efforts, see Iliff, 'The Hogarth Initiative', above note 80, 360.

and NAMMCO agreements. Article III(4) of the ICRW authorises the IWC to 'set up, from among its own members and experts or advisers, such committees as it considers desirable to perform such functions as it may authorise'. Pursuant to this authority, the IWC has created a number of committees, including its advisory Scientific Committee.

Established in 1950, the Scientific Committee is a long-standing advisory body that is currently comprised of some 200 cetacean experts[84] that meet annually and inter-sessionally, as required. The Scientific Committee has a number of sub-committees (both standing and ad hoc), each reporting back to the Committee. The Scientific Committee itself reports directly to the IWC and has its own Rules of Procedure.[85] The Committee is responsible for both the review and production of various documents, the most important being the annual Scientific Committee Report, which is viewed as 'the public face of the work of the Committee'.[86] As such, the Report 'has to serve a number of functions providing a concise yet comprehensive account of the scientific work undertaken for the benefit of (1) the participants; (2) scientists not attending the meeting; and (3) the Commission'.[87] The Scientific Committee's research is supported by a 'Research Fund', which the IWC approves annually.[88]

The IWC has yet to achieve its objective of 'proper and effective conservation and development of whale stocks'. The earliest years of IWC management failed, in large part, due to the utilisation of the Blue Whale Unit (BWU) – a measurement of a species oil yield compared to the blue whale – to set an overall catch quota that ensured oil production and continued over-exploitation, especially in the Antarctic.[89] During this time, the Scientific Committee was populated by a dozen whale biologists who were 'timid' in offering advice that might limit whaling quotas and impact the whaling industry.[90] The 1960s witnessed

[84] Scientific Committee membership is comprised of 'national delegates, invited participants, [and] representatives of specified intergovernmental organisations'. Other scientists and non-governmental organisation representatives can attend the meetings as observers. See further, International Whaling Commission, *Scientific Committee Handbook* (undated), online at: http://iwc.int/scientific-committee-handbook.

[85] International Whaling Commission, 'Rules of Procedure of the Scientific Committee' in *Rules of Procedure and Financial Regulations: As Amended by the Commission at the 65th Meeting, September 2014* (Cambridge: IWC, 2014), 20.

[86] International Whaling Commission, *Scientific Committee Handbook*, above note 84.

[87] Ibid. [88] Ibid.

[89] Ray Gambell, 'International Management of Whales and Whaling: An Historical Review of the Regulation of Commercial and Aboriginal Subsistence Whaling' (1993) 48(2) *Arctic* 97–107, 99.

[90] Aron, 'Science and the IWC', above note 13, 107.

resurgence in the consideration of scientific evidence, and the Scientific Committee expanded its membership beyond cetacean biologists to include quantitative scientists with expertise in population dynamics.[91] During this time, the IWC coordinated a scientific stock assessment using independent experts and its Scientific Committee, culminating in negotiated catch quota reductions that were phased in from 1965 to 1968.[92] The IWC finally replaced the BWU regulatory mechanism with species-specific catch limits and, in 1974, instituted a 'formal management procedure'.[93] Founded on the fisheries principle of maximum sustainable yield (MSY), which accounts for the biological criteria of each stock to set catch quotas at 'a harvest that can be taken for an indefinite time without further depleting the stock', this approach could 'regulate the catches from each stock on an individual basis'.[94] Finally, the Scientific Committee, now populated by 'field experienced biologists . . . [and] population dynamicists', could provide advice independent of the 'needs of the whaling industry'[95] and worked to categorise each stock based on its relationship to MSY and then recommend catch quotas approaching MSY.[96] While attractive in design, this management procedure became unwieldy in application and led to disagreement and uncertainty, further paving the way for the commercial moratorium.[97]

The moratorium was largely the product of political momentum rather than scientific assessment.[98] Indeed, the moratorium of 1982 was adopted by the IWC 'without advice from the Scientific Committee that such a measure was required for conservation purposes'.[99] Because the wording of the moratorium is such that it does not preclude a return to non-zero catch limits for certain species in the future with 'improved scientific knowledge',[100] the IWC did initially work towards crafting

[91] Ibid. [92] Gambell, above note 89, 99. [93] Ibid., 100. [94] Ibid.

[95] Aron, 'Science and the IWC', above note 13, 115. [96] Gambell, above note 89, 100.

[97] Ibid. [98] Aron, 'Science and the IWC', above note 13, 111.

[99] Joji Morishita and Dan Goodman, 'Role and Problems of the Scientific Committee of the International Whaling Commission in terms of Conservation and Sustainable Utilization of Whale Stocks' (2005) 9:2 *Global Environmental Research* 157–166, 158. Scientific Committee advice has not been followed on a number of occasions since the moratorium's introduction. See Andresen, above note 22, 117 (discussing the IWC's opposition to the Norwegian minke take, noting that: '. . . the Scientific Committee concluded in 1991 that a modest Norwegian catch of North Atlantic minke whales did not represent a threat to this population. This finding was set aside by the IWC and the majority still opposes the Norwegian catch, even though it is endorsed by the Scientific Committee').

[100] See International Whaling Commission, *The Revised Management Procedure* (RMP) (undated), online at: http://iwc.int/rmp.

a 'Revised Management Scheme' (RMS).[101] The Scientific Committee conducted an eight-year stock assessment that resulted in the completion of a Revised Management Procedure (RMP), which would serve as the 'scientific element of an overall [management] plan'.[102] The RMP is 'a scientifically robust method of setting safe catch limits for certain stocks' at 'sustainable removal levels'[103] that utilises a 'catch limit algorithm' that is precautionary in nature and provides a 'method for calculating sustainable removal levels' by accounting for other sources of whale mortality.[104] The IWC adopted the RMP in 1994,[105] but no catches would be permitted until the other details of the broader RMS were in place, including an observer scheme, reporting method and enforcement procedure.[106] Work on the RMS has been ongoing since 1994, with little success;[107] indeed, no progress has been made since 2006.[108]

The Scientific Committee currently reports and advises on various issues that seem to extend beyond the ICRW's original mandate. This expansion, enabled by the Scientific Committee's Rules of Procedure,[109] is clearly demonstrated in its 2014 report.[110] Here, in addition to stock assessments and issues related to future RMP implementation, the report also assesses pressing modern threats to whales, including 'non-deliberate human-induced mortality of large whales' (i.e., entanglement and ship strikes), environmental concerns (i.e., pollution, habitat degradation and anthropogenic noise) and even the impact of whale-watching. It also reports on the status of small cetaceans, which are beyond the IWC's regulatory jurisdiction.

[101] Ibid. See also Gambell, above note 89, 101.
[102] Aron, 'Science and the IWC', above note 13, 117.
[103] RMP, above note 100. See also International Whaling Commission, *The Revised Management Procedure (RMP) for Baleen Whales* (undated), online at: http://iwc.int/rmpbw.
[104] RMP (ibid.). See also *The Revised Management Procedure (RMP) for Baleen Whales* (ibid.), section 3.6, entitled 'Adjusting for other sources of human-caused mortality'.
[105] International Whaling Commission, Resolution 1994–1995, *Resolution on the Revised Management Scheme* (1995) 45th Report, 43–44. Note that the IWC declined to adopt the *Revised Management Procedure* in 1993, prompting the Chairman of the Scientific Committee to resign in protest: Heazle, above note 34, 367.
[106] RMP, above note 100. [107] Ibid. [108] Ibid. See further, Jefferies, above note 27, 46.
[109] Rules of Procedure of the Scientific Committee, above note 85, 20 (setting the terms of reference).
[110] International Whaling Commission, *Report of the Scientific Committee*, Doc IWC/65/Rep01 (2014).

2 The *Whaling in the Antarctic* Judgment

The *Whaling in the Antarctic* judgment engages with Australia's challenge to the legitimacy of the second phase of the Japanese Whale Research Program under special permit in the Antarctic, which began in 2005–2006.[111] JARPA II witnessed the annual national issuance of permits pursuant to article VIII of the ICRW to take, hunt and kill 850 minke whales (plus or minus 10 per cent), 50 fin whales and 50 humpback whales.[112] Australia asserted that JARPA II breached the ICRW schedule's prohibitions on killing whales for commercial purposes, on commercial whaling in the Southern Ocean Sanctuary[113] and on the use of 'factory ships or whale catchers attached to factory ships' for killing or treating whales, excepting out the minke whale.[114]

The ICJ's judgment turned on an interpretation of article VIII of the ICRW as applied to the specifics of Japan's Antarctic research whaling program. In its analysis, the ICJ enunciated the following standard of review:

> the Court will assess, first, whether the programme under which these activities occur involves scientific research. Secondly, the Court will consider if the *killing, taking and treating* of whales is 'for purposes of' scientific research by examining whether, in the use of *lethal methods*, the programme's design and implementation are reasonable in relation to achieving its stated objectives. This standard of review is an objective one.[115]

The ICJ ultimately declared that Japan's special permits issued under JARPA II did not fall within article VIII and accordingly violated the schedule.[116] Owing to the programme's ongoing status, the ICJ ordered that any existing permit be revoked and that no further permits be granted pursuant to JARPA II.[117] While this decision has a number of implications for the future of the IWC, and for international environmental disputes before the ICJ, this analysis focuses on the Court's assessment of Japan's reliance on lethal methods of conducting scientific research.

[111] *Whaling in the Antarctic*, above note 14, para 103.
[112] Ibid., para 123 (note that no humpback whales were taken).
[113] See Application Instituting Proceedings filed 31 May 2010 in *Whaling in the Antarctic (Australia* v. *Japan)*, paras 35–36, online at: www.icj-cij.org/docket/files/148/15951.pdf.
[114] See Memorial of Australia in *Whaling in the Antarctic (Australia* v. *Japan)* filed 9 May 2011, vol. 1, 276, online at: www.icj-cij.org/docket/files/148/17382.pdf.
[115] *Whaling in the Antarctic*, above note 14, para 67 [emphasis added].
[116] Ibid., para 247. [117] Ibid., para 245.

The ICJ was satisfied that JARPA II did involve scientific research, but that its design and implementation were not reasonable in light of its stated objectives.[118] In considering the arguments proffered by Australia and Japan, and the expert scientific evidence they each offered, the Court determined that lethal research was 'not per se unreasonable' owing to the fact that some information (i.e., stomach content and ear plug analysis) cannot be obtained using non-lethal techniques.[119] Nonetheless, the reasonableness of Japan's reliance on lethal methods in JARPA II fell on other grounds. First, the evidence suggested that Japan did not sufficiently consider feasible alternatives to lethal methods,[120] despite evidence of 'significant advances in a wide range of non-lethal research techniques' and IWC 'resolutions and Guidelines' that request states to consider whether research objectives can be achieved through non-lethal means.[121] Second, Japan was unable to justify its rigid annual sample sizes that were not altered despite persistent discrepancy between the target sample size and actual annual takes, lending weight to the argument that the sample size setting was 'driven by strictly scientific considerations'.[122] Third, the Court noted a lack of transparency in the sample size setting process and an apparent lack of evidence used in establishing JARPA II sample sizes.[123]

In her Separate Opinion, Judge *ad hoc* Charlesworth adds a gloss to the continued validity of lethal research. She asserts that the precautionary approach ought to apply to the use of lethal research with the effect that it 'requires that non-lethal methods of research be used wherever possible' and that 'lethal methods must be shown to be indispensable to the purposes of scientific research on whales' to be valid under article VIII.[124]

Even though Japan had signalled its intention to abide by the judgment, controversy persists. In November 2014, Japan released its Proposed Research Plan for New Scientific Whale Research Program in

[118] Ibid., para 127. The ICJ further notes at para 133 that: 'The JARPA II Research Plan identifies four research objectives: (1) Monitoring of the Antarctic ecosystem; (2) Modelling competition among whale species and future management objectives; (3) Elucidation of temporal and spatial changes in stock structure; and (4) Improving the management procedure for Antarctic minke whale stocks'.

[119] Ibid., para 135. [120] Ibid., para 144. [121] Ibid., para 137.

[122] Ibid., para 156. Note that Australia maintained that the minke quota was based on Japan's commercial need and funding goals.

[123] Ibid., paras 195–198.

[124] Separate Opinion of Judge *Ad Hoc* Charlesworth in *Whaling in the Antarctic (Australia* v. *Japan: New Zealand Intervening)*, above note 14, 453, para 10.

the Antarctic Ocean (NEWREP-A).[125] In accordance with paragraph 30 of the ICRW's schedule, this document has been submitted to the Scientific Committee for its review and comment.[126] NEWREP-A contemplates a 12-year program that will take 333 minke whales annually and, after surveying the appropriateness of non-lethal research methods in light of its stated research objectives, concludes that non-lethal methods must be supplemented by lethal sampling that enables ear plug, blubber and stomach content analysis.[127] It has been reported that Japan's chief negotiator, Joji Morishita, hopes NEWREP-A will 'trigger or send some message (to international opponents) because we have accepted the ICJ judgment in our research plan'.[128] While compromise remains a valid objective, it is unlikely that NEWREP-A will satisfy those states that oppose lethal utilisation of whales. Bridging this divide will require something much more significant.

III Re-institutionalising Expertise within Cetacean Conservation and Management

This chapter has explored the institutionalisation of scientific experts within the ICRW/IWC regime and has questioned the efficacy of the status quo. Addressing the shortfalls of the regime requires action that reduces the 'malignancy' of its political, ideological and value-based afflictions, with part of the solution resting on the consideration of 'deliberate institutional design[s]' that may motivate political compromise and enhance the Scientific Committee's effectiveness.[129] There are a variety of options available for restructuring the current regime in a manner that restrains arbitrary use of uncertainty, restores the utility of sound scientific evidence and restructures the 'interface between the political and intellectual (scientific) dimensions . . . [where] the task of transforming knowledge into premises for decision making' resides.[130] The most viable options are either an amendment of the ICRW and/or its

[125] Government of Japan, *Proposed Research Plan for New Scientific Whale Research Program in the Antarctic Ocean* (undated), online at: www.jfa.maff.go.jp/j/whale/pdf/newrep–a.pdf [NEWREP-A].

[126] Note that Scientific Committee approval is not required.

[127] NEWREP-A, above note 125, 27–28.

[128] Harumi Ozawa, 'Japan's new whaling plan will prove hunt is science – negotiator', *Agence France-Presse (AFP)*, 26 November 2014, online at: http://usa.news.net/article/2350519/.

[129] See Andresen, above note 22, 111–112.

[130] Ibid., 112.

schedule,[131] or the negotiation of a new international regime that supersedes and replaces the ICRW/IWC regime.[132] I consider the latter option, in the form of an implementing agreement negotiated pursuant to articles 65 and 120 of UNCLOS.[133]

UNCLOS has remained relevant partly because of its implicit recognition 'that some matters would need future resolution via additional agreements or protocols'.[134] One 'important tool' utilised in 'developing the legal framework for the law of the sea' has been the implementing agreement.[135] The most useful example is the 1995 Agreement for the Implementation of the Provisions of the United Nations Convention on the Law of the Sea of 10 December 1982 Relating to the Conservation and Management of Straddling Fish Stocks and Highly Migratory Fish Stocks (UNFSA).[136] The UNFSA expands upon and implements Articles 63 and

131 This option has been explored by the IWC itself in the self-termed 'Future of the IWC' process. See further Iliff, 'Contemporary Initiatives', above note 82. See also Robert L. Friedheim, 'Fixing the Whaling Regime: A Proposal' in Friedheim, *Toward a Sustainable Whaling Regime*, above note 13, 311–335 [Friedheim, 'Fixing the Whaling Regime']; Michael Bowman, '"Normalizing" the International Convention for the Regulation of Whaling' (2007–2008) 29:3 *Michigan Journal of International Law* 293–499, 294.

132 See William Burke, 'A New Whaling Agreement and International Law' in Friedheim, *Toward a Sustainable Whaling Regime*, above note 13, 51–79, 51; Anastasia Telesetsky, Donald Anton and Timo Koivurova, 'ICJ's Decision in Australia v. Japan: Giving up the Spear or Refining the Scientific Design?' (2014) 45:4 *Ocean Development and International Law* 328–340, 335 (considering pro-preservationist states exiting the ICRW/IWC regime to create a new framework that aligns with their enduring preferences).

133 See further, Jefferies, above note 27, chs. 6 and 7.

134 Donald Rothwell and Tim Stephens, *The International Law of the Sea*, 2nd ed. (Oxford: Hart, 2016), 20.

135 James Harrison, *Making the Law of the Sea: A Study in the Development of International Law* (New York: Cambridge University Press, 2011), 113.

136 4 August 1995, 2167 UNTS 3, in force 11 December 2001. The international community is set to commence negotiations in 2016 for a new implementing agreement to conserve and manage biodiversity in areas beyond national jurisdiction. It is widely believed that this new agreement will focus on crafting the legal framework needed to establish high seas protected areas, environmental impact assessments, and the management of marine genetic resources. See *Letter dated 13 February 2015 from the Co-Chairs of the Ad Hoc Open-ended Informal Working Group to the President of the UN General Assembly*, UN Doc A/69/780 (13 February 2015); Jim Crabtree, 'Governments Will Forge First Treaty Protecting Global Oceans', *Environment News Services*, 28 January 2015, online at: http://ens-newswire.com/2015/01/28/goverments-will-forge-first-treaty-protecting-global-oceans/. See further, Elisabeth Druel and Kristina M. Gjerde, 'Sustaining Marine Life Beyond Boundaries: Option for an Implementing Agreement for Marine Biodiversity Beyond National Jurisdiction under the United Nations Convention on the Law of the Sea' (2014) 49 *Marine Policy* 90–97. This new implementing agreement could help lay the groundwork for the kind of cetacean treaty proposed in this chapter by furthering the availability of effective high seas protections.

64 of UNCLOS to address a specific subset of living marine marines, specifically straddling and migratory fish stocks, and as such, it demonstrates the capability for framework obligations to be significantly developed and bolstered by additional agreements. The appropriateness of UNFSA as an analogue for the future of cetacean management and conservation is bolstered by a number of factors. First, it is innovative in its incorporation and application of ecosystem-based precautionary management. Second, it elucidates the duty to cooperate. Third, it promotes and empowers regional management, and fourth, it contemplates innovative compliance and enforcement mechanism and provides recourse to formalised dispute resolution.

In my view, an agreement negotiated to implement articles 65 and 120 of UNCLOS has the potential to modernise cetacean conservation and management.[137] Articles 65 and 120, reasonably interpreted, despite ambiguities, can support an implementing agreement that establishes a new cetacean management regime with the necessary regulatory authority over all cetacean species to address modern threats like by-catch and habitat degradation.[138] This agreement could adopt and apply modern principles of international environmental law and wildlife management, facilitate the promulgation and implementation of conservation and sustainable management measures, and enable compliance, enforcement and recourse to peaceful dispute resolution. Such an agreement may facilitate the necessary compromise between conservation and utilisation, and perhaps even allow the return of a limited commercial take for those cetacean species that can bear it (such as the minke whale). Initially it may appear illogical to assert that achieving comprehensive conservation and management requires a return to a limited commercial take, but this shift is likely part of the compromise required to secure agreement from pro-utilisation states to promulgate regulatory measures that comprehensively address modern threats to cetaceans.

Securing a new implementing agreement to manage all cetacean species will be a daunting task,[139] since it requires replacing an existing regime with new management structures and is predicated on species and

[137] See further, Jefferies, above note 27, 191–193.

[138] Arguably these articles support the negotiation of a new implementing agreement that covers all marine mammal species but a logical starting point for consideration is its expansion to all cetaceans.

[139] See Friedheim, 'Fixing the Whaling Regime', above note 131, 315 (noting that: 'The IWC needs not be thrown out like the baby with the bathwater, and a new whaling regime or regimes need not be created').

issue expansion. Negotiating such an agreement would be resource-intensive and time-consuming, and would be subject to the same political and ideological divisions that currently fracture the IWC. While the possibility of negotiating such an agreement raises many questions that require future exploration, the remainder of Section III will focus on the prospects for re-institutionalising the role of scientific experts in a successor regime and the potential impact this could have on improving the efficacy of international cetacean conservation and management.

A Redefining the Institutional Mandate for the Scientific Committee

The mandate of the IWC has remained unchanged since 1946 and arguably no longer reflects current requirements for cetacean conservation and management. This outdated mandate compromises the utility of institutionalised scientific expertise because the regime's ultimate effectiveness is predicated upon fidelity to its mandate, to which 'it must either commit itself ... or renegotiate'.[140] The reform contemplated here endorses negotiation of a new mandate – one that commits the successor regime to the long-term conservation and sustainable management of cetaceans in a manner that is ecosystem-based and responds to the many threats facing cetaceans. While long-term conservation and sustainable management is not preclusive of lethal uses, it is clearly not driven solely by utilitarian factors. The current scope of the regulatory objectives found in article V of the ICRW is fairly narrow and insufficient to capture what is required to achieve long-term conservation and management, ecosystem-based management and comprehensive threat response.[141]

An expanded mandate and broadened regulatory purpose requires restructuring of the Scientific Committee's role, helping ground future decision-making in science rather than politics.[142] In considering increased functionality for a Scientific Committee, a first-order concern is to recall that its participation must be limited to functions that design, recommend or propose but never usurp the decision-making organ's regulatory function. This is a necessary limit and one that is required to maintain the regime's legitimacy. Fundamentally, the Scientific Committee should remain responsible for providing stock and population assessments

[140] Aron, 'Science and the IWC', above note 13, 118.

[141] ICRW, above note 4, art. V(2)(b).

[142] See Heazle, above note 34, 367 (observing that 'it is the political implications of the issue at hand rather than the science behind it that often have the most influence on the positions governments take').

and for determining the conservation status of cetacean species[143] as part of a robust research programme, and for providing scientific advice, as requested, by the new treaty's decision-making organ, the Secretariat, or other sub-committees. It should also be responsible for designing and recommending a 'Cetacean Management Plan' that functions like the current RMP, but modified as necessary to account for all cetacean species and the whole host of modern threats.[144] In the event of a return to a limited commercial take, the Scientific Committee should be responsible for proposing total allowable catch limits to the regime's regulatory body and for recommending protected and unprotected species and open and closed seasons and waters.[145]

Moving beyond these fundamental functions, a reformed Scientific Committee ought to be positioned to contribute to the mitigation of modern threats, the promotion of animal welfare and the implementation of ecosystem-based management. With respect to addressing modern threats, a new Scientific Committee could be tasked with recommending best-practice guidelines and standards for activities that threaten or otherwise harm cetaceans, including but not limited to (1) cetacean tourism, (2) by-catch mitigation strategies and (3) anthropogenic noise mitigation strategies.[146] Similarly, animal welfare considerations could be contemplated in best-practice guidelines or standards that recommend (1) humane killing techniques and humane killing technologies, (2) education and training programs for those who take or otherwise use cetaceans[147] and (3) methodologies that account for cetacean culture and intelligence.[148]

[143] Convention on Biological Diversity, 5 June 1992, 1760 UNTS 79, in force 29 December 1993, art. 25(2)(a).

[144] See RMP, above note 100 (indicating the role that the IWC's Scientific Committee had in producing the Revised Management Procedure).

[145] See further, Jefferies, above note 27, 229–230.

[146] The IWC's current approach to the production of whale watching guidelines offers a model: see International Whaling Commission, 'General Principles for Whalewatching', as agreed by the Scientific Committee in 1996, online at: http://iwc.int/wwguidelines#manage.

[147] The North Atlantic Marine Mammal Commission (NAMMCO) has produced a number of best-practice killing technique guidelines for different marine mammal species: *Report of the NAMMCO Expert Group Meeting to Assess Hunting Methods for Small Cetaceans* (Tromsø, Norway: NAMMCO, 2011), online at: www.nammco.no/webcronize/images/Nammco/970.pdf.

[148] See Convention on Migratory Species, 11th Meeting of the Conference of the Parties, *Conservation Implications of Cetacean Culture*, UN Doc UNEP/CMS/COP11/Doc.23.2.4 (23 July 2014).

With respect to ecosystem-based management, the IWC's current approach has created two large whale sanctuaries to restrict future commercial hunting, but which do little to regulate other 'human activities that could have impacts on whale populations (e.g., fishing and scientific whaling)'.[149] This shortfall could, at least in design, be addressed by tasking the Scientific Committee with recommending to the regime's decision-making body a network of marine protected areas (MPAs).[150] The creation of a network of MPAs for cetaceans that seeks to manage the habitat and regulate activities in areas of the ocean that are critical to their survival is a necessary objective in achieving long-term conservation and management, as well as increasingly becoming plausible given the current state of scientific knowledge.[151] Such an MPA network would contribute to the international community's Strategic Plan for Biodiversity, which seeks to conserve '10 per cent of coastal and marine areas' through 'well connected systems of protected areas and other effective area-based conservation measures'.[152] This MPA network could include high seas areas as well as areas within national jurisdiction where coastal State consent can be obtained, and could be designed in cooperation with other international organisations to ensure that existing obligations are accounted for and otherwise not prejudiced.[153]

B Elucidating Standards, Qualifications and Limitations

Having contemplated an expanded functionality for the proposed Scientific Committee, it is now appropriate to consider how standards,

149 Doug DeMaster, 'A Review of IWC Whaling Sanctuaries' in *Proceedings of the First International Conference on Marine Mammal Protected Areas*, Maui, Hawai'i, 30 March–3 April 2009, 45–46, online at: http://icmmpa.org/wp-content/uploads/2014/10/FINAL_ICMMPA_PROCEEDINGS_SM.pdf.

150 A marine protected area is a 'a discrete geographic area of the sea established by international, national, territorial, tribal, or local laws designated to enhance the long-term conservation of natural resources therein': Joachim Claudet, ed., *Marine Protected Areas: A Multidisciplinary Approach* (Cambridge: Cambridge University Press, 2011), 2–3. A marine protected area network is 'an organized collection of individual MPAs operating co-operatively and synergistically, at various spatial scales and with a range of protection levels, to fulfill ecological aims more effectively and comprehensively than individual sites could alone': Erich Hoyt, *Marine Protected Areas for Whales, Dolphins, and Porpoises: A World Handbook for Cetacean Habitat Conservation and Planning*, 2nd ed. (Washington: Earthscan, 2011), 88.

151 See, for example, Davidson et al., above note 2; Pompa, Ehrlich and Ceballos, above note 25.

152 Convention on Biological Diversity, Strategic Plan 2011–2020, *Aichi Biodiversity Targets*, Target 11, online at: www.cbd.int/sp/targets/.

153 See further, Jefferies, above note 27, 284–295.

qualifications and limitations can be used to further improve the status quo and to mitigate the effects of the limitations of regulatory science. The first question to consider is, what standard should the Scientific Committee employ in completing its functions? Currently, article V of the ICRW indicates that regulatory decisions are to be made based on 'scientific findings'. By contrast, more recent treaties including UNCLOS and the UNFSA employ a 'best available science standard'[154] for decision-making. Simply altering the language of the standard may be useful in terms of modernising the regime but it does not assist in determining what science should be included and what should be excluded. Further elucidation with respect to the standard would need to appear in an equivalent to the current Rules of Procedure for the Scientific Committee, wherein it is stipulated that the 'science' that is considered or produced must be rational and logical in its design[155] and, to the maximum extent practicable, accord with the recognised standards of the peer review process.[156] The revised rules should also state that while the scientific evidence considered need not be limited to 'conclusive findings', any data that is 'wholly unscientific or unreliable' must be excluded.[157] Further defining the content or source of the information to be utilised is inappropriate because the status and form of available scientific evidence will continually evolve.

This discussion necessitates consideration of how this Scientific Committee – and by extension, the regime's law-making body – should address uncertainty and the risk management associated with incomplete or dynamic information. Despite its frailties, the most appropriate mechanism remains express application of the precautionary principle. To avoid manipulation of the precautionary principle, it is important that any new treaty regime seek to reduce ambiguity by defining the precautionary principle and prescribing its application in light of the regime's mandate and regulatory functions.[158] Precaution, in this application,

[154] The frailties of this standard have been considered, especially in the domestic American context. See Julie Joly, Joel Reynolds and Martin Robards, 'Recognizing when the "Best Scientific Data Available" Isn't' (2010) 29:2 *Stanford Environmental Law Journal* 247–282; Carden, above note 19, 184–194; Darren S. Ryder, Moya Tomlinson, Ben Gawne and Gene E. Likens, 'Defining and Using "Best-Available Science": A Policy Conundrum for the Management of Aquatic Ecosystems' (2010) 61 *Marine and Freshwater Research* 821–828. See also the discussion in Section I(B).

[155] See Heazle, above note 34, 362. [156] Aron, above note 13, 119.

[157] Joly, Reynolds and Robards, above note 154, 251–252.

[158] Article 6 of the UNFSA, above note 136, offers a model for prescribed application of the precautionary principle.

ought not be synonymous with protection and must embody 'a politically acceptable balance between exploitation and conservation priorities'.[159] One possible mechanism to help the scientific standard, as modified by application of the precautionary principle, function properly is to clearly articulate that it imposes a justiciable duty. In so doing, a state who contests the manner in which the available science is defined or put to use in the development of a conservation measure can challenge said measure prior to its implementation.[160]

The second question to consider is to what extent expert participation or membership in the Scientific Committee should be limited. Because science and scientists can both be co-opted for advocacy purposes,[161] it is necessary to consider whether simply restricting participation minimises this occurrence. Aron proposes that the current Scientific Committee could be improved by better IWC management of attendance, in part by 'having specialists who may address specific agenda items while limiting their active participation to those items'.[162] A more measured solution is to allow the Scientific Committee to invite other experts to contribute to its work and for qualified scientific observers from intergovernmental and international non-governmental organisations to fully participate, but to establish qualification guidelines as part of the accreditation process for those who seek participation. It is also appropriate to consider whether similar qualification requirements ought to be established for the members of the Scientific Committee who are appointed by states

159 Heazle, above note 34, 367.

160 This raises a number of questions, including: Which state(s) would be challenged in this sort of dispute? What is the appropriate forum for this sort of challenge? Are legal decision-makers properly positioned to mediate, arbitrate or otherwise resolve such a challenge? While not directly on point, some guidance may be gleaned from the *Southern Bluefin Tuna Cases (New Zealand* v. *Japan; Australia* v. *Japan) (Provisional Measures)*, Order of 27 August 1999, International Tribunal for the Law of the Sea (ITLOS), online at: www.itlos.org/cases/list-of-cases/case-no-3-4/, concerning a challenge to Japan's experimental fishing programme, instituted in response to a zero catch-quota set pursuant to the Convention for the Conservation of Southern Bluefin Tuna, 10 May 1993, 1819 UNTS 360, in force 20 May 1994. ITLOS granted provisional measures prohibiting the experimental programme, but ultimately the Ad Hoc Arbitral Tribunal reversed this award on jurisdictional grounds. The point here is that it may be possible to fashion the scientific obligation in a manner that allows recourse to a dispute resolution process in the event that a state party believes that the duty has been breached.

161 See William Aron, William Burke and Milton Freeman, 'Scientists versus Whaling: Science, Advocacy, and Errors of Judgment' (2002) 52:12 *BioScience* 1137–1140; Tarlock, 'Who Owns Science?', above note 20, 151–152.

162 Aron, above note 13, 119.

parties. In light of the broad scope of work contemplated for the restructured Scientific Committee, these qualification guidelines need not be overly restrictive to achieve their gate-keeping function and could be included in revised Rules of Procedure.

The third aspect to consider is the reasonability of limiting the use of lethal research. Research methodology has progressed to the point that the design and implementation of any large-scale research programme for cetaceans should only utilise lethal techniques when all other methods have been attempted and lethal research is deemed absolutely necessary. While states parties should be encouraged to maintain and develop national cetacean research programmes, tasking the Scientific Committee with primary responsibility for developing and implementing an international research programme further promotes innovation and application of non-lethal scientific techniques and, ideally, negates the need for any ICRW article VIII equivalent.[163] Scientific Committee approval or authorisation ought to be required before any state party can use lethal research as part of its national research programme.[164]

The last point of consideration is mandated transparency. To help ensure that a new Scientific Committee's efforts are both appropriate and duly considered by the law-making body, all of its efforts should be subject to transparency requirements established within the implementing agreement.[165] Transparency enables members of the scientific community external to the regime to critique the approach that is being utilised and to assist in the process translating highly technical issues into a form that lay persons can understand.

C *Networked Experts and Regional Organisations*

A final possibility raised by this proposed re-structuring is an enhanced role for regional organisations and the potential for establishing a global network of scientific experts. Assuming that a new international treaty is possible, enhancing regional implementation and cooperation under the

[163] This reasoning tends to align with that of Judge *ad hoc* Charlesworth in *Whaling in the Antarctic*, above note 14.

[164] See Telesetsky, Anton and Koivurova, above note 132, 335–336 (asserting that the ICJ's reasonableness test might render the Scientific Committee's review of proposed special permits the determinative and *de facto* standard moving forward).

[165] Marc Mangel et al., 'Principles for the Conservation of Wild Living Resources' (1996) 6:2 *Ecological Applications* 338–362, 351 (observing that while scientists should not be the decision-makers, their work should be available to the public in a readily understandable form). See also UNFSA, above note 136, art. 12 (providing an analog for transparency).

auspices of a global regulatory body is one way to further bridge the divide between pro-utilisation and pro-preservation states. The UNFSA operates by empowering RFMOs as the organisations responsible for managing straddling stocks and highly migratory fish species.

With membership organised around impacted coastal states and other states that have a fishing interest in a particular stock, RFMOs now cover most of the world's ocean. A number of regional organisations created by treaty are interested in cetacean conservation and management, including the ASCOBANS, ACCOBAMS and NAMMCO treaty bodies, and the Commission for the Conservation of Antarctic Marine Living Resources created by the Convention on the Conservation of Antarctic Marine Living Resources.[166] None of these organisations threaten the ICRW's primacy because they either expressly defer to the ICRW or are limited to the management of small cetaceans or do not promulgate regulatory measures. The IWC's Scientific Committee has a 'history of co-operation' with many such organisations whose representatives regularly participate in Scientific Committee meetings in a non-voting capacity.[167] Each utilises its own advisory scientific body and the IWC's Scientific Committee.

A new international regime for cetacean management and conservation that entrusts an international body with regulatory decision-making and utilises the sort of reformed Scientific Committee described above leaves considerable room for the regional implementation of globally set standards and programmes. First, it facilitates the use of regional research efforts that work to enhance our understanding of cetaceans and the construction of appropriate international management goals. Each regional organisation's scientific body would then be networked with the possibility of enhanced collaboration and globally oriented participation. Second, it enables formalised cooperation between global and regional advisory scientific bodies. Third, and assuming that a limited commercial take is permitted for certain cetacean species, regional organisations could be responsible for applying to the global body for catch allocations that accord with a global management plan. Such allocations could then be distributed amongst the states participating in the regional arrangement. This approach would expand the role that existing regional fisheries bodies currently play in addressing the marine mammal by-catch problem and empower them with the responsibility of implementing, enforcing and

[166] 20 May 1980, 1329 UNTS 48, in force 7 April 1982.

[167] International Whaling Commission, *Scientific Committee Handbook*, above note 84.

reporting on catch quotas. While this regime could contemplate a new class of regional organisation (i.e., Regional Cetacean Management Organisations), it may also simply approve the participation of existing regional organisations, including those listed above.

Conclusion

Institutional scientific experts occupy a unique position within international decision-making processes, with this chapter having focused on their role for international cetacean conservation and management. Because the IWC's position as an effective international organisation for the conservation and management of whales remains contested, it is necessary to consider improvements and alternatives. The possibility of re-institutionalising the role of scientific experts to improve the comprehensive regulation of our diverse interactions with cetaceans is a logical place to begin since science, despite its shortcomings, remains the most appropriate basis for rational regulation. This basis is also one that pro-utilisation and pro-preservationist states will likely agree upon. Nevertheless, the improved utilisation of scientific expertise is not a panacea.

Cetacean conservation and management will continue to be shaped as much by the forces of the ocean, and by ideological and political agendas, as it is by international institutions. The future of international cooperation in this regard depends on the willingness of all interested parties to work to bridge the divide between utilisation and preservation perspectives in a manner that accounts for competing interests and shifts the focus of this debate from public rhetoric to a meaningful forum where progress towards enhanced international governance can occur. While it is not too late to reform our regulatory relationship with cetaceans, it is necessary to proceed with urgency.

7

Engaging Complexity

Legalising International Arctic Environmental Governance

TAHNEE PRIOR

Environmental change in the Arctic, resulting from both biophysical and socio-economic change, leaves us with informal governance structures that are insufficient to meet the interests and demands of new and old actors.[1] A state change – non-linear, abrupt and with typically irreversible shifts or flips in complex and dynamic systems – will exacerbate the gap between current and required governance structures.[2] Such state change may be driven by climate change, technological innovation, increased resource extraction, migration to the North and potential inter-state conflict. A state change will also have deep effects on the evolution of Arctic norms and worldviews – the moral grounding and anchor of legitimacy of authority in the region – with some evolving more rapidly than others, leading to tension. Consequently, the Arctic requires a flexible governance system that breaks with convention and provides for governance innovation. Yet, what could an international governance structure that accounts for the complexity and rapid change of the Arctic look like and how do we get there?

The ideal scale for governing the transformation of social-ecological systems like the Arctic has been a focus of debate in both international law and international relations, as well as in discussions of global governance.[3] Current intellectual approaches to Arctic

[1] Oran R. Young, 'Arctic Stewardship: Maintaining Regional Resilience in an Era of Global Change' (2012) 26:4 *Ethics & International Affairs* 407–420.

[2] Brian Walker and David Salt, *Resilience Thinking: Sustaining Ecosystems and People in a Changing World* (Washington, DC: Island Press, 2006), 36. See also John H. Holland, *Complexity: A Very Short Introduction* (Oxford: Oxford University Press, 2014).

[3] Eduardo S. Brondizio, Elinor Ostrom and Oran Young, 'Connectivity and the Governance of Multilevel Social-Ecological Systems: The Role of Social Capital' (2009) 34 *Annual Review of Environment and Resources* 253–278.

governance are based on a one-dimensional continuum between realist and ecological legal ontologies. I would argue, however, that neither ontology can accommodate the region's increasingly complex reality and instead I introduce a new dimension that is grounded in a systems perspective.

This chapter, being part of a larger project on translating social-ecological resilience theory into legal doctrine, is divided into three sections. Section I defines governance, generally focusing on the disaggregation of the state and, more specifically, the role of networks in the Arctic. Section II outlines the one-dimensional continuum between realist and ecological legal ontologies in the Circumpolar North. Section III then briefly outlines a reflexive law that could help address the Arctic's increasingly complex reality. Overall, the chapter is fundamentally about institutional design in global environmental governance.

I Governing Environmental Change: Disaggregation and Polycentricity in Arctic Governance

The past 50 years have witnessed an epistemological and ontological shift in our definition, understanding and response to global environmental change and the governance of social-ecological systems.[4] Broadly speaking, there is a need for human societies to steer away from critical tipping points that can lead to rapid irreversible change in the Earth system.[5] More specifically, there is a need for a fundamental reorientation and restructuring of institutions towards more effective Earth system governance.[6] However, our inability to appropriately address long-term complex challenges like climate change can lead to new, or exacerbate existing, governance gaps. We often lack the legal, economic and political experience to manage appropriately issues like deforestation, biological conservation or economic development.[7]

[4] Liliana B. Andonova and Ronald B. Mitchell, 'The Rescaling of Global Environmental Politics' (2010) 35 *Annual Review of Environment and Resources* 255–282, 258.

[5] Jonas Ebbesson and Ellen Hey, 'Introduction: Where in Law is Social-ecological Resilience?' (2013) 18:3 *Ecology and Society* 25.

[6] Frank Biermann et al., 'Navigating the Anthropocene: Improving Earth System Governance' (2012) 335:6074 *Science* 1306–1307.

[7] Robin Kundis Craig, 'Stationarity is Dead – Long Live Transformation: Five Principles for Climate Change Adaptation Law' (2010) 34:1 *Harvard Environmental Law Review* 9–73, 26 and 37; Frances Westley et al., 'Tipping Toward Sustainability: Emerging Pathways of Transformation' (2011) 40:7 *AMBIO: A Journal of the Human Environment* 762–780, 764; Lance H. Gunderson and Lowell Pritchard, *Resilience and the Behavior of Large Scale Systems* (Washington, DC: Island Press, 2002), 3.

Capturing non-linear dynamics is also a daunting challenge and beyond current scientific understanding.[8]

Governance systems include the provision of public goods, the prevention of public wrongs, the internalisation of externalities and the protection of human rights.[9] In the context of global environmental governance, such systems seek to maintain living resources, prevent the degradation of marine ecosystems, internalise the environmental impact of oil spills and strengthen the self-determination of indigenous peoples.[10]

Generally, governance centres on efforts to resolve conflicts, facilitate cooperation and alleviate collective-action problems in an increasingly interdependent world. It defines social practices, assigns roles and guides interactions among actors.[11] These actors co-exist and cooperate across multiple scales and overlapping spheres of authority.[12] States are no longer regarded as the only actors, but are repositioned to participate alongside sub-national governments, transnational corporations, intergovernmental organisations and international and transnational non-governmental organisations, as well as formal and informal markets.[13] But while social institutions are backed by shared goals, they do not necessarily derive from legal or formally prescribed responsibilities.[14]

[8] Eugene A. Rosa, Andres Diekmann, Thomas Dietz Diekmann and Carlo C. Jäger, *Human Footprints on the Global Environment Threats to Sustainability* (Cambridge, MA: MIT Press, 2010), 276.

[9] See Frank Biermann and Philipp Pattberg, 'Global Environmental Governance Revisited' in Frank Biermann and Philipp Pattberg, eds., *Global Environmental Governance Reconsidered* (Cambridge, MA: MIT Press, 2012), 1–25. See also *Arctic Governance in an Era of Transformative Change: Critical Questions, Governance Principles, Ways Forward: Report of the Arctic Governance Project* (14 April 2010), 4, online at www.arcticgovernance.org/.

[10] *Arctic Governance in an Era of Transformative Change* (ibid.). 4.

[11] Andrew Hurrell, *On Global Order: Power, Values and the Constitution of International Society* (Oxford: Oxford University Press, 2008), 14.

[12] William W. Burke-White, 'Complementarity in Practice: The International Criminal Court as Part of a System of Multi-level Global Governance in the Democratic Republic of Congo' (2005) 18:3 *Leiden Journal of International Law* 557–590, 558. See also Philip G. Cerny, *Rethinking World Politics: A Theory of Transnational Neopluralism* (New York: Oxford University Press, 2010); Jan Aart Scholte, *Globalization: A Critical Introduction* (London: Palgrave McMillan, 2005); David Held, *Democracy and the Global Order: From the Modern State to Cosmopolitan Governance* (Stanford: Stanford University Press, 1995).

[13] Miles Kahler, ed., *Networked Politics: Agency, Power, and Governance* (Ithaca, NY: Cornell University Press, 2009); Scholte, *Globalization: A Critical Introduction*, above note 12.

[14] James N. Rosenau and Ernst-Otto Czempiel, eds., *Governance without Government* (Cambridge: Cambridge University Press, 1992), 4.

As a consequence, actors have an interest in monitoring and evaluating governance systems based on factors including efficiency, legitimacy and accountability.

A *The Disaggregation of the State and Networks of Governance*

In 2004, Anne-Marie Slaughter placed a particular focus on the role of networked governance. She identified a 'new world order' where states act in both their aggregate and disaggregated form.[15] She argued that government institutions often delegate tasks to actors who are best adept at developing and implementing policy solutions across local, national, regional and global scales with the aim of minimising governance gaps.[16] The disaggregation of the state occurs in three directions: upward to supra-state and international actors and organisations; downward to cities and communities; and outward to civil society and non-state actors.[17] Disaggregation facilitates the development of networked systems of governance, recognised as distinct phenomena and vehicles for cooperation in global governance. Both horizontal and vertical networks have a non-hierarchical structure that allows them to develop alongside the formalities of traditional intergovernmental cooperation.[18]

Horizontal networks like the Group of 20 or the Organisation for Economic Co-operation and Development are informal and flexible, linking national institutions with their counterparts. Meanwhile, vertical networks like the European Union or the North American Commission for Environmental Cooperation[19] are neither top-down nor bottom-up.[20] They delegate sovereignty to supra-national institutions and are

[15] Anne-Marie Slaughter, *A New World Order* (Princeton: Princeton University Press, 2004), 34.

[16] As discussed in Tahnee L. Prior, 'Breaking the Wall of Monocentric Governance: Polycentricity in the Governance of Persistent Organic Pollutants in the Arctic' (2013) 5 *The Yearbook of Polar Law* 185–232, 192.

[17] Catrien J.A.M. Termeer, Art Dewulf and Maartje van Lieshout, 'Disentangling Scale Approaches in Governance Research: Comparing Monocentric, Multilevel, and Adaptive Governance' (2010) 15:4 *Ecology and Society* 29; David W. Cash et al., 'Scale and Cross-scale Dynamics: Governance and Information in a Multilevel World' (2006) 11:2 *Ecology and Society* 8; Jan Aart Scholte, 'Globalization and Governance: From Statism to Polycentrism,' Centre for the Study of Globalisation and Regionalisation, Working Paper No 130/04, 2004, 4.

[18] Slaughter, above note 15, 13.

[19] The latter created by the North American Agreement on Environmental Cooperation, 14 September 1993, (1993) 32 *International Legal Materials* 1480, in force 1 January 1994, art 10(7).

[20] Slaughter, above note 15, 21–22.

characterised by regularised interaction between similar government units across borders, including various non-state actors.[21] Within a disaggregated system, actors operate at multiple levels based on their ability to provide transnational solutions to global problems that stretch across state boundaries.

Kal Raustiala observed a similar shift in the instruments and mechanisms used by states in adapting to complex and interdependent systems.[22] He argues that transgovernmental networks and soft law – which consists of political arrangements that are generally weak with respect to obligation, precision and delegation – are effective in polycentric systems where treaties may be unnecessary for effective regulation.[23] Informal agreements, like declarations or action programmes, provide vague normative guidance and 'more modest regulation than formal international treaties'.[24] Oftentimes, they are politically and morally binding, retaining a status at times almost equal to hard law, thereby making them an effective means for governing uncertainty.

Harmonisation networks like those required by the North American Free Trade Agreement between the Governments of Canada, Mexico and the United States[25] foster the convergence of national and international law by providing opportunities for cooperation and helping actors comply with and enforce existing treaties and agreements.[26] Information networks, like the International Network for Environmental Compliance and Enforcement,[27] collect, decipher and distil relevant

[21] Kofi A. Annan, *We the Peoples: The Role of the United Nations in the 21st Century* (New York: United Nations, 2000), 70.

[22] Prior, above note 16, 196, with reference to Kal Raustiala, 'The Architecture of International Cooperation: Transgovernmental Networks and the Future of International Law' (2002) 43:1 *Virginia Journal of International Law* 1–92.

[23] Raustiala, above note 22, 86. See also Kenneth W. Abbott and Duncan Snidal, 'Hard and Soft Law in International Governance' (2000) 54:3 *International Organization* 421–456, 422; Brondizio, Ostrom and Young, above note 3, 254 and 270; Michael D. McGinnis, *Polycentric Games and Institutions: Readings from the Workshop in Political Theory and Policy Analysis* (Ann Arbor: University of Michigan Press, 2002), 2.

[24] Timo Koivurova, *Environmental Impact Assessment in the Arctic: A Study of International Legal Norms* (Aldershot, Hants: Ashgate, 2002), 127; Timo Koivurova and Leena Heinämäki, 'The Participation of Indigenous Peoples in International Norm-making in the Arctic' (2006) 42:2 *Polar Record* 101–109, 103.

[25] 17 December 1992, (1993) 32 *International Legal Materials* 289, in force 1 January 1994.

[26] Slaughter, above note 15, 59 and 169; Elinor Ostrom, 'Polycentric Systems for Coping with Collective Action and Global Environmental Change' (2010) 20:4 *Global Environmental Change* 550–557, 552.

[27] The INECE is a partnership of government and non-government enforcement and compliance practitioners from more than 150 countries. See further, http://inece.org/.

knowledge out of a high magnitude of data. They thereby become systems of regulation where 'power flows not from coercive capacity but from an ability to exercise influence through knowledge and persuasion'.[28] Dialogue and collective learning – referring to data on how individual members make decisions and implement solutions, novel ideas and interests, and codes of best practice – can help overcome collective-action problems.[29] Thus, in a state of 'permanent, polyarchic dis-equilibrium', actors use networks to pool information for improved self-regulation.[30] Actors redefine problems, reduce uncertainty and develop solutions. Another promising dimension is the capacity of the networks themselves for socialisation and member support through capacity building and technical assistance.[31]

Network interactions often take place under the auspices of loosely arranged peak organisations, or secretariats. Some organisations have 'material entities possessing physical locations (or seats), offices, personnel, equipment, and budgets', while others do not.[32] Structured by normative guidelines, rather than traditional treaties, these organisations provide technical coordination, monitor processes, adapt rules and develop new standards. They also gather, filter and distribute information in a manner that is accessible to both technical and non-technical audiences.[33] Their ability to act as 'knowledge brokers' by integrating different knowledge systems, as well as bonding and bridging networks of researchers and policy-makers, illuminates new perspectives, redefines problems and helps implement solutions at different levels, potentially shifting the configuration of the system as a whole.[34]

B Polycentricity in Arctic Governance

Geographically, the Arctic is defined by three criteria: above the Arctic Circle, in the case of northern Europe and northwest Russia, and the

[28] Slaughter, above note 15, 7, 55 and 177–178. [29] Ibid., 53–54.

[30] Ibid., 196; Brondizio, Ostrom and Young, above note 3, 271.

[31] Slaughter, above note 15, 195 and 198.

[32] Oran Young, *International Cooperation: Building Regimes for Natural Resources and the Environment* (Ithaca, NY: Cornell University Press, 1989), 32.

[33] Kenneth W. Abbott, 'The Transnational Regime Complex for Climate Change' (2012) 30:4 *Environment and Planning C: Government and Policy* 9.

[34] James Meadowcroft, 'Politics and Scale: Some Implications for Environmental Governance' (2002) 61 *Landscape and Urban Planning* 169–179, 173; Raustiala, above note 22, 49; Brondizio, Ostrom and Young, above note 3, 262.

areas down to 60° north latitude in North America, Iceland and eastern Russia;[35] the marine boundary; and the July isotherm.[36] Based on this definition, the region covers an area of 30 million square kilometres, is rich in natural resources, spans eight countries and 24 time zones, and holds a population of over 4 million, including over 30 indigenous groups. While certain characteristics, like extreme variation in temperature and large areas of permafrost, are shared, others, like language, are not.[37] Despite its distinct regional dynamics, the Arctic has never fit well into traditional forms of governance.[38]

In many ways, Slaughter's 'disaggregated sovereignty' characterises the polycentric nature of Arctic governance. Cultural contact between northern indigenous peoples, the establishment of settlements and cooperation in areas of exploration and trade began long before the nation-state and continued once borders were established.[39] The Circumpolar North has also been 'the locus of significant and suggestive efforts to devise regimes for shared natural resources during the twentieth century'.[40] The period up to the 1920s was regarded as a discovery phase that imagined the region as an uninhabited environmental entity where early explorers and traditional indigenous peoples braved the elements.[41] It was also a period defined by the 1920 Treaty Concerning the Archipelago of Spitsbergen,[42] an

[35] E. Carina H. Keskitalo, *Negotiating the Arctic: The Construction of an International Region* (New York: Routledge, 2004), 33; E. Carina H. Keskitalo, 'International Region-Building: The Development of the Arctic as an International Region' (2007) 42:2 *Cooperation and Conflict* 187–205, 190.

[36] Timo Koivurova, Tanja Joona and Reija Shnoro, *Arctic Governance* (Rovaniemi, Finland: Oy Sevenprint, 2004), 43.

[37] Olav Schram Stokke, Geir Hønneland and Peter Johan Schei, 'Pollution and Conservation' in Olav Schram Stokke and Geir Hønneland, eds., *International Cooperation and Arctic Governance: Regime Effectiveness and Northern Region Building* (London: Routledge, 2007), 78–111, 79.

[38] E. Carina H. Keskitalo, Timo Koivurova and Nigel Bankes, 'Climate Governance in the Arctic: Introduction and Theoretical Framework' in Timo Koivurova, E. Carina H. Keskitalo and Nigel Bankes, eds., *Climate Governance in the Arctic* (Dordrecht: Springer, 2009), 1–26, 12.

[39] Lassi Heininen, 'Circumpolar International Relations and Geopolitics' in *Arctic Human Development Report* (Akureyri: Stefansson Arctic Institute, 2004), 207–225, 207.

[40] Gail Osherenko and Oran R. Young, *The Age of the Arctic: Hot Conflicts and Cold Realities* (Cambridge: Cambridge University Press, 1989), 1; Oran R. Young, *International Governance: Protecting the Environment in a Stateless Society* (Ithaca, NY: Cornell University Press, 1994), 57.

[41] Keskitalo, 'International Region-Building,' above note 35, 192.

[42] 9 February 1920, 2 LNTS 7, in force 14 August 1925.

arrangement that gave Norway sovereignty over the Spitsbergen (now Svalbard) Archipelago in return for Norway's commitment 'to demilitarize the area, grant all parties equal access to the archipelago's natural resources, encourage scientific research, and establish an equitable administrative system'.[43] The 1960s and 1970s were marked by increased Arctic oil and gas exploitation and the simultaneous rise of both environmental and ethnic movements.[44] Norway and Russia, for instance, operated a joint management regime for fisheries in the Barents Sea with parallel monitoring and enforcement procedures.[45] It also saw the signing of the 1973 Agreement on Conservation of Polar Bears.[46]

The 1980s and 1990s witnessed an 'Arctic Boom' resulting from multiple formative events including the end of the Cold War, the 1986 Chernobyl catastrophe, the crossing of sulphur dioxide emissions from the Kola Peninsula into Finland between 1978 and 1988, and the Exxon Valdez oil spill off of the Alaskan coast in 1989.[47] However, a speech in 1987 in Murmansk by Mikhail Gorbachev, then Soviet General Secretary of the Central Committee of the Communist Party, provided particular political momentum for the development of Arctic governance as it stands today.[48] In his speech, Gorbachev focused on six concrete proposals, including the coordination of scientific research, cooperation on environmental protection and the opening up of the Northern Sea Route to foreign ships.[49] Together, these events illuminated the need for and brought down barriers to Arctic governance, which coincided with the second global 'environmental wave', beginning with the 1989 Report on the World Commission on Environment and Development and ending with the 1992 United Nations Conference on Environment and Development.[50]

[43] *Arctic Governance in an Era of Transformative Change*, above note 9, 4.

[44] Keskitalo, 'International Region-Building,' above note 35, 194.

[45] *Arctic Governance in an Era of Transformative Change*, above note 9, 4.

[46] 15 November 1973, (1974) 13 *International Legal Materials* 13, in force 26 May 1976. Four of the eight Arctic states are parties: Canada, Denmark, Norway and Russia.

[47] Keskitalo, *Negotiating the Arctic*, above note 35, 37.

[48] Keskitalo, 'International Region-Building,' above note 35, 194–195.

[49] As reported in Lassi Heininen, 'The Murmansk Speech of 1987' for the *Barents Encyclopedia* (undated), online at: http://bar-enc.didaktekon.se/Editor/Sample-articles /Ex-Murmansk-Speech-S-Heininen-2011-09.pdf.

[50] E. Carina H. Keskitalo, *Climate Change and Globalization in the Arctic: An Integrated Approach to Vulnerability Assessment* (London: Earthscan, 2008), 188.

II Arctic Governance: A One-Dimensional Continuum

A An Ecological Approach to Arctic Governance: The Role of Networks and Soft Law

Developments in the region since the end of the Cold War included state-led region-building through organisations and institutions focused on northern issues, cooperation between regional organisations and northern indigenous peoples, and networks of expert scientific research. These developments took an ecological approach to Arctic governance that underpins soft legal arrangements.[51] The use of soft law in the Arctic, in turn, led to a mosaic of regimes and networks that actors now leverage to cooperatively govern the region.[52] Interactions are facilitated by organisations, including the Arctic Council and the Barents Euro-Arctic Council, and non-binding agreements, such as the Arctic Environmental Protection Strategy. In these fora, information and resources are shared, knowledge gaps are often illuminated and collectively solved, and deliberative equality provides opportunities for social learning, which builds social capital.[53]

1 The Arctic Environmental Protection Strategy and Arctic Council

Transgovernmental networks serve as tools for anticipating and reacting to change in Arctic governance. In 1991, the eight Arctic states – Canada, Denmark, Finland, Iceland, Norway, Sweden, Russia and the United States – adopted the Arctic Environmental Protection Strategy, an informal multilateral and multi-level agreement originally proposed by Finland.[54] The Strategy's social-ecological approach combined

[51] Heininen, 'Circumpolar International Relations and Geopolitics,' above note 39; Lassi Heininen, 'Circumpolar International Relations and Cooperation' in Lassi Heininen and Chris Southcott, eds., *Globalization and the Circumpolar North* (Fairbanks: University of Alaska Press, 2010), 265–306, 277; Abbott and Snidal, 'Hard and Soft Law in International Governance,' above note 23, 422.

[52] Timo Koivurova, 'Increasing Relevance of Treaties: The Case of the Arctic' *AJIL Unbound*, 6 May 2014, online at www.asil.org/blogs/increasing-relevance-treaties-case-arctic-agora-end-treaties.

[53] Prior, above note 16, 191.

[54] *Artic Environmental Protection Strategy*, Rovaniemi, Finland, June 1991, online at: www.arctic-council.org/index.php/en/document-archive/category/556-arctic-environmental-protection-strategy. See further, Keskitalo, *Negotiating the Arctic*, above note 35, 59; Thomas S. Axworthy, *A Brief History of the Creation of the Arctic Council* (Toronto: Walter and Duncan Gordon Foundation, 2011), 1.

Finland's emphasis on the importance of curbing transboundary pollution and Canada's focus on indigenous peoples and the environment.[55] In 1996, the Arctic Council, a high-level intergovernmental forum, subsumed the Arctic Environmental Protection Strategy within its broader mandate. The Council linked the region to global environmental issues and thereby emphasised the importance of environmentally sound management with a focus on 'common Arctic issues' like sustainable development and environmental protection.[56] Later, the Council altered its structure and added a rotating secretariat that is now permanently based in Tromsø, Norway.[57]

The Arctic Council acts as a loosely organised peak organisation, coordinating regimes, addressing overlaps, filling governance gaps, strengthening existing institutions and providing a platform for multi-level and multi-scale cooperation and deliberation.[58] The Arctic Council shapes national policies[59] on environmental protection and sustainable development by promoting cooperation, coordination and interaction among Arctic member states, permanent participants, as well as observer states and organisations. A unique characteristic of the Council is its inclusion of six Arctic indigenous organisations as permanent participants, providing indigenous peoples the opportunity to participate in norm making, frame environmental challenges as social justice issues, lobby member states, share traditional ecological knowledge and gain access to information.[60] Most importantly, indigenous peoples must be consulted prior to a decision being taken.[61] In a legal context, this approach is innovative because indigenous

[55] Timo Koivurova and David L. VanderZwaag, 'The Arctic Council at 10 Years: Retrospect and Prospects' (2007) 40:1 *University of British Columbia Law Review* 121–194; Keskitalo, 'International Region-Building,' above note 35, 190.

[56] Geir Hønneland and Olav Schram Stokke, 'Introduction' in Stokke and Hønneland, above note 37, 1.

[57] Keskitalo, *Negotiating the Arctic*, above note 35, 56.

[58] Raustiala, above note 22, 49; Stokke and Hønneland, above note 37, 149; Slaughter, above note 15, 207–208; Timo Koivurova and Waliul Hasanat, 'The Climate Policy of the Arctic Council' in Koivurova, Keskitalo and Bankes, *Climate Governance in the Arctic*, above note 38, 70 and 78; Young, *International Cooperation*, above note 32, 32.

[59] *Arctic Governance in an Era of Transformative Change*, above note 9, 15.

[60] Henrik Selin and Noelle Eckley Selin, 'Indigenous Peoples in International Environmental Cooperation: Arctic Management of Hazardous Substances' (2008) 17:1 *Review of European, Comparative and International Environmental Law* 72–83, 76; Elana Wilson and Indra Øverland, 'Indigenous Issues' in Stokke and Hønneland, above note 37, 27–49, 34.

[61] Wilson and Øverland (ibid.), 29–30.

peoples often find themselves outside the sphere of influence, facing the inherent limitations of international treaty-making processes.[62] The Arctic Council also grants observer status to non-Arctic states, global and regional intergovernmental and inter-parliamentary organisations, and non-governmental organisations based on their potential to contribute relevant funding and financial resources to the Council's work.[63] Embracing the social-ecological approach of the Arctic Environmental Protection Strategy, the work of the Council has ultimately helped establish the Arctic as a distinct region in both northern and global cooperation.

The Council's work is structured in a systematic soft law manner via a declaration, rules of procedure, two-year work plans and national implementation plans. Adopted under the Iqaluit Declaration,[64] the rules of procedure include guidelines for meetings, the process for submitting project and programme proposals, and role of subordinate bodies. The eight Arctic states have also developed national agencies, whose representatives hold regular meetings, coordinate implementation plans, make an effort to realise recommendations and set out to afford adequate financial resources for joint projects. By avoiding traditional hard law approaches, the Council's current soft law structure provides opportunities for state and non-state actors to build social capital through years of interaction, making it easier for them to adopt codes of best practices and coordinate solutions because they are unlikely to break with convention.

The Council engages scientific and indigenous networks in working groups and task forces to gather extensive scientific data and traditional ecological knowledge that would otherwise be 'impossible for one state, let alone a non-profit or indigenous organisation, to produce independently'.[65] It is largely under the auspices of these groups that governance and legal innovation, in the form of scientific reports and

[62] Ibid.

[63] 'Joint Communique of the Governments of the Arctic Countries on the Establishment of the Arctic Council' (1996) 35 *International Legal Materials* 1386–1387; 'Declaration on the Establishment of the Arctic Council' (1996) 35 *International Legal Materials* 1387–1390, para 3; Koivurova and VanderZwaag, 'The Arctic Council at 10 Years,' above note 55, 130.

[64] Adopted at the First Ministerial Meeting of the Arctic Council, Iqaluit, Canada, 17–18 September 1998, online at: www.arctic-council.org/index.php/en/document-archive/category/5-declarations.

[65] Wilson and Øverland, above note 37, 33–34.

assessments, take place, with examples being the 2002 Arctic Pollution report and the 2004 Arctic Climate Impact Assessment report.[66]

The 2002 Arctic Pollution report by the Arctic Monitoring and Assessment Programme combined scientific data and traditional ecological knowledge to provide evidence of negative exposure to the effects of persistent organic pollutants (POPs) experienced by both Arctic indigenous and non-indigenous communities.[67] This research also significantly contributed to the work of the 2007 Fourth Assessment Report of the Intergovernmental Panel on Climate Change (IPCC) and subsequent legalisation of the international POPs regime.[68] Arctic states pursued the development of a protocol to the Convention on Long-range Transboundary Air Pollution Cooperation[69] on POPs through the United Nations Economic Commission for Europe. The protocol was subsequently scaled up globally to become the Stockholm Convention on Persistent Organic Pollutants.[70] In terms of policy implementation, the Arctic Monitoring and Assessment Programme and the Nordic Environment Finance Corporation partnered to identify specific contaminants, assess their environmental impact and implement small and medium-sized environmentally sound projects in the Russian part of the Barents region.[71] Through their work, the Programme and Corporation identified 42 'hot spots' where projects assist Russian authorities in curbing pollution and supporting regional economic development.[72]

The publication of the Arctic Monitoring and Assessment Programme's high-quality 2004 report on Arctic Climate Impact Assessment – based on field and laboratory experiments, model simulations, observed trends and theoretical analyses – led to a particularly pivotal period in environmental and Arctic governance. Unlike previous reporting, the assessment focused

[66] Arctic Monitoring and Assessment Programme, *Assessment Report: Arctic Pollution Issues* (Oslo: Arctic Council, 1998); Carolyn Symon, Lelani Arris and Bill Heal, eds., *Arctic Climate Impact Assessment* (New York: Cambridge University Press, 2005).

[67] Prior, above note 16, 218. [68] Stokke, Hønneland and Schei, above note 37, 78–112.

[69] 13 November 1979, 1302 UNTS 218, in force 16 March 1983.

[70] 22 May 2001, 2256 UNTS 119, in force 17 May 2004.

[71] Alexei Bambulyak, Svetlana Golubeva and Vladimir Savinov, *Assessment of the Barents Hot Spot Report: Describing the State of 42 Original Barents Environmental 'Hot Spots': Part I – Analysis* (2013), online at: www.barentsinfo.fi/beac/docs/Environment_Ministers_Meeting_4_5_Nov_2013_Inari_HotSpots_Assessment_Report_ENG.pdf.

[72] AMAP Secretariat, *Updating of Environmental 'Hot Spots' List in the Russian Part of the Barents Region: Proposals for Environmentally Sound Investment Projects* (Oslo: Nordic Environment Finance Corporation, 2003), online at: www.barentsinfo.fi/beac/docs/2750_doc_AMAP_Nefco_HotSpots.pdf.

on policy-relevant language, and issues of human and environmental security, which ultimately altered the Council's structure in terms of the role of the secretariat and the agenda of its subsidiary bodies. On a global scale, it significantly contributed to the 2007 Fourth Assessment Report of the Intergovernmental Panel on Climate Change, a scientific intergovernmental body operating under the auspices of the UN.[73]

2 Pan-Arctic Cooperation

Pan-Arctic cooperation beyond the Arctic Council includes the Conference of Parliamentarians of the Arctic Region and Standing Committee of Parliamentarians of the Arctic Region; transnational and national indigenous organisations like the Inuit Circumpolar Council and Saami Council; and the Northern Forum, a collaborative body for sub-national regions from Arctic and non-Arctic states.

3 Regional Collaboration and Bilateral Relations

Regional collaboration in the Arctic includes the Barents Euro-Arctic Council and Barents Regional Council, both attracting membership from Finland, Sweden, Norway, Northwest Russia and the European Commission; the Nordic Council and Nordic Council of Ministers, an inter-parliamentary forum for elected representatives from the Nordic countries; the West Nordic Council between the Faroe Islands, Greenland and Iceland; and pan-Arctic indigenous organisations like the Inuit Circumpolar Council.[74] Academic organisations like the University of the Arctic, scientific bodies like the International Arctic Science Committee and non-governmental organisations like the Arctic Programme of the World Wildlife Fund also fall under the umbrella of pan-Arctic cooperation.[75]

Meanwhile, bilateral relations in the Arctic include the Barents Sea Boundary Treaty between Norway and Russia,[76] ongoing discussions

[73] See Oleg A. Anisimov et al., 'Polar Regions' in Vicente R. Barros et al., eds., *Climate Change 2014: Impacts, Adaptation, and Vulnerability: Part B: Regional Aspects – Contribution of Working Group II to the Fifth Assessment Report of the Intergovernmental Panel on Climate Change* (Cambridge: Cambridge University Press, 2014), 1567–1612.

[74] Heininen, 'Circumpolar International Relations and Geopolitics,' above note 39, 215.

[75] Heininen, 'Circumpolar International Relations and Cooperation,' above note 51, 286.

[76] Treaty between the Kingdom of Norway and the Russian Federation concerning Maritime Delimitation and Cooperation in the Barents Sea and the Arctic Ocean, 15 September 2010, in force 7 July 2011, online at: www.regjeringen.no/globalassets/upload/ud/vedlegg/folkerett/avtale_engelsk.pdf.

between Canada and Denmark regarding Hans Island and the unresolved, yet non-contentious, issues between Canada and the United States regarding the Beaufort Sea. Bilateral relations also exist along the Alaska–Yukon border, where shared governance is taking place via the Yukon River Inter-Tribal Watershed Council, and the Finno-Swedish border, where the municipalities of Haparanda and Tornio act as 'twin cities'.[77]

B A Changing Arctic

A remarkably organic approach to Arctic governance leads scholars and policy-makers alike to hail the region as a laboratory for testing new management strategies and as a prototype for global environmental governance.[78] As Carmack and others note, 'by looking at and understanding the rapid and nonlinear changes that are taking place in the Arctic, we can develop powerful tools to manage and cope with emerging global-scale issues'.[79] But while the Arctic Council's current structure and lack of regulatory politics is generative, fostering cooperation and strengthening existing international law, it has no teeth. It is unable to fully address concerns about environmental governance on a local or sub-regional Arctic scale, which raises questions as to its longevity, influence and accountability.

1 Opening Up the Arctic

While Arctic institutions are often commended for their inclusion of non-state actors, particularly indigenous peoples, it is becoming increasingly 'difficult for Arctic stakeholders to designate specific points in Arctic space as either definitively "inside" or "outside"'.[80] Discussions on the future of Arctic governance often focus on the inclusion of non-Arctic states – six more non-Arctic states were admitted as observers in May 2013 – and its

[77] Joan Nymand Larsen and Gail Fondahl, eds., *Arctic Human Development Report: Regional Processes and Global Linkages* (Copenhagen: Nordisk Ministerråd, 2015).

[78] Oran Young, 'The Arctic in Play: Governance in a Time of Rapid Change' (2009) 24:2 *International Journal of Marine and Coastal Law* 423–442, 424.

[79] Eddy Carmack, Fiona McLaughlin, Gail Whiteman and Thomas Homer-Dixon, 'Detecting and Coping with Disruptive Shocks in Arctic Marine Systems: A Resilience Approach to Place and People' (2012) 41:1 *AMBIO: A Journal of the Human Environment* 56–65, 56.

[80] Hannes Gerhardt et al., 'Contested Sovereignty in a Changing Arctic' (2010) 100:4 *Annals of the Association of American Geographers* 992–1002, 999.

potentially significant impact on regional cooperation (such as their role in negotiating legally binding instruments for the Arctic).[81] Questions pertaining to the degree of new actors' engagement in Arctic Council working groups, for instance, may lead to tension among Arctic Council member states. More specifically, it may lead to stickiness. The inclusion of new actors will likely also raise questions of inclusivity and exclusivity, informality and formality.

A significant example includes the 2008 Ilulissat Declaration under which Canada, Denmark, Norway, Russia and the United States confirmed that the current international legal framework provides 'a solid foundation for responsible management by the five [Central Arctic Ocean] coastal states and other users of the Arctic Ocean through national implementation and application of relevant provisions'.[82] They also reinforced the notion that there is 'no need to develop a new comprehensive legal regime to govern the Arctic Ocean'.[83] The 'Arctic Five' took a similar stance in later meetings on shipping and fisheries.[84] As Michael Byers, writing with James Baker, aptly points out, 'The rules are in place, and they have been for some time'.[85] Still, the non-binding Ilulissat Declaration elicited criticism from three non-coastal Arctic states and six indigenous organisations, all of which were excluded from the meeting. They fear that rapid environmental change in the region is already weakening their participation in key negotiations.

Kankaanpää and Young also highlight the omission of regional administrations, non-indigenous northerners, the private sector, as well as researchers in the humanities and the fields of science, technology, engineering and maths.[86] The absence of local and regional initiatives in multilateral governance structures, despite their active role in practising adaptation, is problematic for three reasons: (1) southern policy-makers

[81] Piotr Graczyk and Timo Koivurova, 'A New Era in the Arctic Council's External Relations? Broader Consequences of the Nuuk Observer Rules for Arctic Governance' (2014) 50:254 *Polar Record* 225–236. See also Sebastien Duyck, 'Drawing Lessons for Arctic Governance from the Antarctic Treaty System' (2011) 3 *The Yearbook of Polar Law* 683–713, 695–696.

[82] 'The Ilulissat Declaration' (2009) 48 *International Legal Materials* 362–363.

[83] Larsen and Fondahl, *Arctic Human Development Report*, above note 77, 224.

[84] As cited in Ibid.

[85] Michael Byers, *International Law and the Arctic* (Cambridge: Cambridge University Press, 2013), 93.

[86] Paula Kankaanpää and Oran R. Young, 'The Effectiveness of the Arctic Council' (2012) 31 *Polar Research* 17176, online at: www.polarresearch.net/index.php/polar/article/view/17176.

should be informed about local impacts in order to avoid making policy decisions that will leave local communities more vulnerable; (2) local and regional administrators should partake in higher-level decision-making processes because they are reliant on them; and (3) a lack of regional and local input may result in uneven scientific assessments.[87]

2 A Changing Arctic: Opportunities for Governance Failure

The Arctic is not static. The 2004 Arctic Climate Impact Assessment, 2007 Fourth Assessment Report and 2013 Fifth Assessment Report of the IPCC all provide empirical evidence of environmental change at a planetary scale.[88] They also highlight incremental and abrupt change to the Arctic. Abrupt non-linear change in the Arctic includes a significant increase in tall shrubs and grasses, a decline of Arctic sea ice in summer at a rate that exceeds earlier modelling projections, the sudden appearance of sinkholes on the Yamal Peninsula as a result of a highly dynamic permafrost system and the release of methane, as well as the accelerated loss of coastal sea ice and sea level rise that is already forcing the relocation of some indigenous communities in Alaska.[89] More specifically, studies have shown that climate change can have non-linear effects on wild reindeer populations in areas like Svalbard, thereby affecting traditional livelihoods.[90] Ultimately, though, the Arctic is not solely a victim of climate change. In fact, a changing Canada Basin – an oceanic basin within the Arctic Ocean – 'feeds back on the global system, with potential impacts on ocean currents and global precipitation patterns'.[91]

Incremental and linear change also highlights that 'physical, biological, and socioeconomic impacts of climate change in the Arctic have to be

[87] Keskitalo, Koivurova and Bankes, 'Introduction' in Koivurova, Keskitalo and Bankes, *Climate Governance in the Arctic*, above note 38, 15; Annika E. Nilsson, *A Changing Arctic: Climate Science and Policy in the Arctic Climate Impact Assessment* (Linköping: Linköping University, 2007), 432.

[88] See Anisimov et al., 'Polar Regions,' above note 73.

[89] Carmack et al., above note 79, 57. See also Anisimov et al., 'Polar Regions,' above note 73; Alexey Portnov, Jurgen Mienert and Pavel Serov, 'Modeling the Evolution of Climate-sensitive Arctic Subsea Permafrost in Regions of Extensive Gas Expulsion at the West Yamal Shelf' (2014) 119:11 *Journal of Geophysical Research: Biogeosciences* 2082–2094.

[90] Nicholas J.C. Tyler, Mads C. Forchhammer and Nils Are Øritsland, 'Nonlinear Effects of Climate and Density in the Dynamics of a Fluctuating Population of Reindeer (2008) 89:6 *Ecology* 1675–1686.

[91] Carmack et al., above note 79, 57.

seen in the context of often interconnected factors that include not only environmental changes caused by drivers other than climate change but also demography, culture, and economic development'.[92] While Arctic inhabitants have adapted historically to environmental change, the complexity of what has been termed as a second state change is an unprecedented challenge for northern communities where the 'rate of change will be faster than social systems can adapt'.[93] In resource-rich areas like the Yamal Peninsula of Western Siberia, as an example, climate change is accelerating access to northern lands for development.[94] Yet it presents a simultaneous challenge to the world's largest area of reindeer herding, which means that grazing lands will shrink as anticipated development activities, alongside infrastructure and pollution, take place.[95] Arctic governance institutions must prepare for disparate positions with indigenous and local communities as they aim to reconcile long-term environmental and social concerns with sustainable economic growth – not a small feat.[96]

New opportunities for resource extraction, transportation and research have drawn the interest of actors from both inside and outside the region.[97] Canadian and Australian mining companies are already investing in and developing projects in Finnish Lapland and Greenland respectively. Access to resources is also a focus of elite networks, like the World Economic Forum and Arctic Business Forum, both seeking to foster business development.[98] However, uncertainty as to the risks associated with resource development on northern communities and ecosystems remains due to a lack of scientific and empirical research. Inadequate resources to manage accidental oil spills in a vast region like the Arctic are only one of the many challenges we are likely to face in this issue area. As Carmack and others point out, 'The Arctic may be home to a vast amount of newly (or soon to be) accessible fossil fuels: the development of these resources will offer tempting short-term gains to some

92 See Anisimov et al., 'Polar Regions,' above note 73.

93 Intergovernmental Panel on Climate Change, *Fifth Assessment Report (AR5)* (Geneva: World Meteorological Organization, 2013).

94 See Anisimov et al., 'Polar Regions,' above note 73. 95 Ibid.

96 See Natalia Loukacheva, ed., *Polar Law Textbook* (Copenhagen: Nordic Council of Ministers, 2010), 53. See also 'The State of the Environment: The Arctic: Social and Economic Background' in *Global Environment Outlook 2000* (Nairobi: United Nations Environment Programme, 1999), ch. 2.

97 Paul A. Berkman and Oran R. Young, 'Governance and Environmental Change in the Arctic Ocean' (2009) 324; 5925 *Science* 339–340.

98 Carmack et al., above note 79, 63.

companies and some countries. However, the amplification effects of continued fossil fuel development will accelerate Arctic sea-ice melt and thereby increase longer term costs to the global economic system.'[99]

A lack of continuity, as evidenced by the Arctic Environmental Impact Assessment and Arctic Economic Council, is also a paradigmatic governance failure in the Arctic. While both are crucial to ensuring sustainable development under pressure to exploit natural resources in the region, they are also at the mercy of Arctic Council chairmanships and the priorities of their two-year tenure.

Seeking to harmonise environmental impact assessments nationally and in a transboundary context, while integrating traditional ecological knowledge and indigenous peoples in decision-making, Arctic states agreed to apply the 1997 Guidelines for Environmental Impact Assessment in the Arctic under the auspices of the 1997 Alta Declaration.[100] They, however, failed to develop a follow-up mechanism to oversee its practical implementation, a clear governance failure partly attributable to a change in the body responsible for the guidelines, which changed from the Task Force on Sustainable Development and Utilization to the Arctic Council Sustainable Development Working Group.[101] Moreover, the recently established Arctic Economic Council, a priority under the Canadian Chairmanship (2013–2015), does not hold the same standing for the subsequent US Chairmanship (2015–2017), leading many to question the Economic Council's sustainability.[102]

Such failures arise from key characteristics of the Arctic's social-ecological systems – interactive causation, non-linearity and path dependency – that are often unexamined by realist and ecological legal approaches to Arctic governance. Consequently, one might expect opportunities for governance failure to increase.

Science and financial resources inadvertently shape our understanding of the region, thereby contributing to governance and legal innovation. However, an underlying driver of governance failure includes gaps

[99] Ibid.

[100] An environmental impact assessment is a procedure designed to ensure that a scientific study is made of the environmental impacts of a proposed activity, with the involvement of all interested parties, before a permit is granted: Koivurova, *Environmental Impact Assessment in the Arctic*, above note 24, 154 and 170.

[101] Ibid., 170–171.

[102] Timo Koivurova, 'Implementing Guidelines for Environmental Impact Assessment in the Arctic' in Kees Bastmeijer and Timo Koivurova, eds., *Theory and Practice of Transboundary Environmental Impact Assessment* (Leiden: Martinus Nijhoff, 2008), 151–174, 172.

in research and data[103] and a lack of funding for logistically and financially constricted organisations like the Arctic Council. In a comprehensive review of the Arctic Climate Impact Assessment report, for example, Nilsson argues that a 'colonial view of the Arctic in which [it] is primarily of interest because of its global role' led to an assessment that placed a stronger focus on the global and the local, rather than the regional scale.[104] While Arctic governance to date has been relatively successful in gathering data and developing networks of cooperation among actors, it is the implementation of rules and regulations that is vitally important and current structures' inability to do so could lead to governance failure.

C A Realist Approach to Arctic Governance: Moving towards an Arctic Treaty System?

Arctic governance is becoming increasingly stagnant, which is reflected in the increasing complexity of its legal system as it seeks to break through system limitations, handle unexpected circumstances and adapt to rapid environmental change. On a one-dimensional continuum, harder legalisation in Arctic governance is premised on a predictive model where laws become increasingly linear, rigid, costly and top-heavy with regulatory prescriptions that cut through dynamical systems to ensure predictability and security.[105] Such legal certainty is useful for economic actors like mining companies who are more likely to invest in long-term activities with pre-decisional environmental impact assessments or cost–benefit analyses in place.[106]

However, rigidity often fails to accommodate or stimulate innovation, does not prioritise risk management and often ignores system

[103] These gaps include 'poor knowledge of coupling among, and thresholds within, bio-geophysical and socioeconomic processes to fully assess the effects of a changing climate, and to separate them from those due to other environmental stressors'. See Anisimov et al., 'Polar Regions,' above note 73.

[104] Keskitalo, Koivurova and Bankes, 'Introduction' in Koivurova, Keskitalo and Bankes, *Climate Governance in the Arctic*, above note 38, 15.

[105] Andreas Duit Victor Galaz, Karatine Echerberg and Jonas Ebbesson, 'Governance, Complexity, and Resilience' (2010) 20:3 *Global Environmental Change* 363–368; Ahjond S. Garmestani, Craig R. Allen and Heriberto Cabezas, 'Panarchy, Adaptive Management and Governance: Policy Option for Building Resilience' (2009) 87 *Nebraska Law Review* 1036–1054, 1037.

[106] J.B. Ruhl, 'Regulation by Adaptive Management – Is It Possible? (2005) 7:1 *Minnesota Journal of Law, Science and Technology* 21–57.

interdependencies.[107] It also sidelines 'the viability of informal, culturally grounded understandings as the basis for societal self-regulation and cohesion'.[108] Regimes are constructed based on different logics with different frameworks for interpreting and resolving problems, and path dependency can ultimately lead to stasis.[109] Constitutionally rooted and layered governmental systems, for example, often lead to trade-offs between small- and large-scale governance, where small-scale systems lack the capacity to deal with complex environmental problems, while larger ones miss the necessary trust and local expertise.[110]

In the Arctic, harder legalisation, by which I mean legally binding obligations that delegate authority to state-sanctioned institutions for interpreting and implementing the law, frames a discourse of geopolitics, high politics and a race for resources.[111] Based on this realist narrative, Arctic and non-Arctic states compete for control over the region's vast natural resources (including oil and natural gas), and the region becomes a theatre for remilitarisation.[112] A realist narrative anticipates a region where Arctic states assert their jurisdictional claims, as when Russia plants its flag on the Arctic seabed and Canadian leaders make annual trips to champion Canadian sovereignty in the region. A realist approach is also reflected in ongoing discussions surrounding the engagement of Russia in Arctic governance amid its geopolitical circumstances in the Ukraine.[113]

Realists argue that harder legalisation helps order relations, reduces transaction costs, strengthens the credibility of commitments, expands available political strategies and resolves problems of incomplete

[107] J.B. Ruhl, 'Adaptive Management for Natural Resources – Inevitable, Impossible, or Both?' (2008) 54 *Rocky Mountain Mineral Law Institute* 11.1–11.33, 11.22–11.23. See also Richard B. Stewart, 'A New Generation of Environmental Regulation?' (2001) 29:1 *Capital University Law Review* 21–182.

[108] Peer Zumbansen, 'Post-Regulatory Law: Chronicle of a Career Foretold,' Faculty Seminar, McGill University Faculty of Law, 18 February 2009, online at: www.mcgill.ca/files/legal-theory-workshop/PZumbansen_Post-Regulatory-Law.pdf.

[109] Jaye Ellis, 'Sustainable Development and Fragmentation in International Society' in Duncan French, ed., *Global Justice and Sustainable Development* (Leiden: Martinus Nijhoff, 2010), 57–75, 18.

[110] Termeer, Dewulf and van Lieshout, above note 17, 32.

[111] Oran R. Young, 'Arctic Governance – Pathways to the Future' (2010) 1:2 *Arctic Review on Law and Politics* 164–185, 173; Abbott and Snidal, 'Hard and Soft Law in International Governance,' above note 23, 421.

[112] Young, 'Arctic Governance – Pathways to the Future,' above note 111, 164–185.

[113] Ellis Quinn, 'Will Russia's Actions in Ukraine Affect Relations in the Arctic Council?' *Radio Canada International*, 21 March 2014, online at: www.rcinet.ca/en/2014/03/21/will-russias-actions-in-ukraine-affect-relations-in-the-arctic-council/.

contracting.[114] It makes the region legible by mapping its terrain, establishes property rights and regulates access to and ownership of resources.[115] It is also said that 'international law provides the very foundations of statehood: principles of sovereignty, recognition, territorial competence, non-intervention, and so on. Violations weaken the international legal system and are self-defeating.'[116]

It is no surprise then that some scholars, policy-makers and non-governmental organisations take a realist approach in advocating for a comprehensive treaty regime (an Arctic Treaty) that is both legally binding and open to legitimate stakeholders from outside the region.[117] Finland's 'Strategy for the Arctic Region', as an example, 'supports the plan to establish the Council as an international treaty-based organisation'.[118]

Multiple developments also signal a move towards harder legalisation in Arctic governance, including the 2008 Ilulissat Declaration;[119] the 2011 Agreement on Cooperation on Aeronautical and Maritime Search and Rescue in the Arctic;[120] the 2013 Agreement on Cooperation on Marine Oil Pollution, Preparedness and Response in the Arctic;[121] the adoption of an Arctic Council Observer Manual for Subsidiary Bodies; and the creation of a Permanent Arctic Council Secretariat.[122] A legally

[114] Abbott and Snidal, 'Hard and Soft Law in International Governance,' above note 23, 451.

[115] Jutta Brunnée and Stephen J. Toope, *Legitimacy and Legality in International Law: An Interactional Account* (Cambridge: Cambridge University Press, 2010). See also James C. Scott, *Seeing Like a State: How Certain Schemes to Improve the Human Condition Have Failed* (New Haven: Yale University Press, 1999).

[116] Abbott and Snidal, 'Hard and Soft Law in International Governance,' above note 23, 427.

[117] See D. Brent Carpenter, 'Warm is the New Cold: Global Warming, Oil, UNCLOS Article 76, and How an Arctic Treaty Might Stop a New Cold War' (2009) 39 *Environmental Law* 15–252; Sanjay Chaturvedi, 'Geopolitical Transformations: "Rising" Asia and the Future of the Arctic Council' in Thomas S. Axworthy, Timo Koivurova and Waliul Hasanat, eds., *The Arctic Council: Its Place in the Future of Arctic Governance* (Toronto: Walter and Duncan Gordon Foundation, 2012), 226–260; Timo Koivurova and Erik J. Molenaar, *International Governance and Regulation of the Marine Arctic: Overview and Gap Analysis* (Oslo: World Wildlife Fund, 2009); Koivurova and VanderZwaag, 'The Arctic Council at 10 Years,' above note 55; Melissa A. Verhaag, 'It Is Not Too Late: The Need for a Comprehensive International Treaty to Protect the Arctic Environment' (2002–2003) 15 *Georgetown International Environmental Law Review* 555–580.

[118] Thomas Nilsen, 'Finland Aims for Arctic Summit' *Barents Observer*, 4 December 2013, online at: http://barentsobserver.com/en/arctic/2013/12/finland-aims-arctic-summit-04-12.

[119] Above note 82. [120] 12 May 2011, Can TS 2013 No 6, in force 19 January 2013.

[121] 15 May 2013 (not yet in force).

[122] Larsen and Fondahl, *Arctic Human Development Report*, above note 77; Koivurova, 'Increasing Relevance of Treaties,' above note 52.

binding International Code for Ships Operating in Polar Waters is due to enter into force in January 2017, adopted by the International Maritime Organization (IMO) under the auspices of the 1974 International Convention for the Safety of Life at Sea (SOLAS Convention)[123] and the Protocol of 1978 relating to the International Convention for the Prevention of Pollution from Ships (MARPOL Convention).[124] Other processes include the draft Nordic Saami Convention, which aims to accommodate the self-determination of the Saami within the territory that they inhabit – a territory that spans four states.[125]

However, some scholars argue that a realist framing of Arctic governance sidelines narratives of cooperation for accounts of conflict and competition.[126] They are concerned with an already overcrowded governance landscape, inflexibility and the likely diminished role for indigenous peoples in decision-making.[127] They also worry about the legalisation of the lowest common denominator and poor implementation of existing hard law agreements.[128] Further concerns include the sovereignty and negotiation costs associated with a comprehensive treaty system, regional seas agreement or framework agreement.[129] If contemporary literature at the intersection of international law and international relations argues that 'the golden age of the treaty as the central tool of international cooperation is ending',[130] then why do we find ourselves returning to harder legalisation in the Arctic?

[123] 1 November 1974, 1184 UNTS 278, in force 15 May 1980.

[124] 17 February 1978, 1340 UNTS 62, in force 2 October 1983.

[125] See further, Nigel Bankes and Timo Koivurova, eds., *The Proposed Nordic Saami Convention: National and International Dimensions of Indigenous Property Rights* (Oxford: Hart Publishing, 2013).

[126] Byers, above note 85, 5.

[127] Duyck, above note 81, 24; Koivurova, Keskitalo and Bankes, 'Conclusions on Climate Governance in the Arctic' in Koivurova, Keskitalo and Bankes, *Climate Governance in the Arctic*, above note 38, 429–445, 416. See also Oran R. Young, 'Arctic Tipping Points: Governance in Turbulent Times' (2009) 41:1 *AMBIO: A Journal of the Human Environment* 75–84.

[128] See Koivurova and VanderZwaag, 'The Arctic Council at 10 Years,' above note 55. See also Protocol to the 1979 Convention on Long-Range Transboundary Air Pollution on Persistent Organic Pollutants (Aarhus Protocol), 24 June 1998, 223 UNTS 79, in force 23 October 2003; Stockholm Convention on Persistent Organic Pollutants, above note 70. Five of the eight Arctic states are party to the Aarhus Protocol, while seven of the eight Arctic states are party to the Stockholm Convention. The United States has signed but not ratified both treaties.

[129] Koivurova and VanderZwaag, 'The Arctic Council at 10 Years,' above note 55, 121.

[130] Raustiala, above note 22, 95.

III Accommodating the Arctic's Increasingly Complex Reality

The current patchwork approach to Arctic governance is insufficient because it incorporates the governance failures of both hard and soft law. Put simply, it is evident that 'in the face of rapid change it is now, more than ever, imperative to close the gap between new knowledge and the corresponding implementation of new policy. Resilience theory offers a useful framework to understand and cope with rapid change and potential regime shifts in the Arctic.'[131]

Scholars and policy-makers alike seemingly acknowledge that the Arctic requires a flexible governance system and seek a structural change that breaks with convention and provides for governance and legal innovation, but there are few bold suggestions for a new approach to Arctic governance and even fewer being implemented.[132] Barret Weber and Rob Shields come to a similar conclusion in noting that 'the urgency in the north is usually presented as something that we ought to be concerned about. But rarely do we hear about plans for concrete action and how real collective movements might begin.'[133] Fundamentally, there is a need for an international governance structure that can account for the complexity of the Arctic region. Otherwise, current institutions like the Arctic Council could become a façade that covers unilateral and uncoordinated policies.[134] As explained by David VanderZwaag, 'A common vision for regional governance has yet to be forged and opinions among academics, NGOs, bureaucrats and politicians continue to clash over the best ways forward.'[135]

The Arctic's complexity – its multiple state and non-state actors, jurisdictions and overlapping fora for decision-making – necessitates a flexible and cross-scale approach, but we are currently at a conceptual and institutional roadblock.[136] In 2014, Byers noted that actors must

[131] Carmack et al., above note 79, 60.

[132] Timothy M. Lenton, 'Arctic Climate Tipping Points' (2012) 41 *AMBIO: A Journal of the Human Environment* 10–22.

[133] Barret Weber and Rob Shields, 'The Virtual North: On the Boundaries of Sovereignty' (2010) 34:1 *Ethnic and Racial Studies* 103–120, 111.

[134] Koivurova and VanderZwaag, 'The Arctic Council at 10 Years,' above note 55, 192.

[135] David VanderZwaag, 'Climate Change and the Future of Arctic Governance: A Slushy Seascape and Hard Questions' in Koivurova, Keskitalo and Bankes, *Climate Governance in the Arctic*, above note 38, 403–429, 403.

[136] See Andonova and Mitchell, above note 4; Rachael Beddoe et al., 'Overcoming Systemic Roadblocks to Sustainability: The Evolutionary Redesign of Worldviews, Institutions, and Technologies' (2009) 106:8 *Proceedings of the National Academy of Sciences of the*

become serious about negotiating and implementing politically significant agreements on issues including oil spills, liability caps, maritime boundaries, continental shelves, international straits, central Arctic Ocean fisheries, demilitarisation of the Arctic Ocean, black carbon and Arctic haze.[137] Yet if predictive modelling is increasingly difficult in the face of the Arctic's second state change, how are we to go about this?

A Designing for Rapid Innovation in the Arctic

Legal mechanisms and regulatory goals must re-orient themselves towards *change*: innovation, adaptation and transformation.[138] But, how can we design a legal system that satisfies both the basic norms of administrative law and adaptive management?[139] I propose a new resilient dimension which underpins a reflexive law that is less rule-bound and is self-correcting, while still respecting basic procedural and organisational norms, such as the scope of participation of non-Arctic states, and follow-up monitoring for the Arctic environmental impact assessment guidelines.[140] For reflexive law to be truly durable, it must operate across scales and levels, and move towards a new model of 'collaborative, multi-party, multi-level, adaptive, problem-solving governance'.[141] This model requires a more comprehensive flow of information regarding environmental conditions and trends, including social behaviour, anthropogenic impacts and policy implementation.[142]

United States of America 2483–2489; Termeer, Dewulf and van Lieshout, above note 17, 29.

137 Statement by Michael Byers speaking at a conference on 'Passing the Arctic Council Torch: A Review of the Canadian Chairmanship and Preview of the Upcoming American Chairmanship' organised by the Centre for Strategic International Studies and the Centre for International Governance Innovation, Washington, DC, 30 September 2014.

138 Craig, 'Stationarity Is Dead,' above note 7, 30; Ruhl, 'Regulation by Adaptive Management,' above note 106, 28.

139 J.B. Ruhl, 'Panarchy and the Law' (2012) 17:3 *Ecology and Society* 31.

140 Jonas Ebbesson, 'The Rule of Law in Governance of Complex Socio-ecological Changes' (2010) 20 *Global Environmental Change* 414–422, 418.

141 Bradley C. Karkkainen, '"New Governance" in Legal Thought and in the World: Some Splitting as Antidote to Overzealous Lumping' (2004) 89 *Minnesota Law Review* 471–497, 473.

142 J.B. Ruhl, 'General Design Principles for Resilience and Adaptive Capacity in Legal Systems: Applications to Climate Change Adaptation Law' (2011) 89 *North Carolina Law Review* 1373–1401, 1398.

B Law as a System: Emergent, Non-linear and Self-organising

Legal systems and the laws that they produce can help or impinge upon our individual and collective ability to respond and adapt to environmental change, fundamentally leading to a normative discussion on law and resilience. Responding to the challenges of complex social-ecological systems, like the Arctic, requires legal systems that can alter as rapidly as the environment is changing. A better understanding of how our ecosystems and legal system interact can provide insight and potentially even solve this dilemma.

Complex adaptive systems, like ecosystems and legal systems, exhibit unpredictable future states where systems may be stable and predictable over some relevant time frame and scale, but are never entirely static as small changes in one condition lead to large changes in other conditions over time.[143] These systems operate on the cusp of order, processing flows of information, learning from and adapting to one another and anticipating behaviour throughout.[144] They are path dependent – with future system states based on previous states – and self-organised around deep structural 'if-then' rules that lend stability to system behaviour following perturbations, like hurricanes or tornadoes.[145] However, if pushed too far, these systems can tip into a state change.[146] What particularly distinguishes complex adaptive systems are their rules that encode patterns of responses to different environmental circumstances. It is also what makes them difficult to simulate.

[143] While there is neither a common definition, nor a commonly accepted way of measuring complexity, there are distinct characteristics that we can identify. Put simply, complexity science seeks to understand and explain how, without the use of a central controller, relatively simple individual components can organise themselves into complex collectives with emergent hard-to-predict behaviour. See further, Melanie Mitchell, *Complexity: A Guided Tour* (Oxford: Oxford University Press, 2009), 4; John H. Holland, 'Complex Adaptive Systems' (1992) 121:1 *Daedalus* 17–30, 21; Yaneer Bar-Yam, *Dynamics of Complex Systems* (Reading, MA: Addison-Wesley, 1997), 10; J.B. Ruhl, 'Law's Complexity: A Primer' (2008) 24:4 *Georgia State University Law Review* 885–911, 894; Michel van de Kerchove and Françoise Ost, translated by Iain Stewart, *Legal System Between Order and Disorder* (Oxford: Clarendon Press, 1994), 11.

[144] Holland, 'Complex Adaptive Systems,' above note 143, 19 and 24; Mitchell, *Complexity*, above note 143, 12.

[145] C.S. Holling, 'The Resilience of Terrestrial Ecosystems: Local Surprise and Global Change' in William C. Clark and R.E. Munn, eds., *Sustainable Development of the Biosphere* (Cambridge: Cambridge University Press, 1986), 292–317, 296; Ruhl, 'Law's Complexity,' above note 143, 902.

[146] Ruhl, 'Law's Complexity,' above note 143, 898–901.

Thinking of law as both a complex adaptive system and tool for managing other natural and social systems can help us better design legal systems for future challenges, like those faced in the Arctic.[147] Law is an emergent property of a legal system;[148] composed of a multitude of actors, ideas, rules and institutions, as well as rights, obligations and responsibilities, that interact and evolve into a network architecture that, over time, lays the foundation of a self-organised structure, giving rise to complex system dynamics.[149] It is path dependent, contains feedback loops and is resilient.[150] A resilient approach measures a system's adaptive capacity and focuses on opportunities for renewal, the emergence of new pathways and the system's ability to discover and generate new laws through the recombination and evolution of existing structures and processes.[151]

As a tool, law can manage other complex adaptive systems like ecosystems with a general acclaim of being able to impose order on social disorder.[152] Yet, with legal certainty comes reductionism, linearity and prediction based on a static understanding of the world.[153] While this can foster trust for adaptation, it often leads us to believe that 'we can isolate parts of ecosystems and adjust them without affecting anything else in the ecosystem [or other systems], when in fact the irreducibility of system behaviour requires us to take ecosystem-level properties into account whenever we touch any part of the system'.[154]

The fragmentation of international law is an often-discussed roadblock that leads to a disconnect between the resilience of legal systems,

[147] J.B. Ruhl, 'The Co-Evolution of Sustainable Development and Environmental Justice: Cooperation, then Competition, then Conflict' (1999) 9:2 *Duke Environmental Law and Policy Forum* 161–185, 163.

[148] Ruhl, 'Law's Complexity,' above note 143, 897.

[149] Ebbesson, 'The Rule of Law,' above note 140, 415; Ruhl, 'Law's Complexity,' above note 143, 895.

[150] Ruhl, 'Law's Complexity,' above note 143, 900; Johan Rockström et al., 'A Safe Operating Space for Humanity' (2009) 461:24 *Nature* 472–475; Craig, 'Stationarity is Dead,' above note 7, 37.

[151] Ruhl, 'General Design Principles,' above note 142, 1388; Carl Folke, 'Resilience: The Emergence of a Perspective for Social-Ecological Systems Analyses' (2006) 16 *Global Environmental Change* 253–267, 253 and 260; Holland, 'Complex Adaptive Systems,' above note 143, 26.

[152] Ruhl, 'Panarchy and the Law,' above note 139; van de Kerchove and Ost, above note 143, 110.

[153] J.B. Ruhl, 'Thinking of Environmental Law as a Complex Adaptive System: How to Clean Up the Environment by Making a Mess of Environmental Law' (1997) 34 *Houston Law Review* 933–1002, 940.

[154] Ruhl, 'Law's Complexity,' above note 143, 903.

the resilience of the laws that they produce and the resilience of the systems that they address.[155] Different legal systems function independently of one another, leading to overlapping and conflicting sets of norms. The isolation of environmental law from human rights law serves as a paradigmatic example where the two frameworks compete because their mandates have simply *not* envisioned solutions for complex issues like climate change.[156] In the Arctic, it is reflected in the often-competing priorities of environmental protection and economic development. Both cases necessitate a better understanding of how different systems evolve. In such a context, a complex systems ontology is particularly useful to better understand the co-evolution of legal systems, social systems and ecosystems, which continually reconstruct their strategies through cooperation, competition and conflict.[157] A resilient whole is thus not necessarily defined by resilient components.[158]

C *A Reflexive Law*

While neither legal certainty nor legal *un*certainty is conducive to sustainable governance, reflexive law could bring us one step closer to a resilient legal system.[159] Such a legal system is less rule-bound, while still respecting basic procedural and organisational norms, like the scope of participation, appeals and reviews in light of novel circumstances, impact assessments, follow-up monitoring and the consideration of alternative options.[160] Reflexive law provides actors with a space to accountably and transparently self-correct in response to change.[161] Actors can implement long-term macro-principles as a part of an overall adaptation strategy (ruling by principle), while decision-makers who are closest to the problem simultaneously design adaptation actions based on local context (ruling by objectives). Comprehensive preservation is impossible and some losses are inevitable. However, reflexive law can

[155] Ibid., 908; Ruhl, 'General Design Principles,' above note 142, 1382–1383.

[156] Siobhan McInerney-Lankford, Mac Darrow and Lavanya Rajamani, *Human Rights and Climate Change: A Review of the International Legal Dimensions* (Washington, DC: World Bank, 2011), 7, 47 and 50; Stephen Humphreys, *Human Rights and Climate Change* (Cambridge: Cambridge University Press, 2010), 11–12.

[157] Ruhl, 'The Co-Evolution of Sustainable Development and Environmental Justice,' above note 147, 168–170.

[158] Ruhl, 'General Design Principles,' above note 142, 1383 and 1388.

[159] Ebbesson, 'The Rule of Law,' above note 140, 416. [160] Ibid., 417.

[161] Westley et al., above note 7, 769.

empower regulators and managers to cope with losses without incurring legal liability.[162]

Unfortunately, reflexive law has yet to be implemented in Arctic governance or elsewhere. Nonetheless, elements of it, such as ecosystem-based management and adaptive management, already exist.[163] Adaptive management and ecosystem-based management, more broadly, resonate with transgovernmental networks and the notion of a disaggregated state, as put forward by Slaughter. The capacity of networks to adapt to and shape change becomes one way of organising and innovating for complex adaptive systems.[164] In her work on social innovation and social-ecological systems, Westley also contends that 'successful adaptive governance systems, often emergent and self-organising, connect individuals, networks, organisations, agencies, and institutions at multiple organisational levels with ecosystem dynamics'.[165]

Ecosystem-based management, implemented through adaptive management, is based on the notion that resilience *should* be managed as a unit rather than through individual regimes and agencies.[166] Six qualities are ideal for such adaptive management:

1. Problem and context dynamically alter in response to environmental conditions and management intervention;
2. Decision-makers have incomplete knowledge of the problem (uncertainty is high), but are able to manipulate features of the problem (controllability is high) without causing substantial or irreversible damage (risk is low);
3. The problem context allows for iterative decision-making;
4. Decision-makers have clear management objectives and the methodological capacity and technological feasibility to use experimentation, option testing, monitoring, assessment, as well as learning to reduce uncertainty and adjust management decisions in policy-relevant time frames;[167]

[162] Ruhl, 'Law's Complexity,' above note 143, 904; Westley et al., above note 7, 770.

[163] Ruhl, 'Panarchy and the Law,' above note 139.

[164] See Michele-Lee Moore and Frances Westley, 'Surmountable Chasms: Networks and Social Innovation for Resilient Systems' (2011) 16:1 *Ecology and Society* 5.

[165] Westley et al., above note 7, 769.

[166] Ruhl, 'General Design Principles,' above note 142, 1373, 1388 and 1390; J.B. Ruhl and Robert L. Fischman, 'Adaptive Management in the Courts' (2010) 95:2 *Minnesota Law Review* 424–484, 430; Ruhl, 'Regulation by Adaptive Management,' above note 106, 53.

[167] Westley et al., above note 7, 770.

5. Decision-makers have sufficient financial and other resources, as well as the necessary stakeholder support to design, implement and adjust management decisions based on novel information; and
6. Adaptive management methods remain within the normative conditions associated with the problem.[168]

In short, by keeping decision-makers linked through weak ties and information, transgovernmental networks can enhance how a system responds to challenges across temporal, spatial, hierarchical or cognitive scales.[169]

Ultimately, adaptive and ecosystem-based management must be implemented through laws and regulations.[170] Yet, how do we develop a framework for translating social-ecological resilience theory into legal doctrine? More practically, how can we adaptively manage a complex adaptive legal system designed to adaptively manage complex social-ecological systems?[171] The latter question may seem like a riddle, but is an immense and impending challenge that will continue to surface in discussions of both global environmental governance and international environmental law.

Research at the intersection of law and resilience is nascent. Aside from a handful of academic case studies conducted with a national focus by a relatively small group of scholars, the practical application of this research is even less developed. While there is no panacea, scholars like J.B. Ruhl, Michel van der Kerchove and Françoise Ost contend that the building blocks of legal systems can be intentionally programmed to respond to high variability and low predictability based on context.[172] The legal system should assume continual, unpredictable and non-linear change instead. It should build upon existing networks – their flows of information, social capital and inherent coerciveness – as a means for organising combinatorial innovation. Decision-makers should transparently 'test hypotheses' by choosing from and combining a range of structures (such as organisations), instruments (such as declarations, treaties and agreements), processes (such as judicial review) and substantive and procedural laws. These legal 'building blocks' are

[168] Robin Cundis Craig and J.B. Ruhl, 'Designing Administrative Law for Adaptive Management' (2014) 67 *Vanderbilt Law Review* 1–87, 19, 23 and 26.
[169] See Moore and Westley, above note 164.
[170] Ruhl, 'Panarchy and the Law,' above note 139. [171] Ibid.
[172] van de Kerchove and Ost, above note 143, 105; Holland, 'Complex Adaptive Systems,' above note 143, 23; Ruhl, 'General Design Principles,' above note 142, 1401.

particularly useful in tailoring macro-principles to localised contexts, such as implementing novel technologies, phasing out existing processes (such as pollutants) or managing locally specific change (such as fisheries management). However, in order for such a reflexive legal system to be effective, it necessitates a steady stream of research funding that can gather, filter, decipher, analyse and broker traditional ecological knowledge and scientific data for both policy-makers and the public. It is this research capability that, ultimately, connects Arctic governance to broader environmental structures.

Conclusion

Within the framework of networked governance, the Arctic becomes a fascinating case study. Theoretically, the legalisation of Arctic environmental governance is interesting due to a combination of governance challenges, including multiple state and non-state actors, jurisdictions and overlapping fora for hard and soft law decision-making. Empirically, it is relevant due to the immediacy of the challenge. Methodologically, the case leads to questions regarding the implications of novel approaches for both international law and international relations.

A one-dimensional continuum between ecological and realist legal ontologies cannot accommodate the Arctic's increasingly complex reality. While an ecological approach allows for generative action, it has no teeth, and a realist approach is unlikely to succeed due to sovereignty costs, negotiation costs and inflexibility. Meanwhile, a patchwork is not an appropriate solution because it incorporates the governance failure of both approaches. I thus introduce a new dimension that is grounded in a systems perspective. A complex systems ontology is crucial because it can help us better understand how alternative proposals for Arctic governance, like reflexive law, could lead to rapid legal innovation. Unfortunately, reflexive law has yet to be implemented. Nonetheless, elements of it, like ecosystem-based management, already exist and suggest that decision-makers move away from prediction and build upon existing networks and expertise in tailoring macro-principles to localised contexts. However, the implementation of reflexive law necessitates financing and committed actors who can maintain steady and unbiased flows of information.

In order to outline and define a reflexive legal system that can account for the complexity of the region, we must return to the drawing board. While scholars call for both governance and legal innovation, demanding a new understanding of sovereignty, space, scale and power, discrepancies in Arctic governance provide evidence for the fact that, in order to clarify a shared vision or 'Northern Strategy', we must first pick apart our current Arctic puzzle. We may ultimately find that the future of Arctic governance necessitates a better understanding of the mental maps of decision-makers and the evolution of legal, social, economic and ecological systems in the region. Future research must distinguish between co-evolutionary processes: the resilience of the current Arctic legal system, the resilience of the laws that it produces and the resilience of other social and natural systems that this law addresses. It must also precisely define a reflexive law for the Arctic and how we can get there.

8

Environmental Government Networks with Asian Examples

HITOMI KIMURA

This chapter examines the increasing prominence of environmental government networks as forms of international governance, with the term 'environmental government networks' inspired by Anne-Marie Slaughter's use of the term 'government networks' to refer to cooperative arrangements across borders between and among government agencies and related regulatory agents that seek to respond to global issues.[1] Drawing on Asian examples, the chapter explains the various types of networks working on environmental issues, their roles and functions, and some of the benefits and limitations of employing networks to address issues of environmental governance. The chapter draws attention to the potential for environmental government networks to facilitate information sharing and coordination between states and officials, and between governments and other stakeholders, while also noting that language differences and divergent geo-political concerns can impede the functioning of these networks. I argue that while these networks possess many of the benefits generally attributed to networks as forms of global governance, such as flexibility, low cost, effectiveness and inclusivity, the existence of environmental government networks also raises the same concerns about network legitimacy and accountability that have been identified in the other chapters within this collection.

The bibliographic details for works published in Japanese have been translated into English by the author.

[1] Anne-Marie Slaughter, *A New World Order* (Princeton: Princeton University Press, 2004), 14. See also Anne-Marie Slaughter, 'Governing the Global Economy through Government Networks' in Michael Byers, ed., *The Role of Law in International Politics: Essays in International Relations and International Law* (Oxford: Oxford University Press, 2001), 178–205 and Anne-Marie Slaughter, 'Global Government Networks, Global Information Agencies, and Disaggregated Democracy' (2002–2003) 24:4 *Michigan Journal of International Law* 1041–1075.

I Overview and Categorisation of Environmental Government Networks

Environmental government networks defy simple classification. Nonetheless, it is possible to distinguish between four main types of networks. I identify these four networks by the following labels: (1) transgovernmental regulatory networks; (2) intergovernmental organisation networks; (3) research-oriented networks; and (4) regional networks.

Transgovernmental regulatory networks are composed of government officials and other regulatory agents from different states whose efforts aim to address environmental issues that are not contained within the borders of a single state. The members of these transgovernmental regulatory networks work in tandem with non-governmental experts and scientific organisations, through various fora, including international conferences, organisational structures and free-standing committees, with a view to securing improved standard-setting and the dissemination of information for the harmonisation of national policies. Examples of these transgovernmental regulatory networks within the environmental sphere include the Intergovernmental Panel on Climate Change (IPCC),[2] the Intergovernmental Platform on Biodiversity and Ecosystem Services (IPBES),[3] and the International Union for the Conservation of Nature (IUCN).[4] The various intergovernmental negotiating committees (INCs) established by the UN General Assembly and the UN Environment Programme (UNEP) also provide additional examples.

The issues attracting the attention of these transgovernmental regulatory networks are varied, but include climate change, biodiversity policy, ecosystems management, chemical usage and sustainable development. Their membership is also varied, with the IPCC attracting membership from 195 countries, the IPBES attracting involvement from 115 governments (as well as another 20 observers) and the IUCN being able to count over 200 government agencies among its members, many of whom work at the local and subnational levels. These networks do, however, share a number of core functions, including scientific assessment, knowledge development and capacity building, as well as negotiation and policy-making support.

With some similarities to the first category, my second category of environmental government networks consists of those government

[2] Online at: www.ipcc.ch. [3] Online at: www.ipbes.net.

[4] Also known as the International Union for the Conservation of Nature and Natural Resources, its website can be found online at: www.iucn.org.

networks that have arisen from the activities of major intergovernmental organisations, often to provide a focal point for environmentally related discussions. Examples include the networks of government officials hosted by major intergovernmental organisations such as the Group of Eight (G8) and Group of Twenty (G20) Environment Ministers Meetings, the Major Economies Meeting on Energy Security and Climate Change (MEM) and the Major Economies Forum on Energy and Climate (MEF).[5] The meetings of ministers and their officials hosted by the bloc of countries known as the BASIC group provide an additional example. Under the BASIC banner, Brazil, South Africa, India and China have committed to act jointly on matters such as greenhouse gas emission reductions.

As with the transgovernmental regulatory networks, the issues attracting the intergovernmental organisation networks cut across the full range of issues affecting the environment, including climate change, energy use and conservation, and biodiversity. However, the membership levels tend to be much lower, and more focused on government, ranging from as few as four and eight member states to seventeen and twenty. The core functions of these networks are agenda setting in a political sense, dialogue facilitation and the formation of common positions.

A third type of government network worth mentioning are the research-oriented networks sponsored or supported by governments that bring together researchers and research-focused organisations to support and encourage information sharing and facilitate interaction between researchers and stakeholders. Compared to other research-oriented networks, this type of government network always involves the presence of governments, but their degree of initiative to take within the operation depends on each government network. Examples include the International Research Network for Low Carbon Societies and the Low Carbon Asia Research Network (LCS-RNet and LoCARNet)[6] and

[5] The Major Economies Process on Energy Security and Climate Change, involving 17 major economies, was an initiative launched by US President George W. Bush in 2007, while the Major Economies Forum on Energy and Climate is an initiative launched by US President Barack Obama in 2009. See further, US Department of State, 'Major Economies Forum on Energy and Climate', online at: www.state.gov/e/oes/climate/mem/.

[6] Online at: http://lcs-rnet.org/. See further Midori Sasaki and Tomoko Ishikawa, 'Promotion of Research towards Low-carbon Societies: Contributions of the International Research Network for Low Carbon Societies (LCS-RNet)' (2012) 165 *Environmental Quarterly* 176–183; Kyoko Miwa, 'International Research Network for

the Asia-Pacific Network for Global Change Research (APN).[7] Here again, membership levels are at more manageable levels so as to support the core functions of providing policy-making support through engagement in a science-policy dialogue and by facilitating interaction between policy-makers and scientists.

Lastly, as the name suggests, regional networks are those government networks that have been established with a deliberate regional focus, including regional government networks focused on environmental issues with a global scale.[8] Asia provides numerous examples of regional government networks, including the Acid Deposition Monitoring Network in East Asia (EANET),[9] the Asian Co-benefits Partnership (ACP),[10] the Asia Pacific Adaptation Network (APAN),[11] the Asian Environmental Compliance and Enforcement Network (AECEN),[12] the Asian Network for Prevention of Illegal Transboundary Movement of Hazardous Wastes,[13] the Asia-Pacific Forum for Environment and Development (APFED),[14] the Tripartite Environment Ministers Meeting among Japan, China and Korea (TEMM)[15] and the Regional 3 R Forum in Asia.[16]

Low Carbon Societies: A Platform for the Scientific Information on LCS Research and Policies' (2011) 160 *Environmental Quarterly* 40–50.

7 Online at: www.apn-gcr.org/. See further, Akio Takemoto, 'Sustainable Development through Scientific Capacity Building under Asia-Pacific Network for Global Change Research (APN)' (2014) 173 *Environmental Quarterly* 45–54; Hiroaki Hashizume, 'Enhancement of Global Change Research in the Asia-Pacific Region: Challenges of the Asia-Pacific Network for Global Change Research' (2008) 150 *Environmental Quarterly* 79–87. See also *Annual Report 2013–2014* (Kobe: Asia-Pacific Network for Global Change Research, 2014).

8 Regarding the current evolution towards regionalism, see Hitomi Kimura, 'Does the Regional or Bilateral Climate Regime Harm the Universality of the Multilateral UNFCCC Process?' in Carter B. Keyes and Olivia C. Lucero, eds., *New Developments in Global Warming Research* (Hauppauge, NY: Nova Science Publishers, 2013), 103–116.

9 Online at: www.eanet.asia. See further, Soichiro Seki, 'Overview of the Second Expert Meeting of the Acid Deposition Monitoring Network in East Asia' (1995) 99 *Environmental Quarterly* 109–130.

10 Online at: www.cobenefit.org.

11 Online at: www.asiapacificadapt.net.

12 Online at: www.aecen.org.

13 Further information is available from the Japanese Ministry of Environment, online at: www.env.go.jp/en/recycle/asian_net/. See also Katsumasa Seimaru, 'Establishment of the Asian Network for Prevention of Illegal Transboundary Movements of Hazardous Wastes' (2005) 136 *Environmental Quarterly* 93–98.

14 Online at: www.apfed.net/.

15 Further information is available from the Japanese Ministry of Environment, online at: www.env.go.jp/earth/coop/coop/english/dialogue/temm.html.

16 Further information is available from the United Nations Centre for Regional Development, online at: www.uncrd.or.jp/index.php?menu=389.

The work of the Asia Pacific Partnership on Clean Development and Climate provides an example of a regional network that was focused on a global environmental issue, until its closure in 2011.[17]

As with the other types of environmental government networks, the target areas can vary, as can the core functions, with the regional networks having focused on policy-making support, information sharing, capacity building and stakeholder dialogue, while also encouraging regional cooperation. The number of governments involved in the regional networks also varies, from as few as three and four, to membership levels of 16 and 17 (for the AECEN and the Regional 3 R Forum respectively). Some regional networks also include organisations and non-governmental groups within their membership (with the ACP providing an example).

II Characteristics of Major Environmental Government Networks

A Transgovernmental Regulatory Networks

The Intergovernmental Panel on Climate Change (or 'IPCC' as it is often called) is an intergovernmental body that was established in 1988 to provide a scientific view on the current state of knowledge in climate change and its potential environmental and socio-economic impacts. Governments take part in the main plenary sessions where the main decisions are made, including the acceptance, adoption and approval of reports. The IPCC assessment reports have influenced and accelerated international negotiations in relation to the United Nations Framework Convention on Climate Change (UNFCCC),[18] the Kyoto Protocol to the UNFCCC[19] and the Paris Agreement.[20] The Paris Agreement is the successor agreement to the Kyoto Protocol and is expected to enter into force in 2016.[21] The networks of scientists interacting with governments provide the latest scientific evidence and data on increased global warming or frequent extreme weather events. Their climate impact analyses have identified specific regions (for example, in Asia and Africa) or issues (such as water security and agricultural production)

[17] Online at: www.asiapacificpartnership.org/english/default.aspx.

[18] 9 May 1992, 1771 UNTS 107, in force 21 March 1994.

[19] 11 December 1997, 2303 UNTS 162, in force 16 February 2005.

[20] On earlier impacts, see Shinya Murase, 'Scientific Knowledge on Climate Change and International Legislation' (2008) 572 *International Issues* 46–58.

[21] UNFCCC, 'Adoption of the Paris Agreement: Proposal by the President: Draft Decision -/CP.21', UN Doc FCCC/CP/2015/L.9/Rev.1 (12 December 2015), online at: http://unfccc.int/resource/docs/2015/cop21/eng/l09r01.pdf.

that are greatly affected by climate change and which require urgent intervention.

The Paris Agreement mentions the need for limiting the temperature increase to 2 degrees Celsius above pre-industrial levels, taking into account results from the IPCC Fifth Assessment Report. It also refers to the more ambitious target of limiting temperature increases to 1.5 degrees Celsius, which reflects the aspirations of the 'High Ambition Coalition' – a bloc formed at the Conference of the Parties in Paris that was led by the European Union, the Marshall Islands and the Alliance of Small Island States (AOSIS) (a number of which are located in Asia). This broadly based network wanted the IPCC to provide a special report on the impacts if global warming was limited to 1.5 degrees Celsius, and the related global greenhouse gas emission pathways. This effort was notable for those in Asia, where it is becoming increasingly difficult to form a single network that speaks with one voice in climate negotiations, in contrast with the unity of the Group of 77 plus China at the third Conference of the Parties held in Kyoto. This lack of unity is due to the significant degree of diversity among the developing countries in Asia, taking into account those with emerging economies such as China and India, members of the Least Developed Countries such as Bangladesh and Nepal, and members of AOSIS such as the Marshall Islands and Tuvalu.

The Intergovernmental Platform on Biodiversity and Ecosystem Services (IPBES) was established in 2012 as an independent intergovernmental body and like the IPCC, it is open to all UN member states. Established 20 years after the adoption of the Convention on Biological Diversity (CBD),[22] the purpose of the IPBES is to assess the state of global biodiversity and ecosystems and to deepen the links between science and policy. From an eligible list of 193 UN member states, 121 countries are members. This network also includes over 20 observers, who are scientists, representatives of non-governmental organisations and indigenous peoples.

The International Union for the Conservation of Nature (IUCN) was established in 1948 as the world's oldest global environmental organisation. It has also become the world's largest professional global conservation network, comprising more than 1,200 member organisations. IUCN includes within its membership more than 200 government agencies and departments, and more than 900 non-government organisations. Funded

[22] 5 June 1992, 1760 UNTS 79, in force 29 December 1993.

by these member organisations, and by bilateral and multilateral agencies, foundations and corporations, IUCN implements projects all over the world. IUCN is also responsible for setting global standards, such as the IUCN Red List of Threatened Species in its capacity as technical advisor to the Convention on International Trade in Endangered Species of Wild Fauna and Flora (CITES).[23] Moreover, the IUCN, by providing scientific knowledge, influences the development of international environmental laws, policies and conventions, such as the Convention on Wetlands of International Importance Especially as Waterfowl Habitat (Ramsar Convention),[24] the Convention Concerning the Protection of the World Cultural and Natural Heritage (World Heritage Convention),[25] CITES and the CBD.[26] Even at the operational stage of a convention regime, IUCN continues to play a core role. For example, IUCN experts conduct research on nominated natural heritage sites and report their findings to the World Heritage Committee.

Environmental government networks such as IUCN coexist with existing international environmental organisations with an intergovernmental focus, such as UNEP, and other international organisations such as the United Nations Educational, Scientific and Cultural Organization (UNESCO).[27] Some of these environmental government networks, especially the transgovernmental regulatory networks identified in the work of Anne-Marie Slaughter, play a pivotal role in bringing an issue to the top of the global agenda and by providing the scientific basis for urging states to engage in standard-setting activities such as treaty-making. As Slaughter explains, government networks, both horizontal and vertical, can coexist with a traditional model of the international system, in which unitary states negotiate formal legal agreements, and operate on an equal plane within international organisations.[28]

An illustrative example can be found in the work of the INCs, established by the UN General Assembly and by UNEP to promote the

[23] 3 March 1973, 993 UNTS 243, in force 1 July 1975. See further, Masahiro Nishii, *Global Environmental Agreements: Evolution, Development and Implementation* (Tokyo: Yuuhikaku, 2005), 375–378.

[24] 2 February 1971, 996 UNTS 245, in force 21 December 1975.

[25] 16 November 1972, 1037 UNTS, in force 17 December 1975.

[26] Above note 22.

[27] Some have suggested that UNESCO taught states the value and utility of science policy organisations: Martha Finnemore, 'International Organizations as Teachers of Norms at the United Nations Educational, Scientific, and Cultural Organization and Science Policy' (1993) 47:4 *International Organization* 565–597.

[28] Slaughter, *A New World Order*, above note 1, 262–263.

negotiation of various international environmental conventions, including the UNFCCC, the Stockholm Convention on Persistent Organic Pollutants,[29] the Convention on the Prior Informed Consent Procedure for Certain Hazardous Chemicals and Pesticides in International Trade (Rotterdam Convention),[30] the Minamata Convention on Mercury[31] and the United Nations Convention to Combat Desertification in Countries Experiencing Serious Drought and/or Desertification, Particularly in Africa (UNCCD).[32] The text of the UNFCCC was adopted after a series of negotiations carried out under the auspices of an INC. In this sense, an INC can be described as a temporal government network set up by the potential parties to promote the negotiation of new conventions in pursuit of specific global policy objectives. States involved in the early stages of the negotiations are also in a better position to protect their national interests by setting the terms for bargaining both the substance and the procedures.[33]

B Intergovernmental Organisation Networks

In 1975, in an attempt to formulate a concerted response to the oil crisis, world leaders from France, the United States, the United Kingdom, West Germany and Japan met for what was to become the first meeting of the Group of Five. The Group of Five was expanded over time to include Italy, Canada and Russia, and the G8 now meets annually to discuss (and set) global economic policy. Since the holding of the Rio Earth Summit in 1992, meetings of first the Group of Seven (G7) and then the G8 Environment Ministers have also been held to discuss global environmental problems.[34] In 1999, a new G20 of Finance Ministers and Central Bank Governors was launched as a forum for informal dialogue among ministers from the then G7, the member states of the European Union, and 11 emerging economies.[35] Over time, the G20 has grown in

[29] 22 May 2001, 2256 UNTS 119, in force 17 May 2004.

[30] 10 September 1998, 2244 UNTS 337, in force 24 February 2004.

[31] 10 October 2013, not yet in force.

[32] 17 June 1994, 1954 UNTS 3, in force 26 December 1996.

[33] Oran R. Young, 'Negotiating an International Climate Regime: The Institutional Bargaining for Environmental Governance' in Nazli Choucri, ed., *Global Accord: Environmental Challenges and International Responses* (Cambridge, MA: MIT Press, 1993), 431–452.

[34] Meeting documentation is available online at: www.g8.utoronto.ca/environment/.

[35] Press Release, 'Finance Minister Paul Martin Chosen as Inaugural Chairperson of New Group of Twenty', Washington, DC, 25 September 1999, online at: www.g8.utoronto.ca /finance/fm992509.htm.

stature to replace the G8 as the premier economic council, but the G8 continues to meet, hosting discussions on climate change, global warming and biodiversity.

Although the declarations adopted by the G8 and the G20 are not legally binding texts, they have political importance in shaping global agendas. The G8 and G20 meetings are attended by heads of state, heads of government and government ministers, along with working-level government officials. Officials are influenced by the meeting outcomes, with Japan, for example, having developed its low-carbon action plan in 2009 to reflect the content of the 'Declaration of Leaders Meeting of Major Economies on Energy Security and Climate Change', adopted at the Tokyo Summit held in July 2008.[36]

Other networks also exist for the facilitation of policy-making between the leading industrialised countries. For example, US President George W. Bush established the Major Economies Meeting on Energy Security and Climate Change (MEM) in 2007 to facilitate an across-governments dialogue on climate change between 17 major economies.[37] Subsequently, the Obama administration launched the Major Economies Forum on Energy and Climate (MEF) in 2009, with one of its stated goals being to generate the political leadership necessary to achieve a successful outcome at the annual UN climate negotiations.[38] Thus, while both fora were established as US-initiated government networks in response to dissatisfaction with the UNFCCC-based multilateral approach, paradoxically, these government networks have been influenced deeply by the UNFCCC-based negotiations in determining their goals and activities.

As mentioned above, the network known by the acronym BASIC consists of environment ministers from the emerging economies of Brazil, South Africa, India and China. It was established at the Copenhagen climate summit in 2009 to formulate a common position in a context where emerging economies were being pressured to adopt similar reduction targets as developed counties. The BASIC countries asked for a legally binding global agreement and ambitious targets for developed countries, but they were successful only in securing relief from targets for developing

[36] The English text of this declaration can be found in the document collection of the Institute of Oriental Culture of the University of Tokyo at: www.ioc.u-tokyo.ac.jp /~worldjpn/documents/texts/summit/20080709.D1E.html.

[37] See above note 5.

[38] Major Economies Forum on Energy and Climate, 'About' (undated), online at: www .majoreconomiesforum.org/about.html.

countries.[39] Climate negotiations have become the touchstone for how environmental treaties are impacting emerging economies.

C *Research-oriented Networks*

Transnational networks of researchers and academics comprise a third type of network. Operating with a relatively high degree of independence from government,[40] these networks are able to claim scientific neutrality and objectivity. An example of one such network is the International Research Network for Low Carbon Societies (LCS-RNet), which was proposed by Japan at the G8 Environment Minister Meeting in 2008, and established by researchers in 2009 as a collaborative platform through which to contribute to both policy-making processes at the national level and international policy-making processes on climate change. The network members include 17 research institutions registered by governments from seven countries (specifically France, Germany, India, Italy, Japan, Korea and the United Kingdom).

A related organisation is the Low Carbon Asia Research Network (LoCARNet), which was set up in 2012 to facilitate the formulation and implementation of science-based policies for low-carbon development in Asia, based on the proposal by LCS-RNet and Japan at the ASEAN+3 Environmental Ministers' Meeting. LoCARNet is a network of prominent researchers, who engage in science policy dialogue and North-South-South collaboration. It also holds side events at Conferences of the Parties (COPs) to influence climate negotiations. The Institute for Global Environmental Strategies (ICES), with its headquarters in Hayama, Japan, serves as a secretariat for both LoCARNet and LCS-RNet.[41]

Some research-oriented networks, however, do not operate independently from government. The Asia-Pacific Network for Global Change Research (APN) is one example. It was established in 1996 as a network of

[39] See further, Lavanya Rajamani, 'The Making and Unmaking of the Copenhagen Accord' (2010) 59 *International and Comparative Law Quarterly* 824–844.

[40] It is thought that British researchers and scientists, for example, enjoy a relatively high degree of independence for their research from the government based on long-held support for the 'Haldane principle', which requires specific research funding decisions to be made independently of government, combined with a more recent movement towards evidence-based policy-making, which requires more economic and scientific robustness to support decisions. See further, Hitomi Kimura, 'Role of Researcher/Academia in Making UK Low Carbon Policy' (2013) 2:3B *Journal of Environmental Science and Engineering* 146–154.

[41] Online at: www.iges.or.jp/en/.

member governments for the promotion of policy-related research related to global change in the Asia Pacific region. Its origins date back to the holding of the White House Conference on Science and Economics Research Related to Global Change in April 1990, when then US President George H.W. Bush invited countries to promote North–South scientific cooperation at the intergovernmental level by creating three regional networks: Europe and Africa; North and South America; and the Asia-Pacific region. The APN secretariat is based in Kobe, Japan.

D Regional Networks

Regionally based government networks focused on environmental issues reflect the regional character of many environmental challenges. In Asia, the regional networks tend to be structured informally and are issue-specific.[42] These networks are not necessarily prominent in setting government policy and agendas, but they can play a crucial role in reducing diplomatic tension between neighbouring countries that have potential territorial disputes.

The Tripartite Environment Ministers Meeting (TEMM) is one example. The TEMM was launched in 1999 to promote dialogue and cooperation among ministers from Japan, China and Korea. TEMM has worked as a platform for discussing crucial regional environmental problems such as air pollution, and has continued to function in times of political and diplomatic tension.

The Acid Deposition Monitoring Network in East Asia (EANET) was established in 1998 at the initiative of Japan to formulate common understandings about the situation of acid rain. As a monitoring network, it also provides a means for sharing basic information among member countries and to promote international cooperation in East Asia. EANET started its operation in 2001, with an intention to also share information about the experiences of Europe and North America. EANET currently has 54 monitoring sites in 13 member states.

Regional networks of states have also developed to address global environmental issues such as climate change. For example, in the Asia Pacific region, an Asia Pacific Partnership on Clean Development and Climate was created, composed of seven major emitters located in the

[42] Hiroshi Ota, 'Possibility of Regional Cooperation on Environmental and Natural Resources in the Northeast Asia' in Shunji Matsuoka, ed., *Environmental Governance in Asia* (Tokyo: Keisoushobou, 2013), 152.

Asia Pacific region (Australia, Canada, China, India, Japan, Korea and the United States). The Asia Pacific Partnership was established in 2006 to enhance partnerships between the public and private sectors and to promote best practices and technologies across a range of key sectors, such as steel and aluminium. The body was initially criticised on the basis that it had established itself as an alternative to the Kyoto Protocol processes. The APP suspended its operations in 2011, when the Global Superior Energy Performance Partnership took up the work of accelerating the transition to a clean energy future.[43]

The Asian Environmental Compliance and Enforcement Network (AECEN) was established in 2005 by environmental agency leaders from 13 Asian countries. Its objective is to improve compliance with environmental legal requirements in Asia. The organisation maintains an environmental impact assessment clearinghouse to share knowledge on international and regional best practices in implementing the assessment. The North American Free Trade Agreement environmental enforcement network is also a regional government network, but plays a stronger role of implementing the agenda and complementing the role of an international organisation.[44]

III The Impact of Environmental Government Networks

Although the IUCN was established in 1948, the great majority of environmental government networks were established in the 1990s, when the world's attention became focused on the scope and extent of transboundary environmental problems. Additional networks concerned with issues of climate change were established in the late 2000s in the lead-up to the negotiation of the Kyoto Protocol. The main functions of environmental government networks are information sharing and capacity building, rather than regulation, although, as will be discussed below, some government networks have had a role in setting standards. These networks have also established a role for scientists, government officials and parliamentarians.

[43] See further, Clean Energy Ministerial, online at: www.cleanenergyministerial.org/Our-Work/Initiatives/ Buildings-and-Industry. See also Takashi Kono, *Objective and Overview of Global Superior Energy Performance Partnership* (Tokyo: Ministry of Economy, Trade and Industry, 2012), online at: www.meti.go.jp/policy/energy_environment/global_warming/pdf/Objective_and_Overview_of_GSEP_METI.pdf.

[44] Slaughter, *A New World Order*, above note 1, 200.

Overall, however, a key distinctive feature of these networks is the role played by governments, with technological innovation having enhanced the facilitation of information sharing and the interaction between and within networks and experts. Asian networks are learning from European governments about the use of blogs and other social media such as Twitter to enhance real-time communication through government networks such as the European Environmental Information and Observation Network (EIONET)[45] – an internet-based information network operated by the European Environment Agency (EEA).[46] The European Commission and national regulatory networks also work together for effective enforcement of various regulations in relation to such matters as electronic communication and energy. The Commission has a supervisory and policy-making role and promotes the establishment of national regulatory networks, while the national regulatory authorities deal with the day-to-day application of the law by using benchmark studies, policy documents and guidelines.[47]

A A Role in the Creation of International Conventions

Some government networks lead to the creation of international conventions. The IPCC and INC, for example, led to the creation of the UNFCCC and the subsequent Kyoto Protocol. The IUCN, under the mandate of what it called 'Project MAR' dealing with the conservation and management of temperate marshes, bogs and other wetlands, was instrumental in bringing about the Ramsar Convention,[48] with the support of the International Waterfowl Research Bureau. The World Heritage Convention[49] was the result of two conventions created by

45 Online at: www.eionet.europa.eu/.

46 Online at: www.eea.europa.eu/. For a Japanese discussion of these communications, see Hiroshi Hosono, 'Utilisation of the Internet in International Information Networks Managed by Administrative Organisations in the USA and European Countries' (1998) 110 *Environmental Quarterly* 104–119.

47 Maartje de Visser, *Network-Based Governance in EC Law: The Example of EC Competition and EC Communication Law* (Oxford: Hart Publishing, 2009); Saskia Lavrijssen and Leigh Hancher 'Networks on Track: From European Regulatory Networks to European Regulatory "Network Agencies"' (2009) 36 *Legal Issues of Economic Integration* 23–55; Leigh Hancher and Pierre Larouche, 'The Coming of Age of EU Regulation of Network Industries and Services of General Economic Interest' in Paul Craig and Gráinne de Búrca, eds., *The Evolution of EU Law*, 2nd ed. (Oxford: Oxford University Press, 2011), 767–769.

48 Above note 24. 49 Above note 25.

UNESCO and the IUCN and, as mentioned above, the drafting of the CITES and the CBD was initiated by the IUCN. The Vienna Convention for the Protection of the Ozone Layer[50] was developed based on discussions within the Coordinating Committee on the Ozone Layer and a subsequent working group set up by the UNEP Governing Council.[51] In most of these conventions, the conferences and meetings of the parties (COPs and MOPs) continue to play a role in creating and maintaining functional government networks even after the adoption of the convention.[52]

B *Encouraging a Role for Scientists, Officials and Parliamentarians*

Environmental scientists and researchers act as experts, advisors and commissioners to governments. In this capacity, they exercise a significant degree of power in relation to how environmental protection measures are formed and implemented.[53] Experts also participate in government networks and contribute to the development or diffusion of law and polices in other countries through knowledge exchange and information sharing. In comparison to purely private networks, government networks are more likely to make a direct impact on government policy-making processes. The relatively high degree of independence and objectivity that is often assumed to accompany the role of scientific expert also contributes to the development and expansion of policy at the global level. However, government officials involved as national delegates in political negotiations under the UNFCCC often participate as scientists and experts in the IPCC. Where national interests are at stake, there is the potential for a clash between experts who try to pursue the truth on climate change and experts who exercise a political role within the networks.

The flexibility of networks is one of their primary advantages. Networks are able to accommodate a changing cast of actors depending on the stage of development of a particular environmental policy or initiative. In Japan, for example, the Kyoto Protocol was at first

[50] 22 March 1985, 1513 UNTS 323, in force 22 September 1988.

[51] Nishii, above note 23, 59, 80–81, 97–98, 116–117 and 165–166.

[52] There are variations, with the Conferences of the Parties for the Ramsar Convention fostering government networks with loose obligations, while the World Heritage Committee under the World Heritage Convention plays the role of a more structured and formal post-adoption government network.

[53] See further, Peter M. Haas with Jan Sundgren, 'Evolving International Environmental Law: Changing Practices of National Sovereignty' in Choucri, above note 33, 401–429. See also the chapter by Cameron S.G. Jefferies in this collection.

considered to be a diplomatic issue rather than an environmental issue, with officials from the Ministry of Foreign Affairs (MOFA) playing a leading role in coordinating with other ministries such as the Ministry of the Environment (MoE) and the Ministry of Economy, Trade and Industry (METI). However, after the United States failed to ratify the Kyoto Protocol, the MoE started to play a leading role, at least at the domestic level.[54] This change in roles was due to the shift in focus from the adoption of the convention, on which MOFA officials have expertise, to a discussion of more specific practices and procedures, which fall within the expertise of MoE and METI officials. Examples include the flexibility mechanisms under the Kyoto Protocol that are further developed as international standards through subsequent COP decisions.

At the implementation stage, officials within the MoE are involved not only in climate-related policy networks but also in other environmental government networks, in collaboration with other relevant ministries if necessary. In Japan, transnational environmental government networks communicate with networks in other countries to adjust domestic laws and policies to reach international standards. Some environmental government networks are based on different divisions within the ministry, with each ministerial division working with a corresponding division within the ministries in other countries. While useful in facilitating information sharing, networking by subdivision can create an impediment to successful policy-making in circumstances where it is necessary to take a holistic approach to certain environmental problems. An example of this is the approach taken to black carbon, which is treated as a discrete problem of air pollution, but which is in fact connected to a far broader issue of climate change.

Language differences are another potential impediment to the effectiveness of networks. Again, taking the example of Japan's involvement in the negotiation of the Kyoto Protocol, officials with the MoE recognised that its scientific officers would need to be conversant in English if they wished to influence the international negotiations. In addition, the MoE did not want its officers to be reliant on officials within MOFA. As a result, MoE has sent officers to universities in English-speaking countries, and to international organisations such as UNEP, the UNFCCC Secretariat, the World Bank and the Asian Development Bank.

[54] Fang-Ting Cheng, *Environmental Diplomacy after the Kyoto Protocol* (Tsu City: Mie University Press, 2013), 7–8.

The role of parliamentarians in environmental government networks has also increased in recent times, but when compared with the role of other stakeholders, it remains relatively limited in scope and impact. (This conclusion is especially true in countries like Japan where the majority of Bills are drafted not by parliamentarians but by government officials.) One example of a network of parliamentarians is the group known as the Global Legislators Organisation for a Balanced Environment (GLOBE), which was established in 1989 on a voluntary basis by parliamentarians from the United States, the EU and Japan to facilitate a global dialogue among legislators on environmental policy positions. In 2005, GLOBE was asked by the G8 to develop a private dialogue among legislators to push the political boundaries with respect to climate change policy.[55] In 2014, UNEP signed a memorandum of understanding with GLOBE to launch a new strategic partnership to increase engagement with legislators and create national foundations for implementing international environmental agreements.[56]

C *Gaining a Role in International Standard Setting*

Transnational environmental standards, and guidelines for their effective implementation and enforcement, are playing an increasingly important role in the domestic legal order, with some so-called soft law arrangements gaining binding force in practice.[57] In some cases, common standards for products or services can be created without formal agreements through vehicles that include private actors and public-private hybrid institutions. Examples include the clean development mechanism (CDM), the ISO 14001 family of standards[58] and the Forest Stewardship Council Standards,[59] which are set by government networks such as the Meeting of the Parties (MOP) to the Kyoto Protocol, the International

[55] Adam Matthews, 'A Role for Legislators' (2009) 15 *Global Governance* 451–455.

[56] United Nations Environment Programme, 'New Agreements Set to Boost Delivery of International Environmental Agreements', Press Release, 27 June 2014, online at: www.unep.org/newscentre/Default.aspx?DocumentID=2791&ArticleID=10929&l=en.

[57] See, for example, Charles Freeland, 'The Work of the Basel Committee' in Robert C. Effros, ed., *Current Issues Affecting Central Banks* (Washington, DC: International Monetary Fund, 1992), 232; Slaughter, *A New World Order*, above note 1, 183. See also the chapter by Cecily Rose in this collection.

[58] See further, International Organization for Standardization, online at: www.iso.org/iso/home/standards/management-standards/iso14000.htm.

[59] See further, Forestry Stewardship Council, online at: https://ic.fsc.org/standards.340.htm.

Organization for Standardization (ISO) and the Forest Stewardship Council (FSC).

To explain further, the CDM Executive Board, a transnational authority, directly sets and operates rules and procedures for the registration of CDM projects.[60] With respect to the ISO standards, the World Trade Organization provides incentives for states to adopt and comply voluntarily, with these incentives serving as tools to remove barriers to international trade and to defend against domestic regulation under the agreements on sanitary and phytosanitary measures and technical barriers to trade. As for the enforcement of the ISO standards, as a non-governmental organisation, ISO has no power to enforce directly the standards it develops. However, a number of ISO standards concerned with the environment have been adopted within legislation and as part of a state's regulatory apparatus, and voluntary standards may also gain force through becoming a market requirement, raising legitimacy questions about ISO's authority to exert control over domestic legal systems in this way. When a regime like ISO opts for strong ex ante requirements, such as certification or licensing, the role of ex post legal enforcement decreases.[61]

As for the FSC Standards, the FSC was established in 1993 to develop international standards for forest management, including guidelines for certification, accreditation, trademark use and governance. To maintain its independence, government institutions and officials are not permitted to become members; however, governments are able to participate in FSC working groups and general meetings as observers, and through this activity, they influence outcomes and extend a non-government network to include a government network.

Conclusion

The primary role of environmental government networks is information sharing and capacity building, rather than regulation. This approach is

[60] Richard Stewart, 'Enforcement of Transnational Public Regulation' and Sabino Cassese, Elisa D'Alterio and Maurizia De Bellis, 'The Enforcement of Transnational Private Regulation: A Fictitious Oxymoron' in Fabrizio Cafaggi, ed., *Enforcement of Transnational Regulation: Ensuring Compliance in a Global World* (Cheltenham: Edward Elgar, 2012), 41–74 and 331–371 respectively.

[61] Fabrizio Cafaggi, 'Introduction: The Transformation of Transnational Private Regulation: Enforcement Gaps and Governance Design' in Cafaggi, *Enforcement of Transnational Regulation*, above note 60, 1–38, 5.

particularly evident in Asia, where language obstacles and differences in national legal systems lead to a preference for non-legally binding approaches to environmental issues. The role of environmental scientists and researchers as experts, advisors and commissioners to governments, however, is as strong in Asia as it is elsewhere. Experts contribute to the development or diffusion of knowledge and information, aided by a degree of independence, as well as professional norms concerning scientific neutrality and objectivity. And yet, despite the benefits of these networks, there remain lingering doubts about their legitimacy and accountability. Legitimacy, however, may ultimately depend on effectiveness,[62] and effectiveness may best be achieved through a variety of networks engaging in a variety of approaches. As the number of countries adopting the standards set by the activities of these networks increases, the legitimacy of both the standard and the network will correspondingly increase. IUCN's Red List of Threatened Species provides an apt example with which to conclude, as the Red List itself is not legally binding, but as more countries enact domestic laws to regulate the species that are listed, so do they make the trading of red-listed species more difficult and less legitimate. This phenomenon can be seen in the case of the polar bear, the giant panda, gorillas, the Pacific bluefin tuna, and recently the Japanese eel.

[62] Anne-Marie Slaughter, 'Power and Legitimacy of Government Networks' in Susan Stern and Elisabeth Seligmann, eds., *The Partnership Principle: Governance in the 21st Century* (London: Archetype Publications, 2004), 1–4.

PART III

Experts, Networks and Institutional Change

9

Non-binding Instruments and Democratic Accountability

CECILY ROSE

In August 2014, executive branch negotiators from the United States reportedly headed to international climate change negotiations with the goal of forging a non-binding agreement rather than a treaty.[1] The Obama administration apparently aimed to avoid the negotiation of a binding treaty that would have to be approved by a two-thirds majority of the US Senate[2] – an unlikely outcome given the prevailing political environment in the Senate. A non-binding instrument, however, would allow the Obama administration to reach an international agreement on climate change without having to subject it to legislative approval, as the US Constitution requires only treaties to be submitted to a vote in the Senate. The Obama administration could also potentially implement such a non-binding agreement without legislative involvement, as the *Clean Air Act*[3] provides statutory authority for the regulation of carbon dioxide by the Environmental Protection Agency – an agency that forms part of the executive branch.[4] The Obama administration's approach towards climate change negotiations raises questions about how the creation of international norms by experts through non-binding instruments impacts democratic governance at the domestic level. Does this form of norm creation leave executive branch negotiators unaccountable to the elected representatives sitting in the legislature?

Much of the existing scholarship on democracy and international law focuses on the right to democratic governance in international

[1] Coral Davenport, 'Obama Pursuing Climate Accord in Lieu of Treaty', *The New York Times*, 26 August 2014.

[2] US Constitution, Art. II, sec. 2, clause 2.

[3] 42 U.S.C. §7401 et seq.

[4] See, for example, Environmental Protection Agency, 'Carbon Pollution Emission Guidelines for Existing Stationary Electric Utility Generating Units; Proposed Rule', 79 *Federal Register* 34830, 18 June 2014.

law – whether such a right exists, and how it may be grounded in international human rights law, for example.[5] This chapter, however, takes as a given the existence of many democratic states around the world, and instead considers the implications of international norm creation for democratic governance in domestic legal systems, particularly within the context of horizontal networks of experts. The chapter specifically examines the widespread use of non-binding instruments for the creation or revision of norms in the international legal field, as opposed to binding instruments, such as treaties. While scholars have discussed the reasons for the widespread use of non-binding instruments, they have devoted relatively little attention to analysing the consequences of this form of norm creation, particularly in domestic legal systems.

Non-binding instruments contain political or moral commitments rather than legal rights and obligations, and are often described and analysed under the rubric of 'soft law'.[6] This chapter, however, deliberately eschews this term, and instead refers to 'non-binding instruments' because of persistent confusion and disagreement among scholars about what 'soft law' means and whether this term ought be used at all.[7] Non-binding instruments embody a huge range of political or moral commitments, many of which closely resemble legal commitments, but for the use of the word 'should' rather than 'shall' or 'must'. Such instruments span the field of public international law, but have played particularly important roles in certain areas such as international environmental law,

[5] See, for example, Thomas Franck, 'The Emerging Right to Democratic Governance' (1992) 86:1 *American Journal of International Law* 46–91; James Crawford, 'Democracy and International Law' (1994) 64 *British Yearbook of International Law* 113; Susan Marks, 'What has Become of the Emerging Right to Democratic Governance' (2011) 22:2 *European Journal of International Law* 507–524; Jean d'Aspremont, 'The Rise and Fall of Democracy in International Law: A Reply to Susan Marks' (2011) 22:2 *European Journal of International Law* 549–570. But see Steven Wheatley, 'A Democratic Rule of International Law' (2011) 22:2 *European Journal of International Law* 525–548.

[6] Philippe Gautier, 'Non-Binding Agreements' in Rüdiger Wolfrum, ed., *Max Planck Encyclopedia of Public International Law* (Oxford: Oxford University Press, 2012), vol. VII, 706–712, para 1.

[7] For a range of views, see Prosper Weil, 'Towards Relative Normativity in International Law?' (1983) 77:3 *American Journal of International Law* 413–442; Christine M. Chinkin, 'The Challenge of Soft Law: Development and Change in International Law' (1989) 38:4 *International and Comparative Law Quarterly* 850–866; Jean d'Aspremont, 'Softness in International Law: A Self-Serving Quest for New Legal Materials' (2008) 19:5 *European Journal of International Law* 1075–1094; Joost Pauwelyn, 'Is It International Law or Not and Does It Even Matter?' in Joost Pauwelyn, Ramses A. Wessel and Jan Wouters, eds., *Informal International Law Making* (Oxford: Oxford University Press, 2012), 125–161.

international financial law and transnational criminal law, especially with respect to corruption and money laundering.[8]

Non-binding instruments take many different forms, from UN General Assembly resolutions and declarations to recommendations, guidelines, principles and standards formulated by experts operating within the context of relatively informal horizontal networks, as well as international organisations like the UN and the Organisation for Economic Co-operation and Development (OECD). Many of these non-binding instruments either lead to or follow up on binding treaties[9] but they may also be free-standing, in that they neither precede nor follow binding instruments.[10]

This chapter focuses on a particular sub-set of non-binding instruments: those that bring about domestic implementation and thus resemble many multilateral treaties. In other words, the focus is on harmonisation efforts, whether in the context of networks of experts or formal international organisations. Like treaties, non-binding recommendations, standards and guidelines often call for changes to domestic legislation or regulations, even though they only represent political or moral, rather than legal, commitments, formally speaking. Although recommendations, for example, do not actually require the enactment of legislation or regulations, domestic implementation is generally forthcoming, in part because of the peer review or monitoring systems that often accompany such non-binding instruments.[11] These binding instruments are thus designed to have

[8] Jürgen Friedrich, *International Environmental 'Soft Law': The Functions and Limits of Nonbinding Instruments in International Environmental Governance and Law* (Heidelberg: Springer, 2013); Chris Brummer, *Soft Law and the Global Financial System: Rule Making in the 21st Century* (Cambridge: Cambridge University Press, 2012).

[9] For example, 'Revised Recommendation of the Council on Combating Bribery in International Business Transactions', OECD Doc C(97)123/FINAL, 23 May 1997; Convention on Combating Bribery of Foreign Public Officials in International Business Transactions, 17 December 1997, (1998) 37 *International Legal Materials* 1, in force 15 February 1999 (OECD Anti-Bribery Convention); OECD Council, 'Recommendation of the Council for Further Combating Bribery of Foreign Public Officials in International Business Transactions', 26 November 2009, online at: www.oecd.org/daf/anti-bribery/44176910.pdf (2009 Recommendation on Further Combating Bribery).

[10] See, for example, Financial Action Task Force, *International Standards on Combating Money Laundering and the Financing of Terrorism and Proliferation: FATF Recommendations* (Paris: FATF/OECD, 2013).

[11] The OECD Working Group on Bribery, for example, monitors the implementation of the OECD Anti-Bribery Convention, above note 9, as well as related recommendations and guidance.

an impact on domestic legal systems in ways that are functionally similar to binding treaties, despite the fact that they do not require legislative approval, as would be necessary for treaties in most (but not all) democratic states.

States are thereby generating international norms that have legal consequences in domestic systems, but they are doing so through non-binding instruments that alleviate the need to seek legislative approval, a process that may be slow, highly political and generally burdensome. Legislatures are uninvolved in the process of concluding non-binding instruments, as executive branch officials or experts instead negotiate and agree to them without having to subject the instrument to a vote in one or both houses of the legislative branch. Legislatures may also be uninvolved in the implementation process, depending on the particular non-binding instrument and the domestic legal system. Non-binding instruments may be implemented through the enactment of domestic legislation, but they may also be implemented through the promulgation of regulations by executive branch officials, or through policy shifts or other extra-legal mechanisms. The regular use of non-binding instruments for the creation of international norms thus raises questions about the political legitimacy of such instruments. Executive branch officials who negotiate non-binding instruments are seemingly unaccountable to legislatures, which often have a prescribed role in approving treaties.

This chapter argues that the loss of accountability that results from the use of non-binding instruments is not as great as it might appear to be at first glance. Oftentimes, the loss of accountability is mitigated by other mechanisms, such as legislative oversight, approval of implementing legislation as opposed to the treaty itself and public consultation processes. This chapter begins by elaborating on the role of legislatures with respect to binding treaties as well as non-binding instruments (Section I), before describing the range of ways in which non-binding instruments may be implemented through both legislative and non-legislative means (Section II). These sections look at the implementation of a number of non-binding instruments concerning transnational crime, international finance and revenue transparency in a range of domestic legal systems. Finally, the chapter concludes by assessing the accountability of non-binding instruments, with a particular focus on instruments produced through the OECD Working Group on Bribery and the Basel Committee on Banking Supervision (Section III).

I The Role of Legislatures in Relation to Treaties and Non-binding Instruments

In democratic states non-binding instruments do not uniformly circumvent legislative involvement in the treaty-making process, as legislatures play a role in approving treaties in most, but not all, democratic states.[12] Out of the 92 institutionalised democracies, as identified through the Polity IV Project, which codes states for purposes of comparative and quantitative analysis,[13] more than two thirds (66 states or 71.74 per cent) require some form of legislative approval of treaties.[14] Conversely, just over a quarter (26 states or 28.26 per cent) do not require any form of legislative approval. Among the 66 states that require some form of legislative approval, 51 states (or 55.42 per cent of the total 92) require the consent of or the approval of the majority of one legislative body.[15] Only 15 out of these 66 states (or 16.30 per cent of the 92 states in total) require the approval of a super-majority of one legislative body or the approval of a majority in two separate legislative bodies.[16] Thus, while the precise role of legislatures in approving treaties varies among democratic states, the overwhelming majority requires some form of legislative approval.

Out of the 26 states that require no legislative approval of treaties, 18 states (half of which are former British colonies) leave treaty making to an individual chief executive or cabinet. The eight other states that require no legislative approval have a rule or tradition of informing the legislative body of signed treaties.[17] (Half of these states are also former British colonies, in addition to the United Kingdom itself.) In these 26 states,

[12] Beth Simmons, 'Appendix 3.2, Ratification Rules', online at: scholar.harvard.edu/files/bsimmons/files/APP_3.2_Ratification_rules.pdf (appendix to Beth Simmons, *Mobilizing for Human Rights: International Law in Domestic Politics* (Cambridge: Cambridge University Press, 2009)).

[13] Center for Systemic Peace, 'The Polity Project: About Polity' (undated), online at: www.systemicpeace.org/polityproject.html.

[14] Center for Systemic Peace, above note 13. Monty G. Marshall and Benjamin R. Cole, Center for Systemic Peace, 'Table 1: State Fragility Index and Matrix 2012'. This chapter includes states that the Polity IV data series categorises as institutionalised democratic regimes, but excludes states that it categorises as uninstitutionalised or weak democratic regimes. These categorizations are based on 'Polity scores' that capture the range of governing authorities, from autocracies, to anocracies, to democracies.

[15] See, for example, Constitution of the French Republic, 4 October 1958, arts. 52, 53(1).

[16] See, for example, US Constitution, art. II, sec. 2, clause 2.

[17] See, for example, the Ponsonby Rule, a practice that has been codified into statutory law by the Constitutional Reform and Governance Act 2010 (United Kingdom), 2010, c. 25, Part 2.

where the legislature has no active role in approving treaties, no real distinction may be drawn between the role of the legislature in approving treaties and non-binding instruments. The legislature simply lacks a role in approving either binding or non-binding instruments.

It may be argued that an accountability gap exists in these 26 democratic states not only with respect to non-binding instruments, but also with respect to treaties. This chapter does not pursue a critique of the treaty-making process in the 26 states that do not require any form of legislative approval, as the focus of this chapter is on accountability in the context of non-binding instruments.[18] That said, the observations made below in Section III concerning accountability-promoting measures could be relevant for analysing the accountability of treaty making in states that require no legislative approval of treaties. Otherwise, the contrast that this chapter seeks to highlight between legislative involvement in treaty making and in the conclusion of non-binding instruments has little relevance for these 26 states.

While the constitutions or statutes of democratic states often specify the need for legislative approval of treaties, they generally make no mention of non-binding instruments. The commitment to non-binding instruments by executive branch officials thus tends to fall into a gap in domestic legal systems, as political or moral commitments that are unregulated by law. The provisions of Germany's Basic Law concerning international law, for example, simply make no reference to non-binding instruments or to their status in the domestic legal system.[19] Non-binding instruments thus fall outside of the scope of Germany's Basic Law, which specifically provides that treaties require legislative approval or consent, while executive agreements do not.[20]

II The Implementation of Non-binding Agreements in Domestic Legal Systems

Although non-binding instruments differ significantly from treaties, when viewed from the formal perspective of ratification rules, they are often functionally quite similar to treaties, as legislatures may be involved in implementing them through the enactment of legislation, just as they

[18] For such a discussion, see Joanna Harington, 'Scrutiny and Approval: The Role for Westminster-Style Parliaments in Treaty-Making' (2006) 55:1 *International and Comparative Law Quarterly* 121–160.

[19] Basic Law for the Federal Republic of Germany, 23 May 1949, as amended, arts. 29, 59.

[20] Ibid., art. 59(2).

would for treaties. In other cases, however, legislatures may play no role in implementing non-binding instruments, as this task may fall instead to officials in executive branch departments or agencies. The following sections briefly review a range of legislative and non-legislative methods for the implementation of a number of different non-binding instruments: two separate OECD recommendations on the tax deductibility of foreign bribes and on foreign bribery more generally;[21] the Basel II Framework (and the associated 2004 Revised Framework), produced through the Basel Committee on Banking Supervision;[22] and revenue transparency standards created through the Extractive Industries Transparency Initiative (EITI).[23]

A *Implementation through Legislative Means*

Non-binding instruments geared towards harmonisation may call for the enactment, amendment or repeal of legislation so that domestic statutory provisions are in accordance with non-binding agreements reached by executive branch negotiators at international organisations like the OECD. In 1996, for example, the OECD Council issued a Recommendation on the Tax Deductibility of Bribes to Foreign Public Officials, which encouraged those OECD member states that did not already disallow the deduction of bribes to foreign public officials to re-examine such tax treatment.[24] This Recommendation actually goes beyond the legal obligations set forth in the OECD Anti-Bribery Convention, which was concluded one year after the Recommendation, in 1997. The Convention itself requires states parties to criminalise the bribery of foreign public officials, but it does not address the issue of tax deductibility.[25] Although many states parties have nevertheless gone beyond the requirements of the Convention by prohibiting the tax deductibility of bribes to foreign public officials in accordance with the

[21] 'Recommendation of the Council on Tax Measures for Further Combating Bribery of Foreign Public Officials in International Business Transactions', OECD Doc C(2009)64, 25 May 2009; 'Recommendation of the Council for Further Combating Bribery of Foreign Public Officials in International Business Transactions', above note 9.

[22] Basel Committee on Banking Supervision, *International Convergence of Capital Measurement and Capital Standards: A Revised Framework* (Basel: Bank for International Settlements, 2004) (2004 Revised Framework).

[23] Online at: http://eiti.org.

[24] 'Recommendation of the Council on the Tax Deductibility of Bribes to Foreign Public Officials', OECD Doc C(96)27/FINAL, 17 April 1996, Recommendation I.

[25] OECD Anti-Bribery Convention, above note 9, art. 1.

1996 Recommendation, there have been a number of laggards, including Bulgaria, Greece, Poland, the Slovak Republic and Turkey.[26] These states have been (or are being) prodded into compliance with the 1996 Recommendation by the OECD Working Group on Bribery, which monitors implementation and enforcement by states parties of the Anti-Bribery Convention as well as associated non-binding instruments like the 1996 Recommendation. Greece, for example, finally amended its *Income Tax Code* in 2006, at the recommendation of the Working Group on Bribery, so that the Code now includes an express prohibition on the deduction of bribe payments to foreign public officials.[27]

Non-binding instruments can also bring about the repeal as well as the amendment of legislation. Like the 1996 Recommendation, the 2009 Recommendation for Further Combating Bribery of Foreign Public Officials in International Business Transactions goes beyond the requirements of the Convention itself. The 2009 Recommendation calls on states parties to encourage companies to prohibit or discourage the use of small facilitation payments, a term that refers to payments made 'to induce public officials to perform their functions, such as issuing licenses or permits'.[28] The Convention not only omitted a criminalisation requirement with respect to such payments, but the Commentaries appended to the Convention specifically clarify that small facilitation payments do not fall within the scope of the Convention's sole criminalisation provision.[29] Nevertheless, most states parties to the Convention did not include an exception for small facilitation payments in their implementing

[26] OECD, 'Update on Tax Legislation on the Tax Treatment of Bribes to Foreign Public Officials in Countries Parties to the OECD Anti-Bribery Convention', June 2011; OECD, 'Phase 3 Report on Implementing the OECD Anti-Bribery Convention in Bulgaria', March 2011, 27–28; OECD, 'Phase 3 Report on Implementing the OECD Anti-Bribery Convention in Greece', June 2012, 34–35; OECD, 'Phase 3 Report on Implementing the OECD Anti-Bribery Convention in Poland', June 2013, 35–36; OECD, 'Phase 3 Report on Implementing the OECD Anti-Bribery Convention in the Slovak Republic', June 2012, 39; OECD, 'Turkey: Phase 2 & Phase 2bis: Follow-Up Report on the Implementation of the Phase 2 and Phase 2bis Recommendations', March 2010, 14–15.

[27] 'Phase 3 Report on Greece', above note 26, 34, para 113; *Income Tax Code* (Greece), art. 31(16).

[28] 2009 Recommendation on Further Combating Bribery, above note 9, Recommendation VI; OECD, *Commentaries on the Convention on Combating Bribery of Foreign Public Officials in International Business Transactions*, 'Article 1: The Offence of Bribery of Foreign Public Officials: Re paragraph 1', para 9, online at: www.oecd.org/daf/anti-bribery/ConvCombatBribery_ENG.pdf.

[29] *Commentaries* (ibid) ('small "facilitation" payments do not constitute payments made "to obtain or retain business or other improper advantage" within the meaning of paragraph 1 and, accordingly, are also not an offence').

legislation that criminalised the bribery of foreign public officials. By the time the OECD Council conducted a review of implementation in 2006, the only outliers were Australia, Canada, South Korea and the United States, each of which expressly established a defence to foreign bribery offences, in keeping with the Commentaries.[30] Canada, however, has since repealed the exception for facilitation payments in the *Corruption of Foreign Public Officials Act*, the legislation that implements the OECD Anti-Bribery Convention.[31]

The 1996 and 2009 Recommendations highlight the use of non-binding instruments to pursue legal reform at the domestic level, beyond that required by the OECD Anti-Bribery Convention, which is itself a limited instrument, with only one criminalisation provision. In the context of the Greek legal order, this means that the Greek legislature ratified the OECD Anti-Bribery Convention in 1998, but never had an opportunity to approve the 1996 Recommendation, which nevertheless had comparable legal consequences in the Greek legal system.[32] The 1996 Recommendation was drafted by members of the Working Group on Bribery, in which Greek government officials participate as experts, as the Working Group includes representatives from all states parties to the Convention. These representatives are generally prosecutors and public servants from departments or ministries of justice, trade, finance, economic affairs and foreign affairs.[33] Their regular involvement in tax or anti-corruption issues in the course of their work at the domestic level allows them to contribute as experts to the Working Group on Bribery. Legislators would normally have no place in the Working Group on Bribery, however, as they lack the expertise needed to make meaningful contributions to the work of this body. Thus, Greek legislators would have had no role in approving or formulating this non-binding

[30] OECD, 'Mid-Term Study of Phase 2 Reports', 22 May 2006, para 57.

[31] 'Canada: Follow-Up to the Phase 3 Report and Recommendations', May 2013, 12–13; *Corruption of Foreign Public Officials Act*, S.C. 1998, c. 34, as amended by *Fighting Foreign Corruption Act*, S.C. 2013, c. 26, s. 3(2).

[32] According to article 28(1) of the Hellenic Constitution, international conventions must be sanctioned by statute, at which point they become an integral part of domestic Greek law and prevail over contrary laws. The Greek Parliament ratified the OECD Anti-Bribery Convention by Law No 2656 of 1998. See OECD, 'Steps Taken to Implement and Enforce the OECD Convention on Combating Bribery of Foreign Public Officials in International Business Transactions', 15 April 2011.

[33] OECD Working Group on Bribery, *Annual Report 2007*, online at: www.oecd.org/daf/anti-bribery/40896091.pdf.

instrument, in contrast to the OECD Anti-Bribery Convention, which it did have an opportunity to approve.

In Canada, however, the legislature did not play a role in approving the Convention, as Canada has inherited the British tradition whereby the power to make treaties rests with the federal executive. Moreover, Canada did not revive the practice of the executive tabling treaties before the legislature until 2008.[34] Consequently, no distinction may be drawn between the Canadian legislature's role with respect to the treaty and its role with respect to the 2009 Recommendation. In both cases, the legislature was uninvolved. In light of the fact that both the Canadian and Greek legislatures had control over the legislative implementation of the OECD Recommendations, one may question whether the lack of an opportunity to formally approve the non-binding instruments really matters from an accountability perspective. It cannot be said, for example, that the legislators had no choice but to implement these recommendations on the tax deductibility of foreign bribes and small facilitation payments. Instead, these legal reforms came about through the normal legislative process, in which the Greek and Canadian legislatures incorporated the recommendations into domestic legislation. Moreover, the legislatures could have opted not to amend or repeal the relevant legal provisions, as the recommendations are, after all, non-binding.

The US government indeed took such an approach, as it opted not to eliminate the exception for small facilitation payments from the Foreign Corrupt Practices Act (FCPA), which implements the OECD Anti-Bribery Convention (though it actually predates the Convention).[35] The US government explained that the executive branch included the Commentaries with the Convention in the transmittal package that it sent to the US Senate for its approval during the ratification process in 1998.[36] The US government consequently considered that a change to the implementing legislation would require consultations with the Senate,

[34] Government of Canada, 'Archived – Canada Announces Policy to Table International Treaties in House of Commons', 25 January 2008, online at: http://nouvelles.gc.ca/web/article-en.do?crtr.sj1D=&mthd=advSrch&crtr.mnthndVl=&nid=374729&crtr.dpt1D=&crtr.tp1D=&crtr.lc1D=&crtr.yrStrtVl=2008&crtr.kw=&crtr.dyStrtVl=26&crtr.aud1D=&crtr.mnthStrtVl=2&crtr.yrndVl=&crtr.dyndVl=.

[35] *Foreign Corrupt Practices Act of 1977*, as amended in 1988 and 1998, 15 U.S.C. §§78dd-1 et seq.

[36] 'Survey #2 on Treatment of Small Facilitation Payments by Members', dated 4 May 2009, in 'Response of the United States: Questions Concerning Phase 3: OECD Working Group on Bribery', 3 May 2010, Annex H, online at: www.justice.gov/criminal/fraud/fcpa/docs/response3-appx-h.pdf.

as well as the amendment of the FCPA by both houses of Congress.[37] The US government thereby took a different approach to a recommendation that effectively modifies a treaty that has been approved by the Senate. In the case of the 2009 Recommendation, the US government displayed an unwillingness to seek Senate approval for what is essentially a modification of the drafters' original agreement on small facilitation payments.

Although this decision may have been motivated more by political considerations than a concern for protecting the role of the Senate in treaty making, it still raises questions about whether legislatures ought to be involved in approving non-binding instruments that effectively modify treaties that were originally subject to legislative approval. If a non-binding instrument were geared towards altering a compromise reached by treaty drafters as a fundamental premise for the conclusion of a treaty, then legislative approval would perhaps be appropriate. In such a situation, the legislature should arguably be given an opportunity to approve a non-binding instrument that alters a balance that was achieved in a prior deal to which the legislature gave its consent. In the case of the 2009 OECD Recommendation, however, the elimination of the exception for small facilitation payments hardly upsets a fundamental compromise achieved during the negotiations of the Convention. Instead, it appears that views among states parties about the criminalisation of small facilitation payments have evolved since the conclusion of the treaty, and have ultimately coalesced into a consensus that exceptions for such payments ought to be discouraged. One may thus question the practical necessity of the US Senate both approving the changes that the 2009 Recommendation makes to the Convention, and approving the legislation that implements this change. Ultimately, when the executive branch pursues the implementation of non-binding instruments through legislative means, the legislature still exercises control over how, or even whether, the non-binding instrument will influence the domestic legal order. As will be explored in Section III, the accountability gap in this context may be negligible.

B Implementation through Non-legislative Means

Non-binding instruments may be implemented in a myriad of ways, beyond the enactment, amendment or appeal of legislation. This section

[37] Ibid.

highlights just some of the non-legislative means by which non-binding instruments may permeate domestic legal systems, in particular regulations, guidelines, policies, self-regulation and memoranda of understanding (MoUs). As shown below, the same non-binding instrument may be implemented through different means (both legislative and non-legislative, binding and non-binding) in various domestic legal systems.

1 Implementation through Existing Statutory Authorisation

The Basel II Framework, for example, has been implemented under existing statutory authority in the United States and in Canada, but through binding regulations in the United States, and non-binding guidelines in Canada. The 2004 Revised Framework[38] adopted by the Basel Committee on Banking Supervision set forth a new methodology for determining minimum regulatory capital requirements for banks, as well as standards to guide the supervisory review process, and disclosure requirements for banks regarding data on their risk exposure and management processes.[39] In the United States, two existing laws provided statutory authority for the promulgation of the regulations that implemented Basel II: the International Lending Supervision Act and the Prompt Corrective Action statute.[40] As analysed by Pierre-Hugues Verdier within the context of a project on 'Informal International Lawmaking', the regulatory implementation of Basel II in the United States proved to be a lengthy and highly controversial process, involving multiple rounds of domestic notice-and-comment procedures as well as congressional oversight in the form of hearings.[41]

The Canadian federal banking regulator, the Office of the Superintendent of Financial Institutions (OSFI), similarly implemented Basel II by exercising its authority under existing legislation.[42] The OSFI,

[38] Above note 22.

[39] As the primary global standard setter for the prudential regulation of banks, the Basel Committee mainly consists of experts or 'professional supervisors' temporarily seconded from member institutions, namely national central banks. See further, Bank for International Settlements, 'About the Basel Committee' (30 September 2015), online at: www.bis.org/bcbs/about.htm?m=3%7C14%7C573.

[40] *International Lending Supervision Act*, 12 U.S.C. §3907; *Prompt Corrective Action*, 12 U.S.C. §1831o.

[41] Pierre-Hugues Verdier, 'US Implementation of Basel II: Lessons for Informal International Lawmaking' in Pauwelyn, Wessel and Wouters, above note 7, 437–467.

[42] *Bank Act* (Canada), S.C. 1991, c. 46, s. 485(2) ('. . . the Superintendent may make guidelines respecting the maintenance by banks of adequate capital and adequate and appropriate forms of liquidity').

however, implemented Basel II by adopting guidelines rather than regulations, because doing so apparently allowed it to avoid extensive procedural requirements under Canada's *Statutory Instruments Act*[43] and government policies that are applicable to the adoption of federal regulations.[44] These procedural requirements include a regulatory impact analysis, a review of the draft regulation by the Department of Justice and an opportunity for public comments. The OSFI did, nevertheless, voluntarily conduct public consultations on drafts of the guidelines before their final adoption.[45] By contrast to the implementation of Basel II in the United States, implementation in Canada did not suffer from any considerable delays or controversy.[46]

The adoption of regulations or guidelines under pre-existing statutory authority could potentially allow regulators in executive branch agencies to promulgate regulations or guidance unanticipated by the legislators who originally enacted the authorising statutes. It could be argued that expert regulators may thus negotiate non-binding instruments in international fora, like the Basel Committee on Banking Supervision, and then return home to implement such instruments through existing statutory authorisation that may have been intended by the legislature for entirely different purposes. Yet in reality, legislation such as the US *Administrative Procedure Act*[47] and the Canadian Statutory Instruments Act helps to prevent the abuse of existing authorising statutes. According to the *Statutory Instruments Act*, for example, the Clerk of the Privy Council, in consultation with the Deputy Minister of Justice, examines proposed regulations to ensure that they do not represent an 'unusual or unexpected use' of the statutory authority.[48] Statutes governing administrative regulation also tend to provide for publication of draft regulations and notice-and-comment rulemaking – potentially significant accountability-promoting measures, as will be discussed in Section III.

2 Implementation without Statutory Authorisation

Non-binding instruments may also be implemented in domestic legal systems outside of the framework of an existing statute that authorises regulations or guidance. In the field of revenue transparency, the EITI has stressed that the non-binding EITI Standard may be implemented by states participating in the initiative through binding legislation, but also

[43] R.S.C. 1985, c. S-22. [44] Verdier, above note 41, 454. [45] Ibid., 455. [46] Ibid.
[47] 5 U.S.C. §500 et seq. [48] *Statutory Instruments Act*, above note 43, s 3(2).

through non-binding means such as MoUs.[49] EITI is a multi-stakeholder initiative established in 2003 and comprised of representatives from companies in the extractive industries, states and civil society groups.[50] The experts involved in EITI thus represent quite different perspectives within the extractives industry. The EITI Standard requires participating states to ensure that companies in the extractive industries publish their payments to resource-rich host states, and the participating states must also publish their revenues so that the two sets of figures may be reconciled.[51]

EITI allows states considerable flexibility in deciding how to implement this Standard. While most states have enacted legislation implementing the Standard, some have instead concluded non-binding MoUs with companies in the extractive industries in order to ensure that the companies report the necessary information to the government. Azerbaijan, for example, opted to implement the EITI Standard through the conclusion of an MoU in 2004 between the Azerbaijani Committee on the Extractive Industries Transparency Initiative, local and foreign companies operating in its extractive industries, and non-governmental organisations.[52] The MoU, which was revised in 2014, provides that oil and gas companies 'shall', twice a year, produce reports detailing the payments made by them to the Azerbaijan government.[53] The Azerbaijani legislature has thus had no involvement in implementing the EITI Standard to which the government made a strong political commitment at a relatively early stage in EITI's existence.[54] The legislature was not even involved in the creation of the Committee on the EITI, which was established by an ordinance passed by the Cabinet of Ministers of Azerbaijan.[55]

49 Anwar Ravat and Sridar P. Kannan, eds., *Implementing EITI for Impact: Handbook for Policy Makers and Stakeholders* (Washington, DC: World Bank, 2012), 128; *The EITI Standard* (Oslo: EITI Secretariat, 2015), online at: https://eiti.org/files/English_EITI_STANDARD.pdf.

50 'Articles of Association' in *The EITI Standard*, above note 49, 46–54.

51 'Requirements for EITI Implementing Countries' in *The EITI Standard*, above note 49, 10–34.

52 For the revised 2014 MoU, see 'Memorandum of Understanding on Extractive Industries Transparency Initiative Implementation in Azerbaijan', online at: www.eiti.az/index.php/en/senedler-2/memorandum.

53 Ibid., paras 1 and 2.

54 Azerbaijan was the first country to achieve the status of EITI compliant: Ingilab Ahmadov, 'EITI in Azerbaijan: Don't Stop Pedalling' *EITI Blog*, 30 March 2012, online at: http://eiti.org/blog/eiti-azerbaijan-dont-stop-pedalling.

55 Ordinance of the Cabinet of Ministers of the Republic of Azerbaijan, No 224, 13 November 2003, online at: www.eiti.az/index.php/en/senedler-2/ordinance2/270-ordinance-of-the-cabinet-of-ministers-of-the-republic-of-azerbaijan-224.

III Assessing the Accountability of Non-binding Instruments

There are many important reasons why experts within state ministries might prefer to generate international norms in a range of fields through non-binding instruments rather than binding treaties.[56] This section begins by highlighting a few of these reasons – adaptability, speed and expertise – before going on to discuss how norm creation through non-binding instruments impacts democratic governance, in particular the accountability of the norm creators to the legislature. Because assessments of accountability will inevitably vary by state and by instrument, the following will focus on the OECD 2009 Recommendation and the Basel II Framework as illustrations of how such analyses may be approached. While the following analyses of the 2009 Recommendation and Basel II Framework conclude with relatively positive assessments of the level of accountability associated with these instruments, it must be admitted that analyses of other non-binding instruments could lead to very different evaluations. Nevertheless, the 2009 Recommendation and Basel II Framework appear to illustrate a general trend, whereby the loss of formal accountability, in the form of legislative approval, may be mitigated by other mechanisms and measures, such as the passage of legislation and public consultation processes at the international and domestic levels.

A The Benefits of Non-binding Instruments

The adaptability and speed of non-binding instruments can make them a more efficient means for generating international norms, as compared with treaties. First, non-binding instruments are well suited to fields in which norms must be capable of adapting in accordance with changing circumstances and evolving views on appropriate normative responses.[57] In the field of international environmental law, for example, non-binding instruments may allow states to attempt to keep pace with climate change, and in the anti-corruption field, non-binding instruments may

[56] For a lengthier discussion of a larger range of reasons, see Anthony Aust, 'The Theory and Practice of Informal International Instruments' (1986) 35:4 *International and Comparative Law Quarterly* 787–812; Harmut Hilgenberg, 'A Fresh Look at Soft Law' (1999) 10:3 *European Journal of International Law* 499–516.

[57] Aust, above note 56, 791.

be revised to reflect evolving attitudes in the business community towards what constitutes impermissible conduct.

While treaties may be modified or amended in accordance with the Vienna Convention on the Law of Treaties,[58] these are relatively cumbersome processes that require states to seek the approval of their legislatures, if such approval is required under the constitution or basic law for the conclusion of treaties. Revisions to non-binding instruments, by contrast, need only be agreed upon by the negotiators, without the extra step of seeking legislative approval of the agreed changes. Treaties may also be updated through the conclusion of protocols, but as protocols are simply treaties by another name, these too are subject to the normal constitutional or statutory rules on treaty making. A non-binding instrument, however, may simply be replaced with a revised and updated instrument, as has occurred in the case of the 40 Recommendations of the Financial Action Task Force.[59] Thus, while treaties are capable of adaptation to an extent, non-binding instruments are considerably more amenable in this respect.

Second, and relatedly, non-binding instruments may represent a faster way of formulating international norms, although in some instances the negotiation of a non-binding instrument may require as much as time as the negotiation of a treaty.[60] The fact that non-binding instruments technically do not create binding legal commitments may speed the norm creation process by increasing the willingness of negotiators to reach agreements, though this suggestion requires empirical support. The absence of legislative involvement in the approval of non-binding instruments may not only enhance the adaptability of these instruments, but also may increase the likelihood that they will be amended or revised relatively rapidly. In addition, because non-binding instruments do not enter into force, as treaties do, domestic approval processes cannot delay their application. It must be acknowledged, however, that not all non-binding instruments are adopted by states after speedy negotiations, as some are the subject of years of work before their conclusion or revision, just as with many treaties.[61] This is

[58] 23 May 1969, 1155 UNTS 331, in force 27 January 1980, arts. 39–41.

[59] The Final Action Task Force (FATF) issued its first set of Recommendations in 1990, and then issued revised Recommendations in 1996, 2003, and 2012.

[60] Aust, above note 56, 789.

[61] The revision process that led to the 2012 version of the FATF 40 Recommendations began three years earlier in 2009.

especially true with respect to non-binding instruments that undergo revisions following public consultations, a process that may take years, as will be discussed below.

Finally, expert government officials commonly draft non-binding instruments, which may be more effective as a result. While treaties are typically drafted by government officials from ministries with competence over the subject matter of the treaty negotiations, and thus may be considered experts in some cases, the average level of expertise among the drafters of non-binding instruments may be considerably higher due to the existence of a network of some sort. In cases where government officials participate in bodies that monitor the implementation of non-binding instruments over the course of many years, they may develop a level of expertise about such instruments and their domestic implementation that would be difficult, if not impossible, to achieve in the context of treaty negotiations.[62] The revision of non-binding instruments may thereby benefit from years of knowledge acquired by government officials who work in the relevant field. The networks that develop around non-binding instruments for the purpose of monitoring and promoting harmonization may therefore be far more robust than in the case of most traditional treaties.

B A Brief Outline of the Concept of Accountability

The efficiency and effectiveness of non-binding instruments may not necessarily conflict with their accountability, despite a common presumption that efficiency and effectiveness are inversely related to accountability.[63] The word 'accountability' has different meanings for different scholars, and thus requires at least a brief explanation of how this word is used in this chapter.[64] In addition, the term 'accountability deficit' is also problematic, as different actors (scholars, journalists and politicians, for example) sometimes use this phrase in an imprecise or politically charged manner that then makes it necessary to revisit what we mean by this term. This chapter draws on the general approach adopted by the 'Informal International Lawmaking' project, which similarly used

[62] For example, the OECD Working Group on Bribery.

[63] Joost Pauwelyn, 'Informal International Lawmaking: Framing the Concept and Research Questions' in Pauwelyn, Wessel and Wouters, above note 7, 13–34, 30.

[64] Mark Bovens, 'Analysing and Assessing Accountability: A Conceptual Framework' (2007) 13:4 *European Law Journal* 447–468, 448.

the concept of accountability to analyse the consequences of informal, or non-binding instruments.[65]

Defined most broadly, accountability refers to responsiveness to people, or, when expressed conversely, disregard of people.[66] This chapter is concerned, in particular, with the responsiveness of executive branch regulators to legislators, but also the responsiveness of these regulators to constituencies affected by the instruments they have negotiated, from citizens in resource-rich states, to multinational corporations and international banks. Defined more narrowly, accountability refers to 'a relationship between an actor and a forum, in which the actor has an obligation to explain and to justify his or her conduct, the forum can pose questions and pass judgement, and the actor may face consequences'.[67] This definition is narrower in part because it refers to ex post rather than ex ante activity, meaning, for example, that expert regulators provide legislators with the text of, and information about, a non-binding instrument only after it has been concluded.[68]

This definition is also narrow because it requires an institutionalised relationship between the actor (i.e., the regulator) and the forum (i.e., the legislature).[69] According to this understanding of accountability, rules and procedures impose certain obligations on the actor with respect to the forum, and they also authorise the forum to impose sanctions or other consequences on the actor.[70] This aspect of the narrow definition of accountability, however, has little relevance for the present examination of the role of legislatures in relation to non-binding instruments. As discussed above, constitutions and basic laws often include rules governing the approval of treaties, while non-binding instruments go without mention. As a result, regulators are not bound by rules that oblige them to submit non-binding instruments to the legislature for approval. Moreover, legislators lack an institutionalised mechanism

[65] Pauwelyn, above note 63; Philipp Dann and Marie von Engelhardt, 'Legal Approaches to Global Governance and Accountability: Informal Lawmaking, International Public Authority, and Global Administrative Law Compared' in Pauwelyn, Wessel and Wouters, above note 7, 106–124.

[66] Pauwelyn, above note 63; Anne-Marie Slaughter, 'Agencies on the Loose? Holding Government Networks Accountable' in George A. Bermann, Matthias Herdegen and Peter L. Lindseth, eds., *Transatlantic Regulatory Cooperation: Legal Problems and Political Prospects* (Oxford: Oxford University Press, 2000), 521–564, 523; Richard B. Stewart, 'Remedying Disregard in Global Regulatory Governance: Accountability, Participation, and Responsiveness' (2014) 108:2 *American Journal of International Law* 211–270.

[67] Bovens, above note 64, 450. [68] Pauwelyn, above note 63, 23. [69] Ibid., 24.

[70] Ibid.

for sanctioning regulators for the negotiation of an instrument that meets with their disapproval, whereas legislators may simply refuse to approve a treaty that they consider unsatisfactory.

This chapter thus takes a somewhat broader approach to accountability, which looks not only at strictly defined accountability mechanisms, which are ex post and institutionalised, but also other accountability-promoting measures.[71] Such measures may be ex ante as well as ex post, and may involve non-institutionalised mechanisms that do not necessarily stem from prescribed rules or procedures governing the relationship between the forum and other actors.[72] In the case of non-binding instruments, this means that appointment procedures, public consultation processes and legislative hearings may all play a role in fostering accountability.[73] As a consequence of this broader approach to accountability, this chapter looks at internal as well as external accountability, meaning accountability to the legislature as well as to stakeholders.

Internal accountability is premised on a delegation model of accountability involving a principal–agent relationship, and it corresponds with a narrower approach to accountability that emphasises institutionalised mechanisms. Executive branch officials have, for example, been entrusted by the legislature with the power to negotiate international instruments, whether binding or non-binding. The principal–agent relationship between legislators and officials involved in negotiating non-binding instruments may, however, be quite attenuated. For example, the legislature may delegate authority to a minister in the executive branch, who in turn delegates authority to a deputy, and so on, until we reach the mid- or senior-level official who represents the state at the OECD Working Group on Bribery. In light of the degree of attenuation that will often exist in situations where a government official is representing the state in the negotiation of a non-binding instrument, it is difficult to conceive of the legislature formally 'sanctioning' such officials, in keeping with the narrow definition of accountability. Such officials are too removed from the legislature, which would typically lack direct supervisory or fiscal control over their decision-making. The less formal, broader mechanisms of accountability may have more relevance in such circumstances, as they will typically involve stakeholders rather than the legislature itself. It should also be noted that officials negotiating non-binding instruments will often have instructions from their foreign

[71] Pauwelyn, above note 63, 26. [72] Ibid. [73] Ibid.

ministry or other relevant department, such that their negotiating positions are not simply left to their discretion.[74]

External accountability, by contrast, is premised on a participation model of accountability that focuses on the relationship between the government official and the actors affected by the non-binding instrument, and thus corresponds with a broader approach to accountability. These actors are external to the domestic legal order, at least in the context of this study, and they may seek to hold negotiators accountable because they must ultimately modify their conduct in accordance with the non-binding instrument, as implemented in the domestic legal order. A broader understanding of accountability can capture the ways in which these external actors – whether citizens, multinational corporations or banks – can participate in holding negotiators accountable by, for example, submitting comments during public consultation processes.

This chapter ultimately approaches accountability from two distinct but complementary perspectives: the democratic perspective, which emphasises popular control, and the learning perspective, which emphasises the enhancement of government effectiveness.[75] The delegation or principal–agent model of accountability reflects the democratic perspective, which focuses on the responsiveness of government officials to the people who have transferred their sovereignty to popular representatives in the legislature through elections.[76] The democratic perspective is the starting point for this study, which begins by questioning whether we ought to be concerned about the lack of legislative control over the approval of non-binding instruments. Given the highly attenuated link between the people and the government officials engaged in negotiating these instruments, this perspective lacks the ability to fully explain the accountability mechanisms at play in this context. The learning perspective, which is associated with the participation model of accountability, thus provides a useful complementary approach. According to this perspective, accountability mechanisms give administrators an opportunity to explain and justify their decisions, and stakeholders an opportunity to ask questions and offer their opinions.[77] The executive branch ideally learns from these exchanges, which help to enhance the effectiveness of governance, particularly the implementation of non-binding instruments. This approach assists in understanding the role of public

[74] Tim Corthaut, Bruno Demeyere, Nicolas Hachez and Jan Wouters, 'Operationalizing Accountability in Respect of Informal International Lawmaking Mechanisms' in Pauwelyn, Wessel and Wouters, above note 7, 310–336, 328.

[75] Bovens, above note 64, 463–464. [76] Ibid., 463. [77] Ibid., 464.

consultation at the international and domestic levels, an accountability-promoting measure to be discussed in the following section.

C *Public Consultation as an Accountability-Promoting Measure*

The 2009 OECD Recommendation builds on the 1997 OECD Anti-Bribery Convention by encouraging states parties to adopt measures on subjects like tax deductibility and small facilitation payments. These issues did not garner a consensus at the time the Convention was negotiated, and therefore were not addressed in the treaty itself. The conclusion of the 2009 Recommendation allowed states parties to update international anti-bribery norms so that they reflect more current attitudes about the bribery of foreign public officials, which have evolved since the mid-1990s. In doing so, the negotiators, who are members of the Working Group on Bribery, were able to draw on years of expertise accumulated through peer review and two phases of mutual evaluations that covered the implementation and enforcement of the Convention in each state party. The formulation of the 2009 Recommendation was not, however, a speedy process. In contrast to the Convention, which was drafted in less than a year on the basis of existing recommendations, the 2009 Recommendation was the product of a three-year process that began with a 2006 study of the implementation of the Convention, and ended with public consultations.

The review undertaken by the Working Group on Bribery included an external consultation process that took place from January to March 2008. On the basis of a consultation paper, the Working Group solicited comments from stakeholders, which it identified as the private sector; the accounting, auditing and legal professions; and civil society organisations; as well as international and regional multilateral organisations and non-party states to the Convention.[78] The Consultation Paper summarised the main issues that had arisen thus far in the implementation of the Convention, and encouraged stakeholders to answer a series of questions set out in the first part of the Paper, in order to further the Working Group's goal of enhancing the Convention's implementation. The Working Group received and published a total of 35 comments on the

[78] Working Group on Bribery in International Business Transactions, 'Consultation Paper: Review of the OECD Instruments on Combating Bribery of Foreign Public Officials in International Business Transactions Ten Years after Adoption', January 2008.

Consultation Paper, from international legal experts, multilateral organisations, civil society, accounting and auditing professionals, and the private sector.[79] Though the number of comments submitted in response to the Consultation Paper was not large, it did at least represent a cross section of stakeholders.

While the 2009 Recommendation escaped ex post, internal accountability in the form of approval by legislators elected by the people, it was the subject of ex ante, external accountability in the form of public consultations. The Working Group explicitly sought the participation of a range of stakeholders, and aimed to gather information, as a part of a sort of learning process about the implementation of the Convention and how it could be improved. This consultation process arguably helps to compensate for the loss of legislative control over the conclusion of the 2009 Recommendation, as the same stakeholders that might normally lobby the legislature or regulators instead had an opportunity to submit their opinions directly to the actors formulating the non-binding instruments.

Public consultations may also enhance the accountability of non-binding instruments when undertaken in domestic legal systems where regulators are considering how to implement a given instrument in the form of regulations under existing statutory authority. The United States, for example, engaged in several rounds of notice-and-comment rulemaking before implementing Basel II through domestic regulations. The US public consultations were in addition to those undertaken by the Basel Committee itself, which issued three separate consultative papers in 1999, 2001 and 2003.[80] By comparison to the consultation process undertaken by the OECD Working Group on Bribery prior to the adoption of the 2009 Recommendation, the Basel Committee's consultation process was far more extensive, as the first consultative paper produced over 200 comments, the second produced 259 and the third produced 187.[81]

Domestic consultation took place in the United States in part because the Basel Committee's proposals had fostered divisions among US banks and US bank regulators, as smaller banks were concerned that they could

[79] OECD, Anti-Corruption Division, Directorate for Financial and Enterprise Affairs, 'Review of the OECD Anti-Bribery Instruments: Compilation of Responses to Consultation Paper', 31 March 2008.

[80] Michael S. Barr and Geoffrey P. Miller, 'Global Administrative Law: The View from Basel' (2006) 17:1 *European Journal of International Law* 15–46; Verdier, above note 41, 445.

[81] Barr and Miller, above note 80; Verdier, above note 41, 445.

not implement the framework cost-effectively. US bank regulators responded to potential resistance from banks as well as Congress by releasing an advance notice of proposed rule-making in August 2003, prior to the adoption of Basel II at the international level.[82] The debate about the application of Basel II to smaller banks influenced ongoing negotiations at the international level, and in October 2003 the Basel Committee issued a revised proposal with a compromise that eventually led to the adoption of the Framework in June 2004. The controversy over Basel II continued in the United States, however, where regulators did not publish a notice of proposed rulemaking until September 2006.

The US public consultation processes thus were ex ante as well as ex post, as the advance notice of proposed rule-making preceded Basel II, and the notice of proposed rulemaking followed it. The comments not only shaped the implementation of Basel II in the United States, but also altered the content of Basel II itself. US regulators did not simply incorporate an international non-binding instrument directly into US regulations, but instead gathered opinions from domestic stakeholders, which then influenced the course of the international negotiations, prior to the final adoption of Basel II. The public consultation processes in the United States complicated international negotiations and contributed to a significantly delayed domestic implementation process, but they also allowed for stakeholders to participate in, and very much influence, the formulation of standards that would affect them.

Conclusion

Although non-binding instruments technically only garner political and moral, rather than legally binding, commitments from states, they often function in ways that are similar to binding treaties, as demonstrated in this chapter. States commonly implement recommendations, codes of conduct and other non-binding instruments as if they were treaties that required incorporation into domestic laws or regulations. The functional similarity between treaties and many non-binding instruments raises questions about the formal distinction between the two types of instruments from the perspective of the legislative branch. In a clear majority of democratic states, the legislature must approve treaties concluded by the executive branch, whereas non-binding instruments do not require any

[82] Verdier, above note 41, 446.

sort of legislative approval. In a minority of democratic states, however, the legislative branch does not play a role in approving treaties, such that no real distinction may be drawn between the role of the legislator in relation to binding and non-binding instruments.

At first glance, it seems that an accountability gap may arise where non-binding instruments escape legislative approval in states where such approval is needed for treaties. It seems that executive branch officials, in the context of expert networks, negotiate non-binding instruments that often have legal consequences for domestic legal orders, without having to seek the approval of, or otherwise involve, the elected representatives of the people who sit in the legislature. Yet, as this chapter has shown, this characterization is too simplistic, as legislatures may enact, amend or repeal laws that implement non-binding instruments, thus exercising control over the manner in which such instruments influence the domestic legal system. In other instances, however, non-binding instruments may escape both legislative approval and legislative control over their domestic implementation, which may be effected through non-legislative means including regulations, guidelines, policies, self-regulation and MoUs. But it would still be too simplistic to argue that these forms of implementation necessarily fall into an accountability gap, as a number of accountability-promoting measures may mitigate the lack of institutionalised, ex post accountability in the form of legislative approval. This chapter highlights, in particular, public consultation processes, which may take place at the international and domestic levels, both before and after the conclusion of non-binding instruments (thus allowing for ex post as well as ex ante accountability). Public consultation may compensate for the absence of internal accountability to the legislature, by allowing for external accountability to stakeholders likely to be affected by the implementation of the non-binding instrument.

As the accountability concerns associated with various instruments will vary considerably depending on the particular instrument and the state in which it is being implemented, this chapter posits a framework for approaching the analysis of accountability in a range of contexts. Because non-binding instruments have legal consequences in domestic legal systems, this form of international norm creation calls for analysis of the accountability of executive branch officials who negotiate these instruments under the auspices of international organisations. The 'golden age of the treaty' may indeed be coming to a close, but this phenomenon ought to be scrutinised rather than celebrated or simply observed.[83] This chapter shows that in some, if not many, circumstances, the mechanisms that help to ensure accountability in the context of non-binding instruments will be less formal and institutionalised, ex ante as well as ex post, and will involve stakeholders as well as (or instead of) legislators themselves. Thus, while non-binding instruments may indeed diminish the role of legislatures with respect to the implementation of international norms, they do not necessarily raise serious accountability concerns.

[83] Kal Raustiala, 'The Architecture of International Cooperation: Transgovernmental Networks and the Future of International Law' (2002) 43:1 *Virginia Journal of International Law* 1–92, 25.

10

Traditional and Modern Designs for an International Law of Sovereign Debt Restructuring

A Way Forward

KEI NAKAJIMA

The external debt of states, as distinct from its internal debt, is normally expressed in foreign currencies, governed by foreign laws and subject to the jurisdiction of foreign courts.[1] These features, in addition to the debtor's status as sovereign, are often perceived as guarantees of the high creditworthiness of sovereign bonds in modern financial markets. However, history shows that sovereign states facing economic or financial crises have frequently declared default on their external debt.[2] It is therefore critically important for foreign private creditors to articulate effective legal schemes by which to stake their claims against defaulting states. Conversely, it is equally vital for defaulting states to defend themselves from a flood of creditor claims in order to secure their remaining assets, and thereby pave the way for a smooth post-crisis recovery. Unlike a private company, a state cannot liquidate itself and cease to exist.[3] Even

Thanks are due to Katayoun H. Nejad, Sayoko Tanaka, and the participants in the fifth 'Four Societies' workshop of 2014 for their comments on an earlier version of this work.

1 Sovereign Insolvency Study Group, 'State Insolvency: Options for the Way Forward' in *Report of the Seventy-fourth Conference Held in The Hague, 15–19 August 2010* (London: International Law Association, 2010), 978–1022, 982 [ILA Sovereign Insolvency Study Group Report 2010].

2 Karl Strupp, 'L'intervention en matière financière' (1925) 8 *Recueil des Cours* 5–124; Jacques Attali, *Tous ruinés dans dix ans? Dette publique: La dernière chance* (Paris: Librairie générale française, 2010), chs. 1 and 3.

3 Francois Gianviti, Anne O. Krueger, Jean Pisani-Ferry, André Sapir and Jürgen von Hagen, *A European Mechanism for Sovereign Debt Crisis Resolution: A Proposal* (Brussels: Bruegel, 2010), 23.

after the declaration of default, a state needs to exist in order to fulfil its duty towards its citizens.[4]

It is against this background that the importance of sovereign debt restructuring as a scheme to reconcile these two competing demands has been repeatedly emphasised. Sovereign debt restructuring can be defined roughly as 'the various techniques used by countries in financial distress to change the debt's original payment terms'.[5] However, this concept has not obtained a fixed legal meaning, and no international mechanism dealing directly with the phenomenon exists. With numerous experts, including not only international lawyers but also economists and financial experts, having put forward various designs for sovereign debt restructuring,[6] one might be able to identify the existence of a loose network of experts struggling with this old and new problem. Although governments have also played a role, it has been relatively modest at least until recently.[7] Bearing in mind the conventional wisdom that the rules of international law are to be made by sovereign states, the international law of sovereign debt restructuring has a distinctive feature in that experts, especially those outside governments such as officers of international financial institutions, lawyers advising on sovereign lending and scholars, have played a significant role in the designing of the rules. Accordingly, their networks have constituted the main arena in which the legal discourse of sovereign debt takes place.

Nevertheless, one might be surprised to learn that the majority of the experts have tended to adhere to centralised and comprehensive, rather

[4] Sir John Fischer Williams, 'Le droit international et les obligations financières internationales qui naissent d'un contrat' (1923) 1 *Recueil des Cours* 289–361, 343.

[5] Michael Waibel, 'Opening Pandora's Box: Sovereign Bonds in International Arbitration' (2007) 101 *American Journal of International Law* 711–749, 712.

[6] See generally Kenneth Rogoff and Jeromin Zettelmeyer, *Bankruptcy Procedures for Sovereigns: A History of Ideas, 1976–2001*, International Monetary Fund Working Paper WP/02/133, August 2002, online at: www.imf.org/external/pubs/ft/wp/2002/wp02133.pdf.

[7] On 9 September 2014, the UN General Assembly decided to elaborate and adopt 'a multilateral legal framework for sovereign debt restructuring processes' in future: *Towards the Establishment of a Multilateral Legal Framework for Sovereign Debt Restructuring Processes*, GA Res 68/304, UN Doc A/RES/68/304 (17 September 2014), para 5. Yet this resolution, initiated by the Group of 77 developing countries and China, faced many abstentions and much opposition. The substance of the proposal is also unknown, with Italy abstaining due in part to the 'the lack of information about the possible elements of the proposed framework': UN Doc A/68/PV.107 (9 September 2014), 8 (Mr. Lambertini).

than decentralised, approaches.[8] As will be discussed below, many of these experts have, with little hesitation, advocated for the ambitious creation of a new international court dealing with sovereign debt disputes, with the most prominent of these proposals being the Sovereign Debt Restructuring Mechanism (SDRM) advocated by the International Monetary Fund (IMF) in 2002. Described as a 'statutory approach' to sovereign debt restructuring, this proposal adheres firmly to a comprehensive and centralised approach. The results of such ambitious attempts were, however, always met with failure, mainly due to their political infeasibility. But if today's experts wish to play a role in the development of global governance networks to address sovereign debt restructuring, it would be hasty to reject these traditional designs simply because they were too optimistic. Instead, it would be much more productive to ask why the experts that were involved felt compelled to adhere to such a centralised statutory approach in the face of the decentralised structure of the international legal order. By identifying the indispensable elements and by putting aside less feasible attempts, international legal discourse among current experts will eventually find a way towards developing a decentralised mechanism for the international law of sovereign debt restructuring.

This chapter is a part of a larger project analysing the legal scheme for sovereign debt restructuring in terms of the conceptual framework of global administrative law.[9] The assumption is that sovereign lending and debt restructuring are governed by a multi-layered bundle of law (debt contracts, contract law generally and public international law including investment treaties) involving various actors and stakeholders (states, citizens of a defaulting state, foreign investors and creditors, private banks, civil society groups campaigning against 'vulture funds' and regional and international financial organisations). If the establishment of a comprehensive system for debt restructuring will be improbable in the near future, one has to explore the mechanism of governance in

[8] Maria Chiara Malaguti, 'Sovereign Insolvency and International Legal Order' (2009) 11:3 *International Community Law Review* 307–326, 321.

[9] See further Benedict Kingsbury, Nico Krisch and Richard B. Stewart, 'The Emergence of Global Administrative Law' (2005) 68:3–4 *Law and Contemporary Problems* 15–61; Benedict Kingsbury and Stephan W. Schill, 'Investor-state Arbitration as Governance: Fair and Equitable Treatment, Proportionality and the Emerging Global Administrative Law', NYU School of Law Public Law Research Paper No 09–46 (19 August 2009), 5–6. See also the chapter by Josephine Toop in this collection.

a non-systematic, hybrid process of restructuring. In this respect, global administrative law will set a conceptual framework that will identify the mechanism of administration in debt restructurings, strengthen the transparency of the process and demand the accountability of the participants, inter alia, governments of defaulting states and holdout creditors.

With this in mind, this chapter reviews the evolution of the traditional designs for sovereign debt restructuring so as to identify the way forward for modern designs. A comprehensive review of scholarly works is not my aim, with this chapter having benefitted greatly from the concise 'history of ideas' from 1976 to 2001 authored by IMF economists Kenneth Rogoff and Jeromin Zettelmeyer concerning the application of bankruptcy reorganisation principles to sovereigns.[10] The aim of this chapter is to grasp the principal characteristics of traditional designs and to identify the continuity and discontinuity between the traditional and possible modern designs for sovereign debt restructuring. Needless to say, such a dichotomy of traditional and modern designs is not offered as the precise picture of previous arguments, but rather as a diagram to find a way towards a decentralised governance mechanism without abandoning the insights of our predecessors.

The chapter is organised into five sections. The theoretical framework for traditional designs and the core problems of sovereign defaults will be identified in Section I. By looking back at a forgotten pioneer in this field in Section II, then, by evaluating the ambitious scholarly projects for an 'international bankruptcy court' in Section III, and the SDRM proposed by the IMF in Section IV, the essential characteristics and limits of traditional designs will be identified. On this basis, the possibility of a modern design for sovereign debt restructuring will be explored in Section V with reference to the contemporary project of the Max Planck Institute for Comparative Public Law and International Law on the exercise of what is termed 'international public authority'[11] and its application to sovereign defaults.

[10] Rogoff and Zettelmeyer, above note 6.

[11] On the difference between the global administrative law project and the project of international public authority, see Philipp Dann and Marie von Engelhardt, 'Legal Approaches to Global Governance and Accountability: Informal Lawmaking, International Public Authority, and Global Administrative Law Compared' in Joost Pauwelyn, Ramses A. Wessel and Jan Wouters, eds., *Informal International Lawmaking* (Oxford: Oxford University Press, 2012), 106–121.

I The Theoretical Framework for Traditional Designs

Sovereign defaults give rise to various complex problems. From the perspective of designing an effective legal scheme, the principal issues that have attracted the continuing interest of experts are the collective action problems of foreign private creditors, and the disincentives and 'moral hazard' of debtor states. These issues have been put forward as the basis for drawing an analogy to domestic bankruptcy law, which in turn serves as a rationale for the creation of a centralised international institution.

A Collective Action Problems and Vultures' Victory

One of the traditional methods used for sovereign financing was a system of syndicated loans in which a limited number of commercial banks participate as the lenders. Within this scheme, banks usually have an interest in continuing their business with both sovereign borrowers and fellow banks. As a result, commercial banks participate in a repeated 'highly transparent prisoner's dilemma' in terms of game theory, which mitigates the incentive to free ride. If a commercial bank does not agree to a debt restructuring plan in which a majority of lenders participate, but instead, acting separately, brings a claim against the defaulting state to obtain the full amount of its credits, that bank might be excluded by its peers from future transactions.[12] As a result, under a system of syndicated loans, the probability of holdout litigation by an individual creditor is relatively limited, with syndicated loans having been the dominant means for sovereign borrowing during the 1970s and 1980s.[13]

In the 1990s, however, the principal scheme for sovereign borrowing shifted from syndicated bank loans to the direct issuance of bonds in capital markets.[14] This shift occurred against the backdrop of the 1989 Brady Plan, which sought to address the debt crisis of the 1980s through the granting of debt relief in exchange for greater collectability and also

[12] Matthias Goldmann, 'Sovereign Debt Crises as Threats to the Peace: Restructuring under Chapter VII of the UN Charter' (2012) 4:1 *Goettingen Journal of International Law* 153–175, 161.

[13] Blaise Gadanecz, 'The Syndicated Loan Market: Structure, Development and Implications' (December 2004) *BIS Quarterly Review* 75; Mattias Audit, 'Introduction générale: dissection du risque souverain', Mattias Audit, ed., *Insolvabilité des états et dettes souveraines* (Paris: Librairie générale de droit et de jurisprudence, 2011), 6.

[14] Anne O. Krueger and Sean Hagan, 'Sovereign Workouts: An IMF Perspective' (2005) 6:1 *Chicago Journal of International Law* 203–218, 209–210; ILA Sovereign Insolvency Study Group Report 2010, above note 1, 985 and 986.

encouraged greater tradability so as to diversify risk more widely.[15] On the one hand, the new scheme made it possible for sovereign states to access broader sources of external financing. On the other hand, debtor states faced a number of atomised private creditors with diverse interests in their bonds.[16] Some creditors wish to instil a long-term relationship with a sovereign borrower, while other creditors, often called 'vulture funds',[17] have interests only in recovering the face value of their bonds. In the words of Matthias Goldmann of the Max Planck Institute, these creditors 'do not participate in repeated games',[18] and therefore exhibit little or no hesitation in initiating holdout litigation against debtor states to enforce their claims before national courts.[19] It is this sort of conduct – or even its likelihood – by creditors that presents what experts term 'collective action problems'.[20] Holdout litigation, even if initiated by a small number of foreign creditors, will adversely affect the whole process of sovereign debt restructuring because it lowers the incentive for the majority of creditors to join in the rescheduling of debts.[21]

A strong argument in support of this business strategy was made by the US Department of Justice in the case of *Allied Bank International* v. *Banco Credito Agricola de Cartag* before the US Court of Appeals.[22] In this case, concerning the default of Costa Rica in 1981, the Department argued in its amicus curiae brief that 'while parties may agree to renegotiate conditions of payment, *the underlying obligations to pay*

[15] Jill E. Fisch and Caroline M. Gentile, 'Vultures or Vanguards? The Role of Litigation in Sovereign Debt Restructuring' (2004) 53 *Emory Law Journal* 1043–1113, 1064. On the principles of the Brady Plan, see Ross P. Buckley, 'The Facilitation of the Brady Plan: Emerging Markets Debt Trading from 1989 to 1993' (1998) 21 *Fordham International Law Journal* 1802–1889.

[16] Krueger and Hagan, above note 14, 210.

[17] Kevin P. Gallagher, *The New Vulture Culture: Sovereign Debt Restructuring and Trade and Investment Treaties*, International Development Economic Associates Working Paper 02/2011, July 2011, online at: www.networkideas.org/working/jul2011/02_2011.pdf. See also Patrick Wautelet, 'Vulture Funds, Creditors and Sovereign Debtors: How to Find a Balance?' in Mattias Audit, ed., *Insolvabilité des états et dettes souveraines* (Paris: Librairie générale de droit et de jurisprudence, 2011), 103–164.

[18] Goldmann, above note 12, 161.

[19] See, for example, *NML Capital, Ltd.* v. *Republic of Argentina*, No 08 Civ 6978 (TPG) (SDNY 23 February 2012); *NML Capital, Ltd.* v. *Republic of Argentina*, 699 F.3d 246 (USCA 2nd Cir. 2012). These cases led Argentina to institute proceedings against the United States before the International Court of Justice in 2014; however, American consent is needed for further steps to be taken in the international proceedings.

[20] Anna Gelpern, 'How Collective Action Is Changing Sovereign Debt' (2003) 22:5 *International Financial Law Review* 19–23.

[21] Waibel, above note 5, 713.

[22] 757 F.2d 516 (USCA 2nd Cir. 1985).

nevertheless remain valid and enforceable'.[23] The idea behind this statement was to criticise Costa Rica's unilateral attempts to restructure private obligations, as confirmed by the statement by the Court of Appeals that 'The Costa Rican government's unilateral attempt to repudiate private, commercial obligations is inconsistent with the orderly resolution of international debt problems'.[24] Subsequently, this case has been viewed widely by experts as illustrating how a single creditor can hold out,[25] with the defaulting state being forced to revise its financial strategies for the repayment of its external debts.[26] Joseph E. Stiglitz, a prominent Nobel laureate in economics, characterised the current legal situation as a 'vultures' victory' because of the absence of a compulsory mechanism equivalent to domestic bankruptcy laws and courts at the international level.[27]

B Disincentives and the Moral Hazard for Debtor States

Difficulties arise not only from the adverse conduct of creditors, but also from the lax behaviour of debtor states. First, debtor governments usually have disincentives to deal with their debt problems seriously. Sovereign debt crises force debtor states to implement austerity measures that entail severe economic distress for their populations, including the cutting of public services and reductions in the number of public employees. In addition, a formal declaration of default will, in effect, close that state's access to foreign financial markets. As a result, governments of debtor states have disincentives to address their debt problems and to negotiate with creditors in the early stages of a financial crisis. Certainly, the expectation of economic recovery might be seen as a justification for deferring debt restructuring (in the sense of 'waiting-for-a-larger-cake'[28]). In the meantime, however, the situation might worsen, resulting in a far more severe crisis. No one can definitively predict the future

[23] Ibid., 519 [emphasis added]. [24] Ibid., 522.

[25] Rogoff and Zettelmeyer, above note 6, 7.

[26] Alice de Jonge, 'Returning to Fundamentals: Principles of International Law Applicable to the Resolution of Sovereign Debt Crises' (2013) 36:1 *Suffolk Transnational Law Review* 1–50, 29 and 30.

[27] Joseph E. Stiglitz, 'The Vultures' Victory' published by *Project Syndicate* (4 September 2013), online at: www.project-syndicate.org/commentary/argentina-s-debt-and-american-courts-by-joseph-e–stiglitz.

[28] Ran Bi, *Beneficial Delays in Debt Restructuring Negotiations*, IMF Working Paper WP/8/38, 2008, 1 and 4.

economic situations.[29] But, because no compulsory bankruptcy proceedings exist, 'the stop early' principle in domestic bankruptcy law, which imposes duties on directors to take actions when their company is insolvent, is not considered feasible for defaulting sovereign states.[30]

Experts have also drawn attention to the so-called moral hazard that is associated with the IMF-led bailouts that have taken place in almost all modern sovereign debt crises.[31] Moral hazard in this context refers to 'distorted incentive structures that induce borrowers . . . to engage in risky financial behaviour, or inadequately monitor the risks they assume, in the expectation that they will be insulated from the adverse consequences of their activities by the public authorities'.[32] Put differently, debtor states will be much less careful about their indebtedness if they can expect such bailouts in cases of emergency. Financial bailouts are also sometimes necessary for defaulting private companies and in particular for commercial banks (ironically often for those considered 'too-big-to-fail'). As a result, experts have recently discussed the drawing up of a so-called 'living will' for banks, which is 'a recovery and resolution plan drawn up *ex ante* with the purpose of using it if a bank gets into difficulties'.[33] However, it has also been suggested that this proposal will be unworkable without a compulsory monitoring mechanism in existence at the international level.

II A Forgotten Pioneer: The League Proposal for an International Loans Tribunal

As illustrated above, experts working within this field have identified the problems arising out of sovereign lending and default and then concluded that these problems share a certain similarity with problems

[29] Goldmann, above note 12, 166.

[30] ILA Sovereign Insolvency Study Group Report 2010, above note 1, 988.

[31] Rogoff and Zettelmeyer, above note 6, 4.

[32] Group of 10, *The Resolution of Sovereign Liquidity Crises: A Report to the Ministers and Governors Prepared under the Auspices of the Deputies*, May 1996, para 5, online at: www.bis.org/publ/gten03.pdf.

[33] Emilios Avgouleas, Charles Goodhart and Dirk Schoenmaker, 'Bank Resolution Plans as a Catalyst for Global Financial Reform' (2013) 9:2 *Journal of Financial Stability* 210–218. According to the authors at 211, 'The main purpose of Living Wills is to achieve *ex ante* benefits. The drawing up of a Living Will should focus the minds of the institution's management and of the supervisors as to what they should expect in the event of an institution's failure. Thus, the drawing up of a Living Will could act as a catalyst for thinking and taking action, as in the wills of individuals.'

arising from corporate bankruptcies. Consequently, it was natural for the experts to draw upon analogies to domestic bankruptcy law so as to address the issues of sovereign defaults. Such analogies were the crux of traditional designs for sovereign debt restructuring. Although Rogoff and Zettelmeyer take the view that the idea of applying domestic bankruptcy principles to sovereigns can be traced back to Adam Smith, they conclude that '[t]he earliest modern reference' for this subject was a work published in 1976;[34] hence their decision to examine proposals published from 1976 on.[35] There is, however, a forgotten pioneer in this field, namely the proposal for an International Loans Tribunal made by the League of Nations in 1939. The League's proposal is worth examining further in that it had already identified the collective action problems discussed above, and had consequently proposed the creation of a permanent international tribunal as a possible solution.

A *Collective Action Requirement for Debt Recovery*

The interwar period saw a great increase in the internal and external indebtedness of states, with the number of sovereign defaults also rising dramatically in this period.[36] Against this background, a 'Committee for the Study of International Loan Contracts' was created by way of a resolution of the Assembly of the League of Nations that was adopted in September 1935, on the initiative of the Netherlands government.[37] The Committee was composed mainly of bank directors, but also included two legal experts among its members. The two legal experts were French law professor (and later a Judge and President of the International Court of Justice) Jules Basdevant and English lawyer Alexander Fachiri.

The committee was mandated to examine the means for improving the content of contracts for future international loans issued by governments or other public authorities. Its terms of reference also made clear that the committee was mandated 'in particular, to prepare model provisions – *if*

[34] Göran Ohlin, 'Debts, Development and Default' in Gerald K. Helleiner, ed., *A World Divided: The Less Developed Countries in the International Economy* (Cambridge: Cambridge University Press, 1976), 207–223.

[35] Rogoff and Zettelmeyer, above note 6, 3 and 4.

[36] Manley O. Hudson, *International Tribunals: Past and Future* (Washington, DC: Carnegie Endowment for International Peace and Brookings Institution, 1944), 204.

[37] *Report of the Committee for the Study of International Loan Contracts* (Geneva: League of Nations, 1939), 5 [League of Nations International Loan Contracts Report].

necessary, with a system of arbitration – which could, if the parties so desired, be inserted in such contracts'.[38] In line with these terms of reference, the committee examined the problems associated with international loans and, notably, drafted a model arbitration clause to be included in future loan contracts.[39] The role of arbitral tribunals was limited strictly to 'that of judges' deciding the rights and obligations of parties, as distinct from the modification of contracts, the latter having essentially a character of negotiation.[40]

In light of the potential holdout strategy of creditors that has been mentioned above, such a 'legalistic' approach might appear to favour foreign private creditors. However, the committee also introduced two schemes to address what have subsequently been called 'collective action problems'. First, in the committee's scheme, not every bondholder had a right to institute proceedings. Rather, a bondholder had to possess 'securities not less than 10 per cent of the amount outstanding'[41] before submitting the case to an arbitral tribunal. By imposing such a 'collective action' requirement, albeit that the threshold might be considered quite low, the committee appears to have addressed the collective action problems now seen in modern terms. Secondly, the committee provided that '*any* party may seize the Tribunal directly by means of a unilateral application',[42] which meant that sovereign bonds disputes might be brought before the tribunal not only by creditors, but also by debtor states.[43]

B *Aspiration for an International Loans Tribunal*

Immediately after finishing its work on the arbitration clause, the committee sensed the limitations with its own approach. As a result, it expressed a strong aspiration to establish a permanent international tribunal. As explained in its report published in 1939:

> The Committee considers that the above suggestions would constitute a considerable step in advance. It is, however, sensible of the fact that a complete solution of the legal difficulties could only be achieved if these questions were taken out of the field of national law by international convention. Under such a convention, *States would undertake to set up an International Loans Tribunal, which would be a single Tribunal with competence extending to all international loans.*[44]

[38] Ibid., 5 and 6 [emphasis added]. [39] Ibid., 9–27. [40] Ibid., 27. [41] Ibid., 26.
[42] Ibid. [emphasis added]. [43] Ibid., 41. [44] Ibid., 27 [emphasis added].

In addition to the two aspects of the model arbitration clause examined above, the committee prepared a 'Draft International Convention' that provides for at least three mechanisms for the settlement of international loan disputes that bear a resemblance to today's investor–state arbitration under the auspices of the International Centre for Settlement of Investment Disputes (ICSID).[45] First, like foreign investors, the draft convention allowed foreign private bondholders to submit directly to the tribunal '[a]*ny disputes* which may arise in respect of any loan to which the present Act has been declared to be applicable'.[46] Secondly, the tribunal adjudicates the dispute 'on the basis of the contracts concluded and of the laws which are applicable, *provided these are not contrary to international law, as well as on the basis of the general principles of law*'.[47] This provision is roughly in line with an early interpretation of article 42(1) of the ICSID Convention, which presupposed the 'corrective function' of international law vis-à-vis domestic law.[48] Thirdly, under the draft convention, the tribunal's decision is final and has 'the same force *as if it had been rendered by a national court of last instance*',[49] which is an approach similar to the requirement that ICSID awards shall be enforced 'as if it were a final judgment of a court in that State'.[50]

However, unlike its draft model arbitration clause, the committee hid this ambitious design for sovereign debt dispute settlement within an annex to its report. The committee explained the reasoning for this as follows:

> The Committee had before it a draft for this purpose, but in present circumstances it would seem difficult to obtain adhesion to such

[45] See further, Convention on the Settlement of Investment Disputes Between States and Nationals of Other States, 18 March 1965, 575 UNTS 159, in force 14 October 1966 [ICSID Convention].

[46] League of Nations International Loan Contracts Report, above note 37, 40 [emphasis added].

[47] Ibid., 41.

[48] *Amco Asia Corporation and others* v. *Republic of Indonesia*, ICSID Case No ARB/81/1, Decision on Annulment, 16 May 1986, para 20. Commentators have questioned this reading: see Emmanuel Gaillard and Yas Banifatemi, 'The Meaning of "and" in Article 42(1), Second Sentence, of the Washington Convention: The Role of International Law in the ICSID Choice of Law Process' (2003) 18:2 *ICSID Review: Foreign Investment Law Journal* 375–411, 408–411; Zachary Douglas, *The International Law of Investment Claims* (Cambridge: Cambridge University Press, 2009), 129 and 130; Rudolf Dolzer and Christoph Schreuer, *The Principles of International Investment Law*, 2nd ed. (Oxford: Oxford University Press, 2012), 292.

[49] League of Nations International Loan Contracts Report, above note 37, 41.

[50] ICSID Convention, above note 45, art. 54(1).

> a Convention. The Committee therefore has not examined this proposal in detail and confines itself to including it in Annex IV for record.[51]

As a result, the League's proposal for sovereign debt dispute settlement tends to be forgotten in the modern discourse on sovereign debt restructuring.[52] To be sure, the basic design remained as a dispute settlement procedure rather than a bankruptcy mechanism.[53] Nevertheless, the proposal qualifies as a pioneer in this field in that it identified a key part of the persisting problem associated with sovereign defaults and attempted to address this by creating a centralised international mechanism.[54] The League proposal should therefore be considered the prototype of traditional designs for sovereign debt restructuring.

III Governance by Analogy: Borrowing from the US Bankruptcy Code

Given the impact of World War II, there was little sovereign borrowing in the 1950s and 1960s. Sovereign credits were then restored through the practice of syndicated bank loans in the 1970s; however, many emerging countries defaulted on these loans during and after the 1980s.[55] It was against this background that legal discourse among experts on the subject of sovereign defaults experienced a resurgence. Various designs were proposed as a solution to the financial crises in these emerging markets, and in particular to the 1995 financial crisis in Mexico.[56] One of the arguments, which seems to have been the backbone of the majority of the experts, was to borrow the ideas of the US Bankruptcy Code, resulting in an ambitious proposition to create an 'international bankruptcy court'.

A *Corporate and Sovereign Bankruptcies: The Basis of the Analogy*

The origins for much of the ideas about an international legal regime governing sovereign debt restructurings can be found in the law of

[51] League of Nations International Loan Contracts Report, above note 37, 27.

[52] Waibel states that: 'This early precursor to the Sovereign Debt Restructuring Mechanism has yet to receive due attention': Michael Waibel, *Sovereign Defaults before International Courts and Tribunals* (Cambridge: Cambridge University Press, 2011), 325.

[53] August Reinisch, *State Responsibility for Debts: International Law Aspects of External Debt and Debt Restructuring* (Vienna: Böhlau Verlag, 1995), 16, note 74.

[54] See also Gustavo Adolfo Olivares Marcos, *The Legal Practice of the Recovery of State External Debt* (PhD thesis, University of Geneva, 2005), 142.

[55] ILA Sovereign Insolvency Study Group Report 2010, above note 1, 985.

[56] See generally, Rogoff and Zettelmeyer, above note 6, 13–23.

corporate financial distress,[57] or, more concretely, in chapter 11 of the US Bankruptcy Code.[58] According to Christopher Oechsli, possibly the first author to refer explicitly to chapter 11 as the model for a state bankruptcy mechanism,[59] the basis of the analogy can be found in the chapter's policy rationale. As Oechsli explained back in 1981:

> Chapter 11 of the Act is designed to *maximize the yield* from the debtor's assets *without withdrawing control from the debtor* or liquidating its assets for the creditors' immediate satisfaction.[60]

Unlike chapter 7 of the same Code, which provides for a liquidation process for companies, chapter 11 leaves open the possibility for a defaulting company to continue to possess control over its business operations (i.e. a 'debtor-in-possession') under the supervision of the courts. In a similar vein, a proposed sovereign debt restructuring mechanism must not undermine the debtor state's sovereignty with respect to economic rehabilitation,[61] because one cannot presuppose that sovereign states can liquidate themselves and put an end to their 'businesses'. There is also a benefit for foreign private creditors, who can expect a higher return in the long term by looking forward to the economic recovery of the debtor state, as this would strengthen the debtor state's repayment capacity.[62] In short, the theoretical basis for the domestic bankruptcy law analogy is the idea that the claims of creditors and the economic needs of debtors can be satisfied simultaneously by legally protecting and restoring the productive status of the latter.

To this end, chapter 11 provides various mechanisms including, inter alia, a trustee with the competence to monitor the debtor's financial status; a creditor committee, which integrates the various interests of the creditors; and a framework for formulating an eventually enforceable rehabilitation plan. However, most of these mechanisms presuppose judicial intervention if circumstances require. Once again, unless an enforcement mechanism exists in the international sphere, the bankruptcy law analogy is deemed to have little feasibility,[63] and as a result,

[57] Robert Rasmussen, 'Integrating a Theory of the State into Sovereign Debt Restructuring' (2004) 53 *Emory Law Journal* 1159–1187, 1174.

[58] Christopher G. Oechsli, 'Procedural Guidelines for Renegotiating LDC Debt: An Analogy to Chapter 11 of the US Bankruptcy Reform Act' (1981) 21:2 *Virginia Journal of International Law* 305–342, 331.

[59] Rogoff and Zettelmeyer, above note 6, 5.

[60] Oechsli, above note 58, 332 [emphasis added]. [61] Ibid. [62] Ibid.

[63] Oechsli's view on this seems to be a bit ambivalent. On the one hand, he predicted optimistically that the '[e]stablishment of a renegotiation plan could continue to be by the

a more ambitious proposal for the creation of an international court has re-emerged for discussion.

B The Proposal for an International Bankruptcy Court

It was probably a lecture given by American economist Jeffrey D. Sachs in 1995 that popularised the very idea of a sovereign bankruptcy mechanism.[64] Consciously or unconsciously, Sachs' proposal followed the previous ideas examined above, and it strongly advocated the establishment of an 'international bankruptcy court'. The main concern was likewise to defend the autonomy of defaulting states during and after financial distress. As Sachs explained:

> *The fact that the debtor is a government is not seen as a reason to forgo the relief of the bankruptcy law, but on the contrary, as a reason to strengthen the relief in order to maintain the political functions of the government,* and to prevent the descent into the Hobbesian world, brought on the by the financial weakness of the state.[65]

Sachs too brought the ideas of domestic bankruptcy law to the international legal plane by stressing the similarity between collective action problems arising out of corporate bankruptcies and of sovereign defaults. He distinguished three stages for the collective action problems, and found solutions in each stage with direct reference to the experience of domestic bankruptcy law.

The first stage occurs at the time of the declaration of default, which prompts a 'creditor grab race' whereby the creditors have an interest not only in satisfying their claims against the defaulted company or state but also in doing so *ahead* of the other creditors.[66] In this regard, Sachs referred to the US Bankruptcy Code, which prevents 'any act to collect, assess, or recover a claim against the debtor that arose before the commencement'[67] of the bankruptcy proceeding. He planned to forestall such a grab race towards defaulted sovereigns by introducing an

agreement and consensus of the parties, and not by imposition from some international institution', but without explaining the feasibility of such an agreement. On the other hand, he emphasised that the IMF could fill a role analogous to the trustee or the bankruptcy court, but put it forward as a choice. See Oechsli, above note 58, 333 and 334.

64 Rogoff and Zettelmeyer, above note 6, 18.

65 Jeffrey D. Sachs, 'Do We Need an International Lender of Last Resort?' Frank D. Graham Lecture, Princeton University, 20 April 1995, 9, online at: http://academiccommons.columbia.edu/item/ac:124041 (emphasis in original).

66 Ibid., 7. 67 11 U.S.C. §362(a)(6).

automatic standstill of the proceedings initiated by foreign creditors before domestic courts.

The second stage takes place during the restructuring itself. Both a defaulted company and a defaulted state need continuing access to capital markets. However, there would be little incentive for foreign private creditors to make a fresh loan to a defaulted entity unless they can obtain a guarantee that the new loan will be paid ahead of the sovereign bonds issued earlier.[68] Sachs again borrowed from the US Bankruptcy Code, which provides that the court may authorise the obtaining of credit or the incurring of debt 'with priority over any or all administrative expenses'.[69] His intention was to attract new loans by prioritizing the repayment of the new loans over that of pre-default bonds.[70]

The third stage is, in Sachs' words, the final reorganisation of the balance sheet. Yet the problem he identified here would relate to the entire process of debt restructuring: foreign creditors, who do not participate in the prisoner's dilemma, would reserve the option either to holdout or to free-ride the outcome of the debt restructuring and, eventually, choose the option more favourable to them. As explained above, that state of affairs adversely affects the process of sovereign debt restructurings. Consequently, Sachs once again referred to the US Bankruptcy Code, borrowing the idea of a so-called 'cram down'[71] whereby the debt reorganisation plan is involuntary imposed by a court, or a majority of creditors, over dissenting creditors.[72]

Unlike the project of the League of Nations, which concealed its ambitions for an international court in an annex, Sachs vigorously and overtly pushed forward the normative argument for a court on the international plane. The existence of the IMF is probably what made his argument possible. In fact, he insisted that 'IMF practices should be reorganised so that the IMF plays a role far more like an international bankruptcy court'.[73] As he explained:

> In the international context there is little formal law covering state insolvency, and certainly no bankruptcy code. Therefore, the question is

[68] Sachs, above note 65, 7. [69] 11 U.S.C. §364(c). [70] Sachs, above note 65, 7.

[71] Ibid., 7 and 8.

[72] 11 U.S.C. §1129(b)(1) provides that: 'the court, on request of the proponent of the plan, shall confirm the plan ... if the plan does not discriminate unfairly, and is fair and equitable, with respect to each class of claims or interests that is impaired under, and has not accepted, the plan'.

[73] Sachs, above note 65, 14.

> mostly a normative one – how should international practice, and specifically IMF practice, be arranged in view of the lessons of bankruptcy law.[74]

Although some doubts were entertained as to the political feasibility of such an institutional reform for the IMF,[75] it was this line of argument that represented the peak of the traditional legal discourse on sovereign debt restructuring, as will be discussed in the next section.

IV Centralised Governance: The Sovereign Debt Restructuring Mechanism

Creditor protection and debt reorganisation are not always in complete opposition. The experience of domestic bankruptcy law indicates that smooth debt reorganisation not only helps recover the debtor's financial situation, but also satisfies the creditors' monetary claims all the more because the recovered debtor is now in a position to produce profits again, a part of which can be used to repay creditors. In other words, the policy goal of bankruptcy law is not always the reconciliation of two competing interests, but sometimes the optimisation or, as much as possible, the maximisation of the interests of all relevant stakeholders. Therefore, following this line of analysis, it might be in the interest of all foreign creditors to participate in sovereign debt restructuring. Nevertheless, holdout strategies are still attractive to creditors insofar as they have to adopt a *maximin* strategy within a prisoner's dilemma. In other words, if the outcome of the debt renegotiation is uncertain, if the economic recovery of the debtor is unpredictable and if other creditors also have the option to holdout, each creditor would be inclined to adopt a holdout strategy to secure *the best of the worst* repayment. That is why statutory bankruptcy law, which deprives creditors of such options and is enforced by a court, is indispensable in a domestic legal system. Therefore, traditional designs of sovereign debt restructuring have presupposed not only the similarity of the goals of domestic bankruptcy law and sovereign debt restructuring, but also

[74] Ibid., 8.

[75] As explained by the Working Party of the Group of Ten: 'Despite their advantages in a national context and some theoretical appeal by analogy in an international context, formal insolvency procedures do not appear to be either appropriate or feasible now or in the foreseeable future as a means of dealing with sovereign debt problems' and thus a proposal that 'focused its attention on procedures that do not require fundamental changes in international laws and conventions and could be implemented more quickly': Group of 10 Report, above note 32, 10 and 11.

the necessity of establishing some compulsory mechanism on the international legal plane.

A SDRM: A Viable Design?

It is against this background that the 2002 proposal for a Sovereign Debt Restructuring Mechanism (SDRM) must be considered remarkable. Introduced by Anne Krueger,[76] while she was serving as the first deputy director of the IMF, the basic structure of the SDRM proposal was in essence the same as previous proposals in that it borrowed the ideas of domestic bankruptcy law and advocated for the establishment of a centralised international mechanism. Since many commentators have already analysed the first official proposal for an SDRM,[77] a remark by Lee Buchheit, a leading expert in the field of international financial law, will suffice to summarise the proposal's historical significance:

> The SDRM was intended to accomplish what the diplomats, gunboat captains, administrators, and judges of the last two hundred years failed to achieve: an effective method by which the official sector could encourage orderly workouts of private sector claims against distressed sovereigns without shouldering the full moral, political, and financial responsibility for these workouts.[78]

Unlike previous proposals, however, the SDRM contained a fairly detailed plan for the implementation of the proposal by way of an amendment of the Articles of Agreement of the International Monetary Fund (IMF Articles).[79] As a result, the significance of the SDRM proposal

[76] Anne O. Krueger, *A New Approach to Sovereign Debt Restructuring* (Washington, DC: International Monetary Fund, 2002).

[77] See, for example, Richard Euliss, 'The Feasibility of the IMF's Sovereign Debt Restructuring Mechanism: An Alternative Statutory Approach to Mollify American Reservations' (2003) 19:1 *American University International Law Review* 107–151; A. Mechele Dickerson, 'A Politically Viable Approach to Sovereign Debt Restructuring' (2004) 53 *Emory Law Journal* 997–1041, especially 1017–1022; Sean Hagan, 'Designing a Legal Framework to Restructure Sovereign Debt' (2005) 36:2 *Georgetown Journal of International Law* 299–402, especially 335–389; Jörn Axel Kämmerer, 'State Bankruptcy' in Rüdiger Wolfrum, ed., *Max Planck Encyclopedia of Public International Law* (Oxford: Oxford University Press, 2012), vol. IX, 489–498, paras 17 and 18.

[78] Lee C. Buchheit, 'The Role of the Official Sector in Sovereign Debt Workouts' (2005) 6:1 *Chicago Journal of International Law* 333–343, 342.

[79] Adopted at the United Nations Monetary and Financial Conference, Bretton Woods, New Hampshire, 22 July 1944, in force since 27 December 1945, as amended, online at: www.imf.org/external/pubs/ft/aa.

lay in its potential political feasibility,[80] rather than in the substance of the idea itself.

The sequence of the strategy for the implementation of the SDRM by way of an amendment of the IMF Articles can be analysed as follows. First, since the IMF is an international organisation attracting the participation from almost all states in the world,[81] it would be more realistic and less cumbersome to revise the existing IMF Articles than to create a new, comprehensive international convention. Second, except for some procedural issues, the IMF Articles can be amended without unanimity among its members. Article XXVIII states that an amendment can be made binding upon the entire membership '[w]hen three-fifths of the members, having 85 per cent of the total voting power, have accepted the proposed amendment'. Moreover, the IMF Articles have been amended several times since their introduction in 1945, which demonstrates that the possibility exists. Third, given the considerable benefits of IMF membership, Krueger thought that 'it is very unlikely that a member would wish to opt out of IMF membership in order to avoid application of the SDRM'.[82]

B The Failure of SDRM: The Dual Roles of the IMF

For the advocates of the SDRM, IMF incorporation was considered the only viable way for rapid implementation. If this path were followed, however, the IMF itself would play the central role in the operation of the proposed SDRM. For some experts, including Jeffrey Sachs, this aspect represented the intended consequence of the IMF's design for an international bankruptcy court, but for others, this situation raised serious doubts about the impartiality of the IMF. Indeed, Krueger realised that the IMF would assume dual roles, which would in turn raise some doubts about its impartiality. As Krueger explained, 'Specifically, the IMF's Executive Board would not be perceived as impartial in this process since the IMF is a creditor and also represents the interest of the sovereign debtor and other bilateral creditors'.[83]

Krueger thought this problem could be overcome through regime design, including the requirement for the decisions of the newly created

[80] Hagan, above note 77, 390.
[81] International Monetary Fund, 'List of Members: Last updated: 12 June 2012', online at: www.imf.org/external/np/sec/memdir/memdate.htm.
[82] Krueger, above note 76, 33–35. [83] Ibid., 34 and 35.

judicial organ to be free from review or interference by other organs of the IMF, particularly the Executive Board.[84] However, scepticism about the IMF's impartiality was the critical factor in the failure of the SDRM project, as subsequently recognised by the IMF itself,[85] and others.[86] The International Law Association's Sovereign Insolvency Study Group, for example, has concluded that the '[c]entral concerns were the double role of the IMF as a creditor and decision-maker'.[87] In any event, the United States, which wields more than 17 per cent of the vote within the IMF and hence has a de facto veto, was opposed to any proposal that would expand the powers of the IMF,[88] partly because of its preference for a decentralised, rather than centralised, approach,[89] and partly because of the opposition from major banks.[90] It was also reported that borrowing countries, including Argentina and Brazil, were adamantly opposed to the SDRM proposal,[91] because it would raise the cost of sovereign financing in foreign capital markets.[92] As a result, the SDRM proposal was doomed to fail, notwithstanding the fact that it was probably the most politically feasible design for sovereign debt restructuring from an historical perspective.[93]

84 Ibid., 35.

85 The International Monetary Financial Committee concluded at its meeting in April 2003 that it was not desirable to move forward to the SDRM: see further, Robert Gray, 'Collective Action Clauses: Theory and Practice' (2003) 35:4 *Georgetown Journal of International Law* 693–711, 693.

86 Dickerson, above note 77, 1020; Kämmerer, 'State Bankruptcy', above note 77, para 18; Christian Walter, 'Debt Crisis' (2011) in Rüdiger Wolfrum, ed., *Max Planck Encyclopedia of Public International Law* (Oxford: Oxford University Press, 2012), vol. II, 1068–1078, para 43.

87 ILA Sovereign Insolvency Study Group Report 2010, above note 1, 1010.

88 Euliss, above note 77, 125 and 126.

89 John Taylor, 'Sovereign Debt Restructuring: A US Perspective', Address given by the US Under Secretary of the Treasury for International Affairs at the conference on 'Sovereign Debt Workouts: Hopes and Hazards' organised by the Institute for International Economics in Washington DC, 1 April 2002, online at: www.iie.com/publications/papers/print.cfm?ResearchId=455&doc=pub.

90 Ross P. Buckley, 'The Bankruptcy of Nations: An Idea Whose Time Has Come' (2009) 43:3 *International Lawyer* 1189–1216, 1213.

91 'G20 Countries Disagree on Debt Defaults', *Central Banking* (11 November 2002), online at: www.centralbanking.com/central-banking/news/1431605/g20-countries-disagree-debt-defaults.

92 Andrea Orzan, *Sovereign Debt Restructuring Mechanism: Who Opposes It and Why?* (Madrid: Fundación CILAE, 2004), 1, online at: www.cilae.org/publicaciones/SDRM.pdf.

93 The IMF's International Monetary and Financial Committee stated in 2003 that 'it is not feasible now to move forward to establish the SDRM', although it added that 'work should continue on issues raised in its development that are of general relevance to the orderly

Traditional designs for sovereign debt restructuring were based to a considerable extent on an analogy with domestic bankruptcy law, aimed at the reconciliation or, if possible, maximisation of the interests of foreign private creditors and defaulting sovereign states. Numerous experts have argued that to attain that goal, it would be necessary to create a centralised international mechanism such as an international bankruptcy court or the SDRM. But while proposals to transplant domestic bankruptcy approaches to the international sphere have attracted attention within the discourse of experts, the proposals to create an effective centralised mechanism have failed repeatedly due to their political infeasibility. Consequently, a modern design for sovereign debt restructuring must also take into effect the decentralised nature of the international legal order.

V Towards a Decentralised Restructuring Mechanism

The post-SDRM period has seen the largest sovereign debt crises in history. Argentina's default in 2001, the ensuing restructurings of its debt in 2005 and 2010,[94] and the Eurozone financial crisis of 2007–2008 brought the issues of sovereign debt back to the centre of financial policy discussion.[95] Against this backdrop, the United Nations Conference on Trade and Development (UNCTAD) launched a study on responsible sovereign financing in 2009. This study led to the adoption in January 2012 of what are termed the 'Principles on Promoting Responsible Sovereign Lending and Borrowing'.[96] UNCTAD's Principles are probably the first comprehensive set of international norms on the subject of sovereign financing.[97]

resolution of financial crises': 'Communiqué of the International Monetary and Financial Committee of the Board of Governors of the International Monetary Fund' IMF Press Release No 03/50, 12 April 2003, para 15.

[94] See Jörn Axel Kämmerer, 'Argentine Debt Crisis' (2011) in Rüdiger Wolfrum, ed., *Max Planck Encyclopedia of Public International Law* (Oxford: Oxford University Press, 2012), vol. I, 579–587, paras 7–10.

[95] Supachai Panitchpakdi, 'Preface' in Carlos Espósito, Yuefen Li and Juan Pablo Bohoslavsky, eds., *Sovereign Financing and International Law: The UNCTAD Principles on Responsible Sovereign Lending and Borrowing* (Oxford: Oxford University Press, 2013), v.

[96] Online at: http://unctad.org/en/PublicationsLibrary/gdsddf2012misc1_en.pdf.

[97] Bodo Ellmers and Konstantinos Todoulos, 'The UNCTAD Principles on Promoting Responsible Sovereign Lending and Borrowing: Explained and Assessed from the Perspective of Eurodad's Responsible Finance Charter', Eurodad Briefing Paper, May 2013, 8, online at: www.eurodad.org/files/integration/2013/05/UNCTAD-Eurodad-principles-briefing.pdf.

Against the background of this soft law evolution,[98] international law experts re-joined the legal discourse on sovereign default that had been led mainly by economists and corporate law experts until the SDRM period. Public law academics Armin von Bogdandy and Matthias Goldmann have argued that existing informal arrangements for sovereign debt restructuring should be reconstructed as an exercise of international public authority,[99] which the two experts (plus another) have advocated as a new approach to international institutional law.[100] As will be explained below, this is one of the most remarkable post-SDRM projects in that it attempts to establish a normative justification for sovereign debt restructuring within the decentralised legal order. It is also worth noting that the international public authority approach also introduces human rights considerations into the arena of sovereign debt restructuring, potentially altering the traditional creditor/debtor dichotomy. This transition to a modern design for sovereign debt restructuring coincides with some new developments in the practice of addressing sovereign debt crises.

A An International Public Authority

Von Bogdandy and Goldmann define the concept of an international public authority as the 'law-based capacity of any international institution to legally or factually limit or otherwise affect other persons' or entities' use of their liberty'.[101] In other writing, they have also explained that this concept serves to complement the concept of global governance because the former is more appropriate for legal analysis than the latter, which does not provide any normative justification for an international institution.[102] To use their words, 'the concept of global governance does

[98] Juan Pablo Bohoslavsky and Carlos Espósito, 'Principles Matter: The Legal Status of the Principles on Responsible Sovereign Borrowing' in Espósito, Li and Bohoslavsky, above note 95, 80–85.

[99] Armin von Bogdandy and Matthias Goldmann, 'Sovereign Debt Restructurings as Exercises of International Public Authority: Towards a Decentralized Sovereign Insolvency Law' in Espósito, Li and Bohoslavsky, above note 95, 39–70.

[100] Armin von Bogdandy, Philipp Dann and Matthias Goldmann, 'Developing the Publicness of Public International Law: Towards a Legal Framework for Global Governance Activities' (2008) 9:11 *German Law Journal* 1375–1400.

[101] von Bogdandy and Goldmann, above note 99, 47. See also Armin von Bogdandy and Ingo Venzke, 'In Whose Name? An Investigation of International Courts' Public Authority and its Democratic Justification' (2012) 23:1 *European Journal of International Law* 7–41, 18.

[102] von Bogdandy, Dann and Goldmann, above note 100, 1376.

not allow for the identification of what the focus of a *legal* discourse should be, i.e. those acts by which unilateral authority is exercised'.[103] They go on to explain that 'In order to provide a basis for legal analysis and to identify phenomena that need justification, we propose focusing on *the exercise of international public authority*'.[104] Thus, for these experts, the concept of global governance is an analytical tool whereas the concept of international public authority focuses on the normative justification of a given international regime.[105]

The application of this concept to sovereign debt restructuring is worth examining because it seeks to establish a normative basis for the construction of sovereign insolvency law within a decentralised legal order. In substance, however, the design provided in the work of von Bogdandy and Goldmann is almost identical to that of the domestic bankruptcy law analogies examined above. For example, they argue for a stay of international and domestic enforcement actions against debtor states during sovereign debt restructuring,[106] an idea that has been advanced frequently by traditional designs as a solution to collective action problems. In this regard, von Bogdandy and Goldmann themselves recognise that they transfer the 'principle of private insolvency law to sovereign defaults'.[107] As they have written, 'It is appropriate to apply a stay by analogy to sovereign defaults, because the only fundamental normative difference between defaulting states and defaulting private entities is that the former cannot be liquidated'.[108] Thus, the substance of their design can be traced back to the same domestic bankruptcy law analogies for which the experts favouring earlier proposals incessantly advocated.

B Emergence of Human Rights Considerations

What makes their experiment remarkable is arguably its novel normative justification, which involves some adjustments to the bankruptcy law analogy. In line with comparable doctrinal attempts to address the current legal order through a lens of global administrative law or the constitutionalisation of international law, von Bogdandy and Goldmann shift their attention from states to citizens as the ultimate source of legitimacy.[109] This insight brings human rights considerations into the

[103] Ibid. [emphasis in original]. [104] Ibid. [105] Ibid., 1381.
[106] von Bogdandy and Goldmann, above note 99, 64 and 65. [107] Ibid., 65. [108] Ibid.
[109] Ibid., 45.

arena of sovereign debt restructuring. The citizens of debtor states are affected greatly by a sovereign debt restructuring, but often lack the power to influence effectively its content. Of course, these citizens are represented by their governments, but defaulting governments have often ignored their responsibility towards their citizens.[110] Recognizing this difficulty, von Bogdandy and Goldmann have argued that 'The protection of fundamental human rights, especially economic, social, and cultural rights, requires a viable state with effective institutions for the maintenance of at least a minimal standard of basic public services such as education, health, and security. States owe this duty to their citizens.'[111]

As a result, the theoretical framework for designing a sovereign debt restructuring has evolved from a traditional dichotomy of foreign creditors versus debtor states to a tripartite structure whereby citizens of a defaulting state can claim their human rights to a minimal standard of living. That change in approach makes citizens autonomous stakeholders, not only in relation to their government while it struggles with a financial bailout, but also in relation to foreign creditors. Thus, von Bogdandy and Goldmann situate their rationale for the automatic stay of proceedings initiated by foreign creditors within the 'need to respect essential human rights',[112] and not just in bankruptcy law analogies, and in this way, the citizens of defaulting states are recognised as autonomous stakeholders within the framework of the modern design for sovereign debt restructuring.

C Developments towards a Decentralised Mechanism

As discussed above, modern designs for sovereign debt restructuring attempt to take human rights into consideration, making the process for sovereign debt restructuring far more complex than that used for a traditional creditor/debtor dichotomy. This complexity leads to the question of whether a modern design for sovereign debt restructuring would be a fortiori infeasible in a decentralised legal order, assuming that traditional design was impossible without a centralised institution. The rest of Section V is devoted to a rough sketch of current developments pointing a way forward for a modern design of sovereign debt restructuring in the absence of a centralised mechanism, which seems

[110] Ibid., 58. [111] Ibid., 61. [112] Ibid., 65.

a much more realistic strategy in light of past efforts and given the decentralised nature of the current international legal order.

First, there has been a gradual emergence of human rights considerations during and after financial distresses. In 1990, the Committee on Economic, Social and Cultural Rights had stressed that that 'international measures to deal with the debt crisis should take full account of the need to protect economic, social and cultural rights through, *inter alia*, international cooperation'.[113] Several years later, in the wake of the Eurozone financial crisis of 2008–2009, the Council of Europe's European Committee of Social Rights concluded that 'the economic crisis should not have as a consequence the reduction of the protection of the rights recognised by the [European Social] Charter' and further stated that 'governments are bound to take all necessary steps to ensure that the rights of the Charter are effectively guaranteed at a period of time when beneficiaries need the protection'.[114] The Committee subsequently found certain labour laws enacted in Greece during the course of the financial crisis to be violations of the European Social Charter.[115]

Another illustration of the emerging role for human rights considerations can be found in a recent ICSID arbitration against Argentina, wherein the respondent invoked the fundamental right of access to water to justify the measures at issue during the course of its debt crisis. In response, the tribunal recognised that:

> [l]'accès à l'eau potable constitue, du point de vue de l'État, *un service public de première nécessité* et, du point de vue du citoyen, *un droit fondamental*. Pour ce motif, en cette matière, l'ordre juridique peut et doit réserver à l'Autorité publique des fonctions légitimes de planification, de supervision, de police, de sanction, d'intervention et même de résiliation, afin de protéger l'intérêt général.[116]

The holding in this arbitral award supports a conception of autonomy for the citizens of a defaulting state vis-à-vis foreign investors and creditors,

[113] Committee on Economic, Social and Cultural Rights, *General Comment No 2 (1990): International Technical Assistance Measures (Article 22 of the Covenant)*, UN Doc E/1990/23 (2 February 1990), 86–89, para 9.

[114] European Committee of Social Rights, *Conclusions 2009 – Volume 1* (Strasbourg: Council of Europe, 2009), para 17.

[115] *GENOP-DEI and ADEDY* v. *Greece*, Complaint No 65/2011, Decision on the Merits (23 May 2012), paras 25–28; *GENOP-DEI and ADEDY* v. *Greece*, Complaint No 66/2011, Decision on the Merits (23 May 2012), paras 56–70.

[116] *SAUR International S.A. c. République argentine*, Affaire CIRDI N° ARB/04/4, décision sur la compétence et sur la responsabilité, 6 June 2012, paras 328–332 [emphasis added].

albeit the human rights considerations were invoked by the government.[117] Further elaboration of this issue remains to be seen.

The second development concerns the traction gained by recent attempts to establish a decentralised governance network to address sovereign debt restructuring. So-called collective action clauses (CACs), which authorise a supermajority of creditors (typically 75 per cent) to amend the conditions of payment of sovereign bonds in a manner that also binds holdout creditors, have gained attention as a viable alternative to the more traditional and centralised approaches favoured by proposals such as SDRM.[118] Indeed, through the Treaty Establishing the European Stability Mechanism (ESM Treaty),[119] Eurozone leaders mandated the inclusion of CACs in all Eurozone bonds issued after 1 January 2013.[120] Since it had been an established practice to insert such a clause in bonds issued under English law,[121] the ESM Treaty can be seen as official support for a decentralised (and contractual) approach to the governance of public debt restructurings.[122]

In addition, some recent international investment agreements now make special provision, whether within the main text or within an annex, to exclude an investor's claim based upon sovereign debts. For example, the United States–Uruguay bilateral investment treaty adopted in 2005 provides in its Annex G that 'no claim that a restructuring of a debt instrument issued by Uruguay breaches an obligation ... may be submitted to ... arbitration ... if the restructuring is a negotiated restructuring at the time of submission'.[123] According to one expert, this Annex was proposed by Uruguay so as to ensure that the treaty regime would

117 The commentary associated with Principle 15 of the UNCTAD Principles, above note 96, explains that: 'The restructuring should be proportional to the sovereign's need and all stakeholders (including citizens) should share an equitable burden of adjustment and/ or losses'.

118 Kämmerer, 'State Bankruptcy', above note 77, para 20.

119 2 February 2012, EU Doc T/ESM 2012/en 59, online at: www.european-council .europa.eu/media/582311/05-tesm2.en12.pdf.

120 Ibid., art. 12(3).

121 Elmar B. Koch, 'Collective Action Clauses: The Way Forward' (2004) 35 *Georgetown Journal of International Law* 665–692, 667; International Monetary Fund, *Strengthening the Contractual Framework to Address Collective Action Problems in Sovereign Debt Restructuring*, IMF Staff Report, 2 September 2014, 17, online at: www.imf.org/exter nal/np/pp/eng/2014/090214.pdf.

122 Regarding the Eurozone CACs, See Christian Hofmann, 'Sovereign-Debt Restructuring in Europe Under the New Model Collective Action Clauses' (2014) 49:2 *Texas International Law Journal* 383–443.

123 Online at: www.ustr.gov/sites/default/files/uploads/agreements/bit/asset_upload_ file748_9005.pdf.

recognise the lawfulness of the debt restructuring that Uruguay had undertaken in 2004 and would allow 'for that kind of flexibility should a similar circumstance arise in the future'.[124] In fact, certain categories of investment claim against a 'negotiated restructuring', which is typically defined as a restructuring where 75 per cent of the bondholders agreed to a debt exchange or other change in payment terms, have been excluded by some investment agreements concluded by Latin American countries.[125] These provisions give sovereign debt restructurings a kind of special status vis-à-vis investment protection, and thereby attempt to find a proper relationship[126] between debt rescheduling and investment arbitration. These developments can also be seen as a step towards the creation of an international legal order for the regulation of sovereign debt restructuring through a network of bilateral treaties.

Conclusion

The aim of this chapter has been to outline the evolution of international designs for addressing the legal issues that arise with respect to sovereign debt restructuring. It described the major projects proposed prior to the IMF's SDRM proposal as being those that favoured a 'traditional design', whereas the recent proposals favour a 'modern design'. Traditional design projects advocate the creation of a centralised international institution based upon a bankruptcy law analogy. They tended to understand sovereign debt restructuring as the dichotomy of foreign private creditors and the debtor state. By contrast, the modern design attempts to find a way towards a decentralised governance mechanism for sovereign debt restructuring. Although it generally follows the bankruptcy law analogy, the analogy is adjusted by the emergence of human rights considerations.

[124] Gallagher, above note 17, 23.

[125] See Colombia-United States Free Trade Agreement, Investment Chapter, art. 10.28 and Annex 10-F (2006); Peru-United States Free Trade Agreement, Investment Chapter, art. 10.28 and Annex 10-F (2006); China-Peru Free Trade Agreement, Investment Chapter, Annex 8 (2006); and Peru-Singapore Free Trade Agreement, Investment Chapter, arts. 10.1 and 10.18 (2008). Different wordings were used earlier. See, for example, Chile-United States Free Trade Agreement, Investment Chapter, Annex 10-B (2003) and Central America-Dominican Republic-United States Free Trade Agreement, Investment Chapter, Annex 10-A (2004).

[126] These investment agreements still allow claims based upon the national treatment standard and the most-favoured-nation obligation, regardless of whether the restructuring in question is 'negotiated' or not: UNCTAD, 'Sovereign Debt Restructuring and International Investment Agreements', *IIA Issues Note*, No. 2, July 2011, 8, online at: http://unctad.org/en/Docs/webdiaepcb2011d3_en.pdf.

This shifts the normative basis of debt workout from states to their citizens, the latter becoming distinctive stakeholders within the legal discourse of sovereign debt restructuring.

Needless to say, this chapter does not present a comprehensive picture of previous scholarly works, but rather a more simplified account referencing the contributions of key experts that is meant to point a way forward. In particular, it did not address in depth the work of those experts who argued for much less centralised approaches at the time of the proposals made by Jeffrey Sachs and the IMF. Thus, the traditional design for sovereign debt restructuring in this chapter must be understood as a reference model used to stand in contrast with the modern design for sovereign debt restructuring. The modern design in this chapter is not just an explanatory note to the recent studies, although this work was deeply inspired by them. It is to be understood rather as a rough sketch of the approach that will likely attract support from future experts in light of new developments on sovereign financing.

The international law of sovereign debt restructuring is, at present, not firmly established. No multilateral convention dealing with this subject matter has been, nor will be concluded, at least not in the near future. For the time being, it is therefore more appropriate to understand the law of sovereign debt restructuring as a complex adaptive system[127] operating within a decentralised international legal order, which gradually adapts, evolves and mutates in line with sporadic and fragmented developments in practice. It is also a system in which various experts will participate with a view to developing proposals for a decentralised approach that is adaptive to such change.

[127] An idea proposed within the context of international investment law: see Joost Pauwelyn, 'At the Edge of Chaos? Foreign Investment Law as a Complex Adaptive System, How It Emerged and How It Can Be Reformed' (2014) 29:2 *ICSID Review: Foreign Investment Law Journal* 372–418, 375.

11

The Fight against Impunity for Core International Crimes

Reflections on the Contribution of Networked Experts to a Regime of Aggravated State Responsibility

MASAHIRO KUROSAKI

The fight against impunity for core international crimes, such as war crimes, crimes against humanity and genocide, is a challenge for the international community as a whole. States and non-state actors such as independent experts both have a role in this fight. The preambles to the Convention for the Prevention and Punishment of the Crime of Genocide (Genocide Convention)[1] and the Rome Statute of the International Criminal Court (ICC Statute)[2] emphasise the importance of international cooperation. Similar provisions aimed at facilitating the suppression of war crimes are found within the four Geneva Conventions of 1949 and the first Additional Protocol of 1977.[3] These treaties encourage or obligate contracting states parties to establish jurisdiction, investigate and prosecute (or extradite) persons suspected of serious

The author would like to thank Larissa van den Herik, Eric De Brabandere, Yannick Radi, Joseph Powderly, the participants of the fifth 'Four Societies' workshop, peer reviewers, and the editors for their invaluable and thoughtful feedback and comments. The usual disclaimer applies.

[1] 9 December 1948, 78 UNTS 277, in force 12 January 1951, preamb para 3.

[2] 17 July 1998, 2187 UNTS 3, in force 1 July 2002, preamb para 4.

[3] Geneva Convention for the Amelioration of the Condition of the Wounded and Sick in Armed Forces in the Field (Geneva Convention I), 12 August 1949, 75 UNTS 31, in force 21 October 1950; Geneva Convention for the Amelioration of the Condition of the Wounded, Sick and Shipwrecked Members of Armed Forces at Sea (Geneva Convention II), 12 August 1949, 75 UNTS 85, in force 21 October 1950; Geneva Convention Relative to the Treatment of Prisoners of War (Geneva Convention III), 12 August 1949, 75 UNTS 135, in force 21 October 1950; Geneva Convention Relative to the Protection of Civilian Persons in Time of War (Geneva Convention IV), 12 August 1949, 75 UNTS 287, in force 21 October 1950; Protocol Additional to the Geneva Conventions of 12 August 1949, and relating to the protection of victims of international armed conflicts (Additional Protocol I), 8 June 1977, 1125 UNTS 4, in force 7 December 1978.

international crimes, and to enact the necessary national legislation. However, the precise regimes under each treaty vary in terms of their scope, nature and legal content, thus offering a piecemeal approach to the problem of impunity.

Adding to this difficulty is the inability of the International Criminal Court (ICC) to arrest and transfer suspects and to gather evidence without state consent. The ICC cannot function properly, nor effectively, without the cooperation of the states parties, with Part IX of the ICC Statute addressing the need for full international cooperation and judicial assistance. States, therefore, have retained a predominant role in the implementation of international criminal law.

As is well known, the obligations to suppress international crimes enshrined in the above treaties are binding on states parties alone due to the *pacta tertiis* principle that treaties do not create obligations for non-parties.[4] This limitation presents the most significant problem for the global fight against impunity. Despite widespread agreement that the core crimes are 'the most serious crimes of concern to the international community as a whole',[5] non-party states to the ICC Statute are not obliged to close the impunity gap, unless they consent to proceedings or are required to do so by a binding UN Security Council resolution.[6] The issue of the obligations of non-party states to fight against impunity has come to a head with the Council's referral of the Sudan and Libya situations to the ICC.[7] These referrals have also led to acute and ongoing tension between the African Union and the ICC,[8] and have given rise to

[4] Vienna Convention on the Law of Treaties, 23 May 1969, 115 UNTS 331, in force 27 January 1980, art. 34.

[5] ICC Statute, above note 2, preamb para 4.

[6] See further Dapo Akande, 'The Effect of Security Council Resolutions and Domestic Proceedings on State Obligations to Cooperate with the ICC' (2012) 10:2 *Journal of International Criminal Justice* 299–324; Göran Sluiter, 'Obtaining Cooperation from Sudan – Where is the Law?' (2008) 6:5 *Journal of International Criminal Justice* 871–884.

[7] Resolution 1593 (2005), adopted 15 March 2005, UN Doc S/RES/1593 (2005); Resolution 1970 (2011), adopted 26 February 2011, UN Doc S/RES/1970 (2011).

[8] On 12 and 13 December 2011, the ICC delivered two decisions on the non-cooperation of Malawi and Chad with respect to the cooperation request for the arrest and surrender of Sudanese President Omar Al Bashir (ICC-02/05-01/09-139 and ICC-02/05-01/09-140), leading to a response by press release from the African Union (AU Press Release No 002/2012, 9 January 2012). See further Dire Tladi, 'The ICC Decisions on Chad and Malawi: On Cooperation, Immunities, and Article 98' (2013) 11:1 *Journal of International Criminal Justice* 199–221. A decision on the non-cooperation of the Democratic Republic of the Congo was issued in April 2014 (Decision No ICC-02/05-01/09-195). The failure of the South African government to arrest Al Bashir further exacerbates the situation. See ICC Press Release No ICC-ASP-20150613-PR1117 (13 June 2015).

legal questions regarding the precise effect and implications of the related Security Council resolutions.

In light of these difficulties, there is merit in looking beyond the treaty-based regimes to strengthen the fight against impunity. This chapter examines the potential for the International Law Commission's 'articles on responsibility of States for internationally wrongful acts'[9] (ILC Articles on State Responsibility) to serve as an independent basis, developed by a respected body of experts, to establish a general obligation for all states.[10] Given that the obligation to suppress the commission of core international crimes is of a peremptory nature,[11] I examine state obligations under article 41 of the ILC Articles on State Responsibility in three areas: (1) to cooperate to bring to an end through lawful means any serious breach of that obligation, (2) to not recognise as lawful the situation created by a serious breach and (3) to not render aid or assistance in maintaining that situation. This regime of 'aggravated state responsibility'[12] can be traced back to draft article 19 on international crimes of states, one of the most controversial issues in the drafting process of the ILC Articles on State Responsibility. However, the move from the idea of state crimes to the concept of aggravated state responsibility represents a victory of state power over the influence of independent experts, and demonstrates the limited potential for development of international law through networks of experts.

The chapter is organised into five sections. In Section I, I present the ILC's regime of aggravated state responsibility. In Section II, I examine the obligations to exercise jurisdiction and to prosecute or extradite under the existing treaty regimes. In Section III, I examine the trigger for invoking the aggravated regime for state responsibility, namely the commission of serious breaches of peremptory norms. I then examine in detail the three duties found in article 41 of the ILC Articles on State Responsibility, focussing on the duty of cooperation in Section IV and the negative duties of non-recognition and non-assistance in

[9] Adopted in 2001 and reproduced in *Report of the International Law Commission*, UN GAOR, 56th Sess, Supp No 10, ch. IV, 43–59, UN Doc A/56/10 (2001).

[10] I use the phrase 'general obligation' in this chapter to refer to both a universal and customary obligation applicable to all states and in the literal sense of a general obligation vis-à-vis a special treaty obligation.

[11] *Prosecutor* v. *Kupreškić*, Judgment of 14 January 2000, Case No IT-95-16 (Trial Ch II) at 203, para 520; *Legality of the Threat or Use of Nuclear Weapons*, Advisory Opinion, [1996] ICJ Rep 226, 257, para 79.

[12] On this concept generally, see, for example, Antonio Cassese, *International Law*, 2nd ed. (Oxford: Oxford University Press, 2005), 262–277.

Section V. I conclude that the regime of aggravated state responsibility, while demonstrating the creative influence of networks of experts, also demonstrates that states retain ultimate control, even over important goals of the international community, such as ending impunity.

I The International Law Commission and the Move from State Crimes to Aggravated State Responsibility

The objective of the International Law Commission, being an institution established by the General Assembly in 1947, is to engage in the progressive development of international law and its codification.[13] Its 34 members shall be 'persons of recognized competence in international law'.[14] The members of the ILC 'should individually possess the qualifications required and that in the Commission as a whole representation of the main forms of civilization and of the principal legal systems of the world should be assured'.[15] The General Assembly therefore intended that the ILC function as a network of experts codifying and developing international law. However, in practice, the ILC works with the input of states, via their representatives on the Assembly's Sixth Committee (the Legal Committee).[16] The ILC Articles on State Responsibility were developed over a long period of time; however, David Caron has criticised the Articles as premature given the state of the law on some aspects of state responsibility, accusing the ILC of possibly 'pushing the limits of its legitimacy to state what the law is'.[17] This accusation may be particularly apt in relation to the regime of aggravated responsibility.

The concept of aggravated responsibility had a long and complex life cycle within the ILC drafting process. This reality reflects the fact that the

[13] *Statute of the International Law Commission*, adopted by General Assembly resolution 174 (II) of 21 November 1947, as amended by resolutions 485 (V) of 12 December 1950, 984 (X) of 3 December 1955, 985 (X) of 3 December 1955 and 36/39 of 18 November 1981, art. 1(1). On the functioning of the ILC, see arts. 15–24.

[14] Ibid., art. 2(1). [15] Ibid., art. 8.

[16] James Crawford, 'The ILC's Articles on Responsibility of States for Internationally Wrongful Acts: A Retrospect' (2002) 96:4 *American Journal of International Law* 874–890, 875.

[17] David D. Caron, 'The ILC Articles on State Responsibility: The Paradoxical Relationship Between Form and Authority' (2002) 96:4 *American Journal of International Law* 857–873, 858. See, however, his comment at 866 that at least one government representative 'has more confidence in the lawmaking integrity of the ILC than that of the Sixth Committee or a diplomatic conference'.

ILC as a network changes over time, with its membership having been replaced entirely between the 1996 draft and the final adoption of the Articles in 2001.[18] The original idea of aggravated state responsibility as a separate category of international wrongful acts came from Special Rapporteur García Amador,[19] and then was later incorporated by his successor Roberto Ago into a draft article under the heading of international crimes and international delicts.[20] The codification work by the ILC, however, had immediately met with a setback since the proposed notion of international crimes of state was so immature under the current status of international law that discussion was preoccupied with its validity at the expense of delineating its legal consequences, above all in relation to the treatment of punitive damages.

Faced with this criticism, Special Rapporteur James Crawford eventually proposed the replacement of the notion of 'state crime' by that of 'serious breaches' of peremptory norms to better reflect extant international law and formulated the substantive legal consequences of those breaches as in the current form of article 41 of the ILC Articles of State Responsibility. He acknowledges that the removal of punitive or exemplary damages was the result of 'nearly unanimous criticisms of governments'.[21] He has also commented that the 1996 draft Article 19 'used inappropriate domestic law analogies'.[22] Both the influence of states and changes to the membership of the ILC as an expert network led to the removal of the concept of state crimes and its replacement with aggravated responsibility.

The aggravated responsibility regime is itself weakened by the lack of full state support. There is still no consensus among states over the recognition of the aggravated state responsibility regime as *lex lata*; some countries like France, Japan, the United Kingdom and the

[18] Ibid., 870.

[19] See further James Crawford, 'International Crimes of States' in James Crawford, Alain Pellet and Simon Olleson, eds., *The Law of International Responsibility* (Oxford: Oxford University Press, 2010), 405–414, 406; Bert Swart, 'General Problems' in Antonio Cassese, Paola Gaeta and John R.W.D. Jones, eds., *The Rome Statute of the International Criminal Court: A Commentary* (Oxford: Oxford University Press, 2002), vol. II, 1589–1605, 1591.

[20] *Fifth Report on State Responsibility by Mr. Roberto Ago, Special Rapporteur*, UN Doc A/CN.4/291 and Add.1 and 2 and Corr.1 (1976), reproduced in [1976] II:1 *Yearbook of the International Law Commission* 3–54; *Draft Articles on States Responsibility: Texts adopted by the Drafting Committee*, UN Doc A/CN.4/L.243 and Add.1 and Add.1/Corr.1 (1976), reproduced in [1976] II:1 *Yearbook of the International Law Commission* 234–248.

[21] Crawford, above note 16, 875. [22] Ibid., 886.

United States appear to remain negative towards it.[23] Despite this, however, it has been supported by other countries such as Argentina, Austria, the Netherlands, the Nordic countries, Poland, Slovakia and Spain,[24] and, most importantly, has been recognised as reflective of custom 'as evidence of a general practice accepted as law'[25] by the International Court of Justice (ICJ), another respected body of experts, in its 2004 advisory opinion on the *Legal Consequences of the Construction of a Wall in the Occupied Palestinian Territory*.[26]

The ILC has no authority to create international law, but the role of codification and progressive development of international law is entrusted to it by those states.[27] Yet, as the Opinion concerning the *Legal Consequences of the Wall* demonstrates, a normative construction by the ILC may be transformed into binding international law decisions of international courts and tribunals. This interactive law-making process is consolidated by the status of both international judges and members of the ILC as experts. Their legitimacy, however, is in part predicated on the court being a regionally balanced group of highly qualified members[28] selected through the state-driven election processes within the UN. It is also worth noting that the statutes of the ILC and the ICJ enable them to 'open the door' to a variety of non-state experts across the world in their interactive law-making process.[29] Understanding a 'network' to mean a system of interconnected groups that 'allows for the participation of

[23] See *Comments and Observations received from Governments*, UN Doc A/CN.4/515 and Add.1–3 (2001), reproduced in [2001] II:1 *Yearbook of the International Law Commission* 64–72.

[24] Ibid.

[25] *Statute of the International Court of Justice*, 26 June 1945, 33 UNTS 993, in force 24 October 1945, art. 38.

[26] [2004] ICJ Rep 136, 197, para 149 *et seq* [*Legal Consequences of the Wall*]. See also *Legality of the Threat or Use of Nuclear Weapons*, above note 11, 231, para 40 (Separate Opinion of Judge Kooijmans).

[27] See articles 1 and 15 of the *Statute of the International Law Commission*, GA Resolution 174 (II), adopted 21 November 1947, as amended by resolutions 485 (V) of 12 December 1950, 984 (X) of 3 December 1955, 985 (X) of 3 December 1955, and 36/39 of 18 November 1981 [ILC Statute].

[28] ILC Statute, above note 27, arts. 3 and 8.

[29] Indeed, articles 16(e) and 25 of the ILC Statute, above note 27, permit the ILC to consult with external scientific institutions and individual experts as well as with other UN bodies in carrying out its mandate, while article 38(1)(d) of the ICJ Statute, above note 28, authorises the ICJ to apply 'judicial decisions and the teachings of the most highly qualified publicists of the various nations, as subsidiary means for the determination of rules of law'.

a wide range of actors' to achieve certain common goals,[30] one can view the ILC and the ICJ as the central hubs of a transnational expert network for universal international law-making in global governance. They function as the state-authorised linchpins, and driving forces, of an interactive law-making process that also takes into account the distribution of power in that network.

The ILC and the ICJ between them have done much to develop the binding nature of the regime of aggravated state responsibility. In addition, one might also be able to claim that Professor (now Judge) James Crawford assumed the role of network hub connecting the ILC to the ICJ in that interaction if one recalls that he was not only the ILC's Special Rapporteur in charge of the regime of aggravated state responsibility but also appeared before the court as an agent for Palestine in the *Legal Consequences of the Wall* case that confirmed the customary law status of the regime. Against this background, the present chapter attempts to explore the potential regulatory power of an expert network of international law from the viewpoint of its contribution of the regime of aggravated state responsibility to the fight against impunity for core international crimes.

The nature of treaty obligations and obligations under the ILC Articles on State Responsibility differ significantly. Most fundamentally, state obligations under treaties such as the Genocide Convention or indeed the ICC Statute are primary obligations, whereas the obligations under the Articles, which largely codify customary international law, are secondary obligations. Interaction between treaty regimes for the prosecution of serious international crimes and the aggravated state responsibility regime can only arise in a case of concurrent or dual responsibility where the criminal conduct of individuals can also directly be attributed to a state as a breach of its own obligations arising from treaty or custom. This chapter examines whether, in such a case, non-parties to the international criminal law treaties have obligations under the aggravated regime in the ILC Articles on State Responsibility and, if so, what obligations arise. André Nollkaemper notes that the law of state responsibility 'is underdeveloped with respect to the aggravated responsibility that characterises cases of concurrent responsibility'.[31] He concludes that 'Now that the

[30] See the chapter by Holly Cullen, Joanna Harrington and Catherine Renshaw in this collection.

[31] André Nollkaemper, 'Concurrence Between Individual Responsibility and State Responsibility in International Law' (2003) 52:3 *International and Comparative Law Quarterly* 615–640, 640.

ICC is starting its work, developing the law on aggravated forms of responsibility – which inevitably will touch on the problems of concurrent forms of state responsibility – should be a key area for the development of international law'.[32]

II Obligations under Treaty Regimes

In order to provide a framework of analysis and to offer a ground for contrast and comparison, it is necessary to set out briefly the relevant treaty provisions on the suppression of core international crimes. These include both international criminal law treaties and international humanitarian law treaties with provisions concerning the prosecution of serious international crimes.[33] These treaty obligations can be divided into two types: ex ante obligations to establish jurisdiction before the event, and ex post or actual obligations to investigate and to 'extradite or prosecute' (also known by the Latin phrase of *aut dedere aut judicare*).

A The Ex Ante Obligation to Establish Jurisdiction

Treaties on the suppression of serious international crimes require or encourage their contracting states parties to establish jurisdiction over treaty crimes. This obligation must be performed in good faith upon ratification of the treaty and in any event prior to the commission of the crimes and the criminal proceedings. Therefore, it is an ex ante obligation, carried out before the event.[34]

Examples of obligations to establish jurisdiction can be found in the Genocide Convention, the Geneva Conventions and the ICC Statute. The Genocide Convention prescribes two types of fora: the court of a state party, which assumes jurisdiction in the territory where the crime took place, and an international penal tribunal whose jurisdiction has been accepted by the states parties.[35] States parties must assert jurisdiction and adopt appropriate national legislation.[36] By contrast,

[32] Ibid.

[33] On the characterisation of treaties concerned with the regulation of armed conflict being considered as part of the field of international criminal law, see Antonio Cassese and Paola Gaeta, *Cassese's International Criminal Law*, 3rd ed. (Oxford: Oxford University Press, 2013), chs. 4 and 6.

[34] *Questions relating to the Obligation to Prosecute or Extradite (Belgium v. Senegal)*, Judgment, [2012] ICJ Rep 422, 451, para 75 [*Belgium v. Senegal*].

[35] Genocide Convention, above note 1, art. VI. [36] Ibid., art. V.

the Geneva Conventions of 1949 adopt a universal jurisdictional approach for grave breaches, but focus on their domestic suppression, providing that each state party 'shall bring such persons, regardless of their nationality, before its own courts in accordance with national legislation'.[37] The ICC Statute establishes a permanent international criminal court that 'shall be complementary to national criminal jurisdictions',[38] asserting that 'it is the duty of every state to exercise its criminal jurisdiction over those responsible for international crimes'.[39]

B The Ex Post Obligations to Investigate and Prosecute or Extradite

States parties to these treaties are obliged, depending on the language of the particular treaty, to investigate, prosecute or, as the case may be, extradite those suspected of committing such crimes. Since such obligations are triggered by the alleged criminal conduct, they can be characterised as being ex post obligations as opposed to the ex ante obligation to establish jurisdiction. The exact scope and content of the obligation varies per treaty, in particular with respect to the obligation to prosecute or extradite.[40]

The Genocide Convention requires 'the state in the territory of which the act was committed'[41] to investigate and prosecute, but it does not contain a clear obligation to extradite. Instead, it states that states parties will 'grant extradition in accordance with their laws and treaties in force'.[42] By comparison, the Geneva Conventions and Additional Protocol I impose explicit obligations to investigate and prosecute (or hand over to others) for grave breaches of their provisions.[43] The ICC

37 Geneva Convention I, above note 3, art. 49; Geneva Convention II, above note 3, art. 50; Geneva Convention III, above note 3, art. 129; Geneva Convention IV, above note 3, art. 146. See also Additional Protocol I, above note 3, art. 85(1).

38 ICC Statute, above note 2, art. 1. 39 Ibid., preamb para 6.

40 See, for example, André Nollkaemper, 'Wither *Aut Dedere*? The Obligation to Extradite or Prosecute after the ICJ's Judgment in *Belgium v. Senegal*' (2013) 4:3 *Journal of International Dispute Settlement* 501–519.

41 Genocide Convention, above note 1, art. VI.

42 Genocide Convention, above note 1, art. VII. On the other hand, Schabas claims that 'An obligation to co-operate in extraditing genocide suspects is set out in article VII': William A. Schabas, *Genocide in International Law: The Crime of Crimes*, 2nd ed. (Cambridge: Cambridge University Press, 2009), 400 and 401.

43 Geneva Convention I, above note 3, art. 49; Geneva Convention II, above note 3, art. 50; Geneva Convention III, above note 3, art. 129; Geneva Convention IV, above note 3, art. 146. See also Additional Protocol I, above note 3, arts. 85 and 88.

Statute does not regulate horizontal *aut dedere aut judicare* schemes.[44] Its preamble asserts 'that . . . effective prosecution must be ensured by taking measures at the national level and by enhancing international cooperation', but the cooperation required by the ICC Statute is between states parties and the ICC, not inter-state cooperation,[45] with Part IX addressing the obligation to cooperate with the ICC.

Without a uniform obligation to prosecute or extradite, various legal questions arise, including the question of the priority to be given to assertions of territorial and national jurisdiction. There is also a question of whether there is, or should be, a hierarchy between the options to extradite and to prosecute, and the criteria regulating both the horizontal (inter-state) and vertical (within the state) dimensions of the complementarity principle. These are matters that have been addressed by the ILC. Based on a nine-year study, the Commission confirmed the diversity of practice in relation to the obligation to extradite or prosecute, concluding that it would be futile to attempt harmonisation, but suggested that transfer of a suspect to an international criminal court or tribunal as a potential third alternative to extradition or prosecution should be included in new treaties.[46]

C The Status and Character of the Above Obligations

Obligations under treaty regimes are binding only on their contracting parties and, at the outside, may qualify as 'obligations *erga omnes partes*', whereby every state party has a common interest in compliance with them and consequently is entitled to make a claim concerning the cessation of an alleged breach by another party.[47] In addition, they are unlikely to be reflective of customary international law given the

[44] As discussed in Dov Jacobs, 'Puzzling over Amnesties: Defragmenting the Debate for International Criminal Tribunals' in Larissa van den Herik and Carsten Stahn, eds., *The Diversification and Fragmentation of International Criminal Law* (The Hague: Brill Martinus Nijhoff, 2012) 305–345, 334.

[45] ICC Statute, above note 2, preamb para 4.

[46] The ILC's final report on the 'Obligation to Extradite or Prosecute (*Aut Dedere Aut Judicare*)' was adopted and submitted to the UN General Assembly for its consideration in 2014: *Report of the International Law Commission*, UN GAOR, 69th Sess, Supp No 10, ch. VI, 139–165, UN Doc A/69/10 (2014).

[47] Ibid., 449 and 450, paras 67–70. The ILC nevertheless goes so far as to argue that a treaty 'may lead to *erga omnes* obligations as well. In other words, all states parties may have a legal interest in invoking the international responsibility of a state party for being in breach of its obligation to extradite or prosecute': ibid., 160, para 47.

variation from treaty to treaty.[48] Although a great deal of attention has been paid to considering the possible customary status of the obligation to extradite or prosecute, there remains no consensus position on this point.[49] It should further be noted that the treaty obligations discussed above only address state cooperation with national and international courts. They exist solely to secure the prevention and suppression of core international crimes. I now turn to an analysis of the regime of aggravated state responsibility, as found in the ILC Articles on State Responsibility, as a means of ensuring a complementary role for non-party states in the fight against impunity.

III Serious Breaches of Peremptory Norms as the Trigger for Responsibility

It must be borne in mind that individual responsibility does not a priori implicate state responsibility for the same conduct, nor vice versa. This position is reflected in the two saving clauses found within the applicable regimes, namely article 58 of the ILC Articles on State Responsibility and article 25(4) of the ICC Statute. Nevertheless, some violations of international law may engage both state responsibility and individual criminal liability, such as situations where crimes are committed by heads of state.[50] However, aggravated state responsibility only arises where there are serious breaches of peremptory norms of international law that are attributable to the state.

The ILC Articles on State Responsibility clarify, to some extent, when a breach can be classified as serious. A serious breach is concerned with not only the character of the obligation breached, but also its intensity. According to article 40(2) of the ILC Articles on State Responsibility, a 'serious breach' exists when a breach 'involves a gross or systematic failure by the responsible state'. The application of this provision thus requires a certain threshold or magnitude of violation. The term 'gross' refers to the intensity (or flagrant nature) of the violation or its effects, whilst the term 'systematic' represents the need for an organised and deliberate violation. As the two characteristics are not

[48] Swart, above note 19, 1591.

[49] While the ILC conceded that no consensus had emerged, it underscored that this did not mean, whatsoever, that it had found that the obligation to extradite or prosecute had not yet crystallised into a customary rule: *Report of the International Law Commission*, above note 48, 160 and 161, paras 49–55.

[50] Nollkaemper, above note 33, 623 and 633.

mutually exclusive, the ILC's experts have suggested that serious breaches will usually be both gross and systematic.[51] They have also suggested that factors such as an intent to violate the norm (particularly in cases of genocide and aggression), the scope and number of individual violations and the gravity of their consequences for the victims will indicate a serious breach.[52]

Be that as it may, the two thresholds of 'gross' and 'systematic' are 'illusory'.[53] Unless specifically required as constitutive elements of the breach as with the specific intent (mens rea) in cases of genocide and aggression, it is understood that the mere fact of the breach could suffice as being 'serious' in the case of peremptory norms due to their status in international law.[54] As the ILC has emphasised, 'it is not intended to suggest that any violation of these obligations is not serious or is somehow excusable'.[55]

IV Cooperation as an Element of the Aggravated State Responsibility Regime

Article 41 of the ILC Articles on State Responsibility sets out three consequences of a serious breach of an obligation arising under a peremptory norm of general international law. These can be described as an obligation of cooperation, an obligation of non-recognition and an obligation of non-aid or non-assistance. The identification of these three obligations leads to the question of whether the treaties on the suppression of international crimes can be complemented by the secondary obligations in the ILC's framework for state responsibility. It is true that both treaty regimes and the aggravated regime under the general law of state responsibility have the same end, namely a communitarian response to jus cogens violations. It has also been said that '[t]he mandatory and unconditional duty for states to cooperate ... is explained by the fact that the international crimes within their jurisdiction violate peremptory norms of international law, in the repression of which all

[51] Commentary to Article 40 of the ILC Articles on State Responsibility, reproduced in *Report of the International Law Commission*, UN GAOR, 56th Sess, Supp No 10, ch IV, 282–286, 285, para 8, UN Doc A/56/10 (2001) [ILC Commentary].

[52] Ibid., 285, para 8. See also James Crawford, *State Responsibility: The General Part* (Cambridge: Cambridge University Press, 2013), 381.

[53] Crawford, *State Responsibility* (ibid.), 381.

[54] Crawford, *State Responsibility* (ibid.), 381.

[55] ILC Commentary (Article 40), above note 57, 285, para 7.

states have an equal interest'.[56] But if this is the case, then one needs to consider how a regime of aggravated state responsibility might interact with treaty obligations of cooperation so as to serve the overarching purpose of suppression of international crimes.

A *The Positive Duty of Cooperation*

When there is a serious breach of a peremptory norm, states have a positive obligation under article 41(1) of the ILC Articles on State Responsibility to cooperate to bring an end to the serious breach by lawful means. Inherent within this obligation are temporal limitations. Once the breach has come to an end, the duty ceases to exist; the temporal limitation does not, however, apply to the obligations of non-recognition and non-aid or non-assistance.[57] It is also worth noting that the state responsibility obligations only become operative when serious breaches of peremptory norms occur – breaches of primary obligations under treaty or customary international law. It therefore seems impossible to elicit any ex ante obligation to establish jurisdiction from the general rules of aggravated state responsibility.

The next question concerns the kind of cooperation required, and the related question of which entities states should cooperate with under the regime of aggravated state responsibility. Since the ILC Articles on State Responsibility are silent on this point, and there is limited state practice on which to draw, the answer appears to be that the form of the required cooperation depends on the circumstances.

Support for this conclusion can be found within the ICJ's jurisprudence. In its advisory opinion concerning the *Legal Consequences of the Wall*, the court recognised a positive duty of cooperation applicable to all states, finding that all states must 'see to it that any impediment, resulting from the construction of the wall, to the exercise by the Palestinian people of its right to self-determination is brought to an end'.[58] This conclusion stands in contrast with the ILC's expert opinion, which found that '[i]t may be open to question whether general international law at present prescribes a positive duty of cooperation', thus

[56] Swart, above note 19, 1594.

[57] See, for example, Eric A. Wyler and Léon A. Castellanos-Jankiewicz, 'Serious Breaches of Peremptory Norms' in André Nollkaemper and Ilias Plakokefalos, eds., *Principles of Shared Responsibility in International Law: An Appraisal of the State of the Art* (Cambridge: Cambridge University Press, 2014), 284–311, 305 and 306.

[58] *Legal Consequences of the Wall*, above note 26, 200, para 159.

concluding that 'paragraph 1 [of Article 41 of the ILC Articles on State Responsibility] . . . may reflect the progressive development of international law'.[59] As a concrete action to bring an end to the serious breach of a peremptory norm, the court required Israel to cease forthwith the construction of the wall, dismantle forthwith those parts of that structure and repeal and render ineffective all legislative and regulatory acts adopted with a view to its construction.[60] By the same token, albeit arising under a different legal framework, the court in its advisory opinion concerning South West Africa (now Namibia) required South Africa to 'withdraw its administration from the Territory of Namibia' in order to fulfil the duty of putting an end to the illegal situation.[61]

As for the entities with which states should cooperate, it must be borne in mind that 'a joint and coordinated effort by all states to counteract the effects of these breaches'[62] was contemplated by the expert members of the ILC, whether or not in an institutionalised way through international organisations such as the UN.[63] It was the ICJ that built upon this by calling upon the UN, in its advisory opinion on the *Legal Consequences of the Wall*, to consider further a response to bring to an end the illegal situation created by the wall.[64] At its core, the regime of aggravated state responsibility foresees a communitarian response.[65] However, even an independent action by one state could be characterised as a communitarian response because the requirement to cooperate with others can be dispensed with in performing the obligation to cooperate under the current state of the regime,[66] although in the view of James Crawford and Simon Olleson, these would be limited to retorsion or possibly countermeasures.[67] As yet, while the ILC Commentary on

[59] ILC Commentary (Article 41), above note 57, 287, para 3.

[60] *Legal Consequences of the Wall*, above note 26, 197 and 198, para 151.

[61] *Legal Consequences for States of the Consequences for States of the Continued Presence of South Africa in Namibia (South West Africa) notwithstanding Security Council Resolution 276 (1970)*, Advisory Opinion, [1971] ICJ Rep 16, 54, para 118 [*Namibia Opinion*].

[62] ILC Commentary (Article 41), above note 57, 287, para 3.

[63] Ibid., 114, para 2. A similar idea can be found within Additional Protocol I, above note 3, art. 89.

[64] *Legal Consequences of the Wall*, above note 26, 200, para 160.

[65] Crawford, above note 52, ch 11.

[66] Pierre Klein, 'Responsibility for Serious Breaches of Obligations Deriving from Peremptory Norms of International Law and United Nations Law' (2002) 13:5 *European Journal of International Law* 1241–1255, 1254 and 1255.

[67] James Crawford and Simon Olleson, 'The Character and Forms of International Responsibility' in Malcolm D. Evans, ed., *International Law*, 4th ed. (Oxford: Oxford University Press, 2014), 443–467, 452, note 36.

article 41 discusses cooperation through international institutions,[68] which could potentially include cooperation with the ICC, it does not specifically suggest investigation and prosecution of international crimes as a form of cooperation to bring an end to a serious breach of a peremptory norm.

B *Obligations in Relation to Investigation and Prosecution*

Within the law on state responsibility, a breach of an international obligation includes both actions and omissions, but does not cover their effects.[69] Hence, the positive duty of cooperation to bring to an end any serious breaches of peremptory norms might become irrelevant where an investigation and prosecution is directed against already completed crimes. On the other hand, there may be a situation in which the duty remains relevant, even in a case of completed crimes, depending on the interpretation of the terms 'breach' and 'bringing to an end'.

It is open to question whether the investigation and prosecution of core international crimes can be regarded as a form of cooperation to bring to an end serious breaches of peremptory norms of general international law. Looking at an example of primary obligations on states, one may recall the provisions concerning grave breaches in the four Geneva Conventions of 1949, which read, 'Once the violation has been established, the Parties to the conflict *shall put an end to it and shall repress it* with the least possible delay' (emphasis added).[70] There are two verbs within this provision worth noting: 'the act of putting an end to it' and 'the act of repressing it'. The purpose of any act of putting an end to it is, by definition, to terminate acts of grave breaches immediately, to the greatest extent possible, with a view to preventing them from expanding and exacerbating damage to the victims of war, while the act of repression might concern the punishment of the persons responsible for those terminated breaches as a means of prevention for the future.[71] The two

[68] ILC Commentary (Article 41), above note 57, 287, paragraph 2.

[69] ILC Articles on State Responsibility, above note 9, arts. 2 and 3. See also ILC Commentary (Article 14), above note 57, 140, para 6.

[70] Geneva Convention I, above note 3, art. 52; Geneva Convention II, above note 3, art. 53; Geneva Convention III, above note 3, art. 132; Geneva Convention IV, above note 3, art. 149.

[71] On the function of the punishment of international crimes, and the connection to the prevention of future crimes, see the preambular paragraph of the ICC Statute, above note 2, which reads, 'Determined to put an end to impunity for the perpetrators of these crimes and thus to contribute to the prevention of such crimes'.

requirements are linked but deliberately separated, a conclusion that is confirmed in the commentaries on the Geneva Conventions published by the International Committee of the Red Cross (ICRC).[72] In other words, the act of bringing to an end is, in a sense, a temporary measure of protection and thus does not fit within the investigation and prosecution phase. Nevertheless, the detention of a head of state as the alleged perpetrator of the ongoing international crimes, as well as the provision of any aid or assistance by lawful means for that purpose, could be considered as the fulfilment by the state of a positive duty in this particular treaty context.

However, if the detention of the head of state does not result in termination of the serious breach, undertaking fact-finding procedures in criminal proceedings might lead to the identification and detention of other high state officials responsible for that breach. Such further arrests might bring the breach to an end entirely. In such a case, if the obligation to cooperate to put to an end the serious breaches by lawful means in some circumstances includes the possibility of cooperation in international criminal processes, all states may, in fulfilling their duty of cooperation, arrest and prosecute (or extradite) the perpetrator and gather evidence in accordance with international law. Needless to say, however, that can be the case only when the serious breaches are already criminalised by national law and thus fall within the jurisdiction of national courts, without the procedural bar of immunity (of which more will be said below).

C *The Obligation to Cooperate with National and International Courts?*

The obligation to cooperate to bring an end to the breach is not aimed specifically at criminal proceedings, nor does the duty require any state to cooperate with any foreign or international court specifically. This is

[72] See Jean S. Pictet, ed., *The Geneva Conventions of 12 August 1949: Commentary* (Geneva: International Committee of the Red Cross, 1952), 606; Jean S. Pictet, M.W. Mouton and A.P. de Heney, eds., *The Geneva Conventions of 12 August 1949: Commentary. II: Geneva Convention for the Amelioration of the Condition of Wounded, Sick and Shipwrecked Members of Armed Forces at Sea* (Geneva: International Committee of the Red Cross, 1960), 272; Jean S. Pictet, Jean de Preux, Frédéric Siordet and A.P. de Heney, eds., *The Geneva Conventions of 12 August 1949: Commentary. III: Geneva Convention Relative to the Treatment of Prisoners of War* (Geneva: International Committee of the Red Cross, 1960), 633; Jean S. Pictet, Oscar M. Uhler and Ronald Griffin, eds., *The Geneva Conventions of 12 August 1949: Commentary. IV: Geneva Convention Relative to the Protection of Civilian Persons in Time of War* (Geneva: International Committee of the Red Cross, 1958), 606.

worth noting in light of the criticism from a number of African states concerning the authority and legitimacy of the ICC.[73] However, the flexibility of the obligation also means that states are not barred from cooperating with courts that have jurisdiction as a means to bring to an end serious breaches of peremptory norms.

The UN has long been the main forum for encouraging international cooperation in the fight against impunity. Acting under Chapter VII of the UN Charter, the Security Council has demanded all parties to cease and desist from committing violations of international criminal law and international humanitarian law. With respect to the situations of the former Yugoslavia and Rwanda, the Security Council has established ad hoc international criminal tribunals for the prosecution of persons responsible for the commission of serious international crimes.

The ILC's regime of aggravated state responsibility suggests that existing institutions can enable states to meet their obligation of cooperation. In the commentary on article 41, the ILC notes that 'Paragraph 1 seeks to strengthen existing mechanisms of cooperation, on the basis that all states are called upon to make an appropriate response to the serious breaches referred to in article 40'.[74] If such 'existing mechanisms of cooperation' have already been established, states may use them as mechanisms for their communitarian responses to fulfil their duty of cooperation.

This could also be relevant to the ICC treaty regime. The ICC is a treaty-based court and not a UN institution, albeit intimately linked to the UN. Indeed, under the ICC Statute, the relationship between the ICC and the UN is envisaged in article 2, and the Prosecutor of the ICC may seek additional information from the UN organs in order to analyse the seriousness of the information received based on article 15(2), not to mention the right of referral by the UN Security Council as prescribed in article 13(b).

V The Negative Duties of Abstention

In addition to the positive duty to cooperate to bring to an end the serious breaches, states have two negative duties under the regime of aggravated state responsibility. These duties are the obligation not to recognise as

[73] See further Asad G. Kiyani, 'Al-Bashir & the ICC: The Problem of Head of State Immunity' (2013) 12 *Chinese Journal of International Law* 467–508.

[74] ILC Commentary (Article 41), above note 57, 287, para 3.

lawful a situation created by the serious breach and the obligation not to render aid or assistance in maintaining that situation. The two duties have also gained recognition from the ICJ, which observed in its advisory opinion on the *Legal Consequences of the Wall* that all states were under obligations 'not to recognize the illegal situation resulting from the construction of the wall in the Occupied Palestinian Territory' as well as 'not to render aid or assistance in maintaining the situation created by such construction'.[75]

Since these duties focus not on the serious breach itself but rather on the situation created by it, the legal nature of the situation must be clarified. A key question is whether the situation created by a serious breach should be regarded as continuing until that breach is punished and any legal injury arising from it is remedied. The answer to this question rests on how one understands the notion of a 'situation' as distinct from the serious breach, particularly the concept of a continuing situation. According to Judge Cançado Trindade, the notion of a 'continuing situation' 'has passed almost unnoticed, and remains virtually unexplored, in doctrinal writings to date, in public international law. Yet, the notion has received some attention in the particular domain of the international law of human rights . . . It has further been acknowledged at not only the jurisprudential level but also at the normative level in recent years, and can no longer be overlooked'.[76]

A 'situation' in article 41(2) of the ILC Articles on State Responsibility is generally understood as a legal claim or fact (fait accompli) relating to status, titles, rights, liabilities or immunities by the responsible state, such as the attempted acquisition of sovereignty and imposition of de facto control over territory, or the creation of a state through the denial of the right of self-determination or recourse to the prohibited use of force.[77] However, the experts do not agree as to whether the assertion of a legal claim must be made by the responsible state or whether any fact created by the serious breach suffices to give rise to a 'situation'.[78] On this, the

[75] *Legal Consequences of the Wall*, above note 26, 200, para 159.

[76] *Jurisdictional Immunities of the State (Germany v Italy)*, Counter-Claim, Order of 6 July 2010, [2010] ICJ Rep 310, 359, para 72 (Judge Cançado Trindade, dissenting opinion).

[77] Crawford, above note 52, 381. See also Martin Dawidowicz, 'The Obligation of Non-Recognition of an Unlawful Situation' in James Crawford, Alain Pellet and Simon Olleson, eds., *The Law of International Responsibility* (Oxford: Oxford University Press, 2010), 677–686, 678.

[78] Dawidowicz accentuates the necessity of the assertion by the responsible state for the obligation of non-recognition saying 'the principle of non-recognition is only applicable where a serious breach of a peremptory norm specifically results in the assertion of a *legal*

ILC commentary remains silent, with all of the examples of state practice cited relating to title to territory or the right of self-determination[79]

Unlike the positive duty to cooperate to bring to an end a serious breach of a peremptory norm, the negative duty of abstention is not dependent on whether the breach is complete in order for a 'situation' to be created by that breach. For this reason, a situation may last even if the serious breach that was created has come to an end. But if the 'situation' in article 41(2) refers only to the assertion of a legal claim or fact by the responsible state, such as a claim to statehood or a title to territory resulting from any serious breaches, no 'situation' would exist until the assertion is made. However, as Andreas Zimmerman and Michael Teichmann rightly suggest, 'No such claims to status or title will, however, normally arise in the context of genocide, torture or violations of basic rules of international humanitarian law'.[80] It would be even more difficult to directly link these situations with the impunity for international crimes.

A The Obligation of Non-aid or Non-assistance

The obligation of non-aid or non-assistance in article 41(2) of the ILC Articles on State Responsibility is more relevant to the investigation and prosecution of international crimes. This duty requires all states to engage in acts of abstention beyond non-recognition.[81] It also goes beyond the question of aid or assistance in the commission of an internationally wrongful act set out in article 16 of the ILC Articles on State Responsibility and deals with the conduct that assists the responsible state in maintaining the situation created by the breach.[82] Hence, while the concept of 'aid or assistance' in article 41(2) is to be interpreted in line with article 16, it does not require subjective intent, such as the 'knowledge of the circumstances of the internationally wrongful act'. According

claim to status or rights by the responsible state – "a situation" all states are obligated not to recognize as "as lawful"': Dawidowicz (ibid.), 678. By contrast, Crawford and Orakhelashvili seem to understand that a situation is not strictly limited to such assertion. Crawford, above note 52, 381 and 382; Alexander Orakhelashvili, *Peremptory Norms in International Law* (Oxford: Oxford University Press, 2006), 282.

79 ILC Commentary (Article 41), above note 57, 288 and 289, paras 5–10.

80 Andreas Zimmermann and Michael Teichmann, 'State Responsibility for International Crimes' in André Nollkaemper and Harman van der Wilt, eds., *System Criminality in International Law* (Cambridge: Cambridge University Press, 2009), 298–313, 308.

81 ILC Commentary (Article 41), above note 57, 291, para 12.

82 Ibid., 290 and 291, para 11. See also Crawford, above note 52, 385.

to the ILC, 'it is hardly conceivable that a state would not have notice of the commission of a serious breach by another state'.[83]

The most significant question to arise in investigating or prosecuting an international crime would be the immunity of states or heads of states. Some scholars have claimed that the loss of immunity in cases of jus cogens violations falls within the regime of aggravated state responsibility since the judgment in the *Ferrini* case by the Italian Supreme Court.[84] However, the immunity of both states and (sitting) heads of state from the jurisdiction of a foreign court is a rule of customary international law, and state practice shows no exception to immunity even in the case of violations of peremptory norms.[85] More importantly, according to the ICJ, immunity is a procedural rule with respect to the jurisdiction of national courts, and not a rule of substance that would conflict with the substantive rule concerning serious breaches of peremptory norms.[86] Furthermore, the ICJ stated that 'recognizing the immunity of a foreign state . . . does not amount to recognizing as lawful a situation created by the breach of a *jus cogens* rule, or rendering aid and assistance in maintaining that situation, and so cannot contravene the principle in article 41'.[87]

Conclusion: The Aggravated Responsibility Regime as a Missed Opportunity

It is important to understand the potential role for the regime of aggravated state responsibility in combating impunity. It would be a stretch to

[83] Ibid.

[84] See, for example, Alexander Orakhelashvili, 'State Immunity and Hierarchy of Norms: Why the House of Lords Got It Wrong' (2007) 18:5 *European Journal of International Law* 955–970, 963–964; Andrea Bianchi, 'Ferrini v. Federal Republic of Germany' (2005) 99:1 *American Journal of International Law* 242–248, 247.

[85] See, for example, *Arrest Warrant of 11 April 2000 (Democratic Republic of Congo* v. *Belgium)*, Judgment, [2002] ICJ Rep 3, 21–22, para 53. See also Hazel Fox and Philippa Webb, *The Law of State Immunity*, 3rd ed. (Oxford: Oxford University Press, 2013), 539; Kiyani, above note 79, 487.

[86] *Jurisdictional Immunities of the State (Germany* v. *Italy: Greece Intervening)*, Judgment, [2012] ICJ Rep 99, 140, para 93. However, the stance of the Institut de Droit International seems to differ from the approach taken by the Court, with the Institut opining that 'Immunities should not constitute an obstacle to the appropriate reparation to which victims of crimes addressed by this Resolution are entitled'. See further Institut de Droit International, 'Resolution on the Immunity from Jurisdiction of the State and of Persons Who Act on Behalf of the State in case of International Crimes', adopted at the Naples session in 2009, online at: www.idi-iil.org/idiE/resolutionsE/2009_naples_01_en.pdf.

[87] *Jurisdictional Immunities of the State*, above note 82, para 93.

argue that the treaty regimes and the regime of aggravated state responsibility have converged to form one single regime of law. The treaties encompass both the ex ante obligation to establish jurisdiction and the ex post obligations to investigate and extradite or prosecute, but their contents focus on criminal proceedings for persons suspected of core international crimes. The regime of aggravated state responsibility, as a set of secondary obligations dependent on the pre-existence of primary obligations under treaty or custom, is limited to ex post obligations triggered by the serious breaches of peremptory norms. Furthermore one of the obligations arising from the regime of aggravated state responsibility, the positive duty to cooperate to bring to an end, may not apply to completed acts, and due to its general character, this obligation of cooperation lacks specific content concerning the investigation and prosecution of the core crimes.

Thus, given that the treaty regimes and the aggravated state responsibility regime do not correspond to each other, it would not be reasonable to derive, for instance, the technical obligations in Part IX of the ICC Statute from the regime of aggravated state responsibility, let alone to imply the ex ante obligation to establish jurisdiction from the aggravated regime's ex post obligations. Neither can a case be made for deriving an obligation to cooperate with national courts and the ICC.

The aggravated state responsibility regime is the result of a missed opportunity, and demonstrates the limits of the influence of networked experts on international law, and the continuing predominance of states. The 1996 draft article 19 on state crimes would have strengthened the fight against impunity by extending international criminal responsibility to states rather than just individuals as contemplated by the ICC Statute and other international criminal courts and tribunals. However, despite the 1996 draft being the product of interactions within the epistemic community of networked international law experts, without the support of states, it could not progress. Instead, under the rapporteurship of James Crawford, a differently constituted ILC conceded the unworkability of the state crimes concept and replaced it with the regime of aggravated state responsibility. Albeit not supported by all states, which could be problematic particularly in terms of implementation of law,[88] it was formulated by the ILC experts and applied by the ICJ judges. This

[88] See, for example, Yasuaki Onuma, 'The ICJ: An Emperor without Clothes? International Conflict Resolution, Article 38 of the ICJ Statute and the Sources of International Law' in Nisuke Ando, Edward McWhinney and Rüdiger Wolfrum, eds., *Liber Amicorum Judge Shigeru Oda* (The Hague: Kluwer Law International, 2002) 191–212.

evolution demonstrates how experts and networks of experts hold the potential to transform international law, but can only ultimately do so if supported by states.

The US Supreme Court once commented in relation to the legal significance of the ICRC commentaries with respect to the Geneva Conventions of 1949, that the reasoned opinions of such experts are, '[t]hough not binding law, … relevant' in legal interpretation.[89] Recall that not only the ICRC but also other experts, such as Francis Lieber, the Institut de Droit International, the Hague Commission of Jurists of 1922–1923, the San Remo Group of Experts of 1988–1994, the Harvard Group of Experts of 2003–2009, and the Tallinn Group of Experts of 2009–2012, have hitherto played significant roles in the development of international humanitarian law of the time.[90] Networks of independent experts continue to be relevant to the development of international law and our understanding of it. Nonetheless, while states may not be the only participants in the international legal system, they still retain their traditional place at its centre.[91] As one commentator has noted, 'International law is still "made" by states, and not by entities such as the International Law Commission'.[92] Nonetheless, the capacity of the ILC to articulate innovative legal concepts such as aggravated state responsibility means that its law-making role cannot be ignored and may continue to develop.

[89] *Hamdan* v. *Rumsfeld*, 548 US 557 (2006), 619, footnote 48.

[90] These experts respectively produced the following opinions: Instructions for the Government of Armies of the United States in the Field, prepared by Francis Lieber and promulgated as General Orders No. 10 by President Lincoln, 24 April 1863, reproduced in Dietrich Schindler and Jiri Toman, eds., *The Laws of Armed Conflicts: A Collection of Conventions, Resolutions and Other Documents*, 4th ed. (The Hague: Brill Martinus Nijhoff, 2004) 3–20; Institut de droit international, 'Les lois de la guerre sur terre: Manuel publié par l'Institut de droit international' (1881–1882) 5 *Annuaire de l'Institut de Droit International* 157–175; Hague Rules concerning the Control of Wireless Telegraphy in Time of War and Air Warfare, reproduced in Schindler and Toman (ibid.), 315–325; Louise Doswald-Beck, ed., *San Remo Manual on International Law Applicable to Armed Conflicts at Sea* (Cambridge: Cambridge University Press, 1995); The Program on Humanitarian Policy and Conflict Research at Harvard University, *HPCR: Manual on International Law Applicable to Air and Missile Warfare* (Cambridge: Cambridge University Press, 2013); Michael N. Schmitt, ed., *Tallinn Manual on the International Law Applicable to Cyber Warfare* (Cambridge: Cambridge University Press, 2013).

[91] Arnold N. Pronto, 'Some Thoughts on the Making of International Law' (2000) 19:3 *European Journal of International Law* 601–616, 602–604.

[92] Ibid., 612.

INDEX

Lightning Source UK Ltd.
Milton Keynes UK
UKOW01n2000220917
309715UK00013B/139/P

9 781107 184428